Early Methodism

in the

Carolinas

The Reprint Company
Spartanburg, South Carolina

This Volume Was Reproduced
From An 1897 Edition
In The
South Caroliniana Library
University of South Carolina
Columbia

The Reprint Company
Post Office Box 5401
Spartanburg, South Carolina 29301

Reprinted: 1972
ISBN 0-87152-090-7
Library of Congress Catalog Card Number: 70-187362

Manufactured in the United States of America on long-life paper.

Very Truly Yours
A M Chreitzberg

EARLY METHODISM

IN THE

CAROLINAS.

BY

REV. A. M. CHREITZBERG, D.D.

PREPARED AT THE REQUEST OF THE SOUTH CAROLINA CONFERENCE.

NASHVILLE, TENN.:
PUBLISHING HOUSE OF THE METHODIST EPISCOPAL CHURCH, SOUTH.
BARBEE & SMITH, AGENTS.
1897.

TO THE

Members of the South Carolina Conference,

OF THE METHODIST EPISCOPAL CHURCH, SOUTH,

IN GRATEFUL REMEMBRANCE OF THEIR KINDNESS SHOWN HIM IN ALL
HIS MINISTERIAL LIFE OF FIFTY-FOUR EFFECTIVE YEARS,
AND NEARLY FIVE OF RETIRED SERVICE,

*THIS RECORD OF THE EARLY STRUGGLES OF OUR
BELOVED CHURCH*

IS AFFECTIONATELY INSCRIBED BY

THE AUTHOR.

AUTHORITIES CONSULTED.

Froude's Worthies.
Ledener's Narrative (unpublished).
Knight's Popular History, 8 volumes.
Ramsey's South Carolina.
Howe's History of the Presbyterians.
Summers's Biographical Sketches.
Strickland's Life of Asbury.
General Minutes of the Methodist Episcopal Church.
Asbury's Journal.
South Carolina Conference Journals.
Old Quarterly Conference Journals.
Deems's Annals, 3 volumes.
Sprague's Annals of the American Pulpit.
Bennett's Virginia.
Shipp's History of Methodism in South Carolina.
Simms's South Carolina.
Abel Stevens's History of Methodism.
Charleston Yearbook.
F. A. Mood's Charleston Methodism.
Autobiography of Bishop Capers.
Autobiography of James Jenkins.
Autobiography of Joseph Travis.
Stray Leaves. By Lucius Bellinger.
Southern Christian Advocate.
Dr. George G. Smith's History of Methodism in Georgia and Florida.
Annual Minutes of the South Carolina Conference.
Rev. Samuel Leard's MS. Lectures.
Communications from Dr. Lovick Pierce, etc.

CONTENTS.

(ix)

ILLUSTRATIONS.

ERRATA.

Page xiii. In contents of Chapter xxix.,
      R. I. Boyd should be R. J. Boyd.
      D. I. Simmons should be D. J. Simmons.
      William A. Fleming should be William H. Fleming.
Page 260. Same corrections as above.
Page xvi. In second paragraph of names under engraving, Sidi H. Brown should be Sidi H. Browne.
Page 12. In poem, "The rock dissembles," should be "The rack dissembles."
Page 13. Eighth line from bottom, Prisleaus should be Prioleaus.
Page 18. Sixteenth line from bottom, Gov. Archibald should be Gov. Archdale.
Page 47. Fourth line from bottom, "courtly Kentuckian" should be "courtly Carolinian," referring to Bishop Capers.
Page 241. Fifteenth line, William Cook should be William Crook.
Page 252. Fifth line from bottom, Anderson should be Andrew.
Page 283. Second line from bottom, Charles Bell should be Charles Betts.
Page 333. T. J. White,* Class 1893. Strike out the D.

SOUTH CAROLINA CONFERENCE, CHARLESTON, S. C., 1870.

On the lower line beginning at the left: David Seal, A. W. Walker, John A. Mood, Thomas Mitchell, R. P. Franks, J. S. Connor, Claudius Pritchard, William H. Fleming, John T. Wightman, A. Nettles, A. J. Stokes, J. T. Kilgo, W. W. Mood, S. Black, Milton Kennedy, Dr. Bond, N. Talley, Bishop Pierce, Dr. Lovick Pierce, T. E. Wannamaker, A. M. Chreitzberg, and John W. Murray.

On the upper line from the left: Charles Wilson, W. C. Power, Sidi H. Brown, S. J. Hill, A. M. Shipp, John W. Kelly, Lewis Crum, J. B. Platt, David Derrick, J. E. Watson, Charles Betts, H. M. Mood, T. Raysor, John Watts, J. W. Crider, J. L. Sifley, William Hutto, John Attaway, Simpson

EARLY METHODISM IN THE CAROLINAS.

CHAPTER I.

America and Protestantism—Romanism and Heretics—Spanish Cruelties to Indians—Raleigh's Protest—Norse Sea Kings—Banner of England—De Allyon—Coligny—Royal Grants—Royal Proprietors—Ledener's Narrative—Indian Tradition—Sullivan's Island—Past and Present Surroundings.

IN no decrees of Almighty God is his hand more clearly seen than in the reservation of North America for Protestantism. Over much of the continent, under France and Spain, Romanism once held sway; but the great Husbandman, not receiving the fruits of his vineyard, let it out to others. The eighth Henry, styled " Defender of the Faith," had somewhat to do with making Britain Protestant, but the greater Elizabeth, his daughter, did more in holding her country wisely and firmly to its mighty principles. Rome, with her pomp and penances, made many automatically religious: simply parasites, with life only in a fallible Church. So He who is the light and life of the world gave the continent to any who could believe and speak in His name. And yet to-day Romish priests teach that America was given by the pope to the Catholics, as if indeed he had any such right. The dominion of the world was once offered to Christ by the devil and rejected. Antichrist seized upon it with avidity, and long has enjoyed it, and "sitteth in the temple of God, showing himself that he is God, . . . whom the Lord shall consume with the spirit of his mouth, and shall destroy with the brightness of his coming."

The time has come when feudalism should cease, and the people with free thought should rule, and mighty commerce should revolutionize the globe. In its colonization Romanism was first—the cross, her emblem, fearfully illustrative of her power; not, indeed, in the crucifixion of self, but of others. If she could be drunk with the blood of the saints, it was no great matter for her sons to revel in the blood of savages. The

(1)

greed for gold brought the Spaniards over the seas, and their wrongs to the Indians cried to heaven for vengeance.

How fearful Raleigh's words in urging the colonization of Guiana: "Who will not be persuaded that now at length the great Judge of the world hath heard the sighs, groans, and lamentations, hath seen the tears and blood of so many innocent men, millions of innocent women and children, afflicted, robbed, reviled, burned with hot irons, roasted, dismembered, mangled, stabbed, whipped, racked, scalded with hot oil, put to the strapado, ripped alive, beheaded in sport, drowned, dashed against the rocks, famished, devoured by mastiffs, burned, and by infamous cruelties consumed, and purposeth to scourge and plague that cursed nation, and to take the yoke of servitude from that distressed people as free by nature as any Christian?" Grant that all this was only to favor his own selfish projects, yet the grand fact of Spanish cruelties to the Indians is clearly in all records.

But not to savages alone was this cruelty shown. Rome's original hate to heretics found exemplification in Coligny's colony under Ribault in Florida, where the colonists were slain and hanged upon the trees, with the inscription, "Not as Frenchmen, but as heretics"; retaliated soon by De Gorges hanging the murderers, with the legend, "Not as Spaniards, but as murderers."

Cruelty is diabolical; to destroy is demoniacal—is never of God, but as punitive, who proclaimed his Son as the Prince of Peace; and that the hate of Rome is held in check in this western world, is undoubtedly of God.

This rich inheritance we enjoy to-day was the fruit of toil and peril. The old Norse sea kings in the eighth and ninth centuries visited these shores. Fierce and cruel, their only wealth in ships and force in swords, they swarmed the seas and plundered everywhere. Worshipers of Thor and Woden, they were like their deities, ruthlessly cruel. They were not to inherit this fair land; but later sea kings—Raleigh, Drake, Blake, and Hawkins—led the way of discovery and settlement. These may have been thought as piratical as the former, but it must be remembered that popery and Protestantism were at deep, deadly, irreconcilable war; the one trusting in the idolatrous mass, the virgin mother, and the saints; the other, in

Christ alone. The purer faith gave a purer life, and with the failing common to humanity they worshiped God and reverenced his law. History declares that "wherever found, in the courts of Japan or China, fighting Spaniards on the seas, or prisoners among the Algerines, founding colonies to grow into enormous transatlantic republics, or in the fiercer polar seas, they are the same indomitable, God-fearing men whose life was one great liturgy." It was men of this caste that crossed the seas and founded on this beautiful coast the empire we inherit. In 1524 De Allyon sought to found a capital for Chicora, as Carolina was originally called, but owing to his perfidy in selling some natives into slavery, failed. Admiral Coligny attempted the same in 1562 near the same site, building Fort Charles, so called after Charles IX. of France. Both failed; if successful, all may have been under the shadowing banners of France and Spain, but "the banner of England blew," and the country rejoiced under the red cross of St. George, to give place eventually and forever to the starry banner of the states.

History declares that Sir John Yeamans falling into disfavor because of his failure at Cape Fear, the command was transferred to Sale, who is described as an octogenarian in feeble health, and said to be a nonconformist and a bigot, terms easily used in accordance with the high prelatical views of the period; yet his letter to Lord Ashley, dated Albemarle Point, June 25, 1670, calls for a minister of religion at that early day; but five hundred acres of land and £40 per annum failed to obtain one. Sale dying in less than a year, the rule devolved on Sir John Yeamans; and Port Royal being too near the Spaniards, Charleston became the seat of permanent settlement, a little over two hundred and twenty years ago.

History records that the first royal grant in Carolina to any lord proprietor was the Heath Patent, August, 1631, under Charles I., some twenty-four years after the settlement at Jamestown and eleven years after the Plymouth landing. The troublous times after in England made it of little effect. Cromwell, some short time after becoming prominent, defeated a candidate for parliament by one vote, who bitterly remarked: "That single vote has ruined both Church and kingdom." It gave to England, however, in the judgment of this latter day, the most kingly man that ever ruled in Britain.

In 1663 Edward Clarendon and others obtained from Charles II. a charter conveying all lands between the thirty-first and thirty-sixth degrees of north latitude. It states: "Excited by a laudable and pious zeal for the propagation of the gospel, we beg a certain country in the parts of North America not yet cultivated and planted, and only inhabited by a barbarous people, having no knowledge of God." These men, as set forth in history, were: Clarendon, mean and covetous; Albemarle, good as a soldier but selfish as a man; Craven, no Christian; Ashley Cooper, afterwards Shaftesbury, the Achitophel of Dryden, highly endowed but an intriguer without principle; Colleton, but little known; the two Berkeleys, wrong-headed and obstinate; and Carteret, neither wise nor honest.

In the Charleston Yearbook for 1883 is given an engraving of the great seal of these lords proprietors. With interest any may view the heavy chirography of the sign manual of each. Nearly all were degenerate cavaliers once mourning defeat under Cromwell, but under the second Charles rewarded for their loyalty with an empire by a dash of the pen. They all have enduring monuments in the soil and rivers of Carolina. Alas! the beautiful Indian Kiahwa and Etiwan changed into the less euphonious Cooper and Ashley. These are monumental. Their memorial before God must be left to the divine mercy.

The grant of territory was enormous, running, as at one time thought, to the Pacific Ocean. They were invested with all the rights, royalties, and privileges within these boundaries. By the "fundamental constitution" a nobility of landgraves, caziques, and barons was created, but failed of recognition early.

One cannot look at the first maps of Carolina without being impressed by the barbaric loneliness as contrasted with its high civilization now. True, most of the magnificent forest growth is gone, but it is replaced by broad acres of cultivation and by a better race than the Indian. One of these maps is without date, but is unquestionably early, for, save along the coast and on each side of the Ashley and Cooper rivers, there are no settlements. It extends some distance above Cape Hatteras and runs down the coast to the gulf. In the northwest is the Appalachian range of mountains, and the interior is dotted over with pictures of the deer, wild hog, beavers, catamounts, and the like, one representing a bowman shooting at an ostrich: a traveler's tale surely, such not being indigenous to the country; like the story Ledener (an unpublished authority) tells of a sand crab's travels, walking in so straight a line, and because of that climbing the tallest pines, and so progressing but a few feet a day. This reminds us of the student's description of a crab: "A fish, red in color, and walks backward." "Good," said the professor "only a crab is not a fish, not red in color, and doesn't walk backward." The narrative of Ledener, although printed, is not yet published. By the courtesy of Dr. Herman Baer, of Charleston, we have been privileged to see it. The date is 1669–70. Had the traveler come down to Albemarle Point, he would have met the founders of old Charleston there and then.

The dedication of Ledener's travels is to Lord Ashley, and is disgustingly fulsome. In it the discovery of the Indian Sea— the Pacific—is apprehended, and the mountains are represented as stooping to his lordship's dominion, rejoicing more in his lordship's deep wisdom and providence than in any advantage of soil or climate.

The map accompanying Ledener's narrative is unintelligible; only the streams in Virginia and North Carolina notable, the Indian names not indicating present places, and the only guess as to localities being the ascent of a mountain to which he gives the royal title. Can this be the King's Mountain in York county? There is no other royal designation of which we are aware.

Anyway, upper Carolina is the point visited, and the manners and customs of the Indians as related at the very time when Charleston was settled are certainly of interest. Ledener states that they were not removed from Virginia by the English, but that they were driven from the northwest by their enemies, and were invited by an oracle to settle where they were some four hundred years before. The then inhabitants were accustomed to feed on raw flesh and fish, and were taught by the newcomers to plant corn and shown how to use it. Their knowledge was conveyed not by letters, but by rude hieroglyphics and tradition; accounts were kept by pebbles and straws and rude leather thongs tied in knots of several colors. For emblems, a stag denoted swiftness; a serpent, wrath;

a dog, fidelity; and by a swan the English were known, because of their complexion and flight over the sea.   They
worshiped one God, Creator of all things, believing he had
but little regard for sublunary affairs, committing them to
good and evil spirits.   From four women—Pash, Sepoy, Aska-
rin, and Maraskarin—they derive the race of mankind.   They
religiously observe the degrees of marriage, limited to differences in tribes; the matching of two in the same tribe is regarded as incestuous, and is punished.   Places of burial are tribal; to
mingle their dust is regarded as ominous and wicked.   Corpses
are wrapped in skins, and provision for use in the other world
is interred with the dead.   Elysium they place beyond the
mountains and the Indian Ocean.   Their councils and debates
were occasions of much judgment and eloquence.

This glance at the past sufficeth for the present; a look at
present surroundings is in order.   From our cottage by the sea
on Sullivan's Island, in which this is written, you look out on
the broad Atlantic and the harbor and bar of Charleston.   The
jetties seeking deeper water for entrance lie just before you,
with the white sails of commerce in the distance, and the roar
of the surf within hearing.   How wonderful the changes of two
centuries, since a feeble band entered this harbor and founded old Charleston at Albemarle Point!   This is Sullivan's Island, a delightful summer retreat fully appreciated by all who
like the balmy breezes from the sea.   In the early days it was
covered with the sand dunes, but now cottages abound, and during four months of the year a goodly number reside here.   All
religious sects are here represented.   A number of Methodist
families make it their summer retreat; among them the successful bankers, George W. Williams and William M. Connor,
Dr. H. Baer, Dr. Cleckly, the Muckenfusses, and Mr. Edwin
Welling.   The last named was foremost in establishing the
Central Church, where all save the Romanists and Episcopalians harmoniously worship.

This is classic ground.   The site of the old Revolutionary
palmetto fort is swallowed up by the sea.   But here is the brick
structure named Fort Moultrie; in its front is the grave of Os-
ceola, the Florida brave who ended his life within its walls.
Yonder is Morris Island, noted in the civil war, the light-
house conspicuous on its sea front.   Here the *Star of the*

EDWIN WELLING.

West, seeking to relieve Fort Sumter, was fired into; and Battery Wagner, stormed at with shot and shell, once there, has been swallowed up by the sea. Higher up the coast is Long Island, where Clinton's forces bivouacked, not daring to cross to aid the British fleet driven from Fort Moultrie. Tradition tells of buried treasure hidden in its sands by Blackbeard, the pirate: mythical, doubtless, as none has ever been found by earnest treasure-seekers. James Island and Fort Johnson are in sight, as also is Fort Sumter, frowning in its ruins. Outside that, outstretching beyond the bar, extending southwardly down the coast, is the harbor royally named Port Royal. Its entrance was recently guarded by Forts Walker and Beauregard, knocked to pieces by the Federal navy. Not far away, nearer Beaufort, are the ruins of De Allyon's Fort Charles. The writer more than fifty years ago, when a missionary to the blacks, often from its ruined ramparts looked out upon the beautiful waters of the bay. Wealth then abounded there and on the neighboring islands, and religiously did many of the inhabitants seek the amelioration of the slave; all is now gone as a dream, and over all are the lines of desolation. Unless fresh life enters these islands, the contented negro in his potato patch will soon equalize them with Hayti and San Domingo.

Calm, bright, and beautiful as is this day in June, 1893, with the overarching blue so typical of peace, and the breezes from the sea, the outspreading waters of this beautiful harbor have often been tossed with tempests, witnessing the hurricane's wild wreck as well as the exercise of man's more baleful passions. Just off the bar yonder in the hurricane of 1740 foundered the good ship *Rising Sun*, Gibson, master; all perishing save a few who had left the ship a day before on a visit to the town. The Rev. Archibald Stobo was among those thus saved, and lived long after, proclaiming the gospel of the blessed God.

On the memorable 28th of June, 1776, Britain's proud navy was humbled before the little palmetto structure contemptuously called a slaughter pen; and in the memory of many now living Federal valor for weeks and months and years vainly strove to break down an endurance equally brave. When Greek meets Greek, all know the issue. But not only was so-called legal warfare famous in these waters, but in that beautiful offing cruised piratical craft, and along that coast sailed

Blackbeard, Bonnett, and Kidd under the black flag. In the eighteenth century some thirty pirates were hanged at Oyster Point and buried at high-water mark; the locality said to be at the junction of Water with Meeting street in Charleston. The beautiful Theodora Alston, daughter of Aaron Burr, sailing from Georgetown, S. C., was captured by them and compelled to walk the plank, finding a grave in the broad Atlantic. Deeds of violence and blood have been common in all ages; diabolical misrule will never end until He comes whose right it is to reign. Just off the wharves of Charleston in colonial times

ST. JAMES CHURCH, GOOSE CREEK, S. C.

a most atrocious massacre of a dozen Indians was perpetrated under order of a chief magistrate. The captain of a sloop was ordered to take them to Barbadoes to be sold into slavery. Declining so to do, he asked the governor where he should send them. The governor with an oath declared, "*I will send them,*" and ordered some Indians to cleave their skulls with hatchets and throw them overboard. This was no representative of the southern slaveholder, of whom Mrs. Harriet Beecher Stowe makes *Le Gree* the type, and as northern sentiment to this day believes, but one of the same Adamic race that, unless divine grace restrains, will make them all as devilish as was this royal governor.

On the surrounding islands are many points of interest. The glamour of romance hangs around many of the old baronial estates. On one of them, and within sound of St. Michael's silvery chimes, is an old mansion with its marble and mahogany adornments still intact, having its covered way leading to the river as the way of escape from the Indians. Tradition has it that in the early days its lordly proprietor, outraged by the attempt of his groom to elope with his daughter, pursued the couple, and overtaking them, without judge or jury hanged the culprit on a tree adjacent.

Not far away, near Otranto, is the old English church of St. James, Goose Creek. This parish was established by an act of assembly, November 30, 1706. The first church here was built in 1707; the present structure was erected in 1713. Over the doorway was in stucco a pelican feeding her young, and the royal arms over the pulpit saved the church from destruction during the Revolution. The present year, 1896, a memorial tablet was erected and unveiled by two young ladies, direct descendants of the Rev. Francis Le Jau, the very first rector of St. James. The tablet is of white marble, and bears the following inscription, in gold letters:

St. James's Parish, Goose Creek.
Established by Act of Assembly
November 30, 1706.
Organized April 14, 1707.
First Church built about 1707.
Present Church built about 1713.
Church consecrated April 17, 1845.

RECTORS.

Rev. Francis Le Jau, D.D., 1707–1717.
Rev. Richard Ludlam, A.M., 1723–1728.
Rev. Timothy Millechamp, A.M., 1732–1748.
Rev. Robert Stone, A.M., 1749–1751.
Rev. James Harrison, A.M., 1752–1774.
Rev. Edward Ellington, A.M., 1775–1793.
Rev. Milward Pogson, 1796–1806.
Rev. John Thompson, 1806–1808.

The rectory of this church was the scene of the exploit of mad Archie Campbell, who with pistol presented compelled Rector

Ellington to marry him to a lady he abducted; tradition stating that the couple lived happily together ever after. The old road, the rectory, the oaks overshadowing, are all intact; the actors in that drama long since dust. Above the church are the Oaks, a fine entrance to one of the old baronial halls, figuring so largely in the Revolutionary story by W. Gilmore Simms. On toward the west is Summerville, and near by once existed Dorchester, named from old Dorchester, Mass. A colony led by Dr. Joseph Lord settled it in 1696. A rare thing in America are the ruins of the old English church, the shell fort, Bethany Church—the lines of desolation over all. Not far away is Middleton Place, with the tomb of Arthur Middleton, one of the signers of the Declaration of Independence; Drayton Hall, headquarters of Cornwallis in 1780, the property having been in the hands of the present owners since 1671; together with other provincial baronial estates.

These are some of the surroundings near the good city of Charleston, S. C. Cyclone-swept and earthquake-shaken, and under a baptism of fire in two wars, she still abides as the queen city of our balmy southland. As it was here in South Carolina that Methodism first built her altars, the city will necessarily occupy a large space in these annals. Looking out into cloudland above us, so typical of human life, we may say with Shakespeare's Antony:

> Sometimes we see a cloud that's dragonish,
> A vapor sometimes like a bear or lion,
> A tower's citadel, a pendant rock—
> The rock dissembles, and makes it indistinct
> As water is in water.

Such always are the mutations in this changing world. The things seen are temporal, only the unseen is eternal.

CHAPTER II.

THE whole North American Continent, then an unbroken
wilderness, offered an asylum to the forlorn, and was embraced by many fleeing from religious persecution. The Puritan, escaping royal and hierarchical tyranny, found in New England, a refuge; the Cavalier, worn out by Roundhead ascend-
ency, found safety in Maryland and Virginia; and many a Huguenot found an asylum in Carolina.

As we have seen the first English settlement failing at Port
Royal in 1670, the site was changed to the banks of the Ashley
in 1671. The only trace of it now is a small hollow running
across the front, once a wide ditch used as a protection from the
Indians. In 1679 a removal was made to Oyster Point, the site
of the present city; and that year thirty houses were built. In
1700 the portions of the province occupied were within the
limits of the Santee and Edisto rivers. Shortly after its settlement, the province was divided into four counties: Berkeley,
Colleton, Craven, and Carteret or Granville. A rapid increase
of population was desired, so that every inducement to immigra-
tion was offered. The revocation of the Edict of Nantes in
1685 influenced this largely.

Soon after the change from proprietary to royal rule in 1729,
vigorous measures were adopted, bounties offered, lands assigned, and other inducements to allure settlers. Protestants
of all nations were invited to come, the Huguenots establishing
themselves on the Santee River and country adjacent; and there
are still found the descendants—Prisleaus, Guerrys, Palmers,
Hugers, Porchers, Mazycks, and others. In the early days,
from the difficulty of obtaining ministers of their own faith,
they became incorporated with the English Church. After
awhile parish privileges failed, and many of their descendants
are numbered with the Methodism of to-day, among them the
Bonneaus, Douxsaints, Bineaus, Du Prees, Du Tarts, Lessenes,
Postells, Remberts, and others.

Many of the poor and unfortunate of Great Britain, Germany, Switzerland, and Holland accepted these offers between 1730 and 1750, settling in Orangeburg, Congaree, and Wateree. Williamsburg was the rendezvous of the Irish, the Swiss settling on Savannah River and founding old Purisburg. This migratory flight of nationalities was by many in the old countries greatly lamented. John Milton represents the genius of Great Britain as a mother "in mourning weeds, with ashes upon her head, and tears abundantly flowing from her eyes, to behold so many of her children exposed at once and thrust from things of dearest necessity because their conscience could not assent to things which the bishops thought indifferent. I shall believe there cannot be a more ill-boding sign to a nation than when the inhabitants, to avoid insufferable grievances at home, are enforced by heaps to forsake their native country." And yet where would have been this great western civilization without it? And where and what would Methodism have been to-day had Anglican bishops nourished it? Of old, God's purpose toward Pharaoh was declared, and his power seen, in the history of Israel. The roll of centuries plainly shows that he makes the wrath of man to praise him in setting up the nations. One declares:

Oh, many a mighty foeman would try a fall with Him—
    Persepolis and Babylon and Rome,
Assyria and Sardis, they see their fame grow dim,
    As He tumbles in the dust every dome.

After the rebellion in 1715 and 1745, many of the vanquished highlanders sought refuge in North Carolina, Flora McDonald, the rescuer of Prince Charlie, for awhile among them.

In South Carolina, up to 1750, the settlements were confined to within eighty miles of the coast; but on the extinction of the Indian claims, and cession of the territory to the king, the upper country began to be settled. Acadia falling into the hands of the English led to the removal of some fifteen hundred French to Charleston, and in 1764 a large number of poor Palatines arrived at the same place. Some two hundred and twelve settlers came from France under their pastor, the Rev. Mr. Gibert, settling at Long Cane, in Abbeville county, and calling their abodes Bordeaux and New Rochelle.

The white population in the Revolution amounted to forty

thousand. After the peace in 1783, many from Europe and the more northern parts of America poured into the state. In 1800 Pendleton and Greenville counties contained thirty thousand souls. The last foreign emigration was in the closing years of the eighteenth century, the occasion the insurrection in San Domingo.

Returning to the earlier date, 1670, it is very certain that no houses for religious worship were built previous to 1680; and for some years after, divine service was but irregularly held anywhere outside of Charleston; and for long years after, as shall be seen presently, many sections were destitute of the gospel until the Methodist itinerant carried it wherever souls breathed in all this broad land.

In 1672 the redistribution of lots in old Charleston shows the names of several pious Huguenots, and in 1679 a petition from Rene Petit was before the council at Whitehall for the transportation of French Protestants to Charleston; but it was not until the opening of the eighteenth century that the Society for the Propagation of the Gospel in Foreign Parts did much in founding parishes and building churches.

In 1672 a lot was reserved in Oyster Point Town, under Governor Yeamans, on which the present St. Michael's stands. The first minister of the Church of England was the Rev. A. Williamson, in 1680, to whom was executed a deed of gift of four acres for a church and rectory. The first church was erected in 1682. Mrs. Afra Cumming, in 1694, gave some seventeen acres adjoining the town, then comparatively of small value, but now constituting the magnificent glebe of St. Philip's and St. Michael's, near Cumming and Wentworth streets in Charleston.

The first communion of any Christian Church outside of Charleston was at Dorchester, February 2, 1696, in the midst of an unbroken forest, surrounded by beasts of prey and savage men, twenty miles from the dwelling of any whites, under an oak, now fallen, and in 1859 fast decaying. This was a colony from old Dorchester, Mass., removing some fifty years after to Georgia. One of the pastors, Rev. Mr. Osgood, being highly esteemed by John Andrew, had his name bestowed upon the infant afterwards Bishop James Osgood Andrew. The lines of confusion now rest on Dorchester, the sole monuments of former habitation being the ruins of an old fort, an ancient church tower, and the graves of the departed.

In the *Pine Grove Echo* of June, 1892, are two engravings, one of the "Old White Church," built in 1696, and the ruined tower of the more pretentious old English St. George's Church, built in 1719.

In the year 1700 five religious denominations were in the province: Episcopalian, French Huguenot, Presbyterian, Baptist, and Quakers. As early as 1670 the want of religious instruction was felt. A letter from Governor Sayle to Lord Ashley dated Albemarle Point, June 25, 1670, shows this. The governor laments the lack of provisions, but insists that "there is *one thing* which lies very heavy upon us, the want of a godly and orthodox minister, which I and many others of us have ever lived under, as the greatest of our mercies." He suggests the employment of a Mr. Sampson Bond, of Oxford. But though the lords proprietors offered eight hundred acres of land and £40 per annum to Mr. Bond, he did not come, the northern colonies securing his services; the more to be regretted as the governor, so solicitous for religious privileges, died March 4, 1671, aged about eighty years.

The "fundamental constitution," by Locke, provided that the Church of England should be the established religion of the colony; but liberty of conscience in religion being secured, population flocked in, and, enjoying a common asylum, the various sects lived in harmony. But in 1698 the Church-of-England adherents obtained the passage of an act settling a maintenance on a minister of that Church. Owing to his worthiness, but little notice was taken of it at the time; but it gave a legal supremacy to the establishment unbroken until the Revolution. Religious supremacy led to political, and the legislative body being mostly Church-of-England men, this soon led to the exclusion of dissenters by a majority of one vote. This led to the usual animosity, and although their petition to the English Parliament was favorably received, but little relief was obtained for nearly seventy years.

Early in the century a law against profanity was passed, as if only in the interests of religion, but evidently leveled at dissenters. Landgrave Smith testified of these legislators "as some of the profanest in the colony themselves." And Mr.

Marshall, rector of St. Philip's, affirmed "that many of the members of the commons house passing the law were constant absentees from divine worship, and eleven of them were never known to receive the Lord's Supper at all." Thus the Church, by law, together with the aid given by England's Society for the Propagation of the Gospel in Foreign Parts, possessed immense advantages over all others. Parishes were formed, and governmental aid was given in the erection of churches. This, with the provision made for society to rest on the aristocratic forms of Britain, gave a coloring to Highchurch claims not yet abated in these later years. But by the advance of knowledge the *historic episcopacy* languished, and has been long since outstripped in the race for dominion by the once despised sectaries. The other colonies to the south of Carolina—Georgia, for instance—were saved from much of this pretentiousness; and we are not surprised at their republican simplicity, and that in Georgia Methodism ranks all other religionists. Yet Dr. Hewett, in his history of these times, speaks of the success of *the Church*, their mild government, with their able, virtuous, and prudent teachers, abating men's prejudices against the hierarchy and giving them superiority over all sectaries. The Presbyterians, however, were a considerable party in the province, and kept up their form of worship in it, erecting churches at Charleston, Willtown, the Islands, Jacksonboro, Indian Town, Port Royal, and Williamsburg. Their ministers, mostly from Europe, were educated, orderly, and zealous. The Independents were formed into a church in Charleston in 1682; the Baptists, in 1685; the French Protestants, in 1700; the German Protestants, about 1750; the Methodists, in 1785; the Roman Catholics, in 1791. From the first decade in the seventeenth century a letter dated Charleston, June 1, 1710, gives the following comparative statement:

$$\left.\begin{array}{lr} \text{All the whites} & 12 \\ \text{Indian subjects} & \text{to the whole as } 66 \\ \text{Negro slaves} & 22 \end{array}\right\} \text{in 100.}$$

The proportion which the several parties in religion bore to the whole and to each other was as follows:

$$\left.\begin{array}{lr} \text{Presbyterians} & 4\frac{1}{2} \\ \text{Episcopalians} & 4\frac{1}{4} \\ \text{Anabaptists} & \text{to the whole as } 1 \\ \text{Quakers} & \frac{1}{4} \end{array}\right\} \text{is to 10.}$$

2

The increase in population from the first settlement in 1670 to 1800 is as follows: 1670, total 150; 1701, 7,000; 1724, 14,000 whites, 18,000 colored, total 32,000. Forty years after, in 1764, 38,000 whites, 85,000 colored, total 123,000. In 1800, by United States census, 196,255 whites, 3,185 free blacks, 146,151 slaves, total 345,591. A glance at the manners and customs of the earlier settlers shows how great changes a century makes. Now roads and bridges and ferries abound where then only the Indian trail existed; and now when railroads speed the traveler, he must then use his own powers of locomotion or be aided by the rude canoe. Beasts of burden were few, and goods and chattels had to be conveyed as best they might. The swamps and branches and the blazes on the trees were the only guide to the traveler. Dirt houses were not uncommon, and excavations in the hillside often gave shelter until a rude cabin could be built.

Outside Charleston in the early days the dwellings were all primitive, and even in the city itself there was nothing palatial until long years after. Between 1730 and 1740 the town consisted of from five to six hundred houses mostly of wood, some covered with clapboards. An earlier date, 1704, shows by Edward Crip's map that but little of the present peninsula was built upon, the western and northern boundaries being the present Meeting and Queen streets. Governor Archibald is profuse in praise of the noble forest growth of the early day, extending out of the city—"that no princes in Europe, by all their art, can make so pleasant a sight."

As to the manners and customs then, Landgrave Smith's account states that the young girls received their beaux at three o'clock P.M., having dined at 12 M., expecting them to withdraw about 6 P.M. Their fathers, obeying the curfew's toll in old England, retired at seven in the winter, and seldom beyond eight in summer. An old history of the Legare family states: "The white inhabitants lived frugally, as luxury had not yet crept in among them; and except a little rum and sugar, tea and coffee, were content with what their plantations afforded. It was customary for families to dine at 12 M. and take tea at sunset, after which the old folks sat around their street doors, or, like good old-fashioned neighbors, exchanged kind greetings with each other from house to house, while the young people assembled in groups to walk or play about the streets. On moonlight evenings the grown girls and young men amused themselves in playing trays ace, blindman's buff, etc. Early hours were much regarded, it being considered a great breach of family discipline for a child to stay out after nine at night."

About 1760 James Duncan, the son of the first settler in Newberry, gives the following description of the manners and customs in the upper country: "The amusements with the first settlers were running foot races, jumping, fiddling, dancing, shooting, blindman's buff, snaffle the brogue, selling of pawns, rimming the thimble, crib and taylor, grinding the bottle, black bear, dropping the glove, swimming and diving, and the like. The dress consisted of hunting shirts, leggings, moccasins with buckles and beads upon them. The men clubbed their hair, and tied it up in a little deer-skin or silk bag, or cued and tied it with a ribbon, sometimes shaving off their hair and wearing white linen caps with ruffles on them. The dress of the women: long-eared caps, Virginia bonnets, short and long gowns, stays, stomachers, quilted petticoats, and high, wooden-heeled shoes."

Of the matter and manner of religious service of those early days only here and there are glimpses of it. Of one thing are we assured, namely, the length of the service—or more properly, the sermon; the canonical twenty minutes of some contrasting vividly with the four to six hours of the others. The old Puritan seemed to consider that the more gloomy the religion the better the type, on the principle, possibly, that bitter medicine is the most curative; and if Sunday could only be made a sorry day, it was all the more acceptable to a sternly juridical deity, and he that could not swallow the "horrible decree," and endure the *nineteenthly,* or the *ninety-ninth* head of a discourse, only gave signs of his gracelessness. True, once Paul preaching long, "until midnight," Eutychus fell down dead; but to one advocating long preaching it might be said that all the difference lay in St. Paul being the preacher. A *"new light"* of the present time in our own bounds insists that from six to seven hours is a moderate length for a sermon.

Sir John Dalrymple, in his history of the Darien settlement, says: "The preachers exhausted the spirit of the people by requiring their attendance at sermons four or five hours long, re-

lieving each other by preaching alternately, but allowing no
relief to their hearers. One of the days for religious service
was Wednesday, and was divided into thanksgiving, humilia-
tion, supplication, in which three ministers followed each other.
As the service of the Church of Scotland consisted of a lecture
with a comment, a sermon, two prayers, three psalms, and a
blessing, the service could not take up less than twelve hours,
during which time the colony was kept close together in the
guard room, used as a church. This in a tropical climate and
at a sickly season. They dampened the courage of the people
by continually presenting hell to them as the termination of life
to most men. The doctrine of predestination carried to extremes
stopped all exertion by showing that consequences depended
not upon exertion at all, but upon election."

An old history in the Legare family tells of an incident between
Solomon Legare and Mr. Stobo, the minister. "Mr. Legare
was strict in the observance of regular hours, and to his great
annoyance the Rev. Mr. Stobo preached sermons of such unusual length that they often interfered with the dinner hour.
Once Mr. Legare got up with his family in the midst of the
discourse, about to leave the church, whereat the preacher
called out, 'Aye, aye, a little pitcher is soon filled'; upon which
irreverent address, the Huguenot's French blood becoming excited, he retorted, 'And you are an old fool!' He went home,
ate his dinner, and returning, listened to the rest of the discourse as if nothing had occurred."

A very great and certainly agreeable change has come over
Christendom in these later times, and the representation of the
divine Father as only sternly juridical, and from eternity de-
creeing eternal death to the race, is more happily and scripturally set forth as the embodiment of love without the slightest
abatement of the necessity for righteousness; and with this
Methodism has had much to do.

CHAPTER III.

AT the time of the settlement of Carolina, Charles II.—his "Sacred Majesty," as flatterers called him, but really the Sardanapalus of the age—with others like him, was reveling at Whitehall; but soon all was to be in the dust. The great Louis XIV. was to sign the edict making France all of one faith, but scattering the noblest of the nation. The second James, the Romish bigot, was to be driven out of the kingdom, and William of Orange to rule; Anne, the nurturing mother of the English Church, was to succeed him, and to deny to Swift the American bishopric. Swift, Harley, and Bolingbroke were to play their parts in Parliament; and Marlborough, after splendid victories, was to become "a driveler and show." Addison and Steele were soon to delight the world with their essays; and soon the humble rectory at Epworth was to have in training, under an incomparable mother, spirits who, though lightly esteemed on earth, should shine as stars in heaven. The Holy Club at Oxford, jeered at by the age, was destined to shake the globe.

The rebound from the strictness of puritanism to the laxity of the Restoration was immense. The secret wickedness of the one, if existent, seemed preferable to the open profligacy of the other. The benefit of the union of Church and State is small to the government, and will always be resisted by many of the governed. As shown by the historian Macaulay, "the training of the High Church under Laud ended in the reign of the Puritans, and the training under the Puritans in the reign of the harlots." The evil was seen and felt even in America, when in Virginia sectaries were whipped, imprisoned, driven from the colony under the Established Church—everything but burned; then the stipends of the clergy, by law enforced, sixteen thousand

(21)

pounds of tobacco, required the labor of twelve slaves to produce it.

Patrick Henry's defense of Walter, Craig, and Childs, sectaries at Fredricksburg, Va., was an overwhelming appeal in behalf of religious freedom. He rose sublimely in the greatness of his theme. "These men," said he, "are charged with—with—what?" Then in low, measured tones he continued: "Preaching the gospel of the Son of God." He paused, and waved the indictment around his head: the silence was painful. Then, lifting his hands and eyes to heaven, he exclaimed, "Great God!" The audience responded by a burst of feeling. The great orator went on with irresistible eloquence, ever and anon waving the indictment round his head, and piercing the conscience of the court with dagger-like questions, till at length he exclaimed in tones of thunder, his eagle eye fixed upon the court, "What laws have they violated?" The excitement had reached the flood. The king's attorney shook with agitation; the court was deeply moved; the presiding justice exclaimed, "Sheriff, discharge those men!"

It is always bad when the fleece is regarded more than the flock —too common among all Church establishments. The clergy of the times rarely sought to reach the hearts of their hearers. Hogarth's "Sleeping Congregation," published in 1736, represents the bewigged preacher droning through his tedious hour, with no attempt to touch the vicious or to rouse the profane. Knight affirms· "From the Revolution to the Rebellion in 1745, the orthodox clergyman had a decided tendency to Jacobitism. After that period he gradually became less earnest in politics, and resolutely applied himself to uphold governments and oppose innovation. He had his own peculiar business in life to perform, which was chiefly to make himself as comfortable as possible. The indecorum, if not the profligacy, of a large number of the English clergy, for a period of half a century, is exhibited by too many contemporary witnesses." In England, the doors of the Established Church being closed against the few adhering to Wesley, the sole alternative was to preach *out* of the church; and in churchyards, on commons, in fields and parks, in market places and private houses, they smote the very foundation of irreligion and vice in the land. Such preaching, from the day of Pentecost

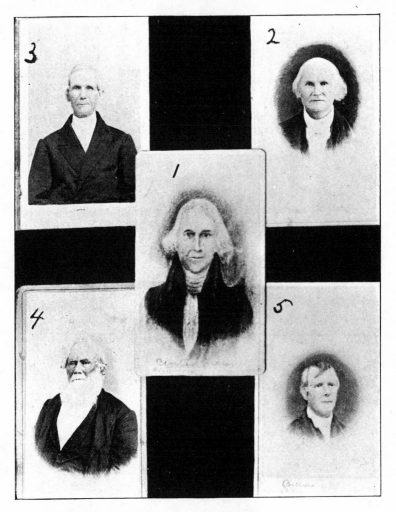

1. JAMES JENKINS.　　　2. WILLIAM CAPERS.　　　3. N. TALLEY.
4. C. BETTS.　　　5. HENRY BASS.

until now, has never been in vain. Few of the regular clergy encouraged or assisted them, yet, unpatronized by power and often unprotected in their civil rights by the magistrates, the society spread. Assistance in preaching was proffered by one and another who, truly converted, felt moved to this work by the Holy Ghost and a love for perishing souls. This was cautiously accepted. Mr. Wesley's testimony concerning these is delivered in the following terms: "It has been loudly affirmed that most of these persons now in connection with me, who believe it their duty to call sinners to repentance, having been taken immediately from low trades—tailors, shoemakers, and the like—are a set of poor, stupid, illiterate men that scarce know their right hand from their left; yet I cannot but say that I would sooner cut off my right hand than suffer one of them to speak a word in any of our chapels, if I had not reasonable proof that he had more knowledge in the Holy Scriptures, more knowledge of himself, more knowledge of God, and of the things of God, than nine in ten of the clergymen I have conversed with either in the universities or elsewhere."

In America an early statute of the neighboring colony of Virginia reads: "Ministers shall not give themselves to riot, spending their time idelie by day or by night, playing at dice, cards, and other unlawful games, but at all times convenient, they shall hear or read somewhat of the Scriptures, or shall occupy themselves with some other honest studies or exercise, always doing the things that shall appertayne to honestee, and endeavor to profit the Church of God, having always in mynd that they ought to excell all others in purity of life, and should be examples to the people to live well and Christianlie." Which nobody can deny.

The stream, however, cannot rise higher than the fountain, and "like priest like people." Intemperance prevailed fearfully; even burials of the dead contaminated the living, not sufficiently sober to inter the dead, and ministers were often disciplined for drunkenness. About 1730 began that series of events which led to the "great awakening." The time had fully come for a genuine revival of religion, which began under Wesley and Whitefield in Europe, and by the Blairs and Tennents in America, and in the closing years of the eighteenth century, by the influence of Methodism, was spread over this continent, and is still spreading over the world.   One little fact few know, that the forests once existing where the city of Charleston now stands was the *oratory* of John Newton—Cowper's Newton—the Olney hymnist, then an officer on a slave ship lying in Charleston harbor.   In a letter dated in 1740 he speaks of "pouring out strong cries and tears amid that shrubbery."   Returning to England, it will be remembered, he became famous as a preacher of righteousness.   Well, what is remarkable?   Only this: the Spirit, moving then over Europe and America, found this poor sinner on a slave ship, as he did Candace's minister in the desert, and sent him with poor, demented Cowper to sing God's praise and power everywhere and in all generations.   The Spirit's work!   Better that than all the mummeries of Rome, the glitter of the historic episcopacy, or the soothings of the decrees; and wherever found, either amid the reputed fanaticism of Methodism or the rodomontade of the Salvation Army, if it turns men to God, it is by nothing less than the Holy Ghost.

Coming near to its advent in Carolina, a glance at the then condition of the country is proper.   The Revolution had wrought great changes in the country, and the long war had doubtless interfered seriously even with the form of godliness then prevalent.   When the Revolution began, all the parish churches were closed, and most of the clergy, originally from Britain, fled the state.   The churches were used as storehouses, even stables, and some of them burned by the British.   At the peace, religion had sadly declined; the churches were again opened, but, because of the lax morality of some of the clergy, closed again.   An idea of the religious destitution, even in the lower parishes, may be formed from Mr. Du Bose's statement, in his "Reminiscences of St. Stephen's," that after his baptism in 1786, by a minister accidentally present and living fifty miles away, he never saw another until twelve years after; as also the fact of his surprise at seeing a Presbyterian minister on his travel of forty miles to a communion, not wondering at his zeal or fidelity, but "because I thought he must be a fool."

With many of the parish churches closed, and only here and there throughout the state a Presbyterian or Baptist congregation, and the usual declension following a long and wasteful war, the time and place were favorable for the introduction of Methodism.   Methodism itself met with no favor, even from its

coreligionists, but under God had to win its triumphs by stalwart use of bow and spear. Like Joseph, "the archers shot at
him and grieved him; but the arms of his hands were made
strong by the hands of the mighty God of Jacob." It sent out
no pioneers seeking goodly places, ran no lines of circumvallation around rich spots, built no fortresses on rich, alluvial
sites, but felt called anywhere and everywhere, and went where
any soul breathed. It hung not around commercial centers,
waiting for mammon worship to compromise with the God of
heaven, but in the city full and wilderness raised the cry,
"Repent, for the kingdom of God is at hand." The old cry
of their "turning the world upside down" never moved them.
Ill names they heeded not, mountain barriers towered in vain,
and flowing rivers stopped not their travel. Bishops and
preachers "wrestled with the floods" of swamps and rivers, but
neither the floods of waters nor the "floods of ungodly men"
made them afraid. They slept by campfires, with saddles for
pillows and the heavens for covering; explored forests, traversed sand hills, dined on the most homely fare at the foot of
forest pines, and preached Jesus and the resurrection everywhere. And, thank God, bishops and other clergy—not in lawn
and crape, it is true, the virtue not in vestments, but in the
Holy Ghost—do it still.

True, at first some of the old Church forms affected them.
Even Asbury for awhile essayed a surplice, gown, and bands;
but all this frippery soon fell off—crape and lawn, poor symbols
of saintship anyhow, were rather in the way in the holes and
corners, dens and caves of the earth they sought out. But
when was Satan ever quiet when God's work was being done?
Slanderous tongues were busy. Reports crossed the Atlantic
concerning "Cæsarism, bishops strutting, soaring," etc. Poor,
dear Mr. Wesley, dazed by the glare and splendor of mitered
priests, palaces, and mighty revenues of Rome and the English
Church, had his wrath greatly excited, and he exclaimed: "Men
may call me a knave, a fool, or a rascal, but never, with my consent, a bishop!" Asbury replied that "he did soar, but it was over
the tops of mountains"; and we know that his episcopal palace was often some hut through which the stars shone, his gar-
dens and pleasant walks the grand old forests, his couch of
ease often the roots of the oak and pine, and a bit of fat bacon

and coarse bread his dainty fare; his annual revenue, *six thousand cents.* As will be seen in these annals, many dear brethren of the old South Carolina Conference have often been along that same route, happy in the love of God. They did soar, but it was in thought to heaven, the palace of the King. Asbury says himself in his journal: "Two bishops in a thirty-dollar chaise, a few dollars between them in partnership. What bishops!" But he adds: "Prospects of doing good are glorious." Ha! any knowing the joy of that experience know it to be more moving than the gold of Ophir. And although we may seem a little in advance of our story, there may as well be put on record here the testimony of Dr. Ramsey, the historian of South Carolina, to the efficiency of their work. He says: "That great good has resulted from the labors of the Methodists, is evident to all who are acquainted with the state of the country before and since they commenced their evangelism in Carolina. Drunkards have become sober and orderly; bruisers, bullies, and blackguards meek, inoffensive, and peaceable; and profane swearers decent in their conversation." Proof enough that their work was from God, and he might have added Christ's own seal to its divinity—" *The poor have the gospel preached unto them.*"

Great was the transformation through the gospel of the Son of God, not only in England, but in America and throughout the world. To know its origin, we must look to the old Epworth rectory in England. It stands intact to-day, ghost room and all, as when the Wesleys inhabited it; the very study where Samuel Wesley was busy with his commentary on the book of Job is existent. Could the old walls speak, what might they not tell of pious ejaculations, and of the patience learned from his prototype? But this writing did little for him. His ode to Queen Mary obtained the Epworth living. Doubtless the good man thought his writings immortal, with no thought whatever of John and Charles save as they annoyed his studies, yet their writings belt the globe, influencing millions. Within those old walls matters usually considered trivial were occurring under an incomparable mother: children were being reared and taught letters and the fear of God. Christ Church, Oxford, came next, with its methodical Fellow and his associates, and their rigid Christian living, so little enlightened then by that "joy of the Lord," the believer's strength.

The year 1736 found the young rector in Savannah, sad, gloomy, and peculiar; bound in the fetters of ecclesiasticism, holding so rigidly to ritual and rubric that nothing less than God's love should unloose, and learning that he who had dared the seas to convert others was not converted himself. Here, when a little over thirty—young, handsome, accomplished, with the best worldly prospects—occurred the Hopkey episode. No scandal accrued, and only the usual nine-days' gossip. Owing to the influence of others, the marriage was not consummated. The Grace Murray affair in England came near proving a tragedy. Wesley was wounded in the house of his friends, and they must have grieved for their fault. The final unhappy marriage was doubtless disciplinary. So if Providence shapes our ends, why quarrel with the mode? But why dwell on these oft-repeated incidents? We note rather the visits of the Wesleys to Charleston as more germane to matters in hand.

John and Charles Wesley visited Charleston for the first time July 31, 1736. Charles was on his way to England. Both were attendants on divine service in old St. Philip's Church. John was invited to preach, but declined. The church was an imposing structure, founded in 1711, and divine service held in it in 1723. It was in the form of a cross, the dim religious light of the interior aiding devotion. Within were many monuments to departed worth. Often has the writer looked reverently on the tall pulpit from which Wesley preached. He witnessed its destruction by fire in 1838. A splendid counterpart, at least in exterior, stands upon its site, lacking, of course, the wealth of marble and glorious memories of the original structure. John's second visit was in April, 1737, and on the 17th he preached from the text, "Whatsoever is born of God overcometh the world"; apparently the spiritual victory as little understood as Christ's teaching to Nicodemus. There were about three hundred hearers present, and but fifty at the communion. Several negroes were present, with one of whom Mr. Wesley conversed. Her replies to his questions showed how little she knew of the Christian religion, leading to his remark: "O God, where are thy tender mercies? Are they not over all thy works? When shall the Sun of righteousness arise on these outcasts of men with healing in his wings?" It was coming, and he was to be one of the agents in the mighty work;

and though fifty years were to pass up to 1787, yet at last should Methodism come and remain. The third and last visit to Charleston was in December, 1737, when, after long and wearisome travel, mostly on foot, he took shipping, and after a stormy passage arrived at Deal, February, 1738—never setting foot again on the American Continent.

Wesley himself was yet in the shadow, and long and bitter was to be the struggle ere he saw the light. "The Holy Club" was formed at Oxford in 1729, for the sanctification of its members. Purification was sought by prayers, watchings, fastings, alms, and labors among the poor. The ascetic struggle was ineffectual. Ten years after, in sight of Land's End, he writes in his journal: "I went to America to convert Indians, but oh, who shall convert me? Who is he that will deliver me from this evil heart of unbelief?" Shortly after, he writes: "This, then, have I learned in the ends of the earth, that I am 'fallen short of the glory of God.' I have no hope but that, if I seek, I shall find Christ. If it be said that I have faith, for many things have I heard from many such miserable comforters, I answer, so have the devils a *sort* of faith, but still they are strangers to the covenant of promise. The faith I want is a sure trust and confidence in God, that through the merits of Christ my sins are forgiven, and I reconciled to the favor of God." He was not far from the kingdom.

In many after conversations with Peter Böhler, the Moravian, who explained the way of the Lord more perfectly, he was led to the hour of the uprising of the Sun of righteousness on his soul as never before. "I felt," he writes, "my heart strangely warmed; I felt I did trust in Christ alone for salvation, and an assurance was given me that he had taken away my sins, even mine, and saved me from the law of sin and death." This personal experience and life from the dead is essentially Methodism. In answer to the question, "What was the rise of Methodism?" in his Conference of 1765, he answered: "In 1729 my brother and I read the Bible; saw inward and outward *holiness* therein; followed after it, and incited others so to do. In 1737 we saw this holiness comes by *faith*. In 1738 we saw we must be *justified* before we are sanctified. But still *holiness* was our point; inward and outward holiness. God then thrust us out to raise a *holy* people.'

CHAPTER IV.

Whitefield — Commissary Garden — Pilmoor — Waccamaw Beach — Hard Travel—Charleston—Purisburg—A Drunken Funeral—In the Theater—Joins the Protestant Episcopal Church—Extemporaneous Preaching—Asbury and His Helpers—Precedence of Methodism—Wightman's Defense of Our Episcopacy.

THE next appearance of germinal Methodism in Carolina was in the person of George Whitefield, in 1738; the vessels bearing Wesley out and Whitefield in passing each other in the Downs. On arriving in Charleston his interview with Garden, the Bishop of London's commissary, was exceedingly kind; but subsequently he had Whitefield arrested for some canonical irregularities. The commissary was honored by Linnæus in giving his name to the beautiful flower Gardenia, of which an old French physician of the city, having a pique against Mr. Garden, said: "That was nothing, for he had called a flower Lucia, after his cook Lucy." His next visit was in 1740. Coming into the state from North Carolina, he writes of the beautiful Waccamaw section, the magnificent sea beach, and the porpoises playing in the ocean. The travelers missing their way, and seeing negroes dancing, there being much talk of insurrection among the slaves, in great fear they made a hurried journey of sixty miles and crossed the ferry from Mt. Pleasant into the city. On Sunday he attended service at St. Philip's, and in the afternoon preached at the white meetinghouse, Congregationalist, just opposite St. Philip's. He doubted if the court end of London could exceed the worshipers in affected finery, gayety, and ill deportment, especially after such judgments, storms, and conflagrations as had lately befallen. He reminded them of this, but seemed as one that mocked. Shortly after he came again, waited on the commissary, meeting with a cool reception. No preaching in St. Philip's now, but to large audiences at the white meetinghouse and in the Baptist and old Scotch churches, preaching at the uncanonical hour of 8 A.M.; at eleven he attended St. Philip's and heard himself berated as a Pharisee, Mr. Garden pouring forth many bitter words against Methodists in general and himself in particular.

(31)

At 5 P.M. he preached in the white meetinghouse yard, the house not large enough to hold the audience. The effect of his preaching could not be otherwise than good, but there was no organization of any sort, and much of his labor was as seed by the wayside.

The next visit to Carolina by any Methodist was some thirty-three years after by one of Wesley's missionaries, Joseph Pilmoor. He had been converted in his sixteenth year, educated at Kingswood School, and traveled four years before coming to America. He was of commanding presence, fine executive ability, and ready discourse. Arriving in America in 1769, after abundant labors in Philadelphia and New York he itinerated extensively; finding his way to Charleston, S. C., in 1773, some thirty-three years after Whitefield. He entered the state at about the same point Whitefield did, in that beautiful Waccamaw section, traveling that same Atlantic beach road opening on the broad ocean through Georgetown, crossing the two Santees, and on to Charleston. There was no other line of travel from the north along the coast; it was the same that Asbury and his pioneers used. One reason why Methodism in the Pee Dee Valley is so strong is because it was favored with the ministry of these early evangelists.

Charles Betts, a modern presiding elder, known to many living, used to be delighted with that ocean-beach travel of more than twenty miles, as he drew rein over his splendid roadsters between his Waccamaw home and Wilmington. And none can travel it to-day without high enthusiasm; but then, like Melrose, it must be

> Viewed aright
> Under the beams of the sweet moonlight.

True, Walter Scott on his own testimony declares he never so viewed Melrose; no matter, it only proves the power of imagination, a mighty faculty in developing anything. But Pilmoor did not find his travel one hundred and twenty years ago of the exhilarating sort. He writes: "The woods were dreary, and I did not see anything but trees for miles together." He got a few blades of Indian corn for his horse, and having a lunch along, man and beast were provided for. After reaching the state boundary he crossed, finding a heavy, sandy road. The tide was in and the beach covered, or this may have been avoided. With but little accommodation for man or horse, and after breaking a wheel and borrowing another, he reached Georgetown. He states: "I have traveled many thousands of miles in England and Wales, and now have seen much of North America, but this day's journey has been the most distressing of all ever met with before; but it is now over, and will never afflict me again." Good, easy man; he had no thought of the pioneers and others who should wrestle with the swamps and swollen rivers, not only once but over and over again, in cultivating Immanuel's lands. He was not accustomed to the corduroy roads of America, and was fearful of that mile between the two Santees, that his horse would break his legs among the trees laid across the mud for a road; he durst not ride at all in the chaise, and reached the inn "covered with dirt." Dear, dear! what tales the missionaries to the slaves could tell of those causeways and rice-field banks in their daily travel, now in the past, but long after Pilmoor's day.

Sunday, January 17, 1773, he called at a church by the wayside, and heard a useful sermon on the necessity of prayer. Monday, 18th, he had a sight of Charleston, but did not get over until late in the evening. An utter stranger, he found his way to a Mr. Crosse's, a publican. Being heartily sick among sons of Belial, he sought private lodgings with Mr. Swinton, "but because family prayer was so uncommon in the cities, and because of the mixed multitude, retired without it." He preached several times in the Baptist and white meetinghouses, afraid of preaching at night because of the mob, but finds his fears, as Asbury and others did not, groundless. He goes to Savannah, and visits Whitefield's Orphan House. On his return he visits Purisburg, and attends a funeral: "Some pretty merry with grog, and talking as if at a frolic, rather than a funeral." These were the times, not much changed yet, of "Rum," "Romanism" not yet blatant, and "Rebellion" not far away. After the funeral they went into the church, when Mr. Zubey gave a sermon— quite appropriate, undoubtedly—on *drunkenness*. He was invited to remain and settle as a parish minister, but states: "However valuable as to earthly things, parishes have no weight with me, my call is to run to and fro." An opinion much modified, as will hereafter be seen. While in the city of Charleston, preaching in the theater, the sons of Zeruiah were too hard for him,

3

table, book, and preacher disappearing through a trapdoor—
used for the ghost in *Hamlet;* but they made no ghost of him,
for springing thence, he adjourned to the yard, exclaiming pleasantly, " Come on, friends, we will by the grace of God defeat
the devil this time!" and there finished his discourse. His
ministry was well received, but left no permanent fruit for
Methodism. He afterwards united with the Protestant Episcopal Church. Dr. Welch, in "Sprague's Annals," says: "In
person he was of portly and noble bearing, and he moved with
an air of uncommon dignity. His countenance was at once
highly intellectual and highly benignant, and his appearance
altogether was unusually prepossessing. The chief characteristics of his ministry were evangelical fervor and simplicity."
He states further his attempts at reading from a manuscript;
"but he would gradually wax warm, his eye kindle, the muscles of his face begin to move, his soul on fire, he would be rushing on extemporaneously with the fury of a cataract; and the
only use made of his manuscript was to roll it up in his hand,
and literally shake it at his audience." The very best use, possibly, to make of such an article in the pulpit. Think of the
early apostles reading from a manuscript with their hearts
aflame with love of souls! Our staid, historic Church folk
cannot abide enthusiasm; and this with the difficulty in their
church service of learning to *"rise and sot"*—as a plain backwoodsman phrases it—interfering with their success among
plain people, notwithstanding their absurd claim of being the
only Church. Dr. Pilmoor died in 1825, in the ninety-first year
of his age.

The fourth visit of Methodism to Carolina, and now with the
determination to remain, was some twelve years after Pilmoor,
by Asbury and his coadjutors in 1785. As to the organization of Churches under the American government, if at all of
any importance, a few dates will fully settle that matter. The
Methodist Episcopal Church was organized December 25, 1784.
In the same year overtures were made to Franklin, in Paris, by
the pope's nuncio, on the subject of appointing a vicar apostolic for the United States; to which congress replied that they
had nothing to do with a subject purely ecclesiastical. In
1786 the pope appointed John Carroll, of Maryland, vicar
apostolic, who was subsequently appointed Bishop of Bal-

DAVID DERRICK. JAMES DANNELLY. W. A. GAMEWELL.

H. A. C. WALKER.   A. M. SHIPP.

timore. In 1789 a general convention of Episcopalians was held, at which the constitution of the new Protestant Episcopal Church, which had been discussed at two previous conventions, was ratified and completed; Bishops White and Provost having been previously ordained by the English bishops. In 1788 the Presbyterians arranged their Church government on a national basis, the Synod of New York and Pennsylvania having been divided into four synods, delegates from which annually met in a General Assembly. So, as far as dates can go, Methodism has the precedence. Dr. William M. Wightman, in his defense of our episcopacy, states:

The time was come for the organization of a CHURCH. There were under Asbury's oversight eighty-three preachers and fifteen thousand members. Methodism began with religion in the heart. Its grand appeal was to the individual conscience. It delivered the testimony of the gospel with all possible stress: "Repentance toward God, and faith toward our Lord Jesus Christ." It sought to bring men from darkness to light, from sin to holiness. This was its first business; and this it did without ordained ministers, without ordinances save the "glorious gospel of the blessed God," without churches, and starting from a "rigging loft" as its point of departure. The only aid it received in money was a donation of £50 from the English Conference. For the first eighteen years it had not among its lay preachers a single man of profound learning or extraordinary mental accomplishments. It was encountered at its outset by the commotions of a Revolution; its cradle was rocked by civil storm and tempest. Who can fail to see that its strength stood in its *religion?* This was its *differentia,* its essential characteristic. Beginning with the religion of the heart, it began from within and worked outward—as genuine Christianity always does. The central functions, the vital forces of the system, being in healthful play, it threw itself, not by mechanical force from without, but by spontaneous energies from within, into those forms of organized life which were the visible extension and manifestation of Church life, in-polity, discipline, and sacraments. This is the philosophy of Methodist *orders.*

Asbury's consecration to the episcopal office proceeded on the ground that episcopacy is not a ministerial order *jure divino*—by divine prescription, of immutable obligation, and clothed with powers emanating directly from God, the channel of Christ's covenanted grace, and therefore indispensable to a Church; but an order *jure ecclesiastico,* originating in the necessities of a connectional body of ministers and members, and holding the exclusive right of ordaining by commission from the Church. For this *jure ecclesiastico* claim, the precedent and practice of Christianity may be adduced; for the *jure divino* right, no solitary passage of Scripture can be pleaded.

The papal theory alone is consistent on this point: the visible Church is a mediator between man and God, the impersonation of Christ, and a depository of grace, sacramental union with which alone gives us access to salvation; the ministry is a priesthood, its powers having come down by perpetual derivation from the apostles; the instrument of transmission is the "sacrament of orders," which is intrusted exclusively to the hands of a bishop. This sacrament of orders impresses an indelible character upon the recipient, and confers sacerdotal grace for the performance of sacerdotal offices. Apart from the virtue of this "sacrament of orders" there can be no true sacraments, nor is there any absolution in the absence of a priest. There is no legitimate priest, therefore, without a bishop, and consequently no valid Christianity outside of this apostolico-succession. This is a theory which one can understand. It is consistent as well as plain. It lacks but one thing: *it is not true.*

To this theory, premises and conclusion, Methodism gives a distinct, unmistakable, utter refutation. It furnishes the demonstration that the spirit and life of Christianity, the birthright and blessing of true inward religion, are to be found outside of this pseudo-sacerdotal system of men and sacraments. It has a priest, "the great High Priest," no more to be exclusively appropriated by a single class of religionists than the light and warmth of the sun. It has a sacrifice—that "once offered"—a sacrifice partaking of divine perfection, wanting nothing to supplement its efficacy; unlimited in its power to save, and undiminished in the fullness of its merit through all generations of the world, and down to the end of time. Any other priest, any other sacrifice, is a grand impertinence. What need have we of other sacerdotal offices when *our* High Priest is able to save them to the uttermost that come unto God by him, "seeing he ever liveth to make intercession for them"? But the sacerdotal character eliminated, then it is matter of not the slightest consequence whether the minister of Christ can trace his genealogy to Linus, Anacletus, or Peter. His call to the ministry is made by the Holy Ghost. The office of the existing ministry is merely to verify that call and countersign his title.

This is as fair a statement as human language can give of the *apology* Methodism makes for being in the world: and we proceed further to illustrate its toils and triumphs.

CHAPTER V.

AT the close of the Christmas Conference and the organization of the Methodist Episcopal Church at Baltimore, Md., in 1784, Bishop Asbury with Jesse Lee and Henry Willis turned their faces southward, hastening on to Charleston. At a Conference "begun at Ellis's Preaching House, Virginia, April 30, 1784, and ended at Baltimore May 28th following," Henry Willis had been sent to Holston, Philip Bruce to Yadkin, Jesse Lee and Isaac Smith to Salisbury, Thomas Humphries to Guilford, and Beverly Allen to Wilmington, N. C. Of the Christmas Conference, the following is on record in the General Minutes:

At this Conference we formed ourselves into an independent Church; and, following the counsel of Mr. John Wesley, who recommended the episcopal mode of Church government, we thought it best to become an Episcopal Church, making the episcopal office elective, and the elected superintendent or bishop amenable to the body of ministers and preachers.

At this Conference the appointments were, for 1785: Georgia, Beverly Allen; Charleston, John Tunnell; Georgetown, Woolman Hickson.

Charleston was the *point d'appui* for the grand work undertaken. Bangs and Andrew state that Henry Willis was the first laborer in the city, induced, possibly, by his greater prominence thereafter; but facts show that John Tunnell was the first. So say the Minutes, and so say the stewards' books, wherein, under date of January, 1786, he received as quarterage £11 11s 9d for the past year's labor. These labors were not confined to the city, but the surrounding country shared in them; and, as will be seen hereafter, the principal rivers gave names to the various circuits formed. While Tunnell was the first in Charleston, James Foster was somewhat in advance of him in the state. Locating on account of bodily infirmity, he formed a circuit among some Virginia Methodist families in Carolina. Reëntering the itinerancy in 1786, he is placed as elder over the Georgia and Carolina work that year, locating in 1787. For some years he was mentally prostrate, wandering among Methodist families and conducting their domestic devotions. There is no record of the time and place of his death.

John Tunnell was said to be "truly an apostolic man. His heavenly-mindedness seemed to shine on his face, and made him appear more like an inhabitant of heaven than of earth." His gifts as a preacher were great. He was sent as a pioneer to the West. He died in 1790 at Sweet Spring, Tenn.

Returning to Asbury's, Willis's, and Lee's first visit to Carolina, their entrance into the state was not that pursued by either Whitefield or Pilmoor, but through Marlborough to Cheraw. Old St. David's, a Protestant Episcopal church, is named as a place in which they had prayer. It is still intact, over a century and a half old. They were entertained in Cheraw by a merchant who had been a Methodist in Virginia. One of his clerks gave them a statement of the religious condition in New England that determined Mr. Lee to seek a further acquaintanceship with that land of steady habits.

Their route was *via* Lynch's Creek, Black Mingo, and Black River to Georgetown, where they arrived February 23, 1785. Georgetown has always been esteemed one of the best soils for Methodism. Two of the happiest years in the life of the writer (1849 and 1850) were spent in its pastorate. He recollects writing up the loose class books, extending from the very beginning, into one solid journal. Were access had to it now, much concerning the early membership could be written.

Bishop Asbury preached on the "Natural Man" and "Spiritual Discernment," very likely regarded as foolishness by those hearing him. But fruit followed in Mr. Wayne opening his house to the preaching, and in his children becoming attached to the Church. On their resuming travel he conducted them to the river, paid their ferriage, and sent them on their way to Charleston with letters to Mr. Wells. Asbury writes of the "barren country in all respects" through which they passed. It had not improved much in 1850; and now, since emancipation, it is more barren than ever. They encountered the two

Santees as usual, of which many missionaries to the slaves of old have vivid recollections.

They came on to Scott's. "The people were merry; their presence made them mute." Next day they met Willis, who had procured a deserted house from the Baptists (probably the old Seaman's Bethel), and gave them Mr. Wells's invitation to his home. Arriving in the city and sending the two on Sunday to preach, Asbury, with good generalship, reconnoitered the field. He attended St. Philip's Church, of which service he says nothing. In the afternoon he attended the Independent meeting, where he "heard a good discourse."

Willis and Lee preached to few in the morning, but to crowds at night. The dearth of religion is mourned over, the Calvinists alone seeming to have any sense thereof. Theaters, balls, and the races absorbed all thought, and the more hidden vices abounded. What degree of religious life existed is unknown; it is very evident that there was but little stirring, awakening preaching in all the town. Ministers looked with suspicion on the newcomers, and even opposed them. Wesley, Whitefield, and Pilmoor had been heard with delight by many, but these men had come to stay, and the old order of things might be disturbed. Many, no doubt, hoped that their wild fanaticism would destroy them; and so, for awhile, the mob was quiet. The bishop's subjects of discourse were: (1) "Now then as ambassadors," 2 Corinthians v. 20; (2) "Rejoice, O young man," Ecclesiastes xi. 9; (3) "He shall reprove the world," John xvi. 8; (4) "The times of this ignorance," Acts xxii. 30; (5) "Ask, and it shall be given," Matthew vii. 7; (6) "Be ready always to give," 1 Peter iii. 15. Here was (1) the commission, (2) retribution, (3) reproof, (4) repentance, (5) prayer, (6) assurance; the series undoubtedly well selected for opening his great commission, and good followed. These men felt all the dignity and responsibility of God's ambassadors. The trumpet gave no uncertain sound. The truth is never powerless, and it is not surprising that opposition was awakened, as at the beginning. But it cannot be suppressed. Racks and gibbets, the stocks and whipping post, bitter mockery and cruel scorn have been alike unavailing.

Knight, in his popular history of England, on Hogarth's "Credulity, Superstition, and Fanaticism, a medley of 1762," remarks:

A new power has arisen. The chief object is the ridicule of Methodism. Whitefield's journal and Wesley's sermons figure by name among the accessories of the piece, where the ranting preacher is holding forth to the howling congregation. Pope had described the "harmonic twang" of the donkey's bray:

> Then, Webster, pealed thy voice; and, Whitefield, thine.

Bishop Lovington had written "The Enthusiasm of Methodist and Papist Compared"; and Hogarth followed the precedent in all ages of despising reformers. The followers of Whitefield and Wesley might be ignorant, superstitious, fanatical. They themselves may have indirectly encouraged the delusions of a few of their disciples; but they eventually changed the face of English society.

Every word true; and Methodism, through Christ's gospel, is to-day engaged in changing not only the face of English society, but of that of the entire world.

This first visit was not without visible fruit. Mr. Wells was converted. "Now we know," says Asbury, "that God has brought us here, and have a hope that there will be a glorious work among the people—at least among the Africans." At the end of the first year (1785) there were thirty-five whites and twenty-three colored in Charleston, and from the stewards' books for that year we gather that $425 was paid to the preachers.

Asbury, this 10th of March, 1785, feeling much love and pity for the people, prepared to leave Charleston, knowing that some were under serious impressions. Crossing at Haddret's Point, he baptized two children, refusing any fee therefor, and hastened on to Georgetown, where he found Mrs. Wayne under deep distress of soul. His objective point was Wilmington, and he deflected from the direct route to go to Kingstree. "Got to Durant's," a name afterwards famous in Methodist annals; "found him a disciple of Mr. Harvey's, but not in the enjoyment of religion. After faithful admonition, left him doubtless a disciple of Christ's." Why this deflection to Kingstree, does not appear, but it may have been to seal to the Church this fruit; and all who know of the Durants, especially the Rev. Henry H. Durant of our day, know the gathering of that harvest was mighty.

The good bishop sped on his way, while Willis and Lee remained in the city. Worship was continued for awhile in the old Baptist meetinghouse. For a time they used it, but one Sunday they found their seats flung out into the streets, and doors and windows barred against them. This they regarded as a mild intimation that they were not wanted there any longer. But this was but as the summer's breeze compared to the wild tornado of persecution following. Turned out into the cold, a kind lady, Mrs. Stoll, opened her house for worship. This proving too small for the increasing congregations, another removal was made to an unfinished house in Wentworth street, and in 1787 the church in Cumberland street was erected.

Pausing for awhile in our narrative, we put on record here the pen portaits of these pioneers—Asbury, Willis, and Lee. The Rev. Thomas Scott about 1790 gives this picture of

FRANCIS ASBURY.

" He was now forty-four years of age, and about five feet eight inches in height. His bones were large, but not his muscles. His voice was deep-toned, sonorous, and clear. His articulation and emphasis were very distinct, and his words were always appropriate. His features were distinctly marked, and his intellectual organs were well balanced and finely developed. His hair and complexion, when he was young, were light, and his eyelashes uncommonly long. His general appearance was that of one born to rule. He was an excellent judge of the character, talents, and qualifications of men for particular stations. When presiding in Conferences, unless when compelled to speak, he sat with his eyes apparently closed; but the eyes were not closely shut, but in constant motion, inspecting countenances."

Joshua Marsden calls him "a dignified, eloquent, and impressive preacher." But his forte was declared by judges to be administration. It is said of him that he would sometimes playfully tease his companion, Bishop Whatcoat. Why not? The gravest may sometimes unbend, if only careful to do so away from a fool. A companion portrait to the above shows how he appeared in old age to the youthful Wightman, afterwards bishop. He states: "Among my earliest recollections is the tolerably vivid impression of a venerable old man, shrunk and wrinkled, wearing knee breeches and shoe buckles, dressed in dark drab, whose face to a child's eye would have seemed stern but for the gentleness of his voice and manner toward the little people. It was the custom of my honored and sainted mother, no doubt at the instance of the bishop himself, to send her children to pay him a visit whenever he came to the city. The last one was made in company with my two younger brothers. The bishop had some apples on the mantelpiece of the chamber when the little group of youngsters, the eldest only some seven years old, were introduced. After a little talk suitable to our years and capacity, the venerable man put his hands on our heads, one after another, with a solemn prayer and blessing, and dismissed us, giving the largest apple to the smallest child, in a manner that left upon me a lifelong impression. I remember, too, how he was carried into Trinity Church and placed upon a high stool, and with trembling voice delivered his last testimony there. An incident trifling in itself may powerfully illustrate character; and the foregoing shows the attention which a chief of a Church extending from Canada to Georgia, with cares innumerable occupying his thoughts, in age and extreme feebleness, was accustomed to pay to *children*—little children."

HENRY WILLIS

was the first preacher ordained by Asbury after his own consecration as bishop, and was ever held by him in the highest esteem, and was selected as one of the pioneers to Carolina. The General Minutes represent him as manly and intelligent, possessing great gifts—natural, spiritual, and acquired. His prominent feature was an open, pleasant countenance. He was of great fortitude; cheerful, without levity; of great sobriety, without sullenness or melancholy; of slender habit of body and feebleness in chest and lungs, but of great energy of address and fervor of mind. Carrying on a large business, he received but little support from the Church, and accumulated a fortune. He continued effective several years, then local, then supernumerary, as the necessities of livelihood demanded, holding on to his grand commission that could not be dispensed with but by unfaithfulness, debility, or death. After thirty years of connection with Methodism, he died in Maryland in 1808, with unshaken trust in God and faith in Christ. Asbury, on visiting his grave, is said to have exclaimed: "Henry Willis! Ah, when shall I look upon thy like again? Rest, man of God."

JESSE LEE.

This other pioneer was one of the giants of the olden time. He became the apostle of Methodism in New England, and once tied Whatcoat in an election to the episcopacy. At this time he was but twenty-seven years of age, and some six years a preacher. He is represented as very large, almost unwieldy, with a fine, intelligent face, impressing one with the idea that he was no common man; of great energy of mind and purpose, with deep insight into the springs of human action; with a voice well-nigh making the house jar when he preached; of excellent humor, often indulged in to the amusement of his friends, but withal of fervent devotion to Christ, his Master. He died triumphantly in his fifty-ninth year and thirty-sixth of his itinerant ministry. His entrance into New England and continued ministry was not without difficulty; those in power regarded it as an intrusion, and predestination, election, reprobation, decrees, and final perseverance met him at every point. The generous hospitality of the South was not there existent. Invited to a house once, the folks left home to avoid him; at another, no one offered him a seat; at another, the whole family slept against time, and he had to leave fasting. Alighting at an inn once and saying he was a preacher and wished to preach in the village, it was asked: "Have you a liberal education, sir?" "Tolerably liberal, madam," said he; "enough, I think, to carry me through the country." To the selectmen he replied that "he did not like to boast of his learning, but hoped he had enough to get on with among them." On one occasion a plan was laid to expose his ignorance before a congregation, when a pedantic lawyer addressed him in Latin. Lee, suspecting a stratagem, replied in Dutch. The lawyer, concluding it was Hebrew, and fearing he had caught a Tartar, retreated. A minister and a lawyer attacking him on doctrinal points, Lee poured hot shot into them. In anger the lawyer said: "Sir, are you a knave or a fool?" "Neither one nor the other," said Lee, "but at present happen to be just *between the two.*" This quieted them.

Two lawyers, referring to his extemporaneous preaching, asked if he did not make mistakes, and if he corrected them. "That depends," said Lee. "If only a slip of the tongue and near the truth, I let it go. For instance, once saying 'the devil was a liar, and the father of lies,' I said '*lawyers.*' It was so nearly correct, I passed right on." The test sermon, to see if he could preach without premeditation, the text given as soon as preliminary services were over, on the subject "And Balaam rose up in the morning and saddled his ass," resulted in the entire discomfiture of the officious parson; Lee showing the rider as the clergyman, the saddle as the salary, and the poor burdened ass as the congregation.

As to his size, the exact avoirdupois is not given, but tradition has it that once in Richmond, crossing a miry street, he was kindly borne over by a colored brother. "Oh, wretched man that I am!" sighed the negro. "You do groan being burdened," was Lee's reply. Eight of the best years of his life were spent in New England, and in that time twenty-five preachers and thirteen hundred members had been gathered.

His stratagem at a camp meeting near Richmond, to put men to sleep rather than to keep them awake, may be noted. At midnight a number of drunken sailors disturbed the camp. Mr. Lee, arising from bed and going into the pulpit, said that they would have a sermon. A burst of noisy merriment followed, but in they came. When all was still, Mr. Lee directed one of the preachers to preach them a sermon. He took for his text, "At midnight Paul and Silas prayed," etc. He had not been preaching long before the stupefying effects of their potations told on the inward and outward man. Mr. Lee called to the preacher, "*Stop.*" Finding none of them stirring, he picked up his hat and said: "Softly! let's go to bed." The next morning, on awakening chilled and around the fires, the sailors regretted being fooled into hearing a midnight sermon.

Whatever may have been the veneration held for Bishop Asbury, the preachers in debate were "not afraid with any amazement" of him or other bishops, for after all bishops are but men. At a General Conference the repugnance of Asbury to a certain measure was shown in his turning his back to the speaker. Mr. Lee, in replying to a speaker who had said, "No man of common sense would use such argument as he had presented," in his rejoinder said: "Mr. President, Brother —— has so said, and I am compelled to believe that the brother thinks me a man of *uncommon* sense." "Yes, yes," said the bishop, turning half round in his chair; "yes, yes, Brother Lee, you are a man of uncommon sense." "Then, sir," said Lee, very quickly and pleasantly, "I beg that uncommon attention may be paid to what I am about to say." It had its effect.

Another instance may occur to many anent H. H. Kavanaugh in the Kentucky Conference at a later date. "Take your seat, brother," said the bishop; "you have talked long enough." "Am I in order, bishop?" was the reply. "Certainly," said the bishop. "Then I shall speak as long as I think fit." And the courtly Kentuckian subsided.

The close of earthly life with Jesse Lee was triumphant; about his last words were: "Glory, glory, glory! Halleluiah! Jesus reigns!"

CHAPTER VI.

THE General Minutes give for the next year, 1786, the following appointments: James Foster, elder; Georgia, Thomas Humphries, John Major; Broad River, Stephen Johnson; Charleston, Henry Willis, Isaac Smith. Beverly Allen, elder; Santee, Richard (Smith) Swift; Pee Dee, Jeremiah Mastin, Hope Hull. These were made at Salisbury, N. C., February, 1786. The bishop had reached Charleston in January, and the incidents of his travel to Salisbury are of interest. It is a pity that they are so meager. What are given in his journal, however, if they do no more, mark the routes pursued by the pioneers.

They crossed Great Pee Dee and Lynch's Creek, on to Black Mingo; lodging at a tavern, they were well used. Preached at Georgetown, "a poor place for religion." Here, they were met by Willis. Came to Wappetaw, and preached at St. Clair Capers's. Thence to Cainhoy by water, and on to Charleston. Sunday, January 15, "had a solemn time in the day and a full house in the evening." All encouraged in the hope of building a meetinghouse this year. Friday, 20th, leaves for Wasmasaw; waterbound, "take to the wild woods." Then on to the Congaree. Lodged where there were a set of gamblers; doubtless remembering the young prophet, betrayed by the elder one, who disobeying the divine injunction, perished (1 Kings xiii. 30): "I neither ate bread nor drank water with them." He left early, riding nine miles; came to a fire, stopped, and "broiling our bacon, had a high breakfast." At Weaver's Ferry they crossed the Saluda. Here once lived a poor lunatic who proclaimed himself God, his wife the Virgin Mary, and his son Jesus Christ. He was hanged for murder at Charleston, promising to rise the third day. "A judicial murder, undoubtedly." At Parrot's log church near Broad River they had some four hundred hearers. Sunday, 29th, preached on Sandy River. The

(48)

floods were out; difficulty in fording streams. Monday on to Terry's; but the old trouble, high waters, made them "go up higher." Coming to Great Sandy River, crossed at Walker's Mill; in danger of losing their horses. Came to Father Sealey's; "stayed to refit, and had everything comfortable." And thus on to John's River and Salisbury, whence he sent the men to the appointments above given. And how gladly would their itinerary, with what they thought, said, and did, be given! But very little is upon record.

James Foster, the first named, retired the next year. All relative to Thomas Humphries, in Georgia, was his welcome from Thomas Haynes, on Uchee Creek, as given by Dr. G. G. Smith. These annals shall have more to say of him. John Major, his colleague—"the weeping prophet"—was remarkable for his pathos and power. Ware says: "He was armed with the irresistible eloquence of tears; was so beloved by the people that they would have risked life to rescue him from insult or injury." He tells of seeing an audience unmoved under a masterly discourse, but melted to tears under a five-minutes' exhortation by Major. Once preaching from the text, "Unto you who believe, he is precious," his voice was lost in the cries of the people. After ten years of itinerant labor, he died in 1788.

Stephen Johnston was only one year in Carolina, but had much success here, doubling the membership. He returned to Virginia, and disappears from the Minutes in 1790. Of Henry Willis, already named, and of Isaac Smith, more to say. Beverly Allen was of gentlemanly bearing, really fine-looking, and at this time of great popularity and usefulness. He has the unenviable notoriety of being the first apostate presbyter in American Methodism. He says in letters to Mr. Wesley at this time: "I was appointed to travel at large through South Carolina, visiting North Carolina and Georgia. . . . At one meeting held in Santee Circuit fifteen or twenty professed conversion. Many called for prayer. Solemn seasons, both in Edisto, Broad River, and Pee Dee circuits. The voices of the people were like the sound of many waters. Great numbers added in the course of this season."

Richard (Smith) Swift ("Smith" is a misprint in the Minutes, no such name before nor after 1786) labored successfully on Santee Circuit, returning a membership of one hun-

4

dred and seventy-eight whites and twelve colored.   He returned to Virginia, locating in 1793.   Jeremiah Mastin and Hope Hull had a most successful year, 1786; an ingathering of over six hundred members and the erection of twenty-two meeting-houses.   Of Humphries and Hope Hull more hereafter.

This, it will be remembered, all occurred in 1786, and measures were taken for the erection of a church on Cumberland street in Charleston, sixty feet long by forty wide.   It was completed in about eighteen months, costing £1,300.   Of it we will have more to say hereafter.

The first session of the South Carolina Conference was held in Charleston, S. C., March 22, 1787.   Where they met is left to conjecture; it may have been in a private house or in Cumberland Church lately built.   It was the beginning of a series of assemblies of which we now see the one hundred and tenth. Its presiding officers were Dr. Thomas Coke and Francis Asbury, both introduced into the episcopacy by as genuine a father in God as ever existed since the apostles' days.   The one in clerical attire, short in stature, of ample rotundity, looking every inch a bishop, and though chimed out of his English parish, with great rejoicing had become the first Protestant bishop in America, and was destined to cross the Atlantic eighteen times at his own charges, to expend his entire fortune for Christian missions, and when near seventy to rest his mortal remains amid the coral groves of the Indian Ocean.   The other, as Stevens says, "not yet fifty years old, in the maturity of his physical and intellectual strength, his person slight but yet vigorous and erect, his eye stern but bright, his brow wrinkled through extraordinary care and fatigue, his countenance expressive of decision, sagacity, and benignity—shaded at times by an aspect of deep anxiety, if not dejection; his attitude dignified, if not graceful; his voice sonorous and commanding."

Of the members present, number and names, there is no record.   By looking at the appointments for 1787 we can only conjecture.   There is no journal extant, and none of the Conference in our archives until 1799, and that but a sheet of foolscap, blotted and blurred and of most horrible chirography, nothing to be compared with the splendid records now existing. Indeed, it may be doubted if any journalistic records, save in the bishop's notebook, obtained in any of these early sessions. It is not until 1801 that Asbury notes in his journal the appointment of "a clerk for the minutes, and another, Jeremiah Norman, to keep the journal." It may be doubted further if very much of parliamentary order prevailed. At a later period "rules of order" were adopted, with which Asbury found fault, and asking how they came into being, McKendree replied: "You are our father, and do not need them; we, your sons, do." Fully mollified, the bishop sat down smiling.

Of course we cannot put on record all the business transacted. We gather from the General Minutes somewhat as to (1) the instruction of the colored people—all are earnestly entreated to care for them, unite them with the society, and to exercise the whole Methodist discipline among them; (2) directions as to books of registry; (3) formation of the children into proper classes, and the truly awakened taken into society; (4) allowance for the married preachers considered too large, and £48 provincial currency allowed them.

Stith Mead, at a later date of 1792, gives the following synopsis of proceedings:

Members present twelve; one received into full connection, two elected to deacon's orders, one located, two admitted on trial, and two called on to relate their Christian experience. Adjournment until next day.

Second Day. Three preachers examined by the bishop before the Conference: first, as to debt; second, faith in Christ; third, their pursuit after holiness. The bishop preached. Hope Hull preached, and Mead called on to relate his experience to the Conference. *In the evening the appointments were read.*

Third Day. All were examined by the bishop as to their confession of faith and orthodoxy of doctrine; two were found to be tending to Unitarianism. All were requested to give as much Scripture as they could recollect as to the personality of the Trinity, especially of the Holy Ghost. Two preachers recanted errors in doctrine and were continued in fellowship. Asbury and Hull preached again. Deep feeling prevailed; the sacrament administered, the services continuing until near sundown. Many sinners were awakened, and ten souls converted.

Fourth Day. Three were ordained elders and two deacons. Conference adjourned about ten o'clock.

The appointments made at this first session in 1787 were: Richard Ivy, elder; Burke, John Major, Matthew Harris; Augusta, Thomas Humphries, Moses Park; Broad River, John Mason, Thomas Davis. Beverly Allen, elder; Edisto, Edward West; Charleston, Lemuel Green. Reuben Ellis, elder; Santee,

Isaac Smith; Pee Dee, H. Bingham, L. Andrews, H. Ledbetter; Yadkin, W. Partridge, B. McHenry, J. Connor; Salisbury, Mark Moore.

A brief reference to each of the above preachers, not already mentioned, is in place. Richard Ivy was a man of quick and solid parts, seeking not himself, his great concern and business to be rich in grace and usefulness; a holy, self-denying Christian; he died in 1795. Of Matthew Harris little is known; he disappears from the Minutes in 1791. Moses Park disappears from the Minutes in 1790. John Mason and Thomas Davis retired in 1788. H. Bingham died the next year, and was buried at Cattle Creek Camp Ground; a plain tablet marks the spot. Edward West located after 1790. Lemuel Green located in 1800. Reuben Ellis was of large body but slender constitution, of slow but sure and solid parts, an excellent counselor and guide; died in 1796. L. Andrews died in 1790. H. Ledbetter, after several years, located, living in upper Carolina, and died in the faith. W. Partridge traveled several years, located some twenty, then reëntered the Conference, traveling a year or two, and died in 1817, exclaiming, "For me to die is gain!" B. McHenry became one of the giants of the West, dying there in 1833. James Connor died in 1789. Mark Moore located in 1799. Travis states concerning him: "He was not a regular itinerant; too unsettled, except in piety and devotion." He lived to a good old age, still a faithful and holy minister.

In 1786 the Broad River, Santee, and Pee Dee circuits are for the first time named. South Carolina in territory is triangular, the Savannah River its base; its apex, the Atlantic. There being few towns, villages, hamlets, the broad streams coursing through its length properly map the territory, giving metes and bounds, and names as well, to the circuits. A glance at the map shows the Savannah River its western boundary; next the Edisto, running half through the state; then the two Santees, soon becoming the Congaree and then branching out into the Saluda, Broad, and Wateree rivers—the Wateree becoming the Catawba, and running up into North Carolina; then next Lynch's River and the two Pee Dees, with innumerable lesser streams all over the state. It is the purpose of these annals to follow as minutely as possible the footprints of the pioneers, and in as chronological order as may be.

H. M. MOOD.　　F. MILTON KENNEDY.　　J. T. WIGHTMAN.
JOHN R. PICKETT.　　　　　　D. J. SIMMONS.

All the Conferences from the first to the fourteenth were held in Charleston, except the eighth session, held at Finch's, which soon after became the site of Bethel Academy. The crowded condition of entertainment in the country induced ever after the selection of cities as the seats of meeting. All these Conferences were presided over by Coke and Asbury jointly, oftener by the last alone, except the twelfth, held by Jonathan Jackson at Asbury's appointment.

Of course it is impossible to note the sessions of Conferences *seriatim.* In the first place, but little is known of the business transacted; and to give the appointments and preachers would overrun our limits to little profit, so we notice only a few of both.

The second session was held March 14, 1788. On his way to it Asbury preached at Beauty Spot, in Marlborough county. Why so called we know not, save that the whole country is lovely. Nothing is said of the building in which service was held, but we remember the huge, barn-like structure once existent at a later day, possibly giving place now to one of more architectural beauty in keeping with the wealth and intelligence of that community. The bishop preached on "The wilderness and solitary place," etc., and on "They weighed for me thirty pieces of silver." They had a gracious, moving time. Then *en route*, resting at Rembert's, Monday found them in their saddles, contending with the swamps of Santee, passing ruined Dorchester, and so on to the city.

Of the business done nothing is known. Asbury, in his journal, notes the riot at the church, causing even the ladies to leap from the windows; Henry Bingham reported dead; and two circuits, Saluda and Waxhaws, added to the appointments. Of the Saluda Circuit there is no definite information. Allied with Bush River in Newberry county, possibly it began in Laurens, taking in Greenville and Anderson. As in 1800 it was united with Cherokee, its boundary presently to be given, this conjecture may not be wrong. The Conference of 1788 (the second) over, Asbury takes up his restless travel, presses on to Cattle Creek, in Edisto Circuit, Gassaway with him; complains that the people are "insensible," "more in love with Christ's messengers than with Christ." Doubtless they had been troubling him about some favorite preachers. Then on to

Broad River, Isaac Smith with him at Finch's. Travels two hundred miles, doubling often for some out-of-the-way appointment, and up often until twelve o'clock at night meetings.

The third session began March 16, 1789. Good reports had; nine hundred increase in membership recorded. No riotous excesses this time, but the city press bitter in its invectives; no wonder, considering the indiscreet action anent slavery. Fourteen preachers stationed in Carolina, among them John Andrew (father of the bishop) on Cherokee Circuit, Humphries, Isaac Smith, and Gassaway. Charleston strangely left blank; Pee Dee Circuit divided into Great and Little Pee Dee, and Cherokee and Bush River first named. On Bush River was William Gassaway. Under that name the record is continuous until changed in 1820 to Newberry Circuit. Farther on in these annals more will be said of that famous charge.

The fourth session, February 15, 1790, was one "of peace and love." Increase, six hundred and thirty members. City Methodists considered "too mute and fearful"; the outside people, "violent and wicked." Asbury, resuming his travel, preaches at Linder's, has "a dry time"; at Cattle Creek, "better"; then on to Chester. He laments the spiritual death wrought by Antinomian leaven; complains of "the leaning to Calvinism," and "the love of strong drink." Whatcoat and himself appoint a night meeting; only "two men came, and they were drunk." Complains of the roads, and the people who "pass for Christians." Thinks a prophet of strong drink might suit them well. And there were some of that sort, if history be a faithful chronicler. In this very year of 1790, Dr. Howe states, "ministers were disciplined for drunkenness, and at funerals often the living were not sufficiently sober properly to bury the dead." Tradition asserts that once hereabout a minister was so far gone in the pulpit as to fall asleep during the singing of the hymns; being aroused by the precentor telling him "it was out," he drowsily replied, *"Fill her up ag'in."* At this session nineteen preachers were stationed.

CHAPTER VII.

The Fifth Session—Elation and Depression—Religious Swearing—Hammet's Arrival—Sixth Session—Mathews Withdraws—Cherokee Circuit —Hard Work, Small Salary—Seventh Session—Eighth Session at Finch's —McKendree—Enoch George—Spiritual Declension—Tabulated Matter in Conference Minutes—Mt. Bethel Academy—Jenkins's Disappointment —Simon Carlisle.

THE fifth session began February 23, 1791. Concerning it but little data exist. On his way to the city Asbury exults in the success of the gospel, rejoices to find "this desert country has gracious souls in it." "How great the change in six years!" "Under Gassaway, on Little Pee Dee, an increase of over eight hundred; the aggregate increase in the Conference, over twelve hundred." And yet he was shortly after much cast down. At Georgetown he preached "a plain, searching sermon; but it's a day of small things." The wicked youths were playing without, and there was inattention within. But great changes require time.

Travis relates of one at Georgetown swearing religiously at a later period. Alas! there are fears that many Church members do it irreligiously. "Brother Roquie, are you happy?" inquired a good woman of one shouting. "Yes, yes; I is happy." She looking him in the face, not incredulously yet without reply, he added: "*I swear I is happy.*" A case for Sterne's recording angel. After all, the good old Frenchman died in the faith, conquering what was long a bad habit.

Bishop Coke attended this Conference, having been shipwrecked off Edisto. He brought Mr. Hammet over from the West Indies. Hammet was disappointed in not receiving the city appointment. James Parks being sent, Hammet pursued the bishop, seeking it for himself. Asbury writes, under date of Charleston, 1791: "I went to church under awful distress of heart. . . . The people claim the right to choose their own preachers, a thing quite new among Methodists. None but Mr. Hammet will do for them. We shall see how it will end." And it was soon seen, culminating in schism shaking the Church in that city to its foundations, resulting in a loss of membership of 27.27 per cent. Mr. Hammet set up for himself, calling his church Trinity, and his people Primitive Methodists. Succeeding for a time, at his death came disintegration, some returning to the old fold, some to other Churches, others to the world. Mr. Brazier, falling heir, sold the church to the Protestant Episcopalians. It was recovered by the trustees, and eventually, with other property, came into our possession. Mr. Hammet died in 1803, and his dust lies in the rear of Trinity Church.

The sixth session began February 14, 1792. It was unusually close in the examination of character, doctrine, and experience. The bishop explained publicly our Church polity, giving reasons for not committing the society in Charleston to Mr. Hammet, who was unknown, a foreigner, and not uniting with the American Church. Philip Mathews withdrew from the connection, his character passing in examination, though Asbury thought "it had been better to subject it to scrutiny." Seventeen years after, in 1809, Travis reports him as feeling the pulses of some converts in Georgetown who were apparently lifeless, and his saying: "Mr. Travis, I want you to pray for me." "Well," said Travis, "kneel down here." "Oh!" was the reply; "I want you to do it privately." There was no rejoinder on the part of Mr. Travis.

At this Conference James Jenkins was admitted. He came near rejection; but it being found that Mathews would withdraw, Jenkins was sent in his place to the Cherokee Circuit. And here for the first time we have accurately stated its boundaries and much relating to the labors of the first preachers. This circuit was formed in 1789 by John Andrew (father of Bishop Andrew) and Philip Mathews. It began near Campbellton, near Hamburg, then up the Savannah River to old Cherokee Town, thence in a line along the Blue Ridge across to Saluda, following the river down, then to the present site of Cokesbury and on to Edgefield, embracing that district together with Abbeville and Pendleton. The last, it will be remembered, has been since divided into two or more counties. It was a six-weeks' circuit, three hundred miles in circumference. Methodism was little known, and that little unfavorably. Here Allen fell; the society he founded, and where he sinned, was entirely broken up, but one man holding fast his integrity. The opposition met with was light compared with other matters demanding endurance. The previous winter had been severe; the large grain crop had to be fed away to the cattle, depending on the wheat crop for sustenance; this failed through the rust; then came drought, in which there was no yield of corn. Famine threatening, the preachers feared they would have to leave—no food scarcely for themselves and horses. For the last there were but three places where corn could be had, musty wheat and grass their only food. The people got through the year by partial supplies from abroad and the abundance of fruit existing. In addition their lives were in danger from the Indians, their chief town being but a few miles from one of the appointments. Attending service once, they indulged in laughter; the chief apologized, saying: "They do not know to whom you were talking; but I know: it was to the Great Spirit." In an attack on the town this chief was killed, causing all families to flee save two, and to these the preachers ministered. There were a few log churches, but in private dwellings, for the most part, religious services were held. Amid it all, souls were converted. The presiding elder, Reuben Ellis, so extensive was his district (the entire state), visited the circuit only twice. On settlement by the stewards, Mr. Jenkins received twenty-two dollars, *including* presents. Souls, however, were converted. At Gribble's a man ran up and requested prayer. All were deeply affected, five joining the Church. An awful circumstance occurred: a youth under awakening hanged himself. Brought up under the teaching of Calvinism, he was driven to despair. Did all this toil and labor pay? One has but to compare the returns of this sixth session with the one hundred and eighth, as set forth in the Minutes, to see, notwithstanding thousands safe in heaven, that thousands more are on the way; the 3,665 members in all Carolina and Georgia, compared with the 72,000 in Carolina alone, giving a good percentage of increase in less than a century.

The seventh session began December 24, 1792. A singular anomaly—two Conferences in one year. The appointments, it will be understood, are for 1793. It was the overlooking the fact of two Conferences in one year that led to the differences of opinion between members of the body in enumerating the sessions of the Conference at a later date. This session was longer than usual. The preaching was so exciting that "the blacks were hardly restrained from crying aloud." Seventeen preachers were stationed. It was the first Conference James Jenkins attended. He says: "It was a source of joy to meet the preachers. Peace and harmony reigned, and their spiritual strength was greatly renewed." James Douthet was received on trial. He had been found by Jenkins the year before, greatly afflicted with rheumatism, trying to flee the call. He labored for thirteen years, located in 1806, and was long a local preacher of great pulpit force; often mentioned by Asbury as "good Father Douthet"; dying in the faith.

It was determined to unite the Georgia and South Carolina Conferences, and the eighth session was accordingly appointed for Finch's, in Newberry county. This Conference was greatly straitened for room: "twelve feet square in which to confer, sleep, and accommodate the sick." The Bethel Academy buildings were not completed, and not dedicated until the next year, 1795. It was a remarkable Conference, not only on account of the union with Georgia, but it was the seat of the first educational enterprise undertaken by the Church in Carolina; and here were gathered some of the mighty men to be developed in after years. McKendree came with Asbury. George was already there. Reuben Ellis, Philip Bruce—Ellis to go back to Virginia, and Bruce to lead the entire sacramental host for the year—Tobias Gibson, N. Watters, Isaac Smith, Joseph Moore, Jonathan Jackson, and James Jenkins were there. William Gassaway had located, but soon after reëntered, doing yeoman service to the cause. Under a great display of divine power, Reuben Ellis preached and Hope Hull exhorted.

Here Asbury was in much affliction, but attended to all his duties. Every attention was paid the Conference, the Presbyterians offering their house of worship. James Jenkins was ordained deacon, the bishop remarking, "You feel the hands of the bishop very heavy, but the devil's hands will be heavier still." McKendree was sent for one quarter to Union Circuit, and removed to Virginia the next year. He had traveled under O'Kelly, and had become prejudiced against Asbury; a closer acquaintanceship satisfied him that Asbury had been misrepresented. He was near six feet in height, robust, weighed a hundred and sixty pounds, strong and active, fair complexion, black hair, blue eyes; his intellect quick, keen, but calm and observant.

His garb was almost Quakerish in its simplicity; a man for the times, leading in triumph the Church in the wilderness. He died in 1835, his last words being, "All is well"; and his dust reposes beside Bishop Soule's, in the Vanderbilt grounds, near Nashville.

Enoch George, like McKendree, was near six feet in height; stout, almost corpulent; energetic, and of military bearing. His form was imposing, face broad, forehead prominent, nose large, eyes blue and deeply set, eyebrows dark and projecting, hair black, tinged with gray; his complexion, from the malaria of the South, sallow. His whole person was stamped with character; his piety profound and tender; one of the most effective preachers of his day. In 1794 he was on the Great Pee Dee Circuit, and this year was sent to Edisto. He himself says:

My labors were of a most painful kind; in a desert land, amongst almost impassable swamps, and under bilious diseases of almost every class, which unfitted me for duty in Charleston or amongst the hospitable inhabitants of the "Pine Barrens." In the midst of all this my mind was stayed on God, and kept in perfect peace. Prospects in general were very discouraging. At my second year in this region, Bishop Asbury inquired if we knew of the conversion of any souls within the bounds of the Conference the past year, and to the best of my recollection the whole of us together could not remember one. At this session of the Conference [1795] nearly all the men of age, experience, and talent located [among them Humphries, Hope Hull, Parks, Ledbetter, McHenry, Coleman Carlisle, and Lipsey]. I was appointed presiding elder and besought the preachers and people to unite as one man, and to seek by fasting and prayer a revival of the work of the Lord in the midst of these years of declension and spiritual death. The Lord heard, and the displays of his power were so manifest that near two thousand members were added to the district in a few months.

Mr. George anxiously sought a change to a more northerly climate, but was denied and sent to Georgia; another trial, as his own district was in peace, but the other full of contention and strife. But that year ended his labor in the South. In 1816 he was elected and ordained bishop, closing his earthly existence in holy triumph in 1828.

From Enoch George's record and from the General Minutes, notwithstanding the unusual strength of laborers in Carolina and Georgia, the returns show a heavy decrease in membership. And here, once for all, with reference to increase and decrease and statistical details in general, these annals need not be encumbered. Tabulated statements will be found in the Appendix giving all information necessary. A study of these will show a singular fluctuation in the membership, arising possibly from persecution, schisms, or rigid discipline. From that review it will be seen that it was not until the eighteenth session in 1804 the numbers were more than ten thousand whites and three thousand colored. After that, the increase was more steady until 1830, falling off more than one-half the next year—40,335 whites and 24,554 colored; and in 1831 in Carolina 20,813 whites and 19,144 colored. Setting off the Georgia Conference explains it. There were no great changes for nearly forty years, when the sixty-fifth session shows a decrease of three thousand whites and nearly four thousand colored, caused by transfer to the North Carolina Conference in 1850; then, some time after, a depletion of ten thousand members, but still the advance was onward. The depletion in colored membership in 1864 was 47,460; in 1865 it was 26,283, gradually growing less until in 1878, when they ceased to be reported. This tabulated statement, with the mortuary record, list of members of the Conference, as also delegates to the General Conference, and other tabulated matter, was the work of the author of these annals when editor of the Annual Minutes from 1870 to 1880; of which he would have said nothing at all if some of them had not been appropriated in another volume without any credit given whatever.

Returning to this eighth session at Finch's, an article from the *Southern Christian Advocate* of 1852, and copied into Deems's Annals for 1856, states:

This section of Newberry was peopled by emigrants from Virginia, among them the Finches, the Crenshaws, the Malones. They were Methodists, and when the subject of a high school was agitated, they entered heartily, and with liberal subscriptions, into the project. Edward Finch gave thirty acres of land and a site for the institution. During 1794 the building was completed, and formally dedicated by Bishop Asbury March 20, 1795, and named Mount Bethel. The Rev. Mark Moore, eminently qualified, was for six years rector, aided by Messrs. Smith and Hammond. The latter, the father of ex-Governor Hammond, took charge after Mr. Moore's retirement, teaching with signal ability for many years. It was largely patronized, even from Georgia and North Carolina. Leading men from Carolina—among them the Caldwells of Newberry, Judge Earle, the first ex-Governor Manning, and William and Wesley Harper—were here academically instructed.

The main building was twenty by forty feet, divided by a partition, with chimneys at each end constructed of rough, unhewn stone. The upstairs was used as lodgings for the students. Several comfortable cabins were also built, as residences for the teachers and as boarding houses. About one hundred yards off, at the foot of a hill, ran a bold spring of pure water. Of this monument of Asbury's zeal in the cause of education nothing scarcely remains except the three chimneys of Father Finch's house, which still stand as solitary sentinels over this classic ground.

Near by is a large graveyard, in which many of the original settlers and some of the students sleep in death. Here, too, in modest seclusion, lie the remains of the Rev. John Harper. A rude stone, some six or eight inches above the ground, bearing the initials "J. H.," marks this grave.

After years of usefulness the academy began to decline, and ceased to exist about 1820, superseded by Mount Ariel and Cokesbury schools.

Of the Rev. John Harper more hereafter. How strange that such entire desolation marks the spot once so noted! In 1851 the Rev. Colin Murchison attempted to establish and build a church, but none now exists. While James Jenkins was on his way to Finch's from Oconee, Ga., with $40 out of $64 allowed him, he fancied that Santee, because Isaac Smith had been there, would be an admirable work. And to it he was appointed; but he had great trouble there, as may hereafter be seen.

This year the second expulsion from the Conference occurred: Beverly Allen in 1792, and Simon Carlisle in 1794. This was a terrible wrong inflicted on an innocent man. Coleman Carlisle, his brother, gives a thrilling relation of the circumstances. Simon reproving a wicked young man, incurred his wrath. Placing a pistol in the preacher's saddlebags, he accused him of theft. Next day, procuring a search warrant, and making oath that he believed Parson Carlisle had stolen his pistol, an officer started in pursuit. Overtaking Mr. Carlisle and making known his business, Mr. C. readily consented to be searched, and, conscious of his innocence, was eager for the examination of his saddlebags. But, alas! out comes the pistol. Carlisle, thunderstruck, knew not what to do, but calmly gave himself up to the officer. He was found guilty; even the Church expelled him. The Minutes ask, "Who have been dismissed for improper conduct?" and his name appears with three others of other Conferences. Now mark the sequel. Two long years he suffered the reproach, and then a wretched young man on his deathbed frantically cried: "I cannot die until I reveal one thing! Parson Carlisle never stole that pistol; I myself put it in his saddlebags." Brother Carlisle was restored to the Church and ministry, dying in peace, a member of the Tennessee Conference, in 1838. It is useless to conjecture why this was permitted concerning an innocent man, while it is written, "All things work together for good to them that love God."

CHAPTER VIII.

The Ninth Session—Rapid Interchange of Preachers—Broad River Circuit—
Incidents—Cowles and Darley—Ivy's Boldness—Philip Bruce—The Tenth
Session—Street Preaching—Bethel Church—Jenkins Denied Orders—
Reuben Ellis—Dark Days—Large Decrease in Membership—Necrological
—Lorenzo Dow.

THE ninth session began January 1, 1795. Little is said of
it anywhere. It was at that time of general depression
when Enoch George says that not a preacher could show one
soul converted. The Minutes tell of short terms of service by
the preachers—three and six months; good generalship in the
bishop, looking not only to celerity of movement, but to a rapid
interchange of place and talent as well. With a celibate ministry
this was easily effected, but not otherwise. Hence such men as
McKendree, George, and others were quartered without mercy.
Quarter enters largely into Methodist nomenclature. Asbury, la-
menting to Jenkins his not getting round his district (the whole
state) but three times, regrets that "he did not get round *quarterly.*" "I told him," said Mr. Jenkins, "that if I had been
quartered, and each part made to travel, I might have done it."

To this session Asbury brought Samuel Cowles and James
Rogers. Cowles and Jenkins were sent to Broad River Circuit,
formed in 1785 by Stephen Johnson. It began in the Dutch
Fork above Columbia, on both sides of Broad River to Pacolet
Springs, parts of Fairfield, Newberry, Chester, and Union counties in it. Within these bounds were Grissom and Partridge,
local preachers. The first Quarterly Conference was at Finch's,
where, in March, Asbury dedicated Mount Bethel Academy.
Preaching with convincing power from "Rejoice evermore," a
young man was converted, and moving West, became a preacher.
At Fish Dam they had a gracious revival, "sweeping the neighborhood." In the interchange of preachers, Enoch George came
up from Charleston, persuading Cowles to take his place there.
His reason for leaving was that "the people there have more
sense than he had." Jenkins, by order of the elder, exchanged
with James Douthet from Saluda, one quarter. Fruit being
plentiful, much brandy led to much wickedness. This he could

(64)

not bear. The wicked called whisky "Jenkins's devil," and invited their friends to partake of it under that name. His opposition to its manufacture and use awakened enmity, and the money value of three months' labor was compensated with eight dollars, half of which he gave to Douthet, gladly escaping to his own circuit again. The last Quarterly Conference was at Sealey's Meetinghouse, once on the road between Richburg and Rock Hill, in Chester county, now no more. Here he heard old Brother Walker, often Asbury's kind host, say " he had been fifty years serving God, and that even yet he was often severely tempted." This greatly encouraged the preacher. This year Mr. Jenkins considered one of the best in his ministry, so far as money was concerned; he received $52 out of $64. No wonder locations were rife; but these men, while working with their own hands for bread, still were freely breaking the bread of life to thousands.

Of Samuel Cowles, Dr. G. G. Smith tells of his being a trooper in the Washington Light Horse at the Cowpens, when, sweeping down upon a dragoon and about to cut him down, the Masonic signal of distress was given and his life was spared. Years after he met his old foe in Thomas Darley, a brother preacher in this Conference. Cowles and Darley both located in 1806.

Richard Ivy died this year. He was admitted in 1777, and was among the first elders, serving several years, mostly in Georgia. In 1793 he was appointed traveling book steward; then his name disappears from the Minutes until the record of his death in 1795. The obituary record states: " Eighteen years in the work, traveling extensively; a man of quick and solid parts; a man of affliction, spending his all, with his life, in the work." In Stevens's History the following is seen:

During the Revolution a file of soldiers surrounded the house where he was preaching, and the officers entered, drew their swords, and crossed them on the table. Ivy was not alarmed, but continued on his subject, "Fear not, little flock," remarking: "Some Christians fear when there is no cause for fear. So it might be now. These men, engaged in defense of their country's rights, meant them no harm." He spoke forcibly on the cause of freedom from foreign and domestic tyranny, glancing from the swords to the officers, as if he would remind them that *this* looked too much like domestic oppression. In conclusion, bowing to the officers and opening his shirt bosom, he said: "Sirs, I would fain show you my heart; if it beats not high for legitimate liberty, may it forever cease to beat." This he said with voice and look thrilling the whole audience. Many sobbed aloud, some cried "Amen," while the soldiers without swung their hats and shouted, "Huzza for the Methodist parson!" The officers shook his hand at parting, and said "they would share with him their last shilling."

Philip Bruce, leading the entire Conference the past year, 1794, was this year stationed in Charleston, with the oversight of Georgetown and Edisto. He was a Virginian, of Huguenot descent, of fine personal appearance, expressive, calm, dignified, and determined; a bachelor, as were most of the early preachers. It is said that he was once near being married, but on consultation with Asbury he was prevailed on to remain single. The dear old bachelor bishop occasionally feared that "the devil and the women would get all his preachers." Mr. Bruce was but two years in this Conference, returning to Virginia, and dying in Tennessee in 1826.

The locations, as seen, were heavy. Hardy Herbert died. He was a youth of genius, pleasing as a speaker, of easy and natural elocution. He died in the faith.

The tenth session began January 1, 1796, and was held in the Cumberland Church, undoubtedly. Members present, twenty preachers and seven graduates, among them Enoch George, Samuel Cowles, J. Humphries, James Jenkins, Jonathan Jackson, Joseph Moore, and Benjamin Blanton. They "began, continued, and parted in peace." The bishop remained in the city some little time. At noon on Sunday an attempt was made to preach in the streets, opposite St. Michael's Church, but it was prevented by the city guard. The bishop held a religious service in the kitchen, while Blanton held a sacramental love feast in the parlor of Brother Wells's house. The city appeared "running mad for races, balls, and plays." He laments the superficial state of religion among the whites; preaches on Sunday from "God is my record," etc., and at night on "Wolves in sheep's clothing." "Some laughed, some wept, and some were vexed." During this visit he preached eighteen sermons, met fifteen classes, wrote about eighty letters, read some hundred pages, visited thirty families again and again, and asks, "But who are made subjects of grace?"

Cumberland Church had now been used several years; the necessity for Church extension was fully felt, and so another church structure is designed, and a lot for burial purposes sought out. Subscriptions were started, but moved slowly. A wealthy gentleman, Mr. Bennett, on being approached as to the sale of a lot, generously gave the trustees the lot on which Bethel Church now stands. There was room enough for a parsonage and a grave- yard, in which the bodies of many of the saints now sleep. Some still live who remember the long, low, dingy building, then deemed quite palatial, where the bachelor preachers dwelt, and for a long time after occupied by families also.

At this Conference James Jenkins was entitled to elder's or- ders, but failed to get them. His proclivity for reproof, his zeal to do right himself and to see that others did so too, did not smooth his path to heaven, and hence he magnified his office at a heavy per cent of discount on his popularity. We shall have much to say of him farther on.

Reuben Ellis died this year. "A man large in body but of slender constitution, of slow but solid parts as counselor and guide. The people of South Carolina well knew his excellent worth as a Christian and a minister of Christ. It is doubtful whether there be one left in all the connection higher, if equal, in standing, piety, and usefulness," say the Minutes.

This ends the first decade of Methodism in South Carolina as an Annual Conference. The growth seemed slow (see table in Appendix). The first Conference numbers were whites, 2,075; colored, 141; and now only 3,862 whites and 826 colored, and yet in 1794 there were as many as 5,192 whites and 1,220 colored. Thus, in not having increase there was absolute loss.

This was about the darkest period in our annals. It will be remembered that but a year or two before not a preacher could call up a solitary soul converted to God during the year. The same in Georgia. Dr. Smith accounts for it there in the lack of laborers. Many things adverse to religion: emigration, po- litical strife, leading men infidels and duelists, the Yazoo fraud, a wide domain, now comprising Alabama and Mississippi, sold by a bribed legislature for a song; the people too busy to at- tend week-day preaching and class meeting; the entire mem- bership in Georgia only 1,028, when five years before they were double that number. As far as Carolina was concerned, the depletion may be traced to the unwise action on slavery, Al- len's fall, the Hammet schism, and the usual opposition of all evil to Christ's kingdom. But amid it all the cry was "On- ward!" and in a few years five instead of four figures (see Appendix) were used to report the numbers—proving the truth of a state jurist's observation that the Methodists were like the calves in Ezekiel's vision, "*they never go backward.*"

Closing the first decade of our Conference, there well may be a pause in the chronological order of the narrative to briefly notice the death of laborers not already named. The necrological record (see Appendix) for the decade is eleven. In addition to those already named, are the following:

Woolman Hickson, the first stationed preacher in Georgetown, S. C.; in 1785, with John Tunnell in Charleston. He was but one year in Carolina. "A man of splendid talents and brilliant genius, whose whole public life was oppressed by physical weakness and suffering." He died and was buried in New York.

James Connor, an undergraduate, in feeble health, dying shortly after in Virginia. "A pious, solid, understanding man, blessed with confidence in his last moments."

Wyatt Andrews, serving but two years, dying in 1790. "As long as he could ride he traveled, and while he had breath he praised God."

John Tunnell, admitted in 1777, dying in 1790; thirteen years in the work—a man of solid piety, great simplicity, and godly sincerity. He was selected as one of the pioneers by Asbury, and stationed at Charleston in 1785. Soon after, he became one of the founders of Methodism in the West. It is said that such was his pathos that a sailor, stopping to listen to his preaching, said to his comrades on rejoining them: "I have been listening to a man who has been dead and in heaven; but he has returned, and is telling the people all about that world."

Lemuel Andrews, "four years in the work; died without any expressions of the fear of death."

Benjamin Carter, "six years in the ministry; a pointed, zealous preacher, and a strict disciplinarian." He was wounded in the war of the Revolution, and died in Georgia in 1792, "blessed with frequent consolations in his last hours."

Hardy Herbert, "a native of North Carolina, but brought up in South Carolina on the banks of the Broad River; a youth of genius, pleasing as a speaker, of an easy, natural elocution." He died in the fear, favor, and love of God.

Ira Ellis was a Virginian; came from Kent Circuit, was stationed in Charleston in 1788, and the next year jointly on the district with Reuben Ellis. We are not advised as to any blood relationship between them. He was said to be much in contrast to Reuben Ellis; of quick and solid parts, undissembled sincerity, great modesty, and with uncommon powers of reasoning. Asbury thought that "with the advantages of education he would have displayed abilities not inferior to Jefferson or Madison." He labored only two years in Carolina, returning to Virginia in 1790, and locating in 1795. There is no account of his death as a local preacher.

Another famous local preacher, and long connected with the Conference, was Thomas Humphries (1783–1820). Of his parentage, birthplace, and early surroundings nothing is on record, and only here and there brief notice of his labors. He was honored in inducting James Jenkins into the Church and ministry; was among the first missionaries to Georgia, and for twenty years labored at his own charges in building up our Zion. In 1783 he was admitted into the connection with Major, Bruce, Ira Ellis, and Lee. For three years he was in Virginia and North Carolina. In 1786 he was sent to Georgia with Major as junior; in 1787, Augusta; in 1788 and 1789, Pee Dee; in 1790, Georgetown. For three or four years his name, though among the elders, does not show among the appointments. In 1795 he is returned as located. In 1796 he was on Great Pee Dee, and continued traveling until finally locating in 1799. Probably possessing wealth and laboring at his own charges, he was not under the usual restrictions of a traveling preacher. Travis states: "He was a good preacher, one of the greatest natural orators of his day; fine-looking, with an exceedingly bright eye, which sparkled and flashed when he was excited. He preached with earnestness and power, and was remarkable for native wit and fearlessness." It was in Georgetown he more than intimated that without repentance the rich and noble would fare as badly as the poor. Lovick Pierce, when on Pee Dee, says: "He lived palatially, was rich as a rice planter, quite popular among the aristocratic, with no discount on his ministry therefore. Faithful in his warnings, a terror to evil-doers, and a praise to all doing well." William Capers, later on, writes of him as "his venerable friend of Jeffers Creek, Darlington, whence having removed to Lodibar, Sumter, he felicitated himself much upon his companionship. In an old Quarterly Conference Journal of the Santee Circuit from 1815, now before us, is a record of the local preachers, twenty-nine in number; the name of Thomas Humphries heads the list, and opposite it is written: "Ob. in the faith, October 20, 1820."

Early in the nineteenth century appeared hereabout the eccentric Lorenzo Dow, a free lance in gospel warfare; the forerunner of latter-day evangelists, with this difference, he received but little encouragement from Church authorities, accorded now to many free from connectional rule, and so promising of disorder and disintegration. Dow could not come under itinerant locality, and so was allowed to rove at his own will. He had been converted under Hope Hull's preaching in New England. Visiting him in Georgia, he found him at his corncrib and saluted him with, "How are you, father?" The hopeful son did not receive much encouragement all the same, being advised to "stick to his work." Although eccentric, Dow was a great polemic, doing valiant battle for the truth. Many anecdotes linger in connection with this singular man. His dropping a coal of fire into the boot of an idealist, who held that all happening was simply imaginary, convinced the learned doctor that that at least was beyond the force of imagination. The stolen ax recovered by his threatening to throw a stone at the offender resulted in its restoration, The thief detected by the expedient of touching the pot under which was placed a rooster, sure to crow upon the guilty hand touching it: all were comfortably at peace when chanticleer made no noise, but guilt was discovered all the same when one hand was not soiled. There is but one memorial of Dow existent in Carolina: at White House Church, Orange Circuit, is a tree with a board in it, used for the Bible when he preached there, now far above a man's head, carried up by the growth of the tree.

CHAPTER IX.

The Eleventh Session — Money No Object — Poor William Hammet — Mr. Wells's Burial—Twelfth Session—No Bishop — Too Much Fire—George Dougherty — Bethel Dedicated — Jenkins's Far-reaching Ministry — His Sleeveless Coat—Weatherley's Calvinism — Conversion of the Pierces — Thirteenth and Fourteenth Sessions — Asbury's Itinerary — Charleston Orphan House—General Conference—Ill Effect of Addresses—Persecution of Dougherty.

RESUMING the narrative chronologically, we reach the year 1797. The eleventh session began January 5, Coke and Asbury presiding. On his way to it Dr. Coke passed through Camden, lodging with Isaac Smith, "formerly an eminent and successful" itinerant preacher. The doctor regrets exceedingly the location of so many able married preachers, "for want of support for their families." He thinks the people "not near so much to blame as the preachers, from a false and most unfortunate delicacy in not impressing it on the consciences of the people." This witness is true; they gloried in not preaching for money, and took the trouble to state it over and over again. No wonder the people were agreeable to the arrangement, and it has taken years to undo the mischief; the tide did not turn until years after, under Capers and Andrew. In the meantime, the loss to the Church was irreparable. Some records from early Quarterly Conference journals will hereafter show upon how low a plane support moved; it will certainly be monumental as to the unselfishness and devotion of our earlier ministry.

The doctor tells of the severe fires in this city and Savannah; mentions "poor William Hammet, now come to nothing," his congregations dwindled to "about thirty whites"; tells of Mrs. Hopeton, "an aged lady of large fortune," who, having been honored with John Wesley's acquaintance, and learning of Hammet, sent for him. The interview "so sickened her of the gospel, he doubted if she would ever attend another gospel meeting." He rejoices in Mr. McFarlain's becoming a pillar of the Church in place of his deceased partner, Mr. Wells. He rather doubts if religion had gained much on this continent since his last visit.

Asbury states that they continued in session six days, sometimes six or seven hours a day; has pleasing accounts of the growth

(71)

of religion; rejoices in the accession of some young men for the ministry, namely, Alexander McCain, William West, R. Gaines, the Floyds—Laomi Floyd withdrawing soon, and the others, save McCain, traveling but a few years. He writes feelingly of the death of Mr. Wells and his burial. Often has the writer, when a child, looked at his tomb in that contracted graveyard, scarcely more than four feet wide, running the length of the church. Old Cumberland gave place to a large brick structure, burned during the civil war. The dust of Wells lies now under the foundation of the large warehouse in Cumberland street.

Measures were taken for the erection of a new church (Bethel). The bishop writes:

If materials fall in their price, and we secure £400, shall we begin? "O we of little faith!" It is a doubt if we had fifty in society when we laid the foundation in Cumberland street, which cost, including the lot, £1,300. The society has been rent in twain, and yet we have worked out of debt and paid £100 for two new lots, and we can spare £100 from the stock, make a subscription for £150, and the Africans will collect £100.

The building committee were Francis Sutherland, G. H. Myers, William Smith, and Alexander McFarlain. The church was dedicated the next year.

From this Conference Jenkins was sent to Georgia; Enoch George, presiding elder. One of his homes was at Bishop Andrew's father's. There were powerful displays of saving grace; souls were converted around the family altars. Here Blanton found a wife in a Miss Huett. Here, at Liberty Chapel, near Greensboro, Enoch George preached so moving a sermon that none of the preachers would open their mouths after him. Jenkins, all in a tremor, exhorted. A man in a uniform fell at his feet, entreating prayer. The mourners often invited themselves to the seekers' bench, the preachers afterwards earnestly inviting them to come; and so that custom began.

The twelfth session began January 1, 1798. A room in the house of Mr. Myers held the body. Judging from the thirty preachers stationed, they must have been crowded if all were present. Among them were Blanton, Gibson, Jackson, Humphries, Jenkins, McCain. Bishop Asbury, detained by sickness, appointed Jonathan Jackson to preside and to station the preachers. Jackson and Blanton were presiding elders. Mr. Jenkins tells: "It was the custom to relate experiences in the

Conference room." While Tobias Gibson was speaking the whole Conference was greatly moved, so impossible was it to resist the spirit with which he spoke. Jenkins preached, and did it as he would have done it in the backwoods. Some said "it had too much fire in it"—not *fox-fire*, or of the sheet lightning sort, you may be assured, but akin to the tongues of fire on the day of Pentecost. Five were admitted on trial, among them a young man about twenty-six years old, who had been a raftsman on the Edisto, and whose educational advantages were better than most at that time, but far from liberal. He had been teaching school at Finch's, hailing from Newberry, and coming with George Clark, preacher in charge on Saluda Circuit. He was ungainly, had lost an eye, his face pockmarked, shoulders stooping, knees bending forward, his walk tottering; his costume a straight coat, knee breeches, stockings, shoes, sometimes fair topped boots with straps at top buttoned to the knee. He was to live but ten years longer, but in that time was to leave an undying record of worth; to become "South Carolina's great Methodist preacher," and to give the first inspiration of education to the Conference. It was George Dougherty, of whom much remains to be written.

Hanover Donnan, admitted at the same time, 1798, located in 1808. Of deep piety, preaching abilities "not splendid," his delivery against him, he studied plainness of speech, and was always deeply solemn and earnest. The others admitted traveled but a short time.

This year Bethel Church was dedicated. As yet there was no pulpit. Blanton, standing on a platform, held the service. The walls were unplastered, and not finished until eleven years later. What memories cluster around this old building! Could the old sounding-board over the pulpit speak, what could it not tell of words of wondrous power! Old Bethel was rolled across Calhoun street, was purchased from us, and is now the property of the Northern Church.

James King and George N. Jones died this year. The first was a victim to the fatal yellow fever. "He gave his life, labors, and fortune to the Church of Christ and his brethren." The latter died triumphantly, "rapt in the vision of God." Both were interred in Bethel graveyard.

From this Conference James Jenkins was sent to Bladen Circuit; Jonathan Jackson, presiding elder. It lay partly in South Carolina and North Carolina, extending from Long Bay to Cape Fear, including Conwayboro, Lumberton, Elizabeth, Smithville, and Old Brunswick Courthouse. There had been a small society in Cape Fear during the Revolution, formed by Philip Bruce and O'Kelly; but the preachers had to leave, and the society was broken up, leaving only three women, who, though without church privileges, were faithful. The preachers had to battle with swollen waters; they raised four new societies. Before leaving this circuit, Jenkins visited Wilmington and talked with Mr. Meredith, who said, speaking of his own flock, that he found these "sheep without a shepherd," and served them. Mr. Meredith was persecuted, even to prison; he preached from the windows to all who would hear him. They had burned his little church. Soon a fearful fire devastated Wilmington. Mr. Meredith gathered his feeble flock in the market place, and told the people that "as they loved fire so well, God had given them enough of it." Five fires occurred later, and no leading man in the work of persecution ever prospered afterwards. In 1800, Mr. Meredith's church and parsonage fell to the Methodist Episcopal Church.

Some of the early ministry of Mr. Jenkins was far-reaching in its influences on Methodism to-day, as witness the following incident. At Conwayboro there were many young people, the children of Methodist parents, so clannish that a breach seemed difficult. Young Henry Durant, our Henry's father, was a captain among them. While Mr. Jenkins preached, the heart of the young man was melted. Opportunity was given to join the Church, and up came Durant, with streaming eyes; young Wilson followed, and all the young men were gained except two. In after years, as is well known, a son of the captain, "our Henry," swept through Carolina, instrumental in good to thousands. Young Gillespie, at old Brunswick Courthouse, also became a convert. Mr. Jenkins labored to influence him, all without seeming effect; but one sentence he could not shake off— "Remember, you have souls to save"; it entered his heart, and kept ringing in his ears. Boarding with a Mr. Balloon, he asked permission to pray in his family. Mr. Balloon, "astonished above measure," consented; the power of God was manifest, he was converted, and a gracious revival followed.

This year the preacher was taken with fever, and had to stop *one* day to take medicine. His appointment was filled, however, by proxy. His homespun coat, given him by his mother, so badly worn, had lost one sleeve from the elbow down. He still traveled one round, "sleeveless in one arm," until a brother exchanged with him, as he says, "giving me the best of the bargain."

The bishop's itinerary on his way to the next session has items of interest; only a few are given on his return journey. The thirteenth session began January 1, 1799, Asbury presiding; Jesse Lee, secretary." This is the first journalistic record in our archives. The Conference held four days; thirty preachers present. Eight were admitted, among them Bennett Kendrick, Lewis Myers, and Britton Capel. There were six locations, among them Thomas Humphries and Mark Moore. The bishop says: "We had great harmony and good humor." Three elders and seven deacons were ordained. On the 20th he preached at Bethel, and in the old church at the last. "A group of sinners at the door; when I took the pulpit, they went off with a shout. I felt what was coming. In the evening there was a proper uproar, like old times." February 3, he preached at Georgetown; Friday, the 10th, at William Gause's; paid a visit to the seashore; saw the breakers—"awfully tremendous sight and sound"; sees the seagulls carrying clams in the air, dropping and breaking them to eat; then on to Old Brunswick, rejoicing in the advancement of the Church there.

This year James Jenkins was sent to Edisto Circuit. This circuit had been enlarged, and extended from Savannah River to within thirty miles of Charleston, and from Coosawhatchie Swamp to Santee River. Mr. Jenkins thought it in a worse condition than any he had ever traveled; "few class papers, and scarcely any class meetings at all." He told them he intended to have order. Some believed he was going to ruin the Church; but he did not. The circuit was formed by Willis. He first preached in a Lutheran church, on Cattle Creek. Jacob Barr, once a Continental officer, heard him. Half atheist as he was, he said: "He must be a god himself, or else a servant of God." He was converted, became a local preacher, and was known more than forty years after as good old Father Barr. His descendants to the fourth generation are attached to Methodism.

At one appointment this year the church was burned. There

were only twenty-six members, thirteen of whom Mr. Jenkins expelled. An incident is worthy of note. Some children near Saltketcher met at the house of a local preacher named Chitty, and engaged in play. The talk turned on religion; from talking they went to praying, and there were several conversions. One appointment was at Mr. Weatherley's. "A Calvinistic sinner," much prejudiced, he barely suffered preaching in his house, closely watching the preachers. He was induced to read Fletcher's "Checks." Maddened by the perusal, "he would dash the book down in a rage"; but persisting, and finding that he had no foundation he could safely trust, he embraced the truth in Jesus, and himself and wife joined the Church. This was in Barnwell county, near the Three Runs. Mr. Weatherley was the uncle of Reddick and Lovick Pierce. They obtained permission from their father to hear Mr. Jenkins, and Lovick Pierce records it as the first pure sermon he had ever heard. The text was, "Happy is that people . . . whose God is the Lord." The preaching was in a manner, tone, power, and spirit perfectly new to all. Conviction and conversions followed; and as to results of that one sermon, count up the good done by the Pierces, their children, and their children's children, and on down to the judgment trump. This was a prosperous year: revivals at nearly all appointments, five new societies raised, and membership nearly doubled. James H. Mellard was a convert this year.

January 1, 1800, opened the fourteenth session. Asbury's journal, as kept while on his way to this Conference, is of interest, if for no more, as marking the routes of travel and recording names of saints at the opening of this nineteenth century.

The bishop crossed the south fork of the Catawba, near the state line, into York county. Wandering in the hickory barrens, they got lost, making it thirty miles to Alexander Hill's. November 1, held a meeting at Josiah Smith's, on Broad River; came to Woods's Ferry, on Broad River, near the mouth of Pacolet River, at Pinckneyville; then over Tiger, and on to Enoree; then on to Colonel B. Herndon's, there meeting Blanton, Black, Norman, and Smith; then, on the 5th, to O'Dell's Chapel, Laurens county, lodging with Henry Davis; next day, to Zoar Chapel, lodging at William Holland's; Thursday, sixteen miles in haste to the funeral of Nehemiah Franks; Saturday and Sunday, Quarterly Conference at Bramlett's. "B. Blanton came; had lost his famous horse; reported $260, and had himself received in four years but $250." "If we do not benefit the people, we have but little of their money. Such is the ecclesiastical revenue of all our order." Then on to Tumbling Shoals and King's Chapel, and to Golden Grove at Cox's Meetinghouse. "It is agreed that this is the best society we have in South Carolina; the land here is rich." Lodged at Deacon Tarrent's; then to Willingham's, on the Indian lands; on to Nash's, Pendleton county, and on to Georgia; and then, by way of Augusta, arrived at Charleston, December 28.

On Wednesday, January 1, 1800, the fourteenth session began; twenty-three members present. The business of the Conference each evening was simply experience meetings. The bishop says: "Slow moved the northern post on the eve of new year's day, bringing intelligence of George Washington's death, December 14, 1799." Think of it! more than two weeks' delay, when now in two seconds the news would flash around the globe. Edward Rutledge, Governor of South Carolina, died January 23. A cloud was over Charleston; pulpits were clothed in black; bells tolling, a paraded soldiery; an oration was delivered, and a marble statue decreed (not erected yet). On the 5th the bishop dined with Jesse Vaughn, and visited Mr. Warnock, steward at the Orphan House, giving high praise to that institution: "No institution in America equal" to it. It is so still, after more than a century's existence.

At this Conference the bishop states: "After encountering many difficulties, I was able to settle the plan for the stations, and to take in two new circuits." These were Natchez and Orangeburg, to which Tobias Gibson and Lewis Myers, respectively, were sent. James Jenkins had been reappointed to Edisto, and was much pleased when Asbury told him that, as Floyd had gone to the Presbyterians, "you must go to Santee in Floyd's place." He obeyed without murmuring. Santee and Catawba had been united some years, extending from St. Paul's, near Nelson's Ferry on Santee, to Providence, within ten miles of Charlotte, N. C.; the river crossed five times every six weeks. Meeting the bishop at Monk's Corner, to conduct him through his work, his horse bruised his leg against a stump; and Asbury, seeing the wound, said: "I wish you were at home." The bishop preached at St. Paul's; then on to Gibson's, Rembert's, Camden, and Horton's. On leaving, the bishop told him he ought to go to the General Conference on the 5th of May, 1800.   Mr. Jenkins says: " We talked much and did little—the salary increased to $80, I thinking $64 quite enough for a single man." He urged the rescinding of the rule about marriage with unawakened persons; lost, but modified by putting them back on trial. They had a long controversy on the use of ardent spirits, "but did nothing on the subject." Addresses were sent to the southern states anent manumission, which, as we shall see, aroused dreadful persecution of the Methodists in Charleston.   At Manchester, one of his appointments on his return, he had trouble. Garrison, his colleague, escaped, " taking to the bushes," but he faced the mob.   The bread for the sacrament was stolen, and the negro worshipers ordered out of the house; but he stood like a lion at bay.   Poor Manchester! the lines of desolation are over it, not a house remaining.   He visited Old Neck, in Marion county.   Greaves, Ellison, and Richardson, famous members of the body, came out of that society.   Spending the night at Woodberry's, his son William upset the canoe.   Often have we heard the boy, then an old man, talk of that accident, done on purpose. The Gauses, Woodberrys, and many others were prominent in later years; the Doziers, Stephensons, and others survive.

In Charleston "the address caused trembling." Mr. Harper, the station preacher, receiving the papers, full of abolitionism, carefully stored them away, and afterwards, being called upon by the intendant of the city, burned them in his presence.   He left satisfied with the preacher's loyalty.   But there was no escape for Methodist preachers.   Mr. Harper was seized by the mob, carried down Meeting street, until, confronted by the city guard, he escaped.   On the next night George Dougherty led the prayer meeting, and though in winter and he feeble in health, they thrust him under a spout, and pumped until he was almost drowned.   A Mrs. Kugley, more courageous than the miscreants assailing him, tore off her apron and thrust it into the spout, while a gentleman, sword in hand, rescued him. The spirit of the man is seen in his reply to his housekeeper's terrified inquiry: "Why, Mr. Dougherty, what have they been doing to you?" Making no triumph of his martyrdom, he simply replied: "Oh, nothing! only pumping me a little." But Heaven was not silent, though seemingly so, at this outrage: a Nemesis followed these men to the bitter end.

CHAPTER X.

ASBURY, pursuing his tireless travel, reaches the beautiful French Broad country, *en route* to Camden, S. C., the seat of an annual Conference for the first time. He set out from Botetourt, Va., on September 16, and on November 14 was "at the foot of the grand mountain division of South Carolina."

Two days' travel brings him to John Douthet's, fifteen miles more to Samuel Burdine's in Pendleton Circuit. The bishop says: "Sister Burdine professes to have known the Lord twenty years; in her you see meekness, gentleness, patience, pure love, and cleanliness." The 19th of November found him at John Wilson's. Here is a sorrowful record from the bachelor bishop: "Benjamin Blanton met me; he is now a married man, and talks of locating." The 22d of November finds him at James Powell's, on Walnut Creek, in Laurens county; then on to King's Chapel, named after the martyr to yellow fever in Charleston; then *en route* to Augusta, Ga. Here "we have a foundation and a frame prepared for erecting, in a day or two, a house for public worship, two stories high, sixty by forty feet. For this we are indebted to the favor of Heaven and the agency of Stith Mead; and what is better, here is a small society." What would he say now of Augusta, Ga.? Crossing the Savannah again, he went on to "Silvador's Purchase," to hold a meeting at a church in Bush River Circuit, near George Connor's. At Abbeville he stopped at John Brunner's, near the courthouse. He says: "Abbeville is a large county, stretching from river to river, and holds better lands than any in the state. Although Bush River Circuit extends through it, there are few Methodists, the most populous settlements being composed of Presbyterians." What would the good man say of Abbeville now —indeed, of all that upper Carolina where Methodism is now most flourishing? Divine love outdoes the "horrible decree" most wonderfully. Then on to Enoree, Tiger, and Broad at Glenn's Chapel, near Broad River: "had an open season and many hearers." "At Glenn's Flat, Chester county, Sealey's Meetinghouse, we kept our Christmas." They lodged at Robert Walker's, eighty years of age, awakened under Whitefield in Fogg's Manor, then living on Sandy River—one of the patriarchs whose name will likely appear farther on. Then, December 26, to Alex. Carter's, on Fishing Creek, crossing the Catawba at Wade's Ferry to old Camp Creek, stopping at John Grymast's, originally from Ireland; then on to John Horton's, on Hanging Rock River. On the 30th they reached Camden.

To go forward a little, this Sealey's Meetinghouse was somewhere in Chester county. Just think of it—two bishops there, and scarcely a ripple on the surface! Now, if only one could get there, what a stir! The writer once besought Bishop McTyeire to attend his Chester District Conference, in that neighhood, and trace the footprints of Asbury, Whatcoat, and others. His reply was flattering, really unctuous: "You are bishop enough." We confess to liking a little oil occasionally, but that was too unctuous; it would have ruined some men; there was too much of it, like that running down Aaron's beard, "even to the skirts of his garment."

This fifteenth session, and the first held in Camden—January 1, 1801—was presided over by Asbury and Whatcoat; Jeremiah Norman, secretary. They sat three hours in the morning and two in the afternoon. Four were received on trial, James H. Mellard and Thomas Darley among them. Of Mellard more hereafter. Darley was once one of Tarleton's troopers. Dunwody called him "a powerful awakening preacher." The Conference had "great union"; some "talked loud, but no improper heat." They were well accommodated at Isaac Smith's, Carpenter's, and two other houses. Mr. Jenkins says: "We dealt closely and faithfully with each other, and the more we talked the better we loved." Mr. Jenkins was appointed presiding elder over the whole state. He was told this would be done at the camp meeting at Camp Creek, on their journey to this Conference. This year measures were taken, in Charleston, to erect a parsonage, of which more hereafter.

On his way to the next session—the sixteenth—in Camden, January 1, 1802, Asbury preached at Cattle Creek. "I lodged

with Sebastian Fanches, and was entertained like a president."
Dear, dear, the types! this was no less than *Funches*. Who in
all that White House country did not know "Jake," a descendant of the old patriarch? The bishop writes of the Four Holes
and Wasmasaw, "originally peopled by the Dutch Presbyterians—they have declined in language and religion, the last reviv-
ing in the present generation—many of whom have joined the
Methodists." The same county is now full of them. At this
Conference two districts were formed in the state—Saluda,
George Dougherty, presiding elder; and Camden, James Jenkins,
presiding elder. About this time camp meetings began to be held,
and though now gone into desuetude, will be hereafter noticed.

On his attending the next session—the seventeenth—again at
Camden, he writes of coming to Henry Culver Davis's, of Newberry District, South Carolina, and states: "The first society formed
at this place declined, and so many removed few were left; this
year they repaired the meetinghouse, and the Lord poured out
his Spirit, and nearly one hundred have been added. I found
that the labors of L. Myers and B. Wheeler had been greatly
blessed in the Broad River Circuit." December 3, at Finch's,
measures were taken to operate Mt. Bethel Academy. "I advised to finish the house for teaching below and lodging above."
Then on to Tiger River to Major Bird Buford's; then to Nathan
Glenn's, on Broad River; then, crossing Broad at Glenn's Flat,
called on the aged Walkers; then on to Chesnut's Ferry, and
into Camden. "It is a trifle to ride in this country thirty miles
without food for man or beast." They held their session—January 1, 1803—in Isaac Smith's house. James Crowder and
John McVean were admitted, and John Harper located. Bennett Kendrick and Thomas Darley were in Charleston this year.
During this year Mr. Jenkins gives some incidents worthy of
note. The "amiable Gillespie," of whom he had written, still
held on to "the one thing needful." At James Guerry's, near
Murray's Ferry, the Guerrys, Muchats, Remberts, and several
other Huguenot families had fled from persecution, and found
a safe retreat on the Santee, called the French settlement. At
first fervent in religion, they declined, the talk about indigo being more common than about religion when they met at church.
John Guerry's father lamented this, and was satisfied that the
Methodists had the life and power of godliness. Nearly all the

6

descendants of the above named persons became Methodists. From Guerry's Mr. Jenkins went to Charleston, but "oh the change for the worse!" "the galleries bare," the product of the address from the General Conference. Then on to Edisto, preaching at Weatherley's where Lovick Pierce was awakened; then on to Cherokee Circuit; then to Saluda at King's Chapel, nearly opposite where Cokesbury now is; next to Fish Dam on Brown River Circuit; on to Union Circuit, then mostly in North Carolina, formed in 1791 by Benjamin Tarrant. In June he again visited Charleston, coming with Brother Dougherty. In a letter from Dougherty to the bishop, after writing of his attention to the negro children, he adds: "The epithet of negro schoolmaster added to that of Methodist preacher makes a black compound sure enough; yet, wonderful to think, the congregations are as large and as serious as they have been at any time since I came to Charleston. The number of blacks that attend on the Sabbath is truly pleasing; yet, alas! I cannot say there is any revival; but I humbly hope the storms in Charleston have taught me some useful lessons. Outward persecution seems to abate, and I am again cheered at the sight of some black faces in the galleries at night."

The eighteenth session was held in Augusta, Ga., January 2, 1804; Coke and Asbury presiding; N. Snethen, secretary. Reaching Columbia, John Harper welcomed Asbury to his house, where they had religious services; then on to Charleston, with sermons by the bishop, Kendrick, Dougherty, and Darley. "I continued a week, lodging in our own house at Bethel, receiving visitors, ministers and people—white, black, and yellow. It was a paradise to me and some others." The bishop's first occupancy of this parsonage is graphically related by Dr. Mood. Bishop Asbury, upon paying a brief visit to the city, toward the end of the year (1803), was permitted, among the first, to occupy the new parsonage. The building had been completed some time, but no steps had been taken to supply it with furniture. Asbury had heard of its erection and completion, and reaching the city, he passed by all of his old stopping places, and went directly to the parsonage, where he hitched his horse, took his saddlebags, and putting them in one of the rooms, sat gravely down upon the doorstep, no one knowing of his arrival. A negro man passing observed him sitting there, and

WASHINGTON STREET CHURCH, COLUMBIA, S. C.

In 1787 the Rev. Isaac Smith, then on Santee Circuit, on passing near the site of the city, occasionally preached at the house of Colonel Thomas Taylor. This was while Columbia was scarcely a hamlet. In 1802 the Rev. John Dunlap, of the Presbyterian Church, and the Rev. John Harper, of the Methodist Episcopal Church, alternately preached in the statehouse. The last named was the first to get a foothold in Columbia. He gave the lot on which the present structure stands. In 1803 the first Christian house of worship was erected in Columbia, and a church consisting of six members organized. In 1807 it was made a station, with G. Daniel Hall pastor. It soon proved too small, and an addition of thirty feet was built. This also becoming unequal to the demand for room, a brick building was projected, under the ministry of William Capers, and dedicated by Bishop Andrew in 1832. Still the cry was for room, and the Rev. William Martin projected and labored for the erection of the Marion Street Charge, which was dedicated by Bishop Capers in 1848. In the fatal year of 1865 the Washington Street Church was destroyed, with a large portion of the city. At that time the membership comprised four hundred white and seven hundred colored people. Utterly impoverished as was the entire South, it became a huge task to rebuild, but under the persevering efforts of the Rev. William Martin the present noble structure was erected; the foundation being laid in 1871, and the edifice dedicated in 1875 by Bishop Wightman. In the shadow of its walls rests the dust of the Rev. William M. Kennedy, N. Talley, William Martin, and other sainted itinerant preachers. Just under the pulpit Bishop Capers, "the founder of missions to the slaves," was interred. The Rev. W. W. Daniel is pastor in 1897.

knowing him, stopped and told him no one lived there. "I know that," said the bishop. "Where do you want to go, sir? I will show you the way." "I want to go nowhere," was the reply. "I will spend the night here." The negro gave information, and soon a number of his friends waited on him; found him still sitting and reading his Bible. "Come, bishop," said one and another; "come, go home with us." "I cannot," said he; "this is the parsonage, and I desire to stay here." "But there is nothing in the house; you cannot stay here," they said. "I do not need much," he replied. "Well," said they, "if you *will* stay, we must try to make you comfortable." Soon two rooms and the kitchen were comfortably furnished. The idea of saying to this worthy prelate just finding a house of his own, "Come to ours"! What would Asbury say to the palatial mansions (many of them) now occupied by his preachers?

The Conference met in Mr. Cantalou's house. The usual business was transacted, but nothing remarkable to note. Methodism during this year (1804) was introduced into Columbia, S. C. J. Harper, a Wesleyan from the West Indies, had been received into the Conference and stationed in Charleston three years, 1799 to 1802. He removed to Columbia, S. C., began a church, and Bennett Kendrick was the preacher in 1805.

The nineteenth session was held in Charleston, January 1, 1805; Asbury and Whatcoat presiding; John McVean, secretary. But little worthy of note was recorded. Benjamin Jones and Tobias Gibson died this year. James Jenkins was superannuated at this Conference.

The twentieth session was held in Camden, December 30, 1805, the same bishops presiding; James Hill, secretary. The two Pierces and James Russell were admitted, and four located. The bishop did not find matters as he wished. "One preacher has deserted his station, and there are contentions among the Africans." He recommended the painting of the new and the enlargement of the old church to eighty feet by forty; enlarging the parsonage and buying a new burying ground. He says: "Religion of a certain kind must be very valuable, since we spend so much to support it. There must be a prodigious revival in the Independent Society—a building of theirs will cost fifty or perhaps one hundred thousand dollars; there is a holy strife between its members and the Episcopalians as to who shall have the highest steeple; but I believe there is no contention about who shall have the most souls converted to God."

A half century after this was written that steeple had got no higher. When this writer was a child the children used to sing:

> Charleston is a Christian place
> And full of Christian people;
> They built a church in Meeting street,
> But couldn't raise a steeple.

It never was finished, and all perished in the burning during the civil war. A handsome structure now occupies its site.

The members reported at this session were 12,665 whites and 4,389 colored. As this closes the second decade of the Conference, dropping for a time the chronological order of the narrative, we sketch briefly some of the heroic workers not already noticed.

HOPE HULL, 1785–1818.

He was born in Maryland, March 13, 1763, and died in 1818, being but fifty-five years old. He was admitted into the connection with a class of twenty-two, several of whom labored in Carolina. He was sent to Salisbury, N. C., in 1785, and to Pee Dee Circuit in 1786. Here doubtless he obtained the *sobriquet* of "The Broadax," for from the first he dealt in stalwart blows, hewing always to the line. His success with Mastin on Pee Dee challenged Coke's admiration, who feared "the sword was too keen for the scabbard." He was a pioneer in Georgia, where he finally made his home, in Burke county in 1788 and Savannah in 1790. The mob was stirred, and he came out of the fire declaring, "My soul has been among lions." Verge and room were requisite for such a man, and it was like binding Samson with cords to confine him to a town; so in 1791 he swept like a cyclone through Georgia, and was afterwards sent to New England. But his heart was in the South, and back to Georgia he came in 1793. In 1794 he traveled with Asbury, and in 1795 located. It was not until after his marriage that Hull located. He had to do it. No man of sensibility could ask a woman to share his lot on $64, or even twice as much, per annum. He became connected with one of the most numerous and respectable families in the state, and his own hands ministered to his necessities. He was not idle in his work for the Church and the education of youth. Franklin College was his debtor for his love, labor, and supervision. His life as a minister was irreproachable. His zeal for God and Methodist doctrine and usage was unabated. He was ready at repartee. A young preacher alluding to his dress thought it would be of advantage to him to be a little more particular. Mr. Hull, with one of his significant looks, replied: "You know, sir, that in a team of horses it is necessary for *one of them to hold back.*" Inquiring once as to the spiritual condition of one in class meeting, he was answered: "I am afraid I am like old Paul, when 'I would do good, evil is present with me.'" "Yes," replied Hull, "and like old Noah, too, you get drunk sometimes." He was of large body and medium stature, large head, curling hair, heavy eyebrows, keen, small eyes, and fine face. He was a natural orator, a fine singer, of strong voice and fine delivery. His descriptive power was excellent, but his majestic gift was in prayer. In his last illness he sent for his brother-in-law, General Merriweather, and said to him in his characteristic style: "God has laid me under marching orders, and I am ready to obey."

DANIEL ASBURY, 1786–1825.

Born in Virginia, February 18, 1762, and dying April 15, 1825, he was a little over sixty-three years old. He was truly one of the heroes of early Methodism. He traveled several years until 1791, then came the inevitable location, and he settled in Lincoln county, N. C., for ten years of farm life. In 1801 he was readmitted, and during his itinerant life was sixteen years on districts, twelve on circuits, one resting, and ten located, thirty-nine years in all. He is represented as of small stature, bald, loss of teeth preventing good pronunciation, with a face thin and furrowed, but its expression always kindly, and eyes indicative of humor. With an intellect above the common order, his opportunities for early culture limited—he says he never heard of a grammar book—yet he was well informed in the Bible, its doctrines, and theology in general; he was by no means unacceptable to persons of culture, and preached with so much sterling sense, earnestness, and simplicity as to merit acceptability. His early training in life was well adapted to enable him to endure the hardships of the itinerancy. Capture by the Indians, a prisoner to the British in Canada, hardened him to perils, and the rough fare of the mountains gave him endurance. A bit of fried bacon and cornbread were dainties compared with cold bread and a cucumber among the Indians. Arrest for preaching and being brought before magistrates never intimidated him, for in that hour it was given him to say and do the right.

From absolute necessity he was some time located; but getting a settled home, by the labor of his wife and children they were supported and he left free to travel, and recompensed by the meagerest pay he gladly broke the bread of life to thousands. As to money, little or much or none, he never slackened his labor for God and souls for one hour. At last came superannuation. He had learned to *commit* and to *submit*, surrendering all to the divine will. On Sunday morning, April 15, 1825, came the last of earth. Apparently more vigorous and cheerful than usual, walking through his yard, suddenly he paused and looking upward as if hearing "the last clear call," fell dead, or rather entered into life. Sudden death in reality is sudden glory.

WILLIAM GASSAWAY, 1788–1823.

The time and place of his birth are unknown, but his connection with the Conference forty-five years, he being converted in early manhood, would bring him to near seventy at his death. Wild and reckless in youth, like the immortal dreamer his conscience was tender as to what many esteemed little sins. Under conviction of sin he would deny himself a draught of water, letting his horse drink, inasmuch "as he was no sinner." His soul athirst for the "living water" found no rest until it sprang up in his soul "into eternal life." A Presbyterian elder led him to the Saviour, as he did many another during his long ministry, William Capers among them; as he said, "that most godly man and best of ministers, William Gassaway," bringing him to Christ. And who that ever read can easily forget that long, dreary sand-hill road from Chesterfield to Sumter, and the high debate between them, of more import than any in philosophic grove or academy, resulting in a lifelong devotion to the Christian ministry? Entering the connection in 1788, local awhile, then reëntering, he finally located in 1813. A gentleman owning a large tract of land in York county gave him some acres, and here for twenty years toiling for his own living, by the gospel of the Son of God he gave spiritual life to many. Here is his grave, the last vestige almost removed. This man an apostle of Methodism, yet his dust will be presently under the plowshare. *"And he died."* Nay, he lives forever. More of him farther on.

JONATHAN JACKSON, 1789–1815.

No time of his birth or place of his death is on record. He was one of the strong men of the Conference, presiding over it in 1798. He was six years on circuits, two on stations, two as supernumerary, and sixteen on districts. He was a real Boanerges, dealing much in the terrors of the law, so that affrighted sinners would sometimes rush away from his preaching. While a presiding elder he was held in high esteem, as one who could bear acquaintanceship. His preaching ability was not great, but his talent for organization was fine. When located he was the same untiring, persevering servant of God. It is on record that forgetting or not recognizing any, even his wife, he knew his Saviour to the end. "And this is life eternal, to know God, and Jesus Christ whom he hath sent."

BENJAMIN BLANTON, 1790–1845.

He was a man of mark, though but eleven years active in the itinerant ministry, and located thirty-one; reëntering, he was superannuated thirteen years, fifty-five in all. In 1796 he was stationed in Charleston; in 1797 presiding elder, dedicating Bethel Church, and was highly esteemed by Asbury. In him were blended the true gentleman and humble Christian. Travis's estimate was: "Cheerful, but never frothy; magnanimous, but not supercilious; fixed, but not bigoted; positive, but not dogmatic; flexible, but not pusillanimous. His house was the itinerant's home, and his library free of access." In love feast he once said that "he thought when he had been forty years in the wilderness he would have been called to cross the Jordan, but now over forty in it, and he was still browsing on the banks of the river." But the call came at last, and praying with unusual power, the next day he slept in death.

CHAPTER XI.

Twenty-first Session, Sparta, 1806—Dougherty and Kendrick—Asbury's Itin-
erary—Twenty-second Session, 1807—The Old Brunswick Circuit—The
Jerks and Dancing Exercise—Everett's Courage—Answer to Prayer—
Brunswick's Worthies—Wilmington, N. C.—James Jenkins—Mob Vio-
lence in Charleston—William Owens Threatened—Outrage from the City
Guard.

RESUMING the chronological order of narrative, we reach
the twenty-first session, at Sparta, Ga., December 29, 1806;
Asbury presiding; Lewis Myers, secretary. In reaching this
Sparta Conference, Bishop Asbury traveled *via* Charleston;
crossed Murray's Ferry; was detained five hours in the swamp;
"heat, mosquitoes, gallinippers, plenty"; reaches the city; finds
all things in good order. "Lewis Myers is an economist." He is
happy that Bethel is finished, and declares, "Should I live long,
I shall set a house in the Northern Liberties of Cooper River."
He did not see it, but new Cumberland is there, nevertheless.
December 26, he reached Sparta. The subject of a delegated
General Conference carried; only two dissenting. Peace was
had respecting the stations; Bishop Whatcoat's funeral discourse
delivered; sixteen admitted on trial, Joseph Travis and John
Collinsworth among them; six located, among them Samuel
Cowles, Thomas Nelson, Hugh Porter, and Levi Garrison. The
last named had left Charleston the year before, on account of
yellow fever.

This was an important session, and it is a privilege to give
Dr. Lovick Pierce's description of affairs. It was sent the writer
when he edited the Minutes of the Conference, on his request-
ing the doctor to give some sketches of the early preachers.
Concerning George Dougherty he writes:

Of him it is only possible to say too much. If no one will flinch from it,
I will say he was South Carolina's great Methodist preacher; at that time
the only member of the Conference that had anything like a classical education, and he only an academic beginning. He was mainly a woods student,
self-built. The extent of his lingual attainments I know not; I only know
that in 1805, he being my first presiding elder, he used to get me to read
from my English Bible for him, while he pored on his Hebrew in the Book
of Genesis. I know also that as far back as I knew him he was incessantly

(90)

engaged to get the Church awake to denominational education, talking on it, begging for it, and after two or three years got his Bethel Academy under way. And now, when the South Carolina Conference is justly proud of her schools and colleges, I bear this testimony fearlessly, that to George Dougherty you owe the first inspiration of educational ambition.

The last Conference he was at [mark, this Sparta Conference] was in the winter of 1806–7. Here he introduced his resolution [and it is recorded on the journals of our Conference] to dismiss forever from the rolls of the Conference any member of it that should run off from his charge for fear of an epidemic. It produced the only high excitement I ever saw in our old Conference. It was debated two days, Dougherty defending it from his seat, too far gone in consumption to stand up. It prevailed by one vote—yeas, fifteen; nays, fourteen. All his glory was in his great mind and heart; he had no personal attractions. He made his way from this Sparta Conference to Wilmington, N. C., and died in March, 1807.

At this same Conference Dr. Pierce writes concerning Bennett Kendrick:

He was in all respects a prince among Methodist preachers; one beautifully symmetrical in person, attractive in address, pure in style, liberal in thought, easy in delivery; indeed, there seemed to be a harmonious sympathy between his mind and his nerves in their influence on his muscles. His whole body seemed to preach, and every motion was a grace. He was at the Sparta Conference, 1806–7, and when his name was called and his character passed, and he, in the prime of life and vigorous health, asked for a location, it came upon us as a sudden shock. He gave his reasons, and as marriage in those days led to location, and as he supposed it would be set down to that cause, he assured us he had no such arrangement on hand or in view, which confounded us but the more. But as a location cannot be denied when the applicant is blameless, he was located. For three mornings he had his horse and sulky ready to leave, and then put up again. The third day, in the morning, he came into the Conference deeply affected, and asked if he might speak. Bishop Asbury, anticipating what was coming, eagerly replied: " Yes, Brother Kendrick, we are always glad to hear you." He stated: " I ask to return to the Conference my location, and to be put back as I was before. I have been ready to leave three mornings, but God forbids my departure; I cannot leave as I am." Then it was that tears of joy flowed freely. Kendrick was restored, and grand provision made for some vacancy. He was appointed presiding elder for Camden District, and went joyfully off, fully persuaded that he had humbly accepted the will of God, concerning himself, at the sacrifice of his own. But in April he died, in the midst of great promise, in our eyes, for years to come. But all flesh is grass, and such men fall as the flower of the grass. So passed away Bennett Kendrick, the brightest star then in our Conference constellation.

This might all have been easily condensed in statement; but what a loss, when so little is on record in our annals from Dr. Pierce's pen!

James Jenkins located this year, with a dozen more. William M. Kennedy, Hilliard Judge, Samuel Dunwody, and James E. Glenn were admitted.

A short while before, the bishop had written in Charleston: "Engaged in closet exercises. I do not find matters as I wish; one preacher has deserted his station, and there are contentions among the Africans." In 1806 the preachers in Charleston were Lewis Myers and Levi Garrison. We may be sure the deserter was not Lewis Myers. The yellow fever was enough to frighten anyone. Two preachers had recently died with it, yet this is about the first instance of desertion, and it led to Dougherty's resolution concerning it. The trouble among the Africans, as will be hereafter seen, culminated in 1815. The bishop had a poor opinion of Charleston Methodism: "Poor, fickle souls! death, desertion, backsliding; unstable as water; light as air, bodies and minds!" He turns his travel northward; buries Abijah Rembert; then on to Rockingham, N. C.; he says: "Here the people would have assembled, but there was a wedding afoot. This is a matter of moment, as some men have but one during life, and some find that one to have been one too many." He was evidently incorrigible in his bachelor proclivities. The Church undoubtedly was his bride, and in her sometimes waywardness he felt that he had as much as he could do to manage matters. Undoubtedly he was so for "the kingdom of heaven's sake"; and his reward, doubtless, will be proportionately great in heaven.

Returning from his northern travel, he came on to the Waxhaws and to Hanging Rock; crossed over Thompson's Creek, near Anson county, N. C., to see George Dougherty, slowly dying, but "his friends had conveyed him away on a bed." Shortly after, Dougherty died in Wilmington, N. C.

The twenty-second session was held in Charleston, January 1, 1807. It sat six hours a day; it was one of great harmony, and there was no trouble in stationing the preachers. "At this Conference," the journal states, "Matthew P. Sturdevant volunteered his services as a missionary to Bigbee [the first of Methodism, save L. Dow's visit in 1803 in Alabama]; was received and elected to the eldership." He was ordained in Bethel Church, and the General Minutes show "Tombecbee, Matthew P. Sturdevant." This charge was connected with Oconee District; but being on the other side of a perilous wilderness, only crossed in thirteen days, it is certain the presiding elder's visits were few and far between. Dr. Lovick Pierce was the elder in 1809, and he states that "he was never there."

Sturdevant was admitted on trial into the Virginia Conference in 1805. In 1807 he was junior preacher on Enoree; for two years on Tombecbee; then, in 1810, Fayetteville, N. C.; locating in 1812. Dr. Anson West, in his "History of Methodism in Alabama," gives a graphic picture of him and his mission. In 1812 Tombecbee was put in the Mississippi District; Samuel Dunwody, presiding elder—his only year on a district; the next year, 1813, he was on St. Mary's, and in the year 1814 he was stationed in Charleston, S. C.

From this Conference Joseph Travis and John Collinsworth were sent to Brunswick Circuit; this had been a part of the old Bladen Circuit. The two preachers were of the same class, both young and inexperienced, the first named mild and loving, the second rather ascetic, but both were zealous and faithful. They had no presiding elder, Kendrick having died, and Jonathan Jackson, appointed in his place, did not reach the circuit until the close of the year. This old circuit lay partly in North and South Carolina, and in the latter state embraced that Waccamaw section so devoted to Methodism.

At one of his appointments, the very first, Travis for the first time met with that strange exhibition called the "jerks" and "dancing exercise"—a vagary not confined to the so-called fanatical Methodists, inasmuch as staid Presbyterians indulged in it. Lorenzo Dow was told that some stakes shown him at a Waxhaw camp meeting were planted for folks taken with the malady to hold on by. No matter if Dow was "taken in" on its turning out that the stakes were used to hitch horses to. It is evident that the sad affliction, or superstition, was known thereabout. Mr. Travis states: "To see persons tumbling down, and jerking hard enough to dislocate their joints, women's combs flying in every direction, and their hair popping almost as loud as wagon whips," was surprising. The conclusion he reached was "that religious people might have the jerks, but that there was no religion in the jerks." He soon had ocular demonstration of their power, leading him almost to conclude that if they were from above, the Lord designed that he should not preach that day;

a more reasonable conclusion, for his maltreatment by the jerks would have been that another power was concerned therein. But to the incident. He was standing on the floor to preach. "Brother Christie, a pious and upright man, the class leader, was standing close by me; and while we were singing the first hymn, Christie looking on the same book, he was suddenly taken with the jerks." The consequence was, the hymn book flew out of the preacher's hand, and the preacher's unfortunate nose was painfully rapped. Mr. Travis was a very pacific man, and felt no sense of reprisal, and, getting over his unjust thoughts of Heaven's design, proceeded with the usual exercises. In his narrative, just before this relation, he tells of Josiah Everett, of Virginia, who, though no "fighting parson," was a man of pronounced eccentricity. Once, preaching in his shirt sleeves, he reproved a son of Belial, who, becoming enraged, made at the preacher in the pulpit; upon which Mr. Everett wheeled round to him hastily, rolling up his shirt sleeves, and exclaiming at the top of his voice, "Do you think that God ever made this arm to be whipped by a sinner? No! no!" at the same time stamping heavily with his foot. The enemy fled, and the sermon was finished as if nothing had happened.

At another time at an appointment where the people seemed rather hardened, while giving out the hymn a thundercloud came up, becoming more and more severe. In time of prayer it was alarmingly so. Mr. Everett prayed for it to come nearer. It came, and he cried out, "O Lord, send the thunder still nigher!" The house appeared to be in a blaze of lightning; then soon came a cry for mercy! mercy! and the results were glorious. Some one went to a magistrate, saying he believed that if Parson Everett had called the third time they would all have been struck dead, and that such a man ought to be legally stopped from traveling at large. The squire asked "if he really thought the parson had power with God," and he answered, "I really do." The reply was: "I can then have nothing to do with such a man. You will have to let him go."

James Russell and John Porter—what boy at Cokesbury in the early days does not remember Porter, the "weeping prophet"?— these were the preachers on Brunswick in 1806. They were both very zealous; of Russell more hereafter. It was a year of revival, and Mr. Travis was afraid that if there were no noise and shouting "no good was done"; hence he became vociferous in preaching, to his great injury, until the Rev. Julius I. Gause kindly whispered that "more faith and less noise" would do equally as well as yelling like a Comanche Indian, if not better. The circuit bordering on Wilmington, N. C., Mr. Travis visited it, and received most excellent counsel from Joshua Wells as to books and study.

There were on Brunswick Circuit in 1807 a number of local preachers: Richard Green, a good preacher and much beloved; Julius I. Gause, of high standing in Church and State; James King, of great pulpit eloquence; Edward Sullivan, an humble, fervent Christian; Dennis Hankins, sincere, devout, and humble, a good preacher. There were many pious, praiseworthy lay members—Brother Gibbs; Peter Gause, a good man, useful and honorable; Mrs. Jane Wilkers, his daughter, an accomplished, thoroughgoing, steadfast Methodist; there were the Durants—Bethel, John, and Thomas; Thomas Frink, Richard Holmes, Robert Howe, and Benjamin Gause, the father, no doubt, of the Marion senator who was such in 1840 when the author traveled the Marion Circuit—a man Falstaffian in proportions, and of as generous a heart as ever beat in human bosom. Long since have they all joined the Church above.

This year, 1807, the bishop passed through Wilmington. He writes: "A high day on Mount Zion." Now what was that Mount Zion? A poor little church, a tumble-down parsonage, and some negro hovels scattered around. It had been willed to him by William Meredith, who finding these sheep had folded them, and going soon after to heaven had given them to Asbury, who had seen the baronial castles and cathedrals and minsters of England—how did they compare with his Mount Zion? As Hyperion to a satyr, or fertile mountain to a barren moor; and yet in his eyes this Mount Zion was superior to all. He felt as David did in carrying the ark to its dwelling place upon Zion, as he sang, "The hill of God is as the hill of Bashan; a high hill as the hill of Bashan." Bashan towered in its glory, looking down upon Zion, in eastern hyperbole, leaping because of its advantage. But David asked: "Why leap ye, ye high hills? this is the hill which God desireth to dwell in; yea, the Lord will dwell in it forever."

James Jenkins located in 1806. He would not have done so

then but for some remarks from Asbury, implying that it was not altogether agreeable for him to occupy a seat in the Conference while not engaged in the regular work. Sure enough; but he was a superannuated preacher, and fully entitled to his seat. There being no provision for supernumeraries yet, and the bishop, jealous for moving cohorts, perhaps thought that this was best. No bishop would likely make any such ruling now. He resided in the lower part of Catawba Circuit, the place not exactly defined, but it was on Sawney's Creek, eleven miles from Camden. Here he wrought on a farm for bread, freely preaching the gospel he loved so well. This year (1807) he attended a camp meeting near Columbia, S. C. The meeting was excellent, notwithstanding great opposition and riot, finally abated by Myers's (the presiding elder's) determination publicly to read out names. In the fall he visited Charleston and preached at Bethel on "He staggered not at the promise." The word was with power, and it was the beginning of a gracious revival. Some one not liking so much noise had some of the negroes put in the workhouse. Some time before (1807) Cumberland Church had been lengthened twenty feet, and Bethel painted, the parsonage enlarged, another burial ground purchased, and the one on Pitt street divided and the southern half appropriated to the blacks. The official board were obliged to take measures to abate the riots so frequently occurring. By enlisting outsiders in this good work, greater peace was secured. A Mr. Cranmer, though no member, and thoughtless concerning piety, took great pleasure in the religious services. A man of powerful frame and no coward, a certain Mr. Brady, a leader in the riots, to his amazement found himself collared, led out of doors, and nicely drubbed by Cranmer. Thus "the earth helped the woman."

This year (1807) Jonathan Jackson and William Owens were the preachers. At a prayer meeting Monday night at Cumberland Church there was a crowd of worshipers. A couple of young men behaved improperly. Owens mildly reproved them, and they became highly angered. Cranmer must have been absent. They seized Owens in the aisle, with the cry, "Pump him!" It seems that the crowd became divided, some saying, "Let him apologize." They were at once in conflict, and Owens, making his escape, safely reached his home. The rioters were lodged in safe quarters by the city guard.

The preaching seemed to need the upholding of an arm of flesh sometimes. Jesse Lee tells the following: "When in New England a man threatened to whip him as soon as he was done. There was present a large athletic man, a recent convert. On dismissal of the congregation he went to the door and cried out, 'Where is the man who wanted to whip the preacher?' A man stepped forth; with one sure and certain blow the young Methodist prostrated him. He called again, 'Any more who wish to whip the preacher?' A second individual stepped up, and down he went. He cried out the third time, 'Any more ready to whip the preacher?' A bully presented himself. After a little tussle he cried, 'Enough!' He called the fourth time, but no response was made."

Another outrage this very year occurred at Bethel Church. While Jonathan Jackson was preaching, to the amazement of the assembly, a large body of the city guard, in full uniform and armed with muskets, surrounded the building. The blacks preferred attending this church as more free from the persecution endured at Cumberland Church. The galleries were crowded. The captain, in full uniform, sword in hand, walked in and commanded the dispersion of the congregation. This was unnecessary, as the clatter of the arms was heard, and the blacks, alarmed, went, and stood not on the order of their going, rushing downstairs, tumbling out of the windows, only to find themselves surrounded by these civic warriors; and they were escorted to the "sugar house," the last possible synonym of sweetness, no explanation ever being given for this extraordinary procedure. Such an assault would not likely be attempted now.

Bennett Kendrick had been appointed (1807) to Camden District, but died early in the year. Jonathan Jackson, then in Charleston, was put in his place, but did not reach the district until in the fall.

7

CHAPTER XII.

Old Journals—Sessions of Quarterly Conference—Old Enoree (Union)—Wil-. liam Gassaway—John Collinsworth—Old Bethel Academy—Local Preachers—Anthony Senter—Origin of Camp Meetings—Collinsworth's Embryo Bishop.

THROUGH the kindness of the Rev. A. H. Lester, and his official board at Union Station, I have before me a relic of the past, in the shape of a Quarterly Conference Journal of the old Enoree Circuit, possibly the only one of the kind as old, extant. This runs back to March 23, 1805, nearly ninety-three years ago. The last record in this book bears date January 7, 1843. I bespeak the favorable action of the board in presenting it to the Historical Society of our Conference, to be held among its archives. The Church of the future may look upon it with delight, in discovering how Methodism won its early triumphs, and how, "not by might nor by power," but by the divine Spirit, it has achieved such glorious results. I would set forth some of its contents, if for no other purpose, to show some of the "metes and bounds" of the early circuits of the South Carolina Conference. One cause of its exactness and consecutiveness may lie in the fact that from 1805 to 1818 Coleman Carlisle was secretary of the Quarterly Conference; another reason is that in 1832 the following resolution carried:

Resolved, That the Recording Steward be requested to purchase a book for the circuit, and that he be requested to record in that book all the minutes in the several old books handed over to him as Recording Steward.

I have tried to trace out the boundaries of these two circuits, but cannot be exact; but who can give correctly the boundaries of the old Saluda District? The first mention of it in the General Minutes is in 1802; George Dougherty, presiding elder. The following appointments were embraced in it: Broad River, Saluda, Bush River and Keowee, Edisto and Orangeburg, and Charleston. The only other district in the state was Camden —James Jenkins, presiding elder—embracing Union, Santee, Catawba, Little Pee Dee, Great Pee Dee, Georgetown, and Bladen; but two presiding elder's districts in all of South Carolina. A line running from Charleston, or more properly from the mouths of the Santees to Columbia, thence upward to Union, and between Union and Spartanburg to the state line, may have been the line of division. In 1803 there was no change save in the increase of appointments. In 1806 Union was left out of Camden District—transferred to Swananoah. In 1802, 1803, and 1804 the eldership was the same. In 1804 the two circuits, Enoree and Sandy River, and Bush River and Keowee, took in all the country above Columbia from the Catawba to the Savannah River. This boundary of course embraced the present counties of Oconee, Pickens, Greenville, Spartanburg, Union, York, Chester, Fairfield, Newberry, Abbeville, Anderson, and Laurens, with parts, doubtless, of Edgefield, Lexington, and Richland. These two respectable circuits were quite compassed in six weeks each; the first by William Gassaway, Hanover Donnan, and Daniel Asbury; and the second by Buddy W. Wheeler, William McKenny, and David Dannelly. The membership in Enoree and Sandy River was 1,186 whites and 131 colored; in Bush River and Keowee, 810 whites and 56 colored. In 1805 Britton Capel was presiding elder on Saluda District, and Enoree Circuit had for its preachers James Hill and W. W. Shepard. James Hill traveled but three years. He was said to possess superior preaching talents; his person manly, manner dignified, and address interesting. He remained pious to the last; but how much did the Church lose in his early location!

The first session of the Quarterly Conference for 1805 was held at Salem Church, March 2 and 3. "Coleman Carlisle chosen clerk." Members present: James Hill, and W. W. Shepard, traveling preachers; George Clarke, Coleman Carlisle, Stephen Shell, David Owen, Nathan Boyd, and William Scott, local preachers; John Glymph, B. Smith, William Seymore, David Croomer, and Lemon Shell, stewards and leaders.

The second session was held at "Horrell's Church House," June 22 and 23. Present, the presiding elder and eleven preachers—John Wallace, Jeremiah Lewis, William Horrell, John Palmer, Coleman Fowler, James Dillard, William Whitby, William Scott, Thomas Humphries, John Briggs, and Nathan Boyd. The usual business was transacted. "The preacher in charge was censured by Brother P., for wearing suspenders." We are greatly relieved by finding that "he was cleared of immoral conduct."

Before noticing further the old Enoree Conference Journal, I would note somewhat of the preacher in charge in 1804, William Gassaway. He entered the connection in 1788, and located in 1814. He is represented as being rescued by Methodism from vice and obscurity, and made a prince in Israel. "Wild and profligate," "a hard drinker," "a famous fiddler," in his youth, and afterwards an ardent saint and apostle. Awakened at a Methodist meeting, he went forward for prayer. The dancing people said, "What shall we do for a fiddler now?" Much was said concerning him; some thought he would not hold out long, others who knew him better said: "He is gone; the Methodists have got him; he will never play the fiddle or drink or fight any more." His convictions were pungent; but, ignorant of the plan of salvation, he hoped to be saved in the use of penance. "Passing a stream once, he allowed his horse to drink, saying, 'You may drink, you are no sinner; but I am, I will not drink.'" Earnestly seeking deliverance, he knew not to whom to go for help but to an elder in the Presbyterian Church, but thought from him to receive no favor, inasmuch as he had asked the Methodists to pray for him. "Think of my surprise," he adds, "when he took me in his open arms, saying to me: 'The Spirit of the Lord is with you. See that you grieve not that Spirit. Make my house your home. I will give you all the help I can.'" This good Presbyterian elder was Joseph McJunkin, of Union District, S. C., a man of genuine piety, who kept him at his house some weeks under Christian instruction. He gave him Baxter's "Saints' Rest." Gassaway took the book, and wandering in the woods, weeping over and confessing his sins to God, sat down to read. He says he had not read long before "the Lord, the King of glory, baptized him with the Holy Ghost and fire from heaven," and that he was fully satisfied of his conversion. He joined the Methodists; had license first to exhort, then to preach, and for more than twenty years labored successfully in Georgia and North and South Carolina. His large family and poor pay induced location, but he continued to labor energetically and successfully. His childlike and absolute faith in prayer led him to commit his way to God. In Camden, S. C., which once formed a part of his circuit, a great revival occurred, and many were converted; among them, a lady whose husband, then absent, was noted for his violent hostility to religion. Returning, he was furious; ordered the withdrawal of his wife, and swore he would cowhide the preacher. But Gassaway was not to be deterred from duty. At the time appointed his enemy sat before him exhibiting wrathfulness, cowhide in hand, prepared to execute his threat. Gassaway prayed, then gave out his text. God being with him, ere he concluded he saw that his persecutor was yielding, and at the close the angry man with streaming eyes knelt and cried out for the prayers of the people as if his last hour were come.

Travis, in his autobiography, states: " When but a youth I was accustomed to hear him preach at my uncle's in Chester District, S. C. He was a sound, orthodox preacher, and on suitable occasions argumentative and polemical; a great lover and skillful defender of Methodist doctrines and usages. He was a pleasant and sociable companion, always cheerful. I never saw him gloomy." One chief honor of this good man lay in his inducting William Capers, of precious memory, into the itinerant ministry. I never pass the spot where old Marshall's Church once stood without recalling the circumstances, and thinking on what seemingly trivial events mighty issues hang; and along that road "that is desert," from Chesterfield Court-house to Sumter, where he urged the argument for his consecration to the work of the ministry, and prevailed. Little did the good man think that he was giving a bishop to the Church, and one of the saintliest spirits to Methodism. Travis states further: "I frequently heard of him after his location; he was the same laborious, zealous, and holy minister of the gospel. He lived to mature old age; ' and he died,' no doubt, as he had lived, 'full of faith and the Holy Ghost.' But where is the periodical, religious or secular, that has recorded his exit?"

Gassaway was the preacher in charge (then called assistant) of the old Enoree Circuit in 1804. The Conference Journal, as I have said, begins in 1805. Two sessions have been noticed; the others for that year are not particularly marked, save in the recommendation of Benjamin Wofford as a traveling preacher to the South Carolina Conference.

The first session for 1806 was held at Lucas's Meetinghouse,

April 5 and 6; B. Capel, presiding elder; Epps Tucker and George Philips, traveling preachers. The following members were present: M. Smith, J. Lucas, John Wallace, James Crowder, Ricketson Lipsey, N. Boyd, T. Humphries, W. Scott, John Wood, John Palmer, Coleman Fowler, W. Horrell, R. Whitby, H. Smith, James McCord, and Moses Morgan. A. L. P., charged with distilling and selling spirituous liquors, was expelled. This Conference is remarkable for giving license to exhort to John Collinsworth, and licensing Joseph Travis to preach—both becoming men of mark in their day.

It is to be regretted that so little is known of the earlier preachers, men who hazarded their lives for the Lord Jesus. Would it not be well for all to put on record any items of interest concerning them? John Collinsworth was licensed to exhort April 5, 1806; January 24, to preach; and in September employed on the Enoree Circuit. In 1807 he and Joseph Travis were admitted on trial in the South Carolina Conference. In 1814 he was the presiding elder on Edisto District; in 1830 transferred to Georgia. Whether he located or died in connection with that Conference, I am unable to state. He was said to be gifted in prayer, and of mighty faith. "F. A. M." relates the incident happening in Virginia, where a fearful hailstorm desolated the crops, seemingly in answer to his prayer. An old planter, riding up to him, demanded: "Are you, sir, the Methodist preacher who prayed the Lord to destroy my crop of tobacco?" He replied: "My name is Collinsworth; I preached yesterday, and prayed the Lord to show his displeasure of raising tobacco." "Well, sir, you are just the man I am after. I am ruined for this season, and I have come to take my revenge out of you, sir," at the same time brandishing a frightful-looking wagon whip. Beginning to dismount, Collinsworth replied: "Well, if I must be whipped for it, I suppose I must submit; but take care before you have done that I do not pray the Lord to overtake you with something worse than overtook your crop." This he had not thought of, and putting spurs to his horse, galloped off speedily.

But returning to the old journal—the General Minutes of 1807 place Lewis Myers on the Saluda District, and William M. Kennedy and M. P. Sturdevant preachers on the Enoree Circuit; yet in all journals of the sessions for that year the last is represented as the assistant, or presiding elder. M. P. Sturdevant was senior by one year.

The first session of the Quarterly Conference was held at Hindman's Meetinghouse, April 4, 1807. "Through grace no charge against any of the members."

The second session was held at Sealey's Meetinghouse, June 13, 1807. A local preacher was censured for performing the marriage ceremony, he being unordained.

The third session was held at Rogers's Meetinghouse, September 20, 1807. As this record contains the full list of official members in the circuit, we give it entire: L. Myers, presiding elder; M. P. Sturdevant, William M. Kennedy, circuit preachers; George Clarke, George Philips, James Dillard, John Watch, John Wallace, W. Young, W. Rowel, Joel Whitten, John Palmer, H. Smith, Thomas Humphries, George Linane, Jerry Lucas, Samuel Harris, Peter Tucker, James Danner, Lemon Shell, Coleman Carlisle, James Gassaway, Jonas Briggs, Coleman Fowler, Richard Whitby, James Crowder, M. Sherbert, Benjamin Wofford, James Mullonax, Andrew Shaw, A. Kennedy, Hugh O'Neal, David Owens, Nathan Boyd, Caleb Davis, Thomas Stokes, Thomas Cunningham, John Terry, and Moses Morgan. "The Conference decrees that the preachers and leaders catechise the children whenever they can."

The fourth session was held December 5, 1807; noted for the mention of Mount Bethel Academy, Lewis Myers, Thomas Dugan, Archy Crenshaw, Dr. Joseph Davis, and Dr. Moore being appointed trustees. This was the first high school among the Methodists in Carolina. The section of Newberry District in which it was situated was settled by emigrants from Virginia. It may be, though I cannot assert positively, the very section of country in which Methodism was first established by James Forster, a local preacher, anterior to its introduction into Charleston. It was evidently a strong point in the interior, for the Conference in 1794 was here held at "Finch's in Fork Saluda and Broad rivers." Thirty preachers were present. They were straitened for room, "having only twelve feet square to confer, sleep, and for the accommodation of those who were sick." Bishop Asbury writes of "resting at dear old Father Yergin's." The Finches, Crenshaws, Malones, and others had been Methodists in Virginia. Edward Finch gave thirty acres of land as a site for the institution. The work began in 1794, and on the visit of Bishop Asbury, March 17, 1795, he prepared subscription papers to be sent abroad, "to raise £100 to finish Bethel School." It ceased to exist in 1820, superseded by Mount Ariel Academy, afterwards the Cokesbury School. After its decline, the settlement, once the garden spot of Methodism in the upcountry, surprising as it may seem, remained for nearly forty years without any regular Methodist preaching. In 1852 the Rev. C. Murchison "took it into" the Newberry Circuit, and organized a society of ten whites and sixteen colored persons.

Returning to the old journal, the first session of the Quarterly Conference for 1808 was held at Fish Dam Meetinghouse, March 12; Lewis Myers, presiding elder; Amos Curtis and John Conon, stationed preachers. A word as to that last name. The secretary's chirography is something "peculiar." Would you believe that the Minutes say the name ought to be John W. Kennon? Alas for "fame"! One "dies for his country" under the cognomen of James Smith, and somebody makes it John Smith. At this session there was nothing of special interest.

The second session was to have been held at Zion, Sandy River, but "the presiding elder being absent, there was no Quarterly Conference, and consequently no business done." The Church improved upon this in after years.

The third Quarterly Conference was held at Rogers's Meetinghouse, October 1, 1808. "Characters examined; through favors, no charges of any consequence against any." Oh, these Methodists! Old Father Jenkins once "shouted aloud"—so happy—when charges were preferred against himself. He regarded it as an evidence of "the love of the brethren"; and pray how far was he wrong? At this Conference two important resolutions were carried:

1. No license to be renewed until applicant had been heard and approved of by the assistant or some experienced preacher.

2. No local preacher to have license renewed unless his gifts are improvable and profitable to the Church.

Ah, if this had been observed everywhere and sacredly, what an arm of strength would our ministry have been, both local and traveling! Is it too late to enforce it now? Threescore years from to-day might not its profit appear?

The fourth session was held December 3, 1808, at Salem Meetinghouse. "A. Center, proposed to travel, and recommended by a majority." The orthography of the name attracts no attention; but write it Anthony Senter, and lo! the change—another name of mark from the old Enoree Circuit:

Anthony Senter was born in Lincoln county, North Carolina, January 28, 1785, and died in Georgetown, S. C., December 23, 1817. Little is known of his early convictions or religious feelings until after his establishment in life. The pious life of one of his neighbors first led him with restless concern to examine the nature of vital religion. In 1806, at a meeting in the Enoree Circuit, he was brought under overwhelming conviction of sin. He went away weeping and praying. On his way home (so overwhelmed was he with the sense of his lost state) he either alighted or fell from his horse, and was found late in the evening lying by the roadside in the utmost agony, pleading with God for mercy. He joined the Church, and soon after entered on the work of the ministry.

From 1809 to 1817 he was a traveling preacher. The last two years he presided over the Broad River District. "A strong mind and a benevolent heart; a single eye and a steady purpose to glorify God; an unwavering faith, fervent love, and burning zeal—these were the exalted attributes of this good man." While able to preach he was indefatigable in the work, and even when so impaired by the fatal consumption as to be prevented from preaching he still traveled from circuit to circuit, assembling the official members, instructing and encouraging them in their work. At last even this was denied him. As the veteran soldier retires from the field faint and exhausted, only retiring because he could do no more, so he reluctantly gave up the toil to die. Reduced to a living skeleton, feeble as a child, and just falling into the grave, his heart could not be separated from the work of God; he still charged himself with its interest and felt its cares. Indeed, with death before him, and the awful glories of the invisible world just ready to be unfolded, like Jacob, gathering up his feet composedly and without dismay, he fell asleep.

Nothing but the usual business of a Quarterly Conference is discoverable in all the records of this old circuit up to March 21, 1813. Then this item is written: "Camp meetings appointed at Salem, at Wofford's, and Fish Dam." A word or two as to their origin and usefulness. Methodism owes its power, next to the divine Spirit, to its aggressiveness. It never waited for the people to call the preachers, but quite the reverse—for the preacher to call the people.   Let every candid mind decide if this is not most in accordance with the command, "Go ye into all the world, and preach the gospel to every creature." The usual and ordinary means of grace might satisfy all the demands of formalism, but they could not satisfy the spirit resolved to storm the very gates of hell to rescue souls from perdition.   No wonder that the early Methodists believed in, and that their true successors still persist in holding, camp meetings.   The decent world and the respectable Church are fully agreed as to all the proprieties that ought to be observed by fashionable people.   These might raise an outcry against them, but this did not deter the men who had the love of souls at heart.   It might be uncanonical to save a soul outside the Church; but uncanonical or not, if there was any hope of success, or even without it, it was attempted; and they did not care a single straw for the opinion of that decent world concerning their ignorance or learning.   Some timid souls are much alarmed for the ark, as was Uzzah when the oxen stumbled; but God is able to take care of his own, ever has done so, and ever will to the end of the world.   Suffer me to put on record something as to the origin of these meetings.   The first notice concerning them in South Carolina is found in James Jenkins's memoirs, about 1802.   He says:

It will be seen that thus far I have said nothing about camp meetings; indeed, until now we had none in this state.   They were becoming quite common in Kentucky and Tennessee, where they commenced about the year 1800, under the labors of William and John McGee—the one a Presbyterian and the other a Methodist minister.   They united on their sacramental occasions, at which the work of the Lord broke out; and such were the gracious results of these meetings that in a very short time multitudes came from every direction; some prepared to remain only a day at a time, others in wagons to stay all night, and soon others again put up small tents and camped during the meeting.   It was not long before other ministers and communities, seeing the good effect of these meetings, were induced to hold similar ones for their own benefit; so that in two years their example was followed by nearly all our Conferences.

Here may be introduced a letter from John McGee, the Methodist, dated October 27, 1800:

Last June, at a sacramental meeting of the Presbyterians at Red River Meetinghouse, the preachers present were Messrs. McCready, Rankin, Hodge, William McGee, and myself; four or five hundred people attended with great seriousness. The Lord's servants preached with much light and liberty, and the people felt the truth and power of the word each day; but the last, which was Monday, was truly a great day. One sermon was preached with the Holy Ghost sent down from heaven. The cry of distressed sinners for mercy was great, while the Lord's people were filled with unspeakable joy.

And thus he continues with details of several other meetings of the same kind. A year or two afterwards, Mr. Hodge, a Presbyterian minister, wrote as follows: "At the time that our Presbytery sat, a vote was carried by a majority of the members for licensing three unlearned men to preach the gospel. The Lord has graciously owned these licentiates, by making them instrumental in the conversion of many."

The ignorant and unlearned men of this day were no less a matter of astonishment than in the days of Peter and John. Their power is accounted for by the fact "that they had been with Jesus."

But to continue from James Jenkins's memoirs: "The Presbyterians held a *general* meeting, as it was then called, at the Waxhaws, on the last of May." He writes to Bishop Asbury from Camden, S. C., June 30, 1802:

Hell is trembling, and Satan's kingdom falling. Through Georgia, South and North Carolina, the sacred flame and holy fire of God, amidst all the opposition, is extending far and wide. The general meeting held at the Waxhaws was on the last of May. Five Methodist, five Baptist, and twelve Presbyterian ministers officiated. The Lord was present, and wrought for his own glory. Sinners were converted on all sides, and numbers found the Lord. One among many remarkable cases I will relate, of a professed atheist who fell to the earth, and sent for Brother Gassaway to pray for him. After laboring in the pangs of the new birth for some time, the Lord gave him deliverance. He then confessed before hundreds that for some years he had not believed there was a God, but now found him gracious to his soul. The Methodists had a general meeting a few days past at the Hanging Rock. There were fifteen ministers—Methodist, Baptist, and Presbyterian—with about three thousand people present.

This is enough, and settles the question as to the first camp meeting held in South Carolina. For many years past they have been kept up at this old Hanging Rock, where they first began, and all over the South the good resulting will not be fully known until the general judgment. Before resuming the old journal, we give this sketch of the Rev. John Collinsworth by Dr. G. G. Smith, of the North Georgia Conference:

No man was perhaps known more widely among Georgia Methodists thirty years ago. He was in many ways a character. Bishop Andrew furnished to Dr. Sprague for his Annals a graphic portraiture of him; and from the old Methodists of Georgia many anecdotes of his peculiar views may be gathered. He was a Virginian by birth, was licensed to preach in South Carolina, and joined the South Carolina Conference in 1807. In 1809, when Augusta, Louisville, and Savannah were in one circuit, he was in charge, with John Rye as his junior. During this year John H. Mann united with the Church in Augusta. He continued to travel for several years, then located from feeble health. His home was in Putnam county, near to that of his lifelong friend, Josiah Flournoy. When his health was restored, he returned to the work, and in it he died on the 4th of September, 1834.

While he was local he cultivated a small farm, and was remarkable for the energy, system, and skill with which he tended it. He was a Methodist of the old type, was very plain in his apparel, and demanded from all the same regard to simplicity. Broadcloth, rings, and ruffles were his abomination. He was a stern Elijah in the pulpit, and in the most solemn and earnest way denounced the terrors of the law upon the guilty sinners who sat under his ministry. Under this appearance of severity of spirit Bishop Andrew, who knew him well, says he carried a gentle, tender heart.

Once he acknowledged that he erred. The story of how that was is substantially as we tell it. He was stationed at Greensboro in 1830. George Foster Pierce, the eldest son of Lovick Pierce, had just graduated, and was in the law office of his uncle, Thomas Foster, studying law. A conversation with James O. Andrew led the young law student to resolve to let the dead bury their dead, while he followed his Master. Application was made by Bishop Andrew to Brother Collinsworth to secure from the Church a recommendation to the Quarterly Conference for license for George Pierce to preach. Uncle Collinsworth did not favor the idea. The young man was too "airy." His hair grew too straight from his forehead. He wore as a Sunday suit blue broadcloth with brass buttons, and cut fashionably at that. He, however, brought the matter before the Church, and was not slow in expressing his disapproval of the request. The Church differed from the preacher, and recommended the applicant. Uncle Collinsworth met him at the door of the church: "Well, George," he said, "these brethren, against my will, have consented to recommend you; but now I tell you, this coat must come off." "But," said the young man, "Uncle Collinsworth, it is almost new, and it is the only nice one I have." "Can't help it; it must come off; a man can't be licensed to preach with such a coat as this on." "But, Uncle Collinsworth, it would not be right to put father to the expense of buying me a new suit." The old preacher was unconvinced; the young applicant was equally decided. "George," said he again, "why don't you brush your hair down on your forehead as I do? It stands up in a most worldly way." "Why, Uncle Collinsworth, if the Lord had wanted my hair to lie down he would not have made it to stand up."

The stern old man went to the Quarterly Conference, decided that George Pierce might do for a worldly lawyer, but he was too "airish" for a preacher—so he told the Conference. They, too, differed with him, and licensed and recommended the future bishop, despite the blue broadcloth. At the Conference in Macon the old gentleman held his peace, though he was decided enough in his opinion.

George went on the Alcovi Circuit, his old pastor to the Sugar Creek Mission. The camp meeting at old Hastings Camp Ground came on, and Uncle Collinsworth was there. It rained, and rained, and rained; the creeks were up, the river almost impassable. One evening, as he entered Sister Pierce's tent, he found George mud-bespattered, just from his circuit, without blue broadcloth or brass buttons. "Why, George, you here?" "You see that I am, Uncle Collinsworth." "Why, how did you get here?" "Partly by land; mainly by water." "Did you swim any creeks?" "Yes, sir; I swam three." "Well, George," he said, kindly laying his hand on his head, "you'll do yet." He lived long enough to be glad that he had been mistaken one time, but not long enough to see how badly. No man doubted the sincere piety of Father Collinsworth. He made no demand of anyone which he did not exact of himself. He lived in a day when stern stuff was needed to keep men at the front, and if he erred it was in the right line. He left quite a family, and his excellent widow passed away only a few years since.

In 1834 the preachers in Charleston were William M. Kennedy, William Martin, and George F. Pierce. The latter supplied the place of William Capers, transferred to the Georgia Conference and stationed in Savannah, Ga. The name in the General Minutes is George W. F. Pierce. He was admitted into the Georgia Conference in 1831; ordained elder in the South Carolina Conference in 1835, and stationed at Augusta. The author, then a youth of fourteen, heard the young preacher in old Trinity (the Hammet building). The text was the first Psalm. The sermon was impressive. There is no telling how much of the young life of the city was affected by it. Doubtless several ministers of the South Carolina Conference were the fruit of that single effort. All but one are now in heaven, and he is looking hopefully to that end.

CHAPTER XIII.

Parsonages—Conferences Contrasted—Benjamin Wofford—Preachers Sent from Enoree—Coleman Carlisle—Support of Ministers—Quarterage and Family Expenses—Meager Estimates—Improper Appropriations—Old District Conferences—Centenary of Methodism in 1839.

RETURNING to the old journal: at the first session held at Mount Tabor, February 16, 1816—Thomas Mason, presiding elder; Reuben Tucker, assistant; Wiley Warwick, circuit preacher—"a plan was proposed to build a glebe or parsonage in the circuit for the traveling preachers"; the glebe, of course, to be procured. This was an early day for such arrangements, yet not early enough by far to prevent the locations so frequent. The parsonage question may well be said to underlie the itinerant system. How much of strength may have been gained to Methodism by an earlier enforcement, can scarcely be computed. One thing is certain: the local itinerancy, so prevalent in some Conferences, would not have obtained had each charge had its preacher's home. Subject an itinerant to the necessity of furnishing such himself, and, as a consequence, he can only travel the length of the tether binding him to his home. Do Methodists glory, and justly too, in the itinerant system? Let them not do it at the expense of extra pressure upon men that are homeless, or induce the necessity of crippling its force. I have heard bishops remark that the South Carolina Conference is more free than some others from this evil. May it not be traceable to the fact of the prominence given this matter?

I have before me the Minutes of the Virginia, South Georgia, and South Carolina Conferences for 1875. The number of parsonages belonging to each is as follows: Virginia, 51; South Georgia, $36\frac{1}{3}$; South Carolina, 74. The one-third of a parsonage has no note of explanation, so it cannot be said certainly what that is. South Carolina has twenty-three more than Virginia, and thirty-eight more than South Georgia. The deficiency in per cent, leaving out the missions in the calculation, is as follows: Virginia Conference, 151 charges, 51 parsonages; deficiency per cent, 66. South Georgia, 95 charges, 36 parsonages; deficiency per cent, 62. South Carolina, 117 charges, 74 parsonages; deficiency per cent, 36. May the review be stimulating to all concerned, and the day be not far distant when every charge shall have its itinerant's home in all our Conferences! [1]

Returning to the old journal, we find that this parsonage matter had its opponents. At the third session, held at Bethel, we find this record: "G. P. censured per the assistant preacher for objecting to the building a parsonage for the married preacher; reproved by the Conference, and admonished."

"November 8, 1816. Benjamin Wofford recommended to the South Carolina Conference as a traveling preacher."

"March 22, 1817. First session at Zoar: Anthony Senter, P. E.; John B. Glenn and Benjamin Wofford, C. P.'s." The second, third, and fourth, no presiding elder, he dying that year. At the second, in the examination of character the record is: "All blameless, except ——, who was found guilty of retailing spirituous liquors. He promised to put away the evil from the Church of God, as directed by the Conference." Mark, this was long before the great temperance reformation.

At the fourth session, held at Wofford's Chapel, December 20, 1817, "Benjamin Rhodes was recommended to the Annual Conference to travel as an itinerant." He continued to travel until 1826, when, stationed in Georgetown, he died. Through somebody's neglect there is no memoir in the General Minutes. Isaac Hartley, a young preacher, was transferred from Rockingham, N. C., to that malarious region at the most unpropitious season of the year to supply the vacant post. He fell likewise. Both Rhodes and Hartley sleep in the Georgetown graveyard. I have heard the presiding elder lament his connection with the transfer, as Hartley was "the only son of his mother, and she a widow." The Conference, for her life, included her in the distribution of its funds.

"January 22, 1818. Ordered, the committee appointed to purchase a parsonage do proceed in collecting money and bring the same into effect." Building a parsonage was not so easy a matter after all. And what good thing in this crooked world is easy?

"February 14, 1818. The following persons were appointed trustees for the parsonage: Coleman Carlisle, Benjamin Hern-

---

[1] Twenty years later there was a noble advance all around. In 1895 the South Carolina Conference numbered 154 parsonages, valued at $218,870.

don, Spilsby Glenn, John Hill, John Odle Hill, and John Mullinax.

"Coleman Carlisle was proposed and employed as a missionary in Laurens District."

"November 6, 1818. Coleman Carlisle was recommended for readmission into the South Carolina Conference. Nathaniel Rhodes and John Mullinax were recommended for admission."

"May 14, 1819. The persons chosen to purchase a parsonage were dismissed, and John Hill, James Mayham, Thomas Hutchins, Z. McDaniel, and Augustus Shands chosen in their place."

"August 14, 1819. Wiley Warwick accused of profane swearing. The Conference judge the said accusation to be a malicious slander."

"November 26, 1819. Wiley Warwick was recommended to the Annual Conference as a preacher of usefulness."

The names of the preachers recommended to the South Carolina Conference from Enoree Circuit, from 1805 to 1820, are as follows: December 7, 1805, Robert Porter, located 1816; April 5, 1806, John Collinsworth, transferred to Georgia 1830; April 5, 1806, Joseph Travis, located 1825; December 4, 1808, Anthony Senter, died 1817; November 7, 1809, John B. Glenn, located 1819; November 30, 1813, Travis Owens, located 1825; December 4, 1815, Benjamin Rhodes, died 1826; November 30, 1817, Benjamin Wofford, located 1820; November 6, 1818, Coleman Carlisle, located 1823; November 26, 1819, N. H. Rhodes, transferred to Georgia 1830; November 26, 1819, Wiley Warwick, transferred to Georgia 1830. Coleman Carlisle and Wiley Warwick were recommended for readmission.

The Rev. Coleman Carlisle passed the greater part of his local life within the bounds of this circuit. The old journal gives evidence of his zeal and usefulness. Three times he entered the traveling ministry, and as often was driven from it by the sheer necessity of making provision for a helpless family. Local or traveling, the word of the Lord was in his bones, and he could not but labor for the cause he loved. Returning from his appointments, with the same horse (hard on the creature, both man and beast) he would plow by moonlight until near midnight, to eke out the scanty disciplinary pittance allowed him, which, small as it was, was still subject to a heavy discount in the payment. He entered the Conference in 1792, traveled three years, and located; entering again in 1801, he traveled three years, and located; and the last time, 1819, traveled four years, and finally retired. He was popular, being sent for from far and near to preach funeral sermons, and receiving for all his long rides and sermons *nothing.* And he was not alone in this, as the long list of locations amply testifies. God was in the movement, or Methodism could never have survived such pressure. Its basal fact was "free grace," and that was confounded with a "free gospel"; so that the idea of cost to any scarcely entered into the calculation. Human nature can endure much, but not everything, and hundreds were forced to provide for those dear to them by location. The Church was long in waking up to the fact that it was God's ordination that they who preach the gospel should live by it; and alas! to-day thousands of her adherents are oblivious of the same fact.

At the time of which I write no provision was made for "family expenses," and at a later day, as those records prove, it was meager at best. The whole machinery for ministerial support was out of shape, as witness the following item, and all the succeeding records.

"February 26, 1820. At a meeting of the trustees of the Methodist parsonage, present Spilsby Glenn, John Hill, John B. Glenn, appropriated to Brother R. L. Edwards two hundred dollars for table or family expenses."

"February 10, 1823. The committee, W. Holland, William Holland, and Benjamin Wofford, estimate the table expenses of Brother Tilman Sneed at one hundred dollars for the present year."

"May 2, 1824. We, the stewards, do agree to give Brother Allan Turner eighty dollars for family expenses, and should he request more, to give it. BENJ. WOFFORD, Sec."

From 1825 to 1830 committees were appointed, but no record of amounts estimated put on record.

June 3, 1831, there is this report: "We, the undersigned, to whom was referred to ascertain what shall be allowed Brother James Stockdale for his family expenses, do report as follows, to wit: That James Stockdale be, and is hereby, entitled to receive the sum of forty dollars, and that said appropriation shall be raised agreeable to Methodist discipline."

8

There is no other record on this subject until July 26, 1836; then this: "The committee report that Brother Crowell be entitled to receive eighty-four dollars, and if his family expenses should be more, the same to be paid if it can be raised."

"July 1, 1838. The committee appointed to estimate Brother Watts's family expenses agree that he be allowed two and a half dollars a week, or one hundred dollars for the year."

Now when it is remembered that what was called the quarterage allowance rarely reached three hundred dollars, the addition for family expenses, as above, made the entire claim exceedingly moderate; yet, moderate as it was, it was seldom met. There are no records of collections and expenditures, as in most journals, or this fact could be put beyond dispute. This raising supplies was a sore subject all these years, as the following records show.

"April 8, 1828. This Conference, in concurrence with the order of the South Carolina Conference, resolved that Enoree Circuit be divided among the stewards thereof; and that they attend personally at every society with subscription papers, for the purpose of making collections for the support of the gospel on the circuit; and that they press upon the congregation, and more particularly upon members of the society, the necessity of their subscribing; and that the same be perpetuated from year to year, unless those who subscribe make known to the stewards their wish to discontinue their subscriptions, or until this resolution is repealed."

"December 27, 1828. Moved by B. B. Gaines, seconded by J. Jennings, that the money which the parsonage sold for be placed in the hands of the stewards, to make up the deficiency of quarterage on the circuit. The motion was carried." Comment is unnecessary.

"May 1, 1829. On motion, resolved that the plan of collecting quarterage be by subscription, and that the names of every member of each society be placed on a paper, and that said paper be presented to each individual; and when this cannot be done by the steward, the preacher in charge be authorized to do the same. And be it further resolved that all the said papers be brought to the third Quarterly Conference."

In this matter of ministerial support I have made a rough estimate of Conference expenditure for the year 1831, the first year after the Georgia Conference was set off. For the support of sixty-four preachers it amounts to $17,100. Call it in round numbers $20,000, which I am satisfied largely exceeds the actual receipts; this would give an average of $312.50. Did ever a religious body of the same respectability, numbers, and wealth get its ministerial service cheaper? The average, per white member, is ninety-seven cents; and including the colored membership, only forty-seven cents.

The first session of the Quarterly Conference for 1820 was held at Ebenezer Meetinghouse, March 2; Daniel Asbury, presiding elder; Griffin Christopher and J. B. Chappel, circuit preachers.

"George Clarke, complained of for putting a school into Ebenezer Meetinghouse," was not censured; but at the second session it was resolved "that no schools, reading or singing, shall be kept in our meetinghouses in future."

"A. S. applied for a dismission as trustee of the parsonage; but in consequence of some embarrassment about the establishment, and as he had taken an active part in getting the house, it was thought not best to grant his request."

I pass over some seven years, nothing unusual appearing.

The third session for 1827 was held at Antioch. Robert Adams, presiding elder; John Mood and William H. Ellison, circuit preachers; John Jennings and Benjamin Wofford, local elders; Wiley F. Holliman, A. Shands, and Benjamin Gaines, licentiates; Z. McDaniel, John Comer, J. C. Mahew, R. Casey, Oliver Kirby, A. Powers, S. Hardy, C. Bogan, and Thomas Humphries, leaders.

The parsonage all these years was a troublesome matter. On motion it was resolved "that the contract between the trustees of the parsonage and Brother B. Wofford with regard to its sale be confirmed." On the question, "Shall the trustees seek out and purchase another parsonage?" it was answered, "They shall."

November 27, 1830, William Whitby was recommended to the South Carolina Conference.

June 30, 1832—Malcolm McPherson, presiding elder; M. C. Turrentine and James Stacy, circuit preachers—the following resolution was adopted:

Whereas this circuit deems it expedient and right that there should be a house provided for the presiding elder's family; and whereas a house is purchased at Mount Ariel (Cokesbury) for that purpose:

Resolved, That this circuit's part be paid out of the avails of furniture of the old Enoree Circuit parsonage.

This was the easiest way of doing it, and likely to carry, nobody being hurt by the operation, but certainly not the best. Such a mixing of interests would not obtain in our day. One's readiness "to sacrifice all his wife's relations for the good of the country" finds its counterpart in this readiness to pay quarterage and buy other property with other people's money. How selfishness will steal into the very sanctuary under religious disguises! The wonder is that even good men often lack the nerve to rebuke it.

"The preacher in charge was complained of for not attending to class meeting strictly enough at Antioch."

"Whereas the Laurens Circuit has passed a resolution to revive the District Conference for Saluda District, and whereas said resolution is offered to this circuit for concurrence, it was moved and seconded that this Conference concur. Motion lost."

What failed to carry then obtains now over all the Southern Church. The class meeting, the Church Conference, the Quarterly, the Annual, and the General Conference seemed to meet all demands; but the present year in the bounds of the Sumter District, in the Santee Circuit—Rev. J. L. Shuford, pastor—a new Conference has originated called the Circuit Conference. Every fifth Sunday such is held, with its delegates, preachers, and stewards, at some point selected. The advantage promised seems to be in bringing about greater unity of action in the churches composing the circuit. May it not be made to supply the place of the "Leaders' Meeting," so hard to be made effective in the country, and now gone into desuetude in the cities? In union is strength, and Methodism loses much of its force just here. The wisdom of Wesley has never been questioned in the institution of the class meeting; its virtual abandonment has been damaging, both spiritually and temporally, the only compensation being in making us like other Churches. When I say class meeting, I do not mean the thing into which it degenerated—of one's getting up, reading a chapter, commenting on it, then prayer and dismissal—but the earnest watch-care of a shepherd over the trust committed to him, and the faithful review by pastors and leaders of the life of each individual.

JAMES H. CARLISLE, LL.D.

In 1833 the name of the circuit was changed to Union. At the second session for this year, "stewards were complained of for not making any collections of consequence to defray the expenses of the circuit."

April 29, 1833, two members were put back on trial six months, and debarred the privilege of taking the sacrament and staying in love feast. Curious penalty for offenses.

January 16, 1836, for the first and only time, there is a record of the churches composing the circuit, namely: Trinity, Chappel, Tabernacle, Fish Dam, Hebron, Bethel, Antioch, Zion, Flat Rock, Wesley Chapel, Sardis, Ebenezer, Mount Tabor, Quaker, Dry Pond, Rogers's, Odle's, Shiloh, Unionville, Fairfield, Rehoboth, and Nob's—twenty-two in all.

The report for Sunday schools for 1835 is full: Angus McPherson, preacher in charge; 480 scholars, 74 teachers, and 32 superintendents—these last quite numerous, some schools having no less than five each. The children forty years ago—how many were gathered into the Church!

August 10, 1839, the centenary of Methodism was observed; William M. Kennedy and William M. Wightman to preach the preparatory sermons at the Flat Rock and Maybinton camp meetings.

We close our extracts from the old journal with a full list of the members of the third session of the Quarterly Conference, held at Bogan's Camp Ground, October 21, 1842—fifty-five years ago. How many now survive? N. Talley, presiding elder; A. McCorquodale and J. R. Pickett, circuit preachers; B. S. Ogletree and J. Jennings, local elders; A. Shands, T. A. Glenn, W. F. Holliman, and J. F. Glenn, local deacons; Miles Puckett, William May, and C. S. Beard, licentiates; Thomas Fowler, exhorter; John W. Kelly and S. L. Malony, examined and licensed; William Hunt, exhorter; J. H. Dogan, steward; T. A. Carlisle, steward and leader; James Epps, B. Dehay, and Caswell Bogan, stewards and leaders; M. Hames, James Gantt, E. Gossett, Sr., Oliver Kirby, W. Foster, E. Gossett, Jr., H. Murph, Henry Wofford, William Farr, Wiley Yarboro, —— Sexton, W. Farrow, —— Miles, R. Gillian, —— Hendricks, A. Shell, —— Hipp, John Sims, Thomas Kumer, W. Clark, P. Tucker, G. Tucker, Thomas Ison, —— Gillian, W. Jennings, —— Thomas, Joshua Bishop, William Mitchell, William Bevis, James Beckwell, R. Lipsey, C. Hames, John Galmon, Perry Stribling, M. Hill, Thomas Young, Lewis Bobo, Wiley Miles, class leaders. A strong Quarterly Conference—nearly sixty members.

January 6, 1844, John W. Kelly and Miles Puckett were recommended to the South Carolina Conference.

This was the old Enoree or Union Circuit, a fruitful nursery of Methodism. Broad River divided Union and Spartanburg counties from Fairfield, Chester, and York, the strongholds of Calvinism; but the care and culture of the early days held this field, and its influence has extended across the river. In Spartanburg Bishop Duncan has his home. James H. Carlisle holds the presidency of Wofford College. Central Church is a gem, and the noble laity exert a gracious influence. Union more than holds its own; in fact, manufacturing enterprises promise a great advance in all this upper country. Well may we rejoice in the early religious culture.

WOFFORD COLLEGE, SPARTANBURG, S. C.; JAMES H. CARLISLE, LL.D., PRESIDENT.

CHAPTER XIV.

THE religious condition of America, before, during, and after the Revolution, was not far from that of the Israelitish commonwealth in Deborah's day. "The inhabitants of the villages ceased," "the highways were unoccupied," and "travelers walked through byways." New gods were chosen; there "was war in the gates," and "not a shield or spear," of heavenly temper keen, "was seen among forty thousand in Israel." Reuben clung to his sheepfolds, Gideon dwelt beyond Jordan, Asher was on the seashore, and Dan abode in ships; and all the while Sisera was at hand. Deborah (see Barbara Heck snatching the cards from the hands of a renegade) "arose, a mother in Israel"; she called to Barak, and bade him take ten thousand of Zebulun and Naphtali and fight; even then, if help came not from heaven, all was lost; but "the stars in their courses fought against Sisera. The river Kishon swept them away." Then sang Deborah: "O my soul, thou hast trodden down strength. Then were the horsehoofs broken by the means of the prancings, the prancings of their mighty ones." No wonder the universal cry was: "Awake, awake, Deborah; awake, awake, utter a song; arise, Barak, and lead thy captivity captive, thou son of Abinoam!" We of this day, who rejoice in the victories won by our fathers, should never forget that "Zebulun and Naphtali jeoparded their lives unto the death in the high places of the field."

We call attention to these veterans who, though little known on earth, have abundant record on high. The very first we notice is the man, as you read back awhile, who was wrongly and maliciously accused of false swearing. From George Bright, in the *Southern Christian Advocate,* we learn that Wiley Warwick was born in Virginia in 1771. He was a moral though irreligious youth, remaining unregenerate until his twenty-sixth year. His marriage at twenty-one to a pious girl brought him under Methodistic influence. In 1796 he was powerfully converted in

Anson county, North Carolina, where he then resided. He was licensed to preach in 1799, and labored as a local preacher until 1804. By persuasion of Bishop Asbury and other preachers he was admitted into the connection. While a local preacher he attended a camp meeting, the first ever held in that section. It was a union meeting, under direction of Dr. Brown, afterwards president of Franklin College, Georgia. Mr. Warwick walked the entire distance, arriving at the three o'clock service. When the sermon was finished, anyone was invited to exhort. Mr. Warwick arose, and under the inspiration of the Holy Ghost, exhorted. The power of God was manifest; people fell in all directions, crying aloud for mercy. From then until Monday morning the good work went on, and eternity will reveal great results.

January 1, 1804, he was admitted into the Conference, held that year in Augusta, Ga. He traveled thirteen years, and failing health induced location. His last year on the Enoree Circuit was nominal, as supernumerary. He remained local until 1821, when he was employed by Bishop George to supply the Union Circuit. At the thirty-sixth session, held in Augusta, Ga., he was readmitted, traveling several years. In 1826 he suffered greatly from a pine splinter in one of the muscles of the thigh; medical skill declined its removal. Having a pad for his saddle, to relieve the pressure, he traveled for years in pain. In 1822, having removed to Habersham county, Georgia, during the journey he got his little finger mashed, forcing amputation. Suffering greatly, he lost two rounds of appointments. At the Conference the presiding elder complained that he had neglected his work. He simply arose and drew forth his inflamed and mutilated hand. It was enough.

While on the Bladen Circuit, in 1806, he was much annoyed by an immersionist named Lindsey. He was very bigoted, and a great enemy to Methodist "circuit riders." Once Mr. Warwick, passing through a low or swampy place, fished out of the mud and water a pair of saddlebags. They were marked with Mr. Lindsey's name in full, and a junk bottle well filled with liquor was first drawn out. At the next house he call for lodgings, but was told that circuit riders could not stay there. He delivered the saddlebags, asking the landlady to inform the parson that they were safe. She began to excuse her preacher, saying he had happened to pass a store that day, and fasting, had taken a little too much liquor, and had thus lost his saddle-bags—begging Mr. Warwick not to tell of the little accident. The rides on this circuit were long. On one stretch there was no house, and necessity compelled him to sleep in the woods, supperless, the earth for a bed, his saddle for a pillow, and the heavens for a covering.

During the thirty years of his efficiency he traveled near 70,000 miles, preached 5,938 sermons, exhorting numberless times, and received $6,392 all told—an average of $110 per annum; rearing a family of five children, and giving them a moderate education. The last years of his life were spent in Dahlonega, Georgia, in a state of sad decrepitude. He was made perfect through suffering. His agony was often so excessive that even morphine gave no aid. No murmur escaped his lips. He died in the eighty-sixth year of his age, the fifty-seventh of his ministry, and the fifty-third of his connection with the itinerancy.

James H. Mellard (1801–1855) was admitted on trial in the South Carolina Conference in 1801, and located in 1810. We are not advised as to his reëntrance into any Conference, but are assured that whether local or traveling he was ever the same zealous, devoted minister of Jesus. Dr. Mood's brief notice in his Charleston Methodism is fully confirmed by T. A. W. (Wayne), of Marion, S. C., in the *Southern Christian Advocate*, with additional particulars incorporated here. James H. Mellard was sent in 1801 to Union Circuit; 1802, Ogeechee, Ga.; 1803–4 to Georgetown, S. C.; 1805, Charleston, S. C.; 1806, Sparta, Ga.; 1807, Cypress; 1808, Savannah; 1809, missionary from Santee to Cooper River. In 1810 he became local. He was in person slim, pale, yet healthy-looking, with an open, lively, pleasant countenance; inviting, cheerful, and familiar, and of most friendly disposition; proving him to be without guile, of great tenderness of soul, and of a noble courage.

Georgetown at that time may have been said to be "Satan's seat." Asbury complains of the men as carried off by intemperance before they could be got hold of. Goodness was at a discount, and depravity at a premium. Few were ever found at religious worship, and Mellard determined to go after them. Mr. Wayne, when a youth, found him on Crosby's platform, near the market, without a herald drawing the crowd. Some in military costume by the aid of drum and bugle were endeavoring to put him down by drowning his voice, but its sonorous notes rose above their din; and they threatened to drown him in Sampit River, but he quailed not, finishing to an orderly dismission. That was enough; the crowds were drawn to the church. A great revival followed, and, quite unusual in our polity then, he was returned the second year. But from the lack of the exercise of discipline there came a falling away; to prevent this he strove, persuaded, entreated even to tears, his tenderness of feeling forbidding the use of the pruning knife. Even before the close of the year he was superseded by Thomas Nelson, a stern disciplinarian. They both domiciled with Mr. Wayne's father. Thomas Nelson, he says, was in stature respectable, with a grave, stable countenance, seldom altered by a smile; inflexible, stern, rigid, of unbending integrity. He taught the little folks to stand in proper attitude at the table before grace was said, and every impropriety of speech or action received correction. Like the ancient Hebrew, he eschewed pork; even the juicy crispness of roast pig, immortalized by Lamb, he could not relish, boiled, roasted, baked, fried, or stewed—he abominated the entire animal. But oh, the power of woman! His marrying a farmer's daughter brought him round, and he even wrote afterwards that "good bacon tasted well." If he had only added "collards," that were a dish to set before a king. The dear, good, ascetic old prophet located in 1803, having been admitted in 1797. The loving disciple, Mellard, was the most popular, and whether traveling or local magnified his office even to the end. Dying triumphantly in 1855, his dust lies near Fort Browder, Alabama, awaiting the resurrection of the just.

George Dougherty (1798–1807), already alluded to, but as one of the sons of "Zebulun and Naphtali, who jeoparded their lives unto the death in the high places of the field," is deserving of more extended notice. He was, by Lovick Pierce's indorsement, South Carolina's great Methodist preacher and first noble martyr. No towering monument marks his grave, and never can: his sacred dust, long sheltered under the porch of the Front Street Church in Wilmington, N. C., was scattered to the winds in the burning of that building years ago. Bishop Andrew gives this portraiture:

None among the men of that day, whose character looms grandly up from the misty past, filled a larger space in the Church. He was born in South Carolina, reared in Newberry District, near the Lexington line, and used to cut ranging timber on the Edisto. He was ungainly in his person, tall, slight, with but one eye; and negligent in dress; but his intellect was of lofty tone, his logical power remarkable, his eloquence at times absolutely irresistible. An example is recorded, when he had to follow without intermission a preacher of another sect, who dealt out lustily opinions which, according to Methodism, were dangerous heresies. Dougherty, on rising, struck directly at these errors; his argumentation became ignited with his feelings; his voice rose till it echoed in thunder peals over the throng and through the forest; dropping polemics, he applied his reasoning in overwhelming exhortation, urging compliance with the conditions of salvation. The power of God came down, and one universal cry was heard through all that vast crowd. Some fell prostrate on the ground; others, rising to flee from the scene, "fell by the way." Dougherty, turning round on the stand to the heretical preacher, dropped on his knees before him, and in the most solemn manner, with uplifted hands and streaming eyes, begged him, in God's name, never again to preach the doctrines he had advanced that day. The scene was overwhelming, and beggars all description.

From a long and admirable paper in Sprague's Annals, from Dr. Lovick Pierce's pen, much could be gathered, but very nearly the whole of it is in Shipp's "Methodism in South Carolina." Dr. Pierce's portraiture of our subject's personality is as follows:

Mr. Dougherty was about six feet in stature, his shoulders a little stooping, his knees bending slightly forward, his walk tottering, and in his general appearance a very personification of frailty. He had lost one eye after he had reached manhood, by small pox, and the natural beauty of a fair face had been dreadfully marred by the ravages of the same malady. His hair was very thin, and he wore it rather long, as was the custom of itinerant preachers in his day. His costume, like that of his brethren generally, was a straight coat, long vest, and knee breeches, with stockings and shoes; sometimes long fair topped boots fastened by a modest strap to one of the knee buttons, to keep the boots genteelly up.

The General Minutes give his appointments as follows: Admitted in 1798, and sent to Santee; 1799, Oconee; 1800 and 1801, Charleston; the next three years, presiding elder on Saluda District; in 1805 and 1806, on Camden District. In 1807 he was superannuated, and essaying to reach the West Indies, was stayed at Wilmington, where he died. In the General Minutes a witness of his death states:

When he spoke of Deity, of providence, or of religion, reverence, gratitude, solemnity, joy, etc., were evidently all alive in his soul. He spoke what he *knew,* and his knowledge of God, his Redeemer and Saviour, inspired his heart with a *confidence* which was neither shaken by the pressure of his afflictions nor the ravages of death. Of his submission and resignation too much could not be easily said. He appeared to be jealous of his own will, and to embrace the will of the Lord, not only without murmuring, but with pleasure; yea, with joy. He spoke of death and eternity with an engaging feeling and sweet composure, and manifested an indescribable assemblage of confidence, love, and hope while he said: "The goodness and love of God to me are great and marvelous as I go down the dreadful declivity of death." His understanding was unimpaired in death, and so perfect was his tranquillity that his true greatness was probably never seen or known until that trying period. He died without a struggle, or scarcely a sigh. He was twenty-six years old on entering the Conference, and only thirty-five at the time of his death.

CHAPTER XV.

RESUMING the chronological order of narrative brings
the twenty-third session of the Conference to Liberty
Chapel, Ga., December 26, 1808. The Conference, about sixty
or seventy members present, was held in Mr. Bush's house, and
religious services were carried on at the camp ground near.
Three missionaries were appointed: James H. Mellard, from
Ashley to Savannah River; James E. Glenn, from Santee to
Cooper River; and M. P. Sturdevant, returned second year, with
M. Burge preacher in charge, to Tombecbee. About three hundred traveling and local preachers were present. Between two
and three thousand persons attended the meeting, many of them
coming one hundred and fifty miles. This was the first visit of
Bishop McKendree to a Carolina Conference, Bishop Asbury
and himself presiding.

It was at this Conference, says Dr. West, that Matthew Sturdevant made his report of the missionary work at Tombecbee.
He was not of robust but rather feeble person, and his travel-
worn attire attested eloquently of the uncleared wilderness. He
told how he had crossed floods, swum rivers and creeks, slept on
the ground, endured hunger and thirst, and heard the howl of
the wolf, the growl of the bear, the scream of the panther, and
the more dreaded whoop of the Indian; the carousals of savage
tribes, and of the no less wicked white settlers, to whom he tendered the gospel message.

In the rejoicing and glory of the noble Alabama Conference
we also rejoice that in her then wilderness that message was
borne by a missionary of the old South Carolina Conference.
The "*Committee on Charity*"—Heaven save the mark!—according to the South Carolina Journal, appropriated to Sturdevant
$74.14. Nor was he the only volunteer to Tombigbee from Car-
olina. Ashley Hewett volunteered, and was appointed to Tombecbee, as will be seen farther on, in the year 1815.

The preachers in Charleston during this year were William Phoebus, and John McVean. The first named, of handsome personal appearance and fine pulpit talents, soon afterwards transferred to New York, dying there in 1831, aged seventy-seven years. The second was regarded as eccentric, later giving evidence of mental derangement. They had been favored with a gracious revival, reporting a gain of forty-two whites and three hundred and ninety-six colored over the preceding year— a goodly number remaining faithful and influential members. The bishop exults over the great and glorious prospects in Charleston and neighborhood. Total increase in the bounds of the Conference, 3,088.

The record in the Conference Journal for 1808 is as follows: "The following brethren purpose to attend the ensuing General Conference, namely: Lewis Myers, Britton Capel, Josias Randall, Wiley Warwick, John McVean, Daniel Asbury, James H. Mellard, William Gassaway, John Gamewell, Samuel Mills, Joseph Tarpley, and Moses Mathews." Afterwards, it will be remembered, delegates were elected.

Sixteen were received on trial, among them William Capers and Urban Cooper. Mr. Jenkins, as local this year (1808), preached at the Wolf Pit, and formed a society, merged now into Smyrna, not far from Ridgeway. He also received an invitation to Winnsboro, from the wife of Captain Buchanan, who had been an officer in the Revolutionary army, and was very highly esteemed by all. There was no organized church here; the courthouse was used for religious services. A minister of another sect using it felt aggrieved that any other should do so, remarking, on Mr. Jenkins's occupancy of it, "that it was like taking the bread out of his mouth." Mr. Jenkins supposed that "if bread was all he was after, it was no matter how soon he lost it." Captain Buchanan doubted if a society could be raised, not dreaming that he should join himself; but at a camp meeting near Camden, in 1809, both himself and wife and Captain Harris and Major Moore were converted and joined the Church; and before the close of 1810 the brick church was erected, giving place in later years to the present house of worship.

The twenty-fourth session was held in Charleston, December 23, 1809. On his way to it the bishop crossed Bush River in Newberry, passing the Quaker settlement. The Friends had

already left for the rich lands on the Ohio, and also to be rid of
slavery. In Judge O'Neal's Annals of Newberry there is an interesting chapter concerning this sect. Now all is a desolation.
He crossed Pacolet, Thickety, and Broad rivers on his way to
Josias Smith's, coming through York to William Gassaway's
near Tirzah Church, *en route* to the Waxhaws. At the Waxhaws
he preached to about four hundred souls; then on Monday had a
cold ride to William Heath's, on Fishing Creek. He preached in
"a log cabin scarcely fit for a stable," some United States officers attending from Rocky Mount. Not a vestige of that humble
temple remains, but a new church was about to be erected near
it in the East Chester Circuit. It may not be generally known
that Rocky Mount came within one vote of being chosen for a
large military establishment long ago. The admirable water
power thereabout may yet be utilized for large factory purposes.
On this visit the bishop was made acquainted with the venerable Mr. Buchanan and wife, then Presbyterians and happy in religion. As noted above, they afterwards became connected with
our Winnsboro Church; indeed, becoming the founders thereof.
As seen, William Capers was admitted in 1809, and was appointed to Wateree Circuit. Objection had been made to his reception
because he had been but five months on trial; but it was over-
ruled, and he was received. Wateree Circuit then extended from
Twenty-five-mile Creek on the west side of Wateree River to
Land's Ford on the Catawba, and on the east side from near
Camden to within twelve miles of Charlotte, N. C. Twenty-four
preaching places were compassed in four weeks, a distance of
about three hundred miles; membership, 498 whites and 124
colored. The present counties of Kershaw, Lancaster, parts of
Fairfield, Chester, and York, were included in it. Within its
bounds James Jenkins resided, and met the young preacher
and gave him a rather poor reception. All who have ever read
William Capers's autobiography remember well the encounter.
Then came the granny's quarter episode, in his giving lessons
on "cleanliness is next to godliness," and the Church trial at
Carter's Meetinghouse in Chester county. Anyone sharing the
hospitalities of Brother Reeves at El Bethel, in Richburg Circuit, may have the site pointed out where stood the church.
There is not a vestige of it remaining, and to look at surroundings none would ever suppose that congregations gathered there,

or that it was ever the scene of a famous Church trial and the first instance of the exercise of Church discipline by the boy preacher, William Capers. It was a *crim. con.* case, and the parties were violent as well as equally divided. A riot ensued, of great violence and profanely boisterous. A woman exclaimed anent the preacher, "He had better go home and suck his mammy!" and the old prophet had spoken of the "eggshell not dropped off," and both aroused all the manhood in the youth, who finally proved the declaration of Bishop Asbury true: "Our boys are men." Ever after, during the year, his ministry was greatly favored at Carter's Meetinghouse.

The present Camp Creek in Lancaster Circuit was one of the appointments that year, and a young lawyer from the courthouse came to the church, inviting Mr. Capers to that place. It happened to be sale day, and the usual accompaniments of carts with cakes and cider, and undoubtedly something stronger, didn't promise much for the sobriety of worship at night. The attempt to preach was made, but interrupted by one stepping forward and bidding the preacher "quit that gibberish and go to his text," and declaring he could preach better than that himself. "Now, Mister, just give me them thar books, and you'll see." At the second appointment the sheriff of the county had a dancing party, and in earnest invited the preacher to attend it. It may be readily concluded that Lancaster Circuit in 1809 did not promise much religiously. This, however, was over eighty years ago, and the beautiful church and handsome parsonage and clever people now show a vast advance over that year. The Millers, Riddles, Mayers, Carters, Lemons, Heaths, Allisons, and Hunters have made it one of the most pleasant charges in the Conference.

In 1809 Joseph Travis was sent to Georgetown, S. C. For four years there had been no preacher appointed, it being served from the adjoining circuits. Mellard had been the last. Mr. Travis was much discouraged; supposing the charge of no account and himself of no account, he might have given up. He found three males and a few females among the whites, but a goodly number of pious colored people. An aged local preacher, William Wayne, gave him some encouragement. Congregations were large but reckless, smoking cigars in church and pelting it with brickbats at night. Attempts were made to waylay him and put him in a pond near by. A gentleman of influence, John Shackelford, met him at the door, saying, "Sir, take my arm, and I will protect you," conducting him safely home. He continued preaching to a crowded but thoughtless congregation until on a certain Sabbath a revival began. Many were converted, and a blessed change was wrought in Georgetown. An incident seemingly trivial, and by some perhaps deemed fanatical in the dedication to God of a babe, occurred this year in Father Wayne's case. He had long lamented the lack of piety in his sons. He and his wife, with their youngest child, were present at a love feast. The aged father, quite happy, takes the little boy in his arms, and holding him as high as he could reach, exclaims, with streaming eyes: "Here, Lord, take Gabriel! O do take Gabriel!" Well, what of it? Oh, nothing, only that Gabriel became a true minister of Jesus, dying in the faith. Something like it occurred in the temple at Jerusalem once, and was thought worthy of record. The Waynes were of the first fruits of Methodism in Georgetown, it will be remembered. Oh, the pity of it, that so many of these are now forgotten! We rescue a few from oblivion, such as Mrs. Sarah Johnson, Mrs. Francis Shackelford, Mrs. Carr, and at a later date Mrs. Beaty, Mrs. Wilson, Mrs. Belin, Mrs. Waterman, as elect women in the Church.

In 1809 Samuel Mills and William M. Kennedy were the preachers in Charleston. Mr. Mills was a thin, spare man, of consumptive appearance; Mr. Kennedy was stout in body, erect, fresh and healthy in appearance. The one was stern, of solemn countenance, always serious in bearing and intercourse; the other of a lively, cheerful aspect, pleasing to all. Mr. Mills was a rigid disciplinarian, almost severe; the other mild, tender, and forbearing. He has a large and excellent record in our Church history. Both were faithful pastors and highly esteemed.

This twenty-fourth session, held late in December, 1809, carries our narrative into the following year, 1810. That year in Charleston three preachers labored—William M. Kennedy in charge; Thomas Mason and Richmond Nolley. Mr. Mason was admitted in 1808 and located in 1812, reëntering, I think, the New York Conference. He was a strong preacher, much beloved, commanding large audiences. Mr. Nolley was tall, thin, and of delicate health; he was remarkable for preaching with his eyes closed, from great timidity.   His closing life as a missionary is fully set forth by Bishop McTyeire.

During this year the city churches were greatly revived. Samuel Dunwody was sent to Georgetown, Joseph Travis to Columbia, and William Capers to Orangeburg.   Of Mr. Dunwody's ministry at that time we have no knowledge, but of the others there are records by their own hands.   In 1810 Mr. Capers was sent as junior to Great Pee Dee Circuit, from which he was shortly removed to Fayetteville, N. C.   Great Pee Dee, then comprehending the Black River and Darlington circuits, stretched from the neighborhood of Georgetown, up through Williamsburg and a part of Sumter District, near Lynch's Creek, opposite to Darlington Courthouse; thence across that creek to a short distance above another, called the Gully; and then downward, toward Jeffers Creek.   Nothing remarkable occurred here, save the story of the witch and the loss of his suspenders, when an eminently pious but weak brother exclaimed: "O, Brother Capers, how I love you! I love to hear you preach; I love to hear you meet class; I love you anyhow.   But, oh, them gallowses! they make you look so worldly, and I know you ain't worldly neither.   Do pull them off."   And he did.   Of his ministry in Fayetteville, N. C., we say but little, as it more properly belongs to North Carolina annals; but we cannot forbear giving the colored preacher Henry Evans's farewell to his people.   Almost too feeble to stand, but supporting himself by the railing of the chancel, he said: "I have come to say my last word to you.   It is this: None but Christ.   Three times I have had my life in jeopardy for preaching the gospel to you.   Three times I have broken the ice on the edge of the water and swum across the Cape Fear, to preach the gospel to you.   And now, if in my last hour I could trust to that, or to anything else but Christ crucified, for my salvation, all would be lost and my soul perish forever."   Could an apostle say more?

Joseph Travis was in Columbia in 1810, and met a kind reception from the Rev. Claiborn Clifton, a wealthy and influential citizen, good lawyer, and excellent local preacher.   At the bar sometimes he would accidentally style the jury "dear brethren."   Yet, as a lawyer, he stood eminently high, esteemed by all.   The first Methodists on record here are Dr. Green, David

COLUMBIA FEMALE COLLEGE; REV. J. A. RICE, D.D., PRESIDENT.

Faust, Esq., Benjamin Harrison, Andrew Wallace, Colonel Hutchinson, Robert Warren, John and Robert Brice. Long since have they been removed to the Church triumphant, and their memory is very precious.

It may not be out of place to state here that Columbia, the capital of South Carolina, is cherished in our annals. Many of the most saintly of God's people have been gathered hence into heaven. It is the seat of our female college, and the Washington and Marion Street churches are flourishing. It is fast becoming a center for cotton factory operations, and the promise of advance civilly and religiously is most flattering.

As something more is to be said of Columbia, we close this chapter here; the next will open with the twenty-fifth session of the Conference, held in Columbia, December 22, 1810. The appointments are noted, and other matters occurring in 1811.

CHAPTER XVI.

IN December, 1810, we find the bishop, on his round of travel, at Winnsboro. Having left Means's hospitable mansion, he remarks: "The generous Carolinians are polite and kind, and will not take our money." On Sabbath at Winnsboro he preached to a few people. Let it be known now that a bishop would preach, and the house would be crowded. On his route to Camden he spent a night with James Jenkins; speaks of his six years' rest and local usefulness, and of his intention of reëntering the Conference; mentions Saint Clair Capers's triumphant death; was some days at Henry Young's, sick. When able to travel he moved on to Columbia, where, in Senator Taylor's house, the Conference was held. Eighty preachers were stationed.

James Jenkins was sent to Santee Circuit. The Catawba Circuit was now separate, but Chesterfield District being added made it quite large. It was a year of great grace among the people. A camp meeting held near Chesterfield Courthouse was very profitable. At his next quarterly visitation, his old friends near Manchester — where the bread for the sacrament had been stolen — paid him another visit, brickbatting the church and discharging pistols while he preached. Mr. Edwin J. Scott, of Columbia, in his "Random Recollections of a Long Life," tells us:

Manchester was on the main road from Camden to Charleston. It was settled, for the sake of health and society, by the rich planters on the Wateree — the Ramseys, Ballards, and others. Besides their residences there were a tavern, a shoe shop, a tailor shop, a blacksmith shop, a schoolhouse, and two or three stores. The largest store was owned by Duke Goodman, who soon after removed to Charleston. He was a leading Methodist and exhorter, or local preacher, and as such was much engaged in mercantile matters. The wicked would say of him that often in giving out the hymn, instead of "*long meter*" he would say "*long staple*." But this may be classed

(138)

with all jeering common to persecutors. Goodman held on his way notwithstanding, highly esteemed and useful to the end. The schoolhouse was used for worship. The village was at one time the terminus of the Wilmington and Manchester Railroad. The lines of desolation are over it now, not a building standing.

We are not surprised at the persecution prevailing in those early days, as drinking and gambling were the everyday occupation of the inhabitants.

William Capers was sent from this Conference to Charleston, and his eloquence, earnestness, and pious zeal produced profound impressions, continuing through a long life. Methodism, on its introduction into the low country of the state, was as favorably received as anywhere else in the United States. Among its first membership in the city were the Stoneys, Westons, Bennetts, and others of the best portions of the community; but before the time of Mr. Capers it had been reduced to a condition of obscurity. The cause for this was not far to seek. Agitation on the slavery question induced suspicion, which came near imperiling any good that may have been done the negro. Under all the obloquy cast upon them, the services of the Church were well attended; but identifying themselves with Methodism was to many out of the question. Numbers who were converted to God under our ministry joined other Churches. Had it been otherwise, the Methodist Church in Charleston might have ranked in worldly respects with the very first in any country.

The nucleus of the Cooper River Circuit was formed this year by the preaching of Mr. Capers at Clemons's Ferry on the Cooper River, and Lenud's Ferry on the Santee River, and the Cooper River Circuit was formed the next year by John Capers. At this Conference Joseph Travis was appointed to Wilmington, N. C. When his name was called his presiding elder, Reddick Pierce, said there was nothing against him. The bishop said he had somewhat, and that was, "he had been studying Greek the past year." Travis acknowledged his guilt, whereupon the bishop remarked upon the danger of preachers neglecting the more important of their work for the mere attainment of human science; the axiom of the day being, "Gaining knowledge is good, but saving souls is better." It is a pity that it had not been found out sooner, as both might very well be carried on together. The next day the good bishop begged Travis not to think hard of his remarks the day before, as he merely designed whipping others over his shoulders.

The twenty-sixth session, its ministrations running into 1812, began December 21, 1811, in Camden. On his way to it the bishop writes: "Hilliard Judge is chosen chaplain to the Legislature of South Carolina, and Snethen is chaplain to Congress! So we begin to partake of the honor that cometh from man; now is our time of danger. O Lord, keep us pure; keep us correct; keep us holy." "Monday 25. We had a serious shock of an earthquake this morning." We have had a much more serious one in our day. Conference held but three days, and was remarkable for harmony and love. It was at this Conference that Lewis Myers made his famous speech anent the marriage of young preachers. Andrew Gramblin had traveled two years with Gassaway, and was eligible to admission and election to deacon's orders—the lady was in all respects a suitable person and of an excellent family—but the speech carried it against him. The young preacher located in 1813, and we remember well his excellent widow long years after, and her house as the preachers' home in Orangeburg.

Joseph Travis was sent to Wilmington, N. C., where upon his advent he met with a most unique reception. He arrived late on Saturday night, and but few knew he was a lame man. On entering the church his lameness induced a bowing motion on his part, and the congregation, believing him to be the most polite preacher they had ever seen, rose *en masse* to return his greeting. Doubtless a broad smile illumined each face on discovering that his politeness was an act of necessity and not of choice.

James Jenkins was appointed to the Wateree Circuit this year. Several new societies were formed, out of one of which came Noah and Sampson Laney, long connected with the Conference.

Francis Ward and Jacob Rumph were stationed in Charleston. The first was seized with fever, terminating in dropsy, from which he never recovered. Jacob Rumph was also taken with fever, which proved fatal. The Minutes say: "He was abstemious, steady, studious, uniform; much in prayer and meditation. In discipline, strict and persevering." He was abundant in the instruction of children, and exceedingly useful. Wrestling

earnestly during his illness for the full witness of sanctification, shortly before his death he exclaimed, "My soul is pure!"
and his prayers were turned to praises. His dust rests in the
Bethel Church cemetery.

This year the presiding elders, leaving out Georgia, were:
Edisto District, William M. Kennedy; Broad River, Hilliard
Judge; Camden, Daniel Asbury; Catawba, Jonathan Jackson.
The first had seven appointments; the second and last, six each;
and Camden, nine.

William Capers was sent to Orangeburg. This was the upper part of the old Edisto Circuit, this year divided into Salka-
hatchie and Orangeburg circuits. It then consisted of thirteen
appointments, traveled in two weeks. It took in the fork of
Edisto for twenty miles up, and the societies between the north
of that river and Beaver Creek; thence downward to the old
state road, opposite Orangeburg, and thence to that place.
Mr. Capers was prevented from going at once to his appointment, finding it necessary, as assistant secretary of the Conference, to pursue after a paper needed by the bishop. After
a rapid journey of several days to and fro, he got partial returns
and reached the bishop, who, an hour after he had left, found the
paper in his own possession. Rather provoking, certainly.

The first quarter of the year on the charge passed exceedingly
well, but the Quarterly Conference brought an appeal from the
administration of the previous year, the preacher in charge being James E. Glenn. The difficulty involved two strong societies, Ziegler's (now Prospect) and Tabernacle, some seven miles
apart. Much feeling, as is usual, was manifested by both parties, all equally respectable. It seemed that the summing up of
the appeal at the request of the presiding elder, William M. Kennedy, by Mr. Capers, had been ungenerously deemed partisan,
although approved by the presiding elder as impartial; and
offense was taken by the Tabernacle people, who declared that
they would no longer hear him preach. The Rev. Osborn
Rogers, of the Congaree Circuit, with no ecclesiastical right so
to do, undertook to serve them, Mr. Capers not opposing. He
met with a prompt rebuke from a pious old sister in class meeting. Upon his asking her how her soul prospered, he was answered that it never had been worse with her than it then was,
and it was likely to be no better as long as he preached there;

that in answer to her usual prayer, the Lord had sent her a preacher, Brother Capers, "but," said she, "not wishing to offend you, I don't know, brother, who sent you." There had previously been earnest entreaty on the part of the people for Mr. Capers's continuance, the malcontents vying with the others to induce a change. He resumed his place. And "for the divisions of Reuben there had been great searchings of heart."

Old Tabernacle was known by the writer when junior preacher in 1841, known again as presiding elder in 1865, and visited once again when on St. Matthew's Circuit in 1887, and then found a desolation and a ruin. How memory ran back upon the past! and many were remembered not now on the earth. Prospect and St. Paul's, in the town of St. Matthews, have absorbed entirely the membership of this dear old church. The descendants of both—among those at Prospect, the Poosers, Laws, Rasts, and others—vigorously uphold the church of their fathers.

During the year Mr. Capers as a young man, and as well when bent with age, found no truce in the immortal conflict all are called to endure. It is only at the end of the warfare that the *Io triomphe* is heard: "Thanks be unto God who giveth us the victory!" The great question pressing on his conscience then was, "Am I not every moment pleasing or displeasing to God?" Upon earnest self-introspection he was dissatisfied as to his religious attainments, and hoped to solve the trouble at a camp meeting—the old Indian fields, where the mighty athletes of the earlier day had struggled and triumphed. He proposed not to be active in it, but to give himself to retirement and prayer after hearing the sermons from time to time. Thus passed several days uncomfortably enough; instead of more light, his mind was more perplexed than ever. Seeing his error, he corrected it by going to work more earnestly for others, and was much relieved, although still unsatisfied. The meeting closed, and he returned to his circuit lacking in faith, in love, and in the assurance of the Holy Spirit—by no means strong and exulting as he had hoped. Riding pensively along the road, musing upon all that had passed at the meeting, and how little it had been improved, his soul was still unrefreshed—like Gideon's fleece, dry in the midst of the dew of heaven. Why was it so? Had he made an idol of the means? Had he overlooked the might of the Saviour? Anyway, he resolved to turn aside into the thick wood.

"There is none here but God; I will even go to him, who has all power in heaven and in earth, with the cry, 'Jesus, Master, heal my blindness; give me faith and love!'" Hitching his horse, he felt pity for the long fast the poor creature should endure before again being unloosed. But it was not so; he had scarcely fallen on his knees, with his face to the ground, before the words of Hebrews xii. 18–24 were applied with power to his mind: "For ye are not come unto the mount that might be touched, and that burned with fire, nor unto blackness, and darkness, and tempest, and the sound of a trumpet, and the voice of words; . . . but ye are come unto mount Sion, and unto the city of the living God, the heavenly Jerusalem, and to an innumerable company of angels, to the general assembly and church of the firstborn, which are written in heaven, and to God the Judge of all, and to the spirits of just men made perfect, and to Jesus the mediator of the new covenant, and to the blood of sprinkling, that speaketh better things than that of Abel." "In that moment how spiritual seemed religion, how intimate the connection between earth and heaven, grace and glory, the Church militant and the Church triumphant! and it seemed to challenge my consent to leave the one for the other." Could he do it? "Instinct said no; and all the loved ones on earth seemed to say no; but the words sounded to my heart above the voice of earth and instinct, 'Ye are come!' and my spirit caught the transport and echoed back to heaven, 'Ye are come!' In that moment I felt, as can only be felt, the exceeding riches of his grace in his kindness toward us through Christ Jesus." He returned to his circuit full of faith and comfort, never losing sight of the fact that it is "not by works of righteousness which we have done, but according to his mercy he saved us, by the washing of regeneration, and renewing of the Holy Ghost." Because of his father's death he was not permitted to remain on this pleasant circuit to the end of the year; and another sore trial was his engagement of marriage, with the intention of locating at the ensuing Conference, the time fixed for the following January 13. But his father's death removing the reasons for his locating, he could not do so with a clear conscience; yet all difficulty was removed by the sweet smile of approval from his betrothed, in willingly accepting the trials then attendant on a traveling preacher's life.

10

CHAPTER XVII.

THE twenty-seventh session was held in Charleston, December 19, 1812; Bishops Asbury and McKendree presiding.
On his way to it Bishop Asbury records his crossing Broad
River at Smith's Ford, his faithful horse, Fox, breasting the
swollen waters safely. Dining in the woods, they came afterwards to Squire Leech's, not far from the present Mount Vernon Church, in Hickory Grove Circuit. The bishop says:
"Brandy and the Bible were both handed to me; one was
enough; I took but one." On to Winnsboro, at Father
Buchanan's. He remarks that "the people here give little
encouragement to Methodism; but the walls of opposition will
fall, and an abundant entrance will yet be ministered unto us;
the craft of learning and the craft of interested religion will be
driven away"—a prophecy long since fulfilled. At Columbia
he preached in the hall of the legislature, members attending; then on to Charleston. The Conference was a good one;
eighty preachers were stationed, with no complaint from any.
Christmas day was held as a fast, and one hundred dined on
bread and water, with a little tea or coffee in the evening. He
declares that funds are low, but rejoices that preachers and
people are inured to poverty.

James Jenkins located again this year. The reason was on
account of a long move, seemingly very inconsistent with the
spirit of an itinerant, and especially such a one as he had
been. But circumstances alter cases. He could have traveled
a charge nearer his home conveniently, but such could not be
had, and it was made known to him that a more distant charge
was to be given him. This, as he never missed an appointment,
would subject him to long absences from home. His wife was in
feeble health, and as he had to cut all the wood used, and to put

his little son on a horse and walk before him to mill, he was forced to take that action. He blamed his presiding elder, Hilliard Judge, but it is not at all unlikely that the presiding elder had his reasons. Bond English once remarked to a preacher: "Never ask why you are changed in appointments; be assured the presiding elder knows more than you do, *why.*" The good man had as much land as he could cultivate on Lynch's Creek, with an outhouse to live in, given him by James C. Postell, and lived by the labor of his own hands, still preaching, without fee, for long, long years. How much Methodism owes to her local preachers is not known on earth, but will be in heaven.

Joseph Travis was sent this year again to Georgetown, where he met with a kind reception, and occupied the parsonage then behind the church in the midst of the graveyard, which served the stationed preachers some thirty-seven years, when, in 1849 and 1850, the writer was the first occupant, as a preacher, of the more commodious house still used as a parsonage. In the five years' absence of Mr. Travis few of the membership had died or backslidden, but he did not find some as earnest in religion as he had anticipated. He laments that the world and its fashions had quenched the ardor and zeal of some of the younger members; but for more than eighty years good old Georgetown has held on its way heavenward, meeting with declensions and revivals as has been the case elsewhere. N. Powers, A. Talley, and James E. Glenn were stationed in Charleston this year. In many records the last name has a B. instead of an E., calculated to mislead. James B. Glenn was another preacher among us, and singularly, if we are not misinformed, the E. in the first name stood for Elizabeth. Of Brother Glenn more will be said. N. Powers was admitted into the connection in 1809, and located in 1818. Alexander Talley was admitted in 1810, locating in 1820. Camden was made a station in 1811, and Henry D. Green was the preacher this year.

William Capers was this year (1813) in Wilmington, N. C., and has left a graphic picture of the church and parsonage. The first was the house erected by Mr. Meredith, and having been paid for chiefly by the weekly collections from the negroes, could not boast of any architectural beauty. Mr. Capers had been ordained elder by Bishop McKendree, December 26, 1812, married on the 13th of January, and by the 21st was in Wilmington, N. C. The parsonage to which he carried his bride was not palatial. It was rather on the shanty order, but of course infinitely better than none. It was of two rooms eighteen by twelve, one above the other, with a sort of stepladder on the outside to get to the upper story, and a shed room attached to serve for a bedroom if necessary—the necessity in a celibate ministry not very pressing. It was quite a good arrangement for a bachelor priesthood, but lacking conveniences for a woman and children. The church was a coarse wooden structure some sixty by forty feet; and yet Bishop Asbury speaks of it as "Mount Zion," and having "high days" therein.

Methodism at this time was regarded as low enough; its followers weak enthusiasts; deemed good enough for the lower orders—negroes especially, who needed to be held in check by the terrors of hell fire. There was but one other church in the place, of the historic episcopacy order, and even that had but one doubtful male communicant, the men being generally much tinctured with the French deistical philosophy; and yet gentlemen and ladies of high position in society were found frequenting the preaching in that humble sanctuary. That good was accomplished is beyond all question. Now what were the doctrines heard there? A master theologian had warned the ages, "Take heed unto thyself, and unto the doctrine." Was there anything of foolish questioning and genealogies, contentions and "strivings about the law," so vain and unprofitable? Anything of vain babbling and opposition of science so called? Anything of priestly functions (save of the one great High Priest); baptismal water, genuflections to east or west; candles lighted or unlit; aught of upholstering haberdashery? Not a whit! But justification by faith and its cognates, original depravity, regeneration, and the witnessing Spirit—these rang throughout this plain sanctuary, moving the white patrician and the negro plebeian to repentance.

Instances are given two years before this time. Mr. Travis states that the Hon. Benjamin Smith, Governor of North Carolina, desired him to call and see his wife, supposed to be unbalanced in her mind. Her head had been shaved and blistered, and after all her treatment by physicians she grew worse. The preacher diagnosed the case at once; instructed and prayed with her. In a few days a carriage drove up to that humble parsonage, and Mrs. Smith, with weeping eyes, entered it, exclaiming: "O sir, you have done me more good than all the doctors put together! You directed me to Jesus. I went to him by faith and humble confidence and prayer. He has healed me, soul and body. I feel quite well and happy." Is there anything of hyperbole or eastern romance in that? Is it not entirely in accordance with the doctrine?

Mr. Capers gives another instance. Mrs. C., of the first class of the upper sort, deeply interested by what she had heard in that humble house of God from the Methodist ministry, under cover of calling upon the preacher's wife, came to consult the preacher. The doubt on her mind was as to the possibility since the apostles' day of common people knowing their sins forgiven. The preacher gave the scriptural proofs freely—received, however, with the old "How can these things be?" Mrs. C. was accompanied by her sister, Mrs. W., who may have supposed herself more level-headed, or at least better established in the old creed, than her sister. And Mrs. W., as a last resort, turning to Mrs. Capers, said: "Well, Mrs. Capers, it must be a very high state of grace, this which your husband talks about, and I dare say some very saintly persons may have experienced it, but as for us it must be quite above our reach. I am sure you do not profess it, do you?" Mrs. Capers blushed deeply, and replied in a soft tone of voice: "Yes, ma'am; I experienced it at Rembert's camp meeting year before last, and by the grace of God I still have the witness of it."

As to the preacher's exchequer. To see him "poor, yet making many rich"; "as having nothing, and yet possessing all things"; to see his seraphic smile, and hear his melting speech uncovering the glory, any earthworm witling might have thought him a "bondholder." Such indeed he was, engaged ever in suing the Almighty Father on his own bond. So do all the faithful until they come into possession of their vast estates in heaven. At this time his finances were at the lowest ebb; his presiding elder was on the way with supplies. A thrip could only buy a fish, and that was all the provision for his guest. How marked the economy and wealth of God! See the prophet at the brook Cherith and at the poor widow's home. And so God deals with his own unto the present hour. He could pour into their lap the treasury consumed in the flame and sunk in the sea; but no, even though they fear bankruptcy, it is still the "drop of oil" and "handful of meal," that they may not have the shadow of independence beyond himself. As the little child remarked, "God hears when you scrape the bottom of the barrel."

The revenue from all sources this year was a few dollars a week, an average of seven. The figures were enormous, 364,000 — *mills*. And much the greater part of this was the cent-a-week collection from the negroes. Long years after, the writer has seen the green-baize-covered table in the preacher's office here, and elsewhere, literally covered with greasy coppers. Fielding once remarked on his income as a magistrate, that his fees were in the dirtiest money of the British kingdoms. Not so here, if you please; every copper had on it heaven's impress and the benediction of Him who blessed the widow's mite and the box of ointment. It was the outcome of pure love to God and man; and mites show this, and sometimes more so, as well as millions.

The Rev. Jesse Jennett, a loving, zealous local preacher, lived in Wilmington then, and for some time before and for long years after, in all over fifty years—known to everyone as the St. John of Wilmington. To his life and labors the Church is greatly indebted. Such was his fine reputation that he was often solicited to become the pastor of another church with a liberal salary, but always declined. Somewhere about 1850 he died in the faith.

At this Conference (the twenty-ninth) Richmond Nolley and John Shrock were transferred to Mississippi and appointed to Tombigbee. Dr. West, in his "History of Methodism in Alabama," gives a vivid description of the Indian troubles encountered by these faithful men, as well as all relating to Nolley's death, as fully recorded by Bishop McTyeire.

After this Conference Bishop Asbury made his way to Georgetown. January 3, 1813, he says: "I preached morning and evening. It was a small time—cold, or burning the dead (?). We have here one thousand blacks and about one hundred white members, most of them women. The men kill themselves with strong drink before we can get at them." On to Wilmington. "There is little trade here and fewer people; of course there is less sin. I was carried into the church, preached and met the society. Lord, be merciful to me in temporals and spirituals! William Capers is married; he is twenty-three, his wife eighteen." It would almost seem as if the good bishop thought no one ought to marry until near seventy.

Mr. Travis gives an item or two concerning the General Conference of 1812, the very first delegated General Conference in our Church. The delegates from the South Carolina Conference were Lewis Myers, Daniel Asbury, Lovick Pierce, Joseph Tarpley, William M. Kennedy, James Russell, James E. Glenn, Joseph Travis, Hilliard Judge, and Samuel Dunwody. (For all after delegations see Appendix.) The election of local preachers to orders was before the Conference. Those in favor took the ground both of expediency and necessity. Jesse Lee was adverse, arguing that "the bishop *could not,* in good conscience, ordain to elder's orders unless the form of ordination was changed, it requiring each to devote himself to the ministry. How could this be done when engaged in the usual avocations of life?" When he sat down, seemingly carrying the house with him, one Mr. Asa Shen arose in reply, declaring that "the same form required of one to be ordained that he should *rule well his own family.* Mr. Lee had made this promise twenty years ago, and has not fulfilled it to this day." Mr. Lee shook his sides with laughter, and the vote was against his measure. Upon what curious matters do large privileges rest after all!

The presiding elder question was up also—as to making the office elective—but was not carried, and likely never will be. This year nineteen were admitted on trial, among them James O. Andrew, afterwards bishop.

The twenty-eighth session was held at Fayetteville, N. C., January 14, 1814; Bishops Asbury and McKendree presiding. "A spiritual, heavenly, and united Conference." Twenty deacons were ordained, eighty-five preachers stationed, fifteen admitted, twenty located, and one, Lewis Hobbs, died. In 1811 he went to Mississippi as a missionary, in 1813 was stationed at New Orleans, and in 1814 returned to Georgia, dying triumphantly.

The twenty-ninth session was held at Milledgeville, Ga., December 21, 1814; Bishops Asbury and McKendree presiding. This was the last South Carolina Conference attended by Asbury. He presided at all the rest except the twelfth session, which was presided over by Jonathan Jackson. At this session one hundred characters were examined; six admitted, twelve located, and ten elders and twenty-two deacons ordained. Bishop Asbury served under great feebleness. He remarked on the great peace, love, and union prevalent. On his northward journey he mentions the death of Dr. Ivy Finch, only thirty years of age, who was killed by his horse running away near Columbia, S. C. He was the son of one of the early Methodists, Edward Finch, the bishop's dear friend.

The thirtieth session was held in Charleston, December 23, 1815; Bishop McKendree alone presiding. At this session Ashley Hewett responded to a call for volunteers for Mississippi, and made his perilous journey through the Indian territory. Farther on we record the singularity attending his death.

From this onward we shall not attempt a minute record of the Conference sessions. The reader is referred to the Appendix, where all information as to time, place, officers, and numbers is given. A complete record of every individual member as to admission and removal will there be found also.

CHAPTER XVIII.

The Hammet Schism—Its Success and Early Decline—Dr. Brazier—Rev. Israel Munds—Bennett Kendrick—Sale of the Church—Its Recovery—Holding the Fort—Henry Muckenfuss—The African Schism—Great Loss of Members — Sole Memorial—African Disintegration — Old Bethel—Crowded Houses—Literal Interpretation of Scriptural Figures—Wings of Silver—The Great Schism of 1834.

CHARLESTON has been the only place in the bounds of the Conference affected by schism. These, while embittering for awhile all Christian feeling, are now happily ended. The Hammet schism, seriously affecting the spread of Methodism for more than two decades, began early. It originated in an attachment of some to a preacher of no ordinary ability, the Rev. William Hammet, affecting and bringing under a severe strain one of the first principles of Methodist itinerancy—the surrender on the part of preachers and people of the right of choice as to men or places. There was but one way to meet this—in steadily holding to our principles, even though there should be the loss of valuable members. The fifth session of the Conference held over one day in compliment to Dr. Coke, shipwrecked off Edisto. On his arrival with Mr. Hammet, who preached to the great delight of all, an effort was made to retain him in the city. The appointments had all been arranged by Bishop Asbury, and the Rev. James Parks, who was afterwards made rector of Cokesbury School in Maryland, designated as the preacher. The clamor was great to have Mr. Hammet supplant him. On the bishop's departure he was pursued in order to get a change. Mr. Asbury was unyielding, and the trouble began. Mr. Hammet encouraged the disaffection, anathematized Asbury, complained of insult by the American preachers, and attempted to make out the whole of American Methodism a schism from Mr. Wesley. He began preaching in the market place for awhile to large numbers, setting up, as he called it, the Primitive Methodist Church, and eventually succeeded in erecting the first Trinity Church, with parsonage and outbuildings on Hasell street, all deeded in fee simple to himself. In 1792 there was a loss reported in the membership of eighteen whites and thirty-seven colored; and there was no large increase among the whites until 1807, some sixteen years afterwards, when eighty were reported.

Matters ran on in the usual course, but little is left upon record. Mr. Hammet served his congregation until early in 1803, and his health failing he died on May 15. For a year or two his people had no minister. The deed by which he had held the property of Trinity Church provided that in case of his death Mr. Brazier should succeed him, he having a life interest therein, and afterwards to be at the disposal of the congregation. Mr. Brazier was written to and came, preaching a short time, but by no means with general acceptation. A rupture in the congregation of St. Philip's (Episcopal) Church led Mr. Frost to seek to secure Trinity for his adherents, and proposals were made for its purchase. In the meanwhile a number of the congregation of Trinity were making arrangements to secure the services of Bennett Kendrick, then (in 1804) stationed in the city, and who has left upon record some incidents connected therewith. It seems that while some were in favor of a transfer to the Conference others were opposed to it. Some desired him to leave Cumberland and to confine himself to Trinity; if he would do this, they would abandon the idea of employing another preacher. Dr. Brazier stated that "if he had any idea of renouncing the Methodist Episcopal Church, and would join them, all difficulty would be removed immediately." This Mr. Kendrick regarded as "a grand insult," and was about to reply warmly, when Mr. Pilsbury said "they would not require me to join them immediately, but they thought if I continued with them throughout the year, I should become so attached to them as never to leave them." This was no better than the first proposal, and Mr. Kendrick remarks: "I strove not to let a passion stir, and replied, 'I do not see why I may not be as useful to you by being a member of the old church as if I were to join yours.' Pilsbury answered that 'I might'; and there stands the business to-day."

It is quite evident that Dr. Brazier was moving cautiously, making one proposal after another, only to change, keeping in view his ultimate sale of the property. Arrangements were sought to be made for Mr. Kendrick to confine his labors to Trinity. This he could not do, and he determined to get Dr.

Brazier to say whether he would stand to his first agreement or not. In the interview he was informed by the doctor that he should make over the church to Mr. Munds and Mr. Mathews, and that he expected all the pious part of the society would leave Trinity and go to Cumberland, and he advised Mr. Kendrick to receive them. In the meanwhile Mr. Pilsbury was active in trying to secure a large part of the membership for Mr. Kendrick, and finally, as he says, "he (Mr. Mathews) takes the fold by paying its worth, and I the flock without money or price." Mr. Kendrick finally states that "if Brother Dougherty would have agreed to stay in town and attend to the Cumberland people, I would have kept the Trinity people together in the new church, even at the risk of my reputation and what evils I might have suffered. Some of our official members pressed me hard to do so, and promised me their assistance." This was the end of the matter, so far as Mr. Kendrick was concerned, it being impossible for Mr. Dougherty, who was the presiding elder, to remain in the city.

The property was finally sold for $2,000, pews erected, and the church formally dedicated according to the forms of the Episcopal Church. This aroused the membership, and they instituted proceedings at law for its recovery. While the suit was pending, their counsel informed them that if peaceable possession of the property could be obtained it would aid in its recovery. So when service was held by Mr. Frost one of the Trinity members slipped the keys of the church into her gown pocket, and there was no small ado over their loss. Messengers were dispatched for reënforcements, and they entered, barring up the doors and windows, and there remained for several months, until the suit was decided. It is on record that one Charlestonian was born within those sacred walls. Upon the decision of the court in their favor arrangements were made for the transfer of the property and membership to the Methodist Episcopal Church. Unfortunately no dates are accessible; but the Minutes show that it was not until 1810 that three ministers were stationed in Charleston, four stationed in 1811, two in 1812, and three in 1813, with this record in Bishop Asbury's journal: "Sunday, December 12, 1813. I preached in Trinity Church. We have it now in quiet possession."

Of Dr. Brazier there are no records extant, and no person living who can give any information concerning him. Of the Mr. Munds mentioned, a few survive who knew him. He never connected himself with the Methodist Episcopal Church, although he was a steady worshiper therein, and held in high esteem by all. One of the first members of Trinity Church, whose birth antedated the Revolution, and who as a boy witnessed the defeat of the British off Sullivan's Island, was Mr. Henry Muckenfuss, born in 1766 and died in 1857, in his ninety-first year. He was the brother-in-law of William Hammet, and was connected with Trinity Church from its very beginning. An English queen declared that if her heart was examined after death Calais would be found inscribed upon it. So great was his love for Trinity, the same may have been said of Mr. Muckenfuss. According to Dr. J. T. Wightman, Mr. Muckenfuss had but three thoughts—the artillery, Trinity Church, and heaven. For near seventy years he was an official member of Trinity, and has left a number of descendants strongly devoted to Methodism, in Charleston, S. C.

One examining the return of members in the General Minutes cannot but be surprised at the rapid increase, and as sudden decrease, in so short a period in the colored membership. In 1812 there were 3,128 reported, and in 1817 the number was 5,699, giving an increase of 2,571 members in five years; and then in 1818 the entire colored membership was 1,323, showing the unprecedented decrease of 4,376 members in one year. Something uncommon must have occurred to produce such a change; and the more so, as there was, with but little fluctuation, an increase among the whites of seventy-two members. There could be no lack of care and zeal in the ministry, consisting of such men as Dunwody, Capers, Ward, Powers, Senter, Hodges, Andrew, Myers, and Bass.

In 1815 Anthony Senter, a strict disciplinarian, being in charge, caused a careful revisal of the colored society. On a close examination of their financial matters much corruption was found to exist. Hitherto they had held their Quarterly Conferences separately, and their collections were disbursed by themselves. Restraints were placed on these, and offense was taken. Then began secret agitation, and much disaffection existed, to so great an extent that two of their number had obtained ordination from the African Church in Philadelphia.

Attempts were made to secure Bethel Church for themselves, on the ground that the colored people had contributed largely to its erection. These movements of course were secret until their plans were fully matured. Then the erection of a hearse house by the trustees on their portion of the burial lot adjoining Bethel Church being the pretext, and no attention being paid to their protest, at one fell swoop nearly every leader gave up his class paper, and four thousand three hundred and seventy-six members withdrew, only one thousand three hundred and twenty-three remaining. After great exertion they

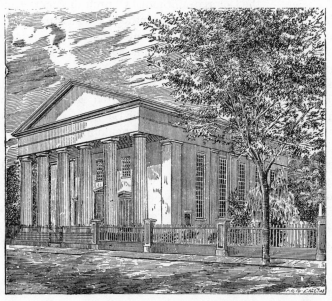

BETHEL CHURCH, CHARLESTON, S. C.

succeeded in erecting a neat church structure at the corner of Hudson and Calhoun streets, calling themselves the African Church. Such a large withdrawal affected greatly the congregations, and the loss of their responses and hearty songs of praise was largely felt.

It was an unfortunate time for the movement. Rumors of insurrection were in the air, and the attempted revolt in 1822, when a large number of leaders of that movement were hanged, put an end for the time being to their separate existence. Not a vestige of their church structure remains, and all that is monumental of this sad schism is the lone burial lot aforesaid. Numbers returned to the Methodist Episcopal Church, some to the Scotch Presbyterian, the rest nowhere.

The African disintegration came at the end of the great civil war, and by it the Southern Methodist Episcopal Church was despoiled of the fruits of near a century's labor. In 1864 the return of colored members was 47,461, and in 1865 this was diminished to 26,283; a loss in one year of 21,178. There was a large declension yearly, and twelve years afterwards the colored members ceased to be reported at all. While the establishment of the Colored Methodist Church in America saved a few to the influence of the Methodist Episcopal Church, South, far the larger number went into other Church establishments; the northern army chaplains aiding largely the disintegration.

The author vividly recalls his pastorate at Bethel Church in 1862. There were near fourteen hundred colored communicants. Morning and afternoon of the Sabbath were devoted to the whites, with the usual monthly communion service to the colored in the afternoon, while every Sabbath night was given to them separately in old Bethel. This service was always thronged —galleries, lower floor, chancel, pulpit, steps and all, almost from floor to ceiling. The preacher could not complain of any deadly space between himself and congregation. He was positively breast up to his people, with no possible loss of the *en rapport.* Though ignorant of it at the time, he remembers now the cause of the enthusiasm under his deliverances anent the "law of liberty," and "freedom from Egyptian bondage." What was figurative they interpreted literally. He thought of but one ending of the war; they quite another. He remembers the sixty-eighth Psalm as affording numerous texts for their delectation, *e. g.,* "Let God arise, let his enemies be scattered"; His "march through the wilderness"; "The chariots of God are twenty thousand"; "The hill of God is as the hill of Bashan"; and especially, "Though ye have lain among the pots, yet shall ye be as the wings of a dove covered with silver, and her feathers with yellow gold." It is mortifying now to think that his comprehension was not equal to the African intellect. All he thought about was relief from the servitude of sin, and freedom from the bondage of the devil; and as to the wings of silver and feathers of yellow gold, that was only strong hyperbole for spiritual good. But they interpreted it literally in the good time coming, which of course could not but make their ebony complexion attractive, very. He doubts if they realize it now any more than the "forty acres and a mule" promised them. But really these meetings were richly enjoyable, the more so as there was very little of a temporal nature to enjoy under the dreadful restrictions of war. They showed their appreciation of their pastor by the presentation of a purse of value on his leaving them. But the war ended at last, and then came the army chaplains and disintegration. Their chief rulers hoped to absorb all, white and colored, folds and flocks, but they were hugely disappointed. Rich and powerful as they were, they were not able to purchase the humblest white member. They began parceling out the chief stations and offering rich inducements to presumed renegades. The Southern ministry, leaders and neophytes, sprang to the encounter as never before, and under God rescued the Church from ruin. The Southern Church, mauger the affected doubt of the Northern Church, had done its full duty to the slave. The record is with God, and the reward on high.

The great loss in the colored membership in 1817 was after seventeen years, in 1834, largely recovered, to such an extent that the churches were straitened for room to accommodate them. An arrangement long in use, as under Bishop's Asbury's direction, was to seat the aged and infirm negroes on the lower floors of the churches; and to some extent half of the seats along the walls had been appropriated to free persons of color. This became a source of annoyance, not only on account of racial prejudices, but also because of the lack of room for the whites on crowded occasions. Favors to a few soon began to be supposed accorded to all, and the seating of the whites became so interfered with that complaints were common, and after awhile they clamored for a change. This culminated presently in the forcible ejection of some of the colored people. It was concluded that the slaves should all go into the galleries, and the boxes be so arranged as to seat the free colored people. But alas! when has Satan ever been absent from church quarrels? Disagreement was engendered; a contest between the young and the old white members ensued. There were criminations and recriminations, rejoinders and surrejoinders, with not much admixture of Christian charity, resulting at last in the expulsion of nine and the instant withdrawal of one hundred and sixty-five others. This was the heaviest blow Methodism ever received in Charleston, resulting in the formation of the Protestant Methodist Church, which was finally absorbed in the Wentworth Street Lutheran Church, in that city.

It might be well to say that the Bethel Church of the engraving on page 157 must not be confounded with old Bethel, which was the first structure erected on that site. That building was placed in the rear, and used for the Sunday school; afterwards it was moved across the street, and sold to the Northern Methodist Episcopal Church. The present handsome lecture room was the gift of one of our merchant princes, Francis J. Pelzer, a leading member of Methodism in Charleston. The present church structure has been lately remodeled in its interior. The heavy, unsightly galleries, made necessary once for the accommodation of the colored people, have been removed, and the auditorium is one of the handsomest in the city. The Academy of Arts on west Broad street, once used as a church, was sold long ago. The old St. James Chapel on King street has long been merged in the handsome Spring Street Church of to-day.

CHAPTER XIX.

AS already seen, the circuits took the names of the rivers
flowing through the state. The more methodical plan for
these annals is to take the original circuits, with their changes,
and as far as may be give all now known concerning Methodism,
and this chronologically if possible.

The old Santee Circuit is the first named, as early as 1786, in
the General Minutes; and as it embraced the most frequented
route of the pioneers, it must be first in order. It was formed
one year previous to the first Conference held in South Carolina.
The appointment of Beverly Allen, elder, and Richard Smith (*sic*)
—evidently a misprint for Swift, there being no Richard Smith
then in the Conference—was made at Salisbury, N. C., February
1, 1786. Messrs. Tunnell and Willis had been one or two years
before in Charleston, and may have traversed its territory; but
James Jenkins, who traveled it in 1794, says it was formed by
Richard Swift.

The river Santee divides the counties of Georgetown and
Williamsburg from Berkeley, then skirting the lower part of
Clarendon separates it from Orangeburg up to where the Congaree enters it, known after that as the Wateree; dividing Richland from Clarendon and Sumter, and changing its name above
Camden to Catawba; dividing Fairfield from Kershaw, Chester
and York from Lancaster, and running through the famed Waxhaws beyond Charlotte into North Carolina. Thus it will be
seen that it takes in very nearly the heart of the state. This was
the original Santee Circuit of 1786. Six years later, in 1790, Catawba Circuit was set off. In 1794 its boundaries were in the
counties of Sumter, Kershaw, and a part of Richland. In 1795
it was called Santee and Catawba; in 1797, Santee, Catawba,
and Camden, so remaining until 1803; it was then called Santee,
Wateree, and Catawba until 1805; then Santee alone, and so remained until 1808, when William Capers "rode with Gassaway";

11 (161)

Chesterfield county in part was then added, its extent being from Gainey's Meetinghouse, four miles above the courthouse, its upper appointment, to Taw Caw, now St. Paul's, its lowest. In 1809 Wateree was set off, with William Capers preacher in charge. From an old Quarterly Conference Journal in our possession it seems that these boundaries were unchanged up to 1831. Churches known to be in Chesterfield county are mentioned in the journal. It will be seen that within these boundaries, where in 1797 there were but four hundred and fifty-three white and one hundred and thirteen colored members, there are now thousands of members, with a wealth of Sunday schools, churches, and parsonages having no existence then.

In 1811 Camden was made a station, with Samuel Mills preacher in charge. It was in this circuit, in 1787, that Isaac Smith, on the banks of the Santee, consecrated himself afresh to God. The spot is unknown, but no matter; "neither in this mountain nor at Jerusalem," but everywhere may men worship the Father. Only here and there do we catch glimpses of the pioneers and their work; they were too busy making history to record it. In 1794 James Jenkins was the preacher in charge. On his way to the Conference at Finch's he tells how of all places most desirable was this Santee Circuit, and only because of Isaac Smith's having been there it "must be in a good condition." But at Marshall's, some miles below Columbia (Camden more likely), his troubles began. An old, disorderly member, of influence, had not been expelled. Isaac Smith told him he must do it, and he, who like Knox feared not the face of man, "did it at once." The year was an exceedingly sickly one, many dying.

In 1800 Santee and Catawba were reunited, and James Jenkins was reappointed to it. It reached then from Nelson's Ferry on the Santee to within ten miles of Charlotte, N. C. The preachers crossed the Santee River five times on every round of six weeks.

In 1808 Catawba was cut off and Chesterfield added. The preachers were Jonathan Jackson, William Gassaway, and William M. Kennedy. William Capers was with Mr. Gassaway, and came to Smith's (afterwards Marshall's); here he was drawn on to exhort. Then they went across to Chesterfield, to Knight's (Fork Creek). Here William Capers first received the Spirit of adoption. Thence they rode along that dreary sand-hill road in Chesterfield leading to Sumter Courthouse. The high debate between them was more important in results than any in academic groves, fixing for all time, and eternity too, Capers's relation to God and the Church. Then came the Taw Caw camp meeting and the conversion of Joseph Galluchat under his ministry; then his licensure and launching out on his career of usefulness.

In 1811 the Catawba Circuit was taken off and Chesterfield added, making the circuit still larger. James Jenkins was again the preacher in charge. Here he met with much persecution; was publicly posted at Sumterville and Owens's Meetinghouse, but God was "within the shadow" and watched over him. At Clark's, near Lodibar, there was a gracious revival. One poor sinner undertook to make sport of the whole, and was told by James C. Postell that if not careful God would kill him yet. Shortly after, his horse running away with him, he was instantly killed. Mr. Jenkins was called to a camp meeting, Samuel Mills, from Camden, supplying his place on the circuit. In the lower part of the circuit, from malaria he took the fever and died. Before his death he endeavored to tell of his work to Mr. Jenkins, and about some disorderly members. All that could be made out was, "There is dirt below"; explained afterwards by a local preacher's arrest for drunkenness, who was expelled, lost his property and character, dying suddenly. Mr. Mills was greatly lamented. The night before his death he was much engaged in prayer and preaching, rising to his feet and dismissing congregations. His last words were Luke xxii. 28, 29. His body rests in the old Quaker burying ground at Camden, with other preachers of the Conference.

In 1814 William Capers was preacher in charge on Santee, a most convenient appointment, as he himself declares. "All went on so uniformly as to furnish nothing for recollection"; yet it was the most eventful year in his life. The outlook for a living by his ministry was so dreary as to enforce location. Then came the loss of his beloved wife, and his after entrance on an itinerant life, never to locate again. The author knows of his declaration to a young wife whom he had just married to a preacher: "If you would not sip sorrow all your life, never do you let that man locate." And she never did. His experience was dearly purchased; the desire of his eyes was removed at a stroke, and though feeling exquisitely the blow, he never called in question the divine goodness. Pleasant as were the surroundings at Lodibar, and Rembert's not far distant, he tore himself away to fulfill the great work assigned him.

The Quarterly Conference Journal for Santee Circuit is in hand. It contains the rules governing local preachers and exhorters, adopted in 1814. The journal is a record from December, 1816, to November 26, 1831, a period of fifteen years. It is valuable as one of the few official records surviving, and as giving the names of the official members of the past. We put on record here as not likely to be recorded elsewhere a list of twenty-seven local preachers, namely: Elders—Thomas Humphries, James Jenkins, Aaron Knight, Thomas D. Glenn, Henry D. Green, John S. Capers, James Parsons, John Russell; Deacons—Thompson S. Glenn, John Bowman, Thomas Anderson, Henry Young, James C. Postell, Edward Skinner, Gabriel Capers, James Mangum, Nathan Grantham, John Marshall, Sherrod Owens, James Newberry, James Hudson, Richard Knight, William Hudson, William Brockinton, Isaac Richburg, Henry H. Schrock, John Humphries. A number of these will be recognized as once members of the Conference, and as having done most excellent work for the Church either as itinerant or local preachers.

The first Quarterly Conference recorded was held at Bradford's Meetinghouse, December 7, 1816; Anthony Senter, presiding elder; Nicholas Talley and William Harris, circuit preachers; local preachers present, Thomas D. Glenn, Alexius M. Forster, John S. Capers, John Bowman, Gabriel Capers; steward, Charles Williams; class leaders, William Brunson, Robert A. Sullivan, John Smith. Nothing but the usual business was transacted. The first record of the churches is in 1821, namely: Clark's, Green Swamp, Branch Meetinghouse, Taw Caw, Rehoboth, Oak Grove, Owens's, Marshall's, Bethel, Knight's, Zion, Stephens's, Bethany, Bethlehem, Russell's, Rembert's, Providence—seventeen in all. In 1823 four more are added, namely: Mulberry, New Prospect, Robertson's, and Zoar. In 1830 Sumterville takes the place of Green Swamp. From the record it would seem that hearing appeals, references, and licensures was the only business transacted. It was not until 1823 that the numbers received and expelled were reported. In 1827—under the ministry of Robert Adams, presiding elder, George W. Moore and Sherrod Owens—at one Quarterly Conference 464 whites and 293 colored were received on trial.

Santee Circuit has ever been regarded as a first-class appointment, financially as well as otherwise, yet how moderate the expenditure! The following are the full returns from each church for 1821: Rembert's, $70.25; Clark's Meetinghouse, $48.18; Green Swamp, $31.95; Knight's, $35.22; Bethel, $18.75; Bethlehem, $14.06; Bethany, $4.36; Branch Meetinghouse, $2; Taw Caw (now St. Paul's), $9.12½; Rehoboth, $6.87½; Oak Grove, $1.25; Owens's, $8.93¾; Marshall's, $7.30; Zion, $3.12½; Stephens's, $5.68¾; Providence, $15.25; Russell's, $24.50; Judith, $3.50; total, $310.31, for the payment of Daniel Asbury, presiding elder, and Anderson Ray and Nathan Grantham, circuit preachers. In 1826 the amount collected for R. Adams and S. Dunwody was $343.06¼. In 1827, the year of the great revival under George W. Moore, there is only one financial exhibit, amounting to $56.18¾, with this note: "Deduct bad money, five cents, which the secretary has added and not deducted, making the return $56.23¾." Rather bad bookkeeping, undoubtedly. If a trial balance sheet had been called for, there would have been difficulty. But there was improvement, as in 1828 the dignity of a surplus carried to the Annual Conference plainly shows. Here is the record in full. The stewards settled with the traveling preachers as follows:

Whole amount collected.................................$350 18¾

Robert Adams, presiding elder, quarterage.......$ 36 00		
Traveling expenses.......................... 5 00		
Family expenses........................... 30 00	71 00	
Jo P. Powell, quarterage........................ 100 00		
Traveling expenses 11 68	111 68	
William Ellison, quarterage..................... 100 00		
Traveling expenses........................ 11 00	111 00	
	293 68¾	
Surplus sent by Brother Powell to Conference...............	56 50	
	$350 18¾	

There are no quarterly exhibits, or we would give the amounts from each church, that each might share the honor of the surplus. But the noble Santee Circuit did better than that the next year, 1829, mauger the surplus. Here are the returns under the secretary's signature:

Whole amount collected...............................$419 00
Disbursed as follows:
    Robert Adams, presiding elder..............$ 34 00
    Samuel Dunwody, quarterage.......$240 00
        Family expenses.............. 45 00 =285 00
    William Young, junior preacher............ 100 00=$419 00

But in 1831 there was still greater improvement in the finances, as the returns show:

Collected........ ....$483 24
Disbursements:
    William M. Kennedy, presiding elder.......$129 62
    William M. Wightman..................... 134 04
    J. J. Allison.............................. 219 58=$483 24

Surplus carried to Conference............................$ 31 47½

It is very evident that these men could never be made rich in this world's goods at this rate of expenditure, and the supreme wonder is how men of any intelligence could suppose that such a rate of expenditure would give a man a living. Within these boundaries, from 1786 to 1831, for nearly half a century, it was difficult to raise a support, or what was considered such, of $500 for three preachers. Now, within the same boundaries, in 1893 $8,163.51 was collected, giving an average support of about $630 to each of thirteen preachers; but it took two generations to advance the Church thus far. Truly the labor of travel now is not near such as the fathers endured. Evidently these venerable men had everything of labor, with the poorest earthly recompense, on a much larger scale than we have hearts for. We here put on record some other names of official members.

1817: James C. Postell, Thompson S. Glenn, James Jenkins, James Hudson, local preachers; James Rembert, Sherrod Owens, F. L. Kennedy, Jesse Woodard, Sinclair Limebacker, Samuel W. Capers, John Marshall, George Laws, Samuel Bennett, Thomas Watson, class leaders.

1818: Nathan Grantham, James Mangum, Ed Skinner, Lewis Gainey, John Stephens, Charles Pigg, local preachers.

1820: John Houze, Matthew Meek, class leaders.

1823: Richard Spann, William L. Brunson, Isaac Richburg,

Samuel Bennett, William Murphy, George Turner, Henry Shrock, Henry Stokes, class leaders; Hartwell Macon, steward.

1828: James E. Rembert, Thomas Jenkins, Willis Spann, class leaders.

1829: Caleb Rembert, steward; Thomas Commander, Henry Stokes, Richard Benbow, A. Alexander, William Fullerton, William Bell, class leaders.

1831: Adam Benbow, James Tennant, class leaders; John H. Ragen, M. J. Blackman, W. L. Brunson, stewards; Elias Durant, Robert McLeod, class leaders.

From Dr. Burgess's "Chronicles of St. Mark's" we learn of some later local preachers. William Lewis, for many years ordinary of Sumter District, often preached at Oak Grove. James Parsons was clerk of the court for many years, and often preached at Oak Grove. The "cities of refuge" was his favorite subject of discourse, and his choice hymn "Blow ye the trumpet, blow." He removed to Mississippi in 1859. The Rev. H. C. Parsons of precious memory was his son. John S. Richardson, a son of Judge Richardson, often preached at Oak Grove. Sherrod Owens, long a local preacher, lived on Taw Caw. He was for a short while connected with the Conference, and long used as a supply in mission work. He was indebted to his wife for a knowledge of the alphabet. He was quite earnest in pulpit labor and exceedingly popular with all. Preaching once on "Let brotherly love continue," pausing, he said with great force, "But it must exist first." J. Rufus Felder lived near Wright's Bluff. Dr. Burgess joined the Church under his ministry, at Oak Grove, in 1848. Blacksmith Billy, a colored preacher, is kindly remembered by Dr. Burgess.

In 1833 Dr. Burgess notes the formation of the Sumterville Methodist Female Benevolent Working Society. It was one of the first women's aid societies in the Santee Circuit, and these names are worthy of record: Sarah Glenn, *née* Capers, sister of William Capers (first Mrs. Guerry, afterwards Mrs. Glenn), Jane D. Moses, Martha A. Walsh, Elizabeth D. Glenn, Lucy K. Macon, Martha A. Du Bose, Elizabeth Ballard, Margaret A. Bostick, Maria M. Fluitt, Sarah W. Durant, Mary N. Durant, Sarah Mellett, Louisa Williams, Mary A. Bowen, Eliza A. Williams, Theresa C. Wilder, Caroline M. Brunson, Sarah Daniels, Elizabeth Flowers, Mary Williams, Eugenia P. Poole. An elect lady, Mrs. Mary Ann Eliza Canty, deserves a memorial. For more than forty years her house was the preachers' home. Her departure from the Church militant was made with the declaration, "All bright, all bright."

The financial report of the Santee Circuit for 1893, as given in the Annual Conference Minutes of that year, is as follows, the four charges named then constituting the circuit:

Summerton, 94 members, paid for salaries	$ 301 87
St. Paul's (old Taw Caw), 172 members, paid for salaries	256 45
Andrew Chapel, 144 members, paid for salaries	273 12
St. James, 83 members, paid for salaries	158 12
Total	$ 989 56
And in 1895 a total of	$1,021 23

Sumter Station, 1823–1893. These dates are here placed, not that the Sumter Station was then first set off, nor that a church was then erected, for that was not done until 1827, and it was not made a station until 1851; but from an early day—1785, perhaps —there had been Methodist preaching in or near it. It is on record that at a house of Mr. Maple's there had been preaching. Green Swamp was within two miles of Sumter, built probably about 1790. Richard Singleton and Richard Bradford were connected therewith. It is stated of the latter that previous to his conversion he entertained Hope Hull, and, so suspicious were the times concerning Methodist preachers, he watched him closely to see if he loved liquor. Bradford died in the faith in 1826. In 1823 James Jenkins began preaching in Sumterville. Green Swamp being inconveniently far away, and many without conveyances, the people gladly attended his ministry in the village. At length, at a Quarterly Conference held at Fork Creek, November, 1823, the following persons were appointed trustees of the intended church structure: Richard Bradford, Hartwell Macon, James Parsons, Wiley F. Holliman, William Lewis, William L. Brunson, Mason Reams, Henry Young, and Francis L. Kennedy. But the church was not dedicated until July, 1827, by the preacher in charge, George W. Moore. The Green Swamp membership at once transferred, and that church no longer appeared on the journal.

In 1831 a revival was held in Sumter Church by the Revs. William M. Wightman and Allison, assisted by the Rev. H. A. C. Walker. In 1844, thirteen years after, this structure was found too small. It had never been ceiled or plastered, and had become quite dilapidated. Two acres of land were obtained near the old site, and a building seating four or five hundred persons was erected, the galleries accommodating some two or three hundred more. The Revs. Samuel Townsend and J. H. Chandler were the preachers on the Sumterville Circuit. The new church was dedicated in 1847 by the Rev. H. Spain; text, Genesis xxviii. 17, "This is none other but the house of God."

In 1851 a petition representing the male members, signed by W. L. Brunson, J. Hervey Dingle, and W. Lewis, was sent to the South Carolina Conference at Georgetown, and Sumter was made a station. The Rev. W. W. Mood writes that on May 18, 1885, under the pastorate of the Rev. H. F. Chreitzberg, ground was broken for the present brick structure, little Genevieve Hyatt moving the first soil. The church was dedicated by Bishop Duncan, May 27, 1888; text, Acts i. 8. William L. Brunson and James Hervey Dingle were for many years pillars of the church in Sumter, and are deservedly held in grateful remembrance.

Rembert Church was one of the oldest in Santee Circuit—indeed, in the state; it was some twelve miles from Sumter, on the road to Camden and Statesburg. Bishop Asbury frequently preached there; and in this neighborhood was his favorite resting place from the severe, labors of travel, the little rest he allowed himself to take in his tireless round of a continent. "Rembert Hall" and "Perry Hall" are often mentioned in his journal. Caleb Rembert and Abijah Rembert were the sons of Captain Caleb Rembert, of "Rembert Hall." Abijah was the father of Colonel James E. Rembert, a gentleman of the old school, and so favorably known in later years. His father, Abijah, died in 1805 at the age of sixty-two years. In Colonel Rembert's house the author has seen the portraiture of five generations. The original chapel has long since vanished. A camp ground at one time surrounded the site, and here the fathers ministered often. Parley W. Clenny, who was sent to fill the vacancy caused by McNab's flight, died on the ground, Dr. Whitefoord Smith preaching his funeral sermon. The present church makes a goodly appearance from the road; repaired and repainted, and the undergrowth cut away, it makes a pretty sight. It is now in the Oswego Circuit. Bless the foreign nomenclature creeping into our country! Denmark, for instance.

Manning Station is an offshoot from the Santee Circuit, and the circuit was formed in 1860. Oak Grove, not far from the village, was an appointment. St. Mark's Church was attached to it in 1861. This neighborhood was formerly connected with the parish of the Protestant Episcopal Church. A singularity in connection with the original St. Mark's Church was that it was built on the dividing line between Prince Frederick and St. Mark's parishes, now Williamsburg and Clarendon counties, on the north side of the Santee public road. A new church was built for the Methodists. The Rev. John R. Pickett was about the first of the preachers serving this section. In 1889 Manning was made a station, and it was served for three years by the Rev. Henry M. Mood, who in 1895 finished his second term of very acceptable service there.

CHAPTER XX.

IN addition to what has been said of Rembert's and Lodibar, the two prominent places in the old Santee Circuit, there is much more to be said of their earlier history; and through the kindness of the Rev. Samuel Leard, who, from his long residence in that old, historic circuit, is well prepared to narrate events, we place on record much of interest. Rembert's he calls classic, because it was the residence of men and women who in point of descent, intelligence, and respectability were the peers of the most aristocratic in the land. He calls it Methodistic, in that it furnished some of the finest illustrations of a pure life, conjoined with the most fervent piety and devotion to God and to his cause. The "high hills of Santee," situated just below, and on the borders of Wateree and Santee rivers, had been famous before and during the Revolution for the wealth, intelligence, and refinement of its inhabitants, and exercised great influence over the social and intellectual characteristics of the earlier settlers. Mr. Leard's acquaintance with the section began in the second quarter of the present century, while the history of Methodism runs back into the last quarter of the eighteenth century. Asbury states, "January 6, 1802. I rode twenty miles to James Rembert's" (Rembert Hall). This was about a mile from the present church. "December 20. I came here to enjoy a little rest; preached at Rembert's Chapel. Great change in this settlement; many attend preaching with seriousness and tears." And thus at various seasons in his long ministry. In 1812 he mentions the death of the elder Capers, father of the first Bishop Capers. He was a patriot of the Revolution born in the parish of St. Thomas, October 13, 1758; died in this neighborhood, and was buried in the graveyard on Dr. Dick's place, now owned by Dr. Henry Abbott. He was buried October 12, 1812, and on the tombstone is this legend: "My father, my father, the chariot of Israel, and the horsemen thereof!" Another stone bears the following: "In memory of Mrs. Anna Capers, wife of Rev. William Capers, and the only daughter of Mr. John White, of Georgetown District, born February 20, 1795; born again September 14, 1811; died December 30, 1815. Admired by all who knew her, and beloved as admired, and amiable as beloved, and pious as amiable"; concluding, as characteristic of her, with St. Paul's inimitable description of Christian charity. Another memorial stone is inscribed to the first wife of Samuel Wragg Capers: "Mrs. Elizabeth W. Capers, died March 29, 1818; aged 19 years, 2 months, and 9 days. *Esto fidelis ad mortem, et dabo coronam vitæ tibi.*"

Another distinguished family was the Remberts. James Rembert was of Huguenotic extraction. In addition there were the Messrs. Caleb, Samuel, James, Jr., and Abijah Rembert, all living in the first quarter of the present century, and contributing by their energy and piety to the building up of Methodism. There was a Mr. John Rembert and his son, Captain James Rembert, near Bishopville; the widow of the elder becoming the wife of the Rev. Allan McCorquodale. James E. Rembert, son of Abijah Rembert, for many years a steward and liberal supporter of the Church, was born in 1800, and died March 20, 1883. He and his wife were received into the Church by Thomas Mabry in 1822. The Young family was one of the oldest and most useful in the Rembert settlement. The Rev. Henry Young was for many years a Methodist, and for twenty years a local preacher. He died at the age of seventy years in 1835. The Rev. William M. Kennedy and his brother, Francis L., found excellent wives in this household. The last named spent the greater part of his life in this neighborhood, and exerted a noble influence. He was a man of property and of fine moral character. He died November 12, 1837, having been a member of the Church for twenty-seven years. Brother Francis Henry, his son, joined the Church under the Rev. A. McCorquodale's ministry. He died March, 1875. Nicholas Punch was an old and faithful member here. Among the local preachers remembered were the brothers John B. and James E. Glenn. Years afterwards they became citizens of Abbeville. The Rev. John B. Glenn, once an itinerant, was a Virginian by birth, and a blacksmith by trade. He was a tall, bony, wiry man, of great boldness and determination of character; a fine, simple, earnest man of God. He married the widow of Le Grand Guerry, a sister of William Capers. James Elizabeth Glenn was, in physical development, entirely different from his brother—gigantic in person, with a full-rounded face, ample dimensions, florid complexion, a voice like a trumpet, and faculties naturally of the highest order. He was greatly polemic, set for the defense of the gospel, the champion of Methodism in Abbeville and surrounding counties. He was the founder of Tabernacle Academy, afterwards Cokesbury School; the instrument in securing S. Olin for his school, and also in his conversion. He wrought at the handicraft of a carpenter, building churches literally as well as spiritually. He had the capabilities of a bishop, and the humility of a child; was a favorite with the young, hunting with the boys on Mulberry and Coronica creeks, and was their defender from all oppression. He emigrated to Alabama, founding the Glenville village and school. Our loss was the gain of that noble state. More is to be said of him in the sequel. The Rev. Noah Laney, for a long time an itinerant, found a wife in this excellent community. The Rev. Elias Frasher, another local preacher, a descendant of Lord Lovat, the Jacobite, was a man of fine personal appearance, well educated, and a perfect gentleman in and out of the pulpit. He was possessed of considerable wealth, and exerted a good influence during his life.

The Rev. William Guerry, a nephew of Bishop Capers, lived between Rembert's and Lodibar. He resembled the bishop in style and manners, and became a member and minister in the Protestant Episcopal Church. Alexius M. Forster was long associated with Lodibar as teacher and minister, and afterwards connected with the South Carolina Conference. Willis J. Spann was long identified with Rembert's. He was of slender form, of an active, nervous temperament, of fine conversational powers, and deeply religious. He was a strong pillar at Rembert's.

Colonel Sinclair Deschamps, the founder of Mechanicsville, and long a resident at Sumter, was once a member at Rembert's. Of Huguenotic origin, he was tall and slender in person, of ardent temperament, and quick in mind and action; a gentleman in manners, a Methodist from principle, and a zealous supporter of the Church. Brother Thomas Boone was also a member. He has a son who is an esteemed minister of the North Carolina Conference. The McLeods were numerous, and noted for their fine Christian character. Daniel McLeod, near Lodibar, Moses, Oliver, Robert L., N. B., and Roger D. McLeod were all devoted Methodists and firm supporters of the Church. The Rev. Henry D. Green is worthy of special notice. He was a native of Georgetown District, born in 1791. He entered the South Carolina Conference in 1810, and traveled five years. He married a Miss Mathews, of Camden, S. C., and settled not far from Rembert's Church, of which he was among the earliest organizers. From small beginnings he became wealthy, and his home was elegant and well furnished. He was a good planter, a kind master, and a devoted husband. His second marriage was to a Miss Abbott, of Camden. Their house was the preachers' home. He was a student with a fine library, and his profiting as a theologian was conspicuous. As a preacher he had the eloquence of thought, but his voice was not strong, and a certain hesitancy of speech hindered fluency. He could preach a thoughtful sermon, full of good sense and instruction and of unbounded sympathy, and he has left behind him a reputation of exalted Christian worth. Mr. Leard describes the last visit paid him. He was alone, his wife not long dead, his children all married and gone. His servants had followed the prevailing example, and nearly all of them had left. He could not but speak of his great loss in the death of his wife, and the broken up condition of the country, and the ruined state of his neighbors and himself. He was asked his age, and replied that he was seventy-six, and added if it were possible to go back and live his life over, there were but five years he desired to repeat —when he was a poor traveling Methodist preacher.

The last camp meeting at Lodibar attended by Mr. Leard was in 1850. It was then a splendid camping ground, with fine tents and preaching stand, and the *elité* of the country in attendance; the surroundings forming a great contrast with the simplicity, ease, and freedom of former days. What had been gained in elegance and refinement was overbalanced by loss in simplicity and power. Bishop Capers, with the Rev. Samuel W. Capers, the presiding elder, and some twenty preachers were present. A severe reproof had been given for some improper conduct, and the effect was electric and disastrous. An apology had been withheld until there was a ferment of passion. With great difficulty peace and harmony were restored to the demoralized congregation.

The Rev. James Jenkins lived for several years in this community. By eminence he was one of the most heroic founders of Methodism in the Santee country—indeed, in the entire state. He was then aged, and his tall, erect form, independent bearing, and cast-iron expression of features made an indelible impression on all seeing him. He was at that time a superannuated preacher, almost blind, yet he moved about with an energy most surprising. Entering the Conference in 1792 and dying in 1847, he had for fifty-five years served in the ministry. Some called him "Thundering Jimmie," and others the "Conference Currycomb." He was always ready for the correction of any wrong in manners or morals, and yet all apprehension of rebuke was mingled with unqualified reverence and respect. His style of preaching was very plain and simple; he seemed utterly oblivious to all surroundings, and had but one purpose, and that was to rebuke sin unsparingly and to urge the necessity of vital godliness. He would often give utterance to an animated shout, sometimes displeasing to a modern congregation. He was an Elijah or a John the Baptist of the early Church. His whole bearing in the pulpit was most impressive. His almost sightless eyes, his thin, long, white locks, and his fearlessness in proclaiming the truth, made you feel deeply.

Bishop Capers in early life being identified with this Lodibar section, his residence here for a year may be recalled with propriety. The farm upon which he settled was here, he having located to provide for the comfort of his almost adored young wife. Her early death subverted all his plans, and as soon as he could he reëntered the traveling connection, never to locate but in the grave. There were but few parsonages at that time for the accommodation of any. Of the one occupied in Columbia, S. C., soon after, he has left a graphic picture in his autobiography. He would in familiar intercourse give other items not therein published. One of these occurred with the Rev. Samuel Leard, to whom he related the manner of the stewards in the settlement of church dues. The meetings were once a week, when all collections were reported and weekly expenditures settled up.

And it was in no mean city, and one also with several wealthy members, that this occurred. On one occasion, among other things, one-half bushel of corn was reported as bought. "Brother Capers," said a steward, "I see here a half bushel of corn; how is that? You do not keep a horse; what use did you have for corn?" Dr. Capers replied: "Well, brother, the presiding elder came, and he had a horse. I always make it a rule for him to stay at the parsonage, and hence I was obliged to have the corn." You see he "acknowledged the corn." What else was to be done under the circumstances? "But, Brother Capers," continued the steward, "why did you not send the presiding elder and his horse over to my house, and thus save the expense to the church?" "No, brother," replied the doctor, "I always claim the presiding elder, and must provide for his horse as well as for himself; but if not allowed, *scratch it out.*"

Again, in reviewing the account, a steward said: "Look here, Brother Capers, I see a half pound of tea is charged; would not coffee be cheaper?" "Perhaps so," said the doctor; "but my wife likes a cup of tea occasionally, and I cannot refuse to afford her that little luxury; but if you think it too expensive, *scratch it out.*"

All this may be thought only a burlesque on economy. But it is on record from another source that at least one of that board of stewards, and a wealthy man at that, was so economical, according to his own son's testimony, that he "saved shoe leather by always seeking a soft place to put down his foot."

Mr. Leard, on the bishop's relation of the above, becoming quite indignant, could stand it no longer, and springing to his feet, exclaimed, "How could you stand it, bishop?" "Softly, my brother, softly," said the bishop. "Ever since God took away my Anna, I could endure anything for the privilege of preaching the gospel of Christ." And the dust of that lovely woman, whose premature death changed the elegant, gifted, and eloquent William Capers into the self-denying, laboring martyr, rests in that lonely graveyard near Lodibar.

The Capers family have long been distinguished for piety, fine personal presence, intelligence, and most of them as eloquent preachers of the gospel. They were descendants of Major William Capers, of Revolutionary fame, who married Mary Singletary, daughter of John Singletary, of St. Thomas's Parish,

BUNCOMBE STREET CHURCH, GREENVILLE, S. C.

Methodism was established in Greenville between 1833 and the end of 1835, by the Rev. Thomas Hutchins, who preached in the courthouse. In 1836 a church was built, which was served by the circuit preachers until 1841, when Greenville was made a station, with the Rev. W. P. Mouzon as preacher in charge. In February, 1873, the congregation moved from the old church, corner of Church and Coffee streets, into the handsome building now used, fronting on Buncombe street, from which the church takes its name. It was dedicated by Bishop Doggett, the Rev. E. J. Meynardie being the preacher in charge. It has at present a membership of four hundred and thirty-five. St. Paul's Church, Greenville, and the Mission Church were both formed from the congregation of the Buncombe Street Church. The Rev. William A. Rogers is the pastor for 1897.

12

S. C.; another daughter, Anna, marrying Beverly Allen. The family make up a remarkable ministerial record: Rev. William Capers, D.D., one of the bishops of the Methodist Episcopal Church, South; Rev. Gabriel Capers, Rev. John S. Capers, Rev. Samuel W. Capers, Rev. Benjamin H. Capers, Rev. Thomas Humphries Capers, Rev. James Capers, Rev. William Tertius Capers, Rev. John S. Capers, Rev. Richard Thornton Capers, and Rev. Ellison Capers, now bishop in the Protestant Episcopal Church.

The Chesterfield Circuit, as we have seen, was a part of the Santee Circuit, and its history may be noted in the next chapter.

CHAPTER XXI.

WE may offend in noticing minutely some matters; the opprobrium engendered would not be risked for that alone. As to the motive, the writer is willing to leave it to the developments of the judgment day, hoping that others, if much concerned about it, may afford to do likewise. Offending the sensitiveness of any would be avoided if possible; but must the truth be suppressed because painful? Besides, is there no sensitiveness on the part of others, often charged with base self-seeking, who, though giving the best of denial by a life-long endurance, are silent from necessity?

One object has been to show that at several points in our Conference territory during the same decade, from 1830 to 1840, however meager the support, the work has gone on. True this is no new thing in Methodism existing to-day. But the novelty lies in the fact that but few comparatively know it. Year after year the preachers are furnished churches, and whether supported or not the supply does not fail. This is so contrary to all human action, and so like offering a premium for default, that many are ready to conclude the lack of support is mythical. What better can these old records do than to give up their testimony? The covering-up process does not aid advancement; hiding facts in the minds of officials and covering over delinquent charges may minister to a pseudo-charity, but militates ever against the truth and progression.

If any portion of the country may have urged poverty as the cause of failure in sustaining Church operations, this wire-grass, sand-hill section had reason to do so. Save along the borders of the streams, all was land of the poorest description; yet it will be seen that it was not far behind some of the richer territory of the Conference. Indeed, I am clearly of the opinion that poverty, though always urged, is the very least cause of failure in this direction. This may appear in the sequel.

The Chesterfield Circuit, although Methodism existed within

(180)

its boundaries from the very beginning, was incorporated with other circuits until 1832. Bordering on North Carolina, it was one of the first sections of the state visited by the apostolic Asbury. Under date of February 17, 1785, he writes of the Cheraw Hills, and his spending some time in prayer in the church at that place—none other than the present Episcopal Church, which antedates the Revolution. Others of the fathers soon followed. The Rev. Hugh Craig, long a local preacher in this circuit, remembers the gift of a little catechism to himself, when a child, by the famed George Dougherty. Within its boundaries, at Old Fork Creek (Knight's Meetinghouse), William Capers was converted, and along "that dreary sand-hill road leading from Chesterfield Courthouse to Sumterville" struggled concerning his call to preach, and conquered. Within its territory those elect ladies, Mrs. Blakeny and Mrs. Blair, domiciled and cheered the itinerant in his rounds with all their abounding wealth afforded. Of a later day are the Williamses, Craigs, Chapmans, Lucases, and others, whose praise, if not in this, will be in another and more enduring book.

The first session of the Quarterly Conference for 1832 was held March 17, at Chesterfield Courthouse. William Kennedy, presiding elder; John M. Kelly, preacher in charge; Allen Rushing, local preacher; L. Ogburn, exhorter; John Burnett, M. K. McCaskill, James C. Brown, and John D. Price, leaders. Other members present were: Hugh Craig and John Stephens, local preachers; James Wright, William Hudson, William Morse, J. W. Hudson, C. Therell, Haywood Chapman, A. McInnis, Alexander Cassidy, J. McLean, K. Bennett, Edwin Odum, Henry Wallace, and William Moss. In 1833, B. Dozier, Alexander McNair, W. H. Wadsworth, William Hall, Thomas Sweat, Clement Cogdell, Elias Fraser, William L. Morse, Tyre McHaffy, and Isaac Hall were added. In 1834 Charles Pigg, O. Gatledge, Andrew Miller, and Peter Stewart appear. In 1839 O. Jordan, Dr. Charles Williams, J. B. Nettles, Hugh Blakeny, Jesse Gibson, and William Ingram are recorded. In 1841 M. J. McDonald, Donald McDonald, J. Stephens, A. Miles, J. McCrary, E. Ellis, M. Talbert, and S. P. Murchison are added.

In 1832 there were admitted on trial 206 whites and 128 colored. The churches, with payments for the entire year, were: Society Hill, $28.20; Mt. Zion, $5; Sardis (Stephens's), $2.91;

Fork Creek, $34.28; Smyrna (McHaffy's), 81 cents; Taxahaw, $11.81; Zion, $5; Pleasant Hill, $5; Courthouse, $34.70; Shiloh, $2.57; Bear Creek, $7.98; Mt. Olivet, $9; New Prospect, 72 cents; Public collections, $25.18.   Total collected, $173.16.

Traveling expenses.................................	$ 6 50
Paid presiding elder	50 00
Paid preacher in charge.............................	116 66
Total...	$173 16

Membership, 474 whites; average per member, 38 cents.

In 1833, same presiding elder; A. B. McGilvary, preacher in charge.   First quarter, 43¾ cents; second quarter, $65.75; third quarter, $36.43; fourth quarter, $73.18¾; stewards' meeting, $48.01.   Total collected, $223.81.

Traveling expenses	$ 8 50
Paid presiding elder	50 00
Paid preacher in charge.............................	165 31
Total...	$223 81

Average per member, 42 cents.

The yearly collections for the support of presiding elders and preachers for the next years are as follows:

1832. John M. Kelly, preacher in charge	$173 16
1833. A. B. McGilvary	223 81
1834. William Brockington...........................	213 99
1835 to 1840 imperfect.	
1841. George R. Talley	228 82
1842. J. M. Bradley	329 15
1843. Abel Hoyle	253 89
1844. A. M. Chreitzberg.............................	358 52
1845. John Watts....................................	196 04
1846. M. A. McKibben	212 31
1847. W. L. Pegues	130 35
1848. M. A. McKibben................................	212 31
1849. W. L. Pegues	273 53
1850. A. Nettles....................................	239 35
1851 and 1852 imperfect.	
1853. D. W. Seal....................................	235 65
1854. D. W. Seal....................................	433 49
1855. Daniel McDonald	141 26
1856. S. Jones	246 15
1857. S. Jones	212 53
1858. E. J. Pennington..............................	199 66
1859. E. J. Pennington..............................	367 60
1860. Jesse S. Nelson...............................	320 07

1861 to 1867 imperfect.

1868. Oliver Eady $330 00
1869. J. C. Hartsell 380 00
1870. J. Sandford 577 72
1871. J. B. Platt 635 00
1872. J. B. Platt 797 00
1873. A. Ervine...................................... 680 00
1874. A. Ervine...................................... 623 30
1875. J. C. Russell 680 00
1876. J. W. Murray 756 44
1877. J. W. Murray 813 19
1878. J. W. Murray 646 97
1879. J. W. Murray 788 54
1880. C. D. Rowell.................................. 855 00
1881. C. D. Rowell.................................. 844 61
1882. C. D. Rowell.................................. 814 78
1883. C. D. Rowell.................................. 819 59
1884. J. W. McRoy 721 80
1885. J. W. McRoy 601 21
1886. W. H. Whitaker 682 79
1887. W. H. Whitaker 818 44

This shows a very creditable increase in ministerial support. How it will be in the future remains to be seen. This once large circuit is now cut in half.

A tabular statement for five years will show the amounts contributed by each church, and an aggregate for five years' ministerial labor as low as could be reasonably expected:

CHURCHES.	1844.	1845.	1846.	1847.	1848.	Total.
Society Hill	$ 33 18	$ 40 00	$ 30 00	......	......	$ 93 18
Fork Creek...............	55 02	37 02	36 90	$ 49 60	$ 33 25	211 69
Damascus	85 50	40 00	65 00	38 00	13 00	241 50
Mt. Zion	6 00	......	......			6 00
Zion	4 00	6 50	7 00	6 25	9 75	33 50
Bethel	40 17	20 02	1 00	1 50	......	62 69
Friendship...............	10 00	5 00	4 25	3 00	......	22 25
Prospect................	8 50	2 61	7 50	1 00	2 00	20 61
Mt. Olivet	13 75	......	7 50	50	1 50	23 25
Courthouse	66 53	25 56	28 87	22 00	27 00	169 96
Shiloh	10 00	1 50	8 60	50	1 00	21 60
Pleasant Hill	5 00	1 42	......	......		6 42
Sardis	9 87	10	1 25	1 50	2 87	15 59
Public collections........	11 00	23 60	14 43	7 50	40 67	97 20
	$358 52	$203 33	$212 30	$130 35	$131 04	$1,025 44

This record from the Quarterly Conference Journal here closes. We would like to have the figures covering the war period, but they are not at hand. From 1868 to 1875 there are returns showing a healthy increase in the finances, and giving promise of improvement still greater in the coming years:

Year.	PREACHER IN CHARGE.	Amount Collected.	Average.
1868	O. Eady	$330 00	75
1869	J. C. Hartsell	380 00	81
1870	J. Sandford	577 82	87
1871	J. B. Platt................................	635 00	79
1872	J. B. Platt................................	797 00	$1 02
1873	A. Ervine	680 00	97
1874	A. Ervine	623 30	85
1875	J. C. Russell	680 00	89

But let us run back into the past and in the light of contrast view the improvements hereabout. The names of York, Chester, Lancaster, and Chesterfield proclaim our connection with English history from an early period in the seventeenth century. With the reigns of the pedant James and the untrustworthy Charles, the profligate son, and the monkish brother who for love of Rome threw away his kingdom and crown, this upper country of Carolina had but little to do. It was not until near the close of the eighteenth century that any settlement of importance was made therein. About the middle of the said century hereabout tribes of Indians, the Catawbas and Waterees, were masters of the whole. Bands of traders supplied the necessities of the Indians and their own in the way of barter, reaping a rich harvest from the unsuspecting natives. What a blessing to think nobody now wants to cheat his neighbor! Oh, no; not one, nowhere!

But it is religious and not civil matters in hand just now. It will be remembered how nearly Dean Swift came to being made bishop of America. What the record would have been had the queen's disinclination to him been overcome, who can conjecture?

All know John Wesley's plea to the bishop of London to ordain preachers for America, rejected with disdain—the people so few, the country so far. Alas for human foresight! What might not the Church of England have gained by his compliance, yet what might not the country have lost by the complex machinery not fitted for the wilderness?

Chesterfield was doubtless named from the courtly earl whom the great English lexicographer so snubbed in his dedication of his great dictionary. His body long since dust, here he has an imperishable monument to his memory. This Chesterfield Circuit is monumental in another sense; at least its name has been associated with Methodism many years, and some old documents in my possession will show that amid all discouragements of the past there has been a steady increase, promising still more of success in coming years. The circuit itself, though Methodism existed in its boundaries from the very beginning, was incorporated with other charges until 1832, sixty-five years ago. Bordering on North Carolina, it was one of the first sections of the state visited by the apostolic Asbury as early as 1785. And though ignorant and unlearned men, just like Peter and John, they built up a great Church nevertheless; and their sons are laying the foundation broad and deep for mightier conquests in the twentieth century, now near at hand.

At Society Hill we had but little success. There was some difficulty as to the site of the church in 1834. The road to it was fenced up, entailing a lawsuit; a resident minister using his influence against us, and finally falling sadly. There were strong friends there, however—Dr. Hoges, James and William Houze, and Mrs. Snipes. In 1844 Dr. Charles Williams resided there, and was very influential.

The old Fork Creek Church, while in Santee Circuit and for years after, was ever noted as fruitful. It is still to the front in Jefferson Circuit.

Camden Station has ever been a place of importance in Methodist annals. It was the seat of ten Conferences, and was once in connection with Santee Circuit, but in 1811 was set off as a station, so remaining until now. The Quarterly Conference Journal from 1839 to 1854 is before us. But little save the usual inquiries is on record. The members of the first Quarterly Conference, held February 9, 1839, were H. Spain, presiding elder; B. Thomas Mason, preacher in charge; S. W. Capers, Thomas Berry, and A. Purifoy, local preachers; John R. Joy, class leader and exhorter; J. S. Depass, James Dunlap, James C. West, W. C. Workman, stewards. At other sessions Phineas Thornton, T. S. Mood, F. B. Rush, A. V. Pritchard, J. N. Gamewell.

In 1852 a resolution was offered by J. N. Gamewell, requiring financial reports yearly from the board of stewards; but no attention was paid to the same thereafter.

Camden has been favored with remarkable men and women. To those noted above may be added the names of two elect ladies, Mrs. Amelia Haile and Mrs. Sarah Ciples, who gave the present parsonage, and made provision for servants and everything needed for the comfort of the pastors. Thurlow Caston, an able lawyer, was exceedingly useful to the church; he died in early life. Dr. Zemp was for years a steward, and had much to do with the erection of the present handsome church structure. It was enterprised during the ministry of the Rev. H. F. Chreitzberg in 1875, and set apart for worship some two or three years after. The elect ladies noted above surely deserve some memorial for their liberal gift of a parsonage, bank stock, servants, and the like to the Camden Church.

The Wateree Circuit was set off, as seen, in 1809; so remaining until 1833, when Wateree was confined to the mission work, and in 1834 Lancaster Circuit in its place, sweeping up into the Waxhaws. In 1870 Lancaster Courthouse was made a station and the Lancaster Circuit changed into Hanging Rock. In 1809 it will be remembered how faultless was the ministry of William Capers, and it was not until 1833 or 1834 that any attempt was made to build a church at the courthouse. James Jenkins with J. J. Allison held a two days' meeting at that time, preaching in the courthouse. They were kindly entertained by Colonel Witherspoon. He states that Frederick Rush was the preacher in charge, but the Minutes say differently. They were R. Adams and S. Armstrong. Rush was on the Wateree Mission. Ten whites and thirteen blacks were enrolled, and a Brother Brummet appointed leader. In a year or two afterwards a church was built. In 1835, with James C. Postell, another meeting was held by James Jenkins. There was then a comfortable house of worship and a number of members. Among the first members were the Beckhems, Mayers, Brummets, Millers, Riddles, and others. As we have seen, the original Santee Circuit ran up to near Charlotte, N. C. The introduction of Methodism there is worthy of note, and may be seen at length in James Jenkins's autobiography. Dr. Dunlap, with Mrs. Martin, mother of the Rev. William Martin, were among the first to join. Dr. Dunlap was the son of the lady subjected to the fearful ordeal in the graveyard of the Waxhaws Presbyterian Church in the last century. In 1788 Saluda Circuit and the Waxhaws were added to the appointments. Michael Burdge was the preacher in charge.

The Waxhaws were long famous in Methodist annals, and are often mentioned in Bishop Asbury's journal. It was attractive to him because of the Catawba Indians near by, and Burdge was sent to labor specially with them. Coke and Asbury visited the tribe and preached to them through an interpreter. A rude structure was improvised and the tribe attended, but they were more concerned about the present than a future life. All efforts since to Christianize them have been abortive. At a late date a few women may have been seen in attendance on worship at Friendship Church in the present Leslie Circuit. Some were members there who seemingly were not full-blooded Indians. The Waxhaws are known to fame as the birthplace of Andrew Jackson. At the old church he attended school. In that graveyard his father is buried, and thither the wounded were carried from the Buford massacre during the Revolution. That old graveyard witnessed a scene in the latter part of the eighteenth century most disgraceful to civilization: the disinterment of a corpse, after months of burial, to prove the guilt or innocence of one accused of murder. The widow of the dead man was compelled to touch the corpse to see if, according to the superstition of the time, it would bleed. The lady, afterwards Mrs. Dunlap, by the general sentiment of the community was held entirely innocent.

Some distance from the Waxhaws Presbyterian Church, on the road to Charlotte, once stood the Methodist Waxhaws Church. Near it, and not far from the road, stands a conglomerate formation neatly poised on a narrow shelf of rocks, and named by the writer, "The Sachem's Pipe." The folklore of the country states that the little children would look with open-eyed astonishment to see it move, which it would inevitably do on hearing a cock crow; not readily seeing that their disappointment lay in the rock being so hard of hearing.

Bishops Asbury and McKendree in their travel in this neighborhood once sought shelter with a good old Associate Reformed Presbyterian. To their request to stay all night the answer was: "That is as ye behave yourselves."

" Well, Mr. Mc——, we are Methodist preachers—"

"Hoot mon," was the sudden reply, "of all people in the warld I hate them the most!"

"But why?" was the rejoinder.

" Why, they get drunk and tell lees."

" Who says so?" was the inquiry of the bishop.

" Why, our good mon the meinester."

" Does he get drunk?" was next asked.

"Weel, not often," was replied.

After being admitted, they asked liberty to pray, and were told, "Pray, mon, as much as ye like."

Their request to sing a hymn was indignantly refused with a " No, that ye sha'n't! "

The Waxhaws Presbyterian Church for a long time was the center of religious influence in this section. Camp meetings were once held there. At one time a well-to-do population lay along the Catawba River. Emigration and the emancipation of the slaves have much reduced its prosperity. The old graveyard contains the dust of several generations. Methodism at the Waxhaws has always had a good representation. Lying directly in the route of travel of the pioneers, it was favored with their early ministry; and it has long retained a deep spirituality of character. The present church structure is small, but it is expected that a more commodious one will soon be erected.

From the Waxhaws came James Russell, an uncultured backwoodsman, but who, like Burns the plowman, had natal gifts, and the matchless sweep of whose oratory charmed the erudite Olin. Of him more is to be said hereafter.

Michael Burdge had peculiar honor as the first missionary—indeed, the only one ever sent to the Catawba Indians at the Waxhaws in 1788. He traveled four years; located in 1807; sought readmission into the Conference, and after a year or two obtained it; was honored, with Sturdivant, as a missionary to Mississippi; labored under difficulties subjecting him to complaint and trial, and was finally set down in the General Minutes as expelled from the Oneida Conference in 1819. Dr. Anson West, in his " History of Methodism in Alabama," has pretty thoroughly traced his history, and has shown from the journals of the Oneida Conference that he was not expelled for criminality, but imprudence. He was afterwards connected with the

LITTLETON STREET METHODIST CHURCH, CAMDEN, S. C.

Methodism was introduced into Camden about 1787. Isaac Smith has the honor of being its founder. For thirteen years it had no "set place" of worship. During the pastorate of the Rev. James Jenkins a church was erected. The building was very plain and inexpensive. Once or twice it was enlarged to accommodate the increased audiences. It stood near the present jail.

In 1825, under the leadership of the Rev. Malcolm McPherson, a new church enterprise was started. This resulted in the plain edifice on De Kalb street. It was occupied February 6, 1828, the first service being the forty-second session of the Annual Conference over which Bishop Soule presided. The negroes now own and use this house for a church. In 1860 a lot was bought on Monumental Square, and the corner stone of a new church was laid with grand and imposing ceremonies. The civil war caused this to be abandoned. After the sale of the De Kalb street property a small house was purchased on Hampton Square and used as a church. This was only a temporary expedient.

In 1875, under the leadership of the Rev. H. F. Chreitzberg, D.D., the handsome Littleton Street Church was begun. A few years later it was completed, while the Rev. J. O. Willson, D.D., was pastor. The dedicatory sermon was preached by the pastor under whose leadership it was begun. On that occasion Dr. Chreitzberg preached a magnificent sermon. This building is a perfect gem. Dr. F. L. Zemp, chairman of the building committee, deserves much credit for making this enterprise such a success.

During the pastorate of the Rev. J. Thomas Pate, D.D., in 1896, the building was found to be too small, and was enlarged twenty feet. A splendid pipe organ was also placed in the church. It is now one of the very best churches in the state.   J. T. P.

Methodist Protestant Church, and represented it in their General Conference in 1838.

We have a much better record of another of the honored missionaries sent from the South Carolina Conference to Mississippi. In response to a call for volunteers at the thirtieth session held in Charleston, S. C., December, 23, 1815—William McKendree, bishop—A. Hewitt was sent to Tombigbee. His long travel through the Indian country tested his courage, his life often being in jeopardy.

Ashley Hewitt was recommended by a Quarterly Conference held in Enoree Circuit in 1810. He served faithfully in his Conference until transferred. Dr. Anson West's portraiture seems to be of no flattering kind, and yet has an offset in his end as related by Joseph Travis. "In stature he was tall and lean, blue eyes and hair of light color, a fair complexion, a mouth large enough to indicate a fluent speaker, and a pleasant countenance. He was a quiet, sedate, matter-of-fact man, possessing a sound judgment, medium attainments, and moderate abilities. He had neither genius nor fancy. As a preacher he had but little or no variety, and was almost entirely destitute of emotion and of action. In 1830 he located."

The Rev. Joseph Travis writes of an intimate acquaintanceship with Hewitt, and of his being highly esteemed in his missionary fields, both in Mississippi and Louisiana. He gives a singular relation concerning his death scene. His daughter, Elizabeth, was taken sick with himself the same day. Intelligence was brought him that she was dead. He asked, "Did she profess religion before she died?" The answer was, "No." "Then she is not dead. God will not permit her to die until she is converted. I have trusted my heavenly Father too long to doubt it, and he has heard my prayer too frequently now to turn a deaf ear to my dying request in behalf of my beloved child." But she was laid out, when to the astonishment of all, after lying thus about an hour, she opened her eyes, and said, distinctly: "Glory to God, my sins are forgiven, and I am going safe to heaven." Her father died the same day.

CHAPTER XXII.

HAVING traced the first named circuit (Santee), the next
established the same year (1786) was the Great Pee Dee,
divided two years after, in 1788, and called the Great and Little
Pee Dee; Little Pee Dee, as far as the number of members
goes, being the greater. The first named, in 1788, reported 885
whites and 50 colored, and in 1789 only 369 whites and 39 colored; while Little Pee Dee reported 598 whites and 20 colored
members.

In 1796 James Jenkins traveled the Great Pee Dee Circuit,
and states that it embraced portions of Williamsburg, Sumter,
Darlington, and Marion counties; the larger part of Marlboro
county being in the Little Pee Dee Circuit. The whole of the
Pee Dee Valley, one of the fairest portions of the state, has always been favorable to Methodism. The country was early pre-
empted by the pioneers, and is held firmly to the faith up to
this hour. By putting on record all now known of that early
day, and taking the Santee, Congaree, and Broad rivers as the
line, very nearly one-half of the state will have been brought under review. It is sad that so little is on record concerning the
early work and workers. Only here and there are incidents
noted, and unless put on record permanently very little will be
rescued from oblivion.

The Great Pee Dee Circuit, as we have seen, was formed by
Jeremiah Mastin and Hope Hull in 1786. They did yeoman
service, calling forth the high approval of Coke. Where it began we are not informed, but it must have been in Britton's
Neck, on its lower end, the river proving, from the difficulty of
crossing it, an exceedingly great barrier. In more modern times
to reach Georgetown often required seven miles of ferriage.

The old Neck Church for a long time served the necessities
of the people, the old Ark, lower down in the fork of the rivers,
being more recently established. A glance at the map shows

(192)

the Great Pee Dee River running down from North Carolina, and with Georgetown, Florence, Darlington, and Chesterfield counties on the western side, dividing those counties from Horry, Marion, and Marlboro.

The Pee Dee Valley, it will be remembered, was entered by Bishop Asbury, and early mention made of Bennettsville, Beauty Spot, etc. The next notice in the journal is on February 2, 1790, concerning Flowers Meetinghouse, on the north side of Marion Courthouse. It stood near a large oak in the yard of General William Evans. James Jenkins, then a youth, had gone to conduct the bishop on his way to the fourth session of the South Carolina Conference in Charleston. The journal states: "On February 2, 1790, we came to Flowers Meetinghouse. We had a lively stir; one soul found peace, and I had freedom in preaching." Mr. Jenkins states: "Glory! glory! glory be to God! I was that soul." It seems that soon afterwards he was accustomed to hearty shouting, a matter quite common then, but now largely gone into desuetude. Some did not like it even then. One said that "it was a new religion, and the old members must get it," but added, "If this be religion, I pray the Lord to keep me from it." Mr. Jenkins naïvely adds: "I fear his prayer was answered." He says further: "Ever after this, in public and private, I have praised the Lord aloud whenever I have felt like it; for if I can help it, I don't choose to help it." And why should any man's liberty be restrained by another man's conscience? True, by it he earned the *sobriquet* of "Bawling Jenkins," but what of that? Some of the wicked said that even the apostles at Pentecost were drunken.

The years pass on, and with them the tide of life. Sugg, Herbert, Lilly, Bonner, Tolleson, Lipsey, Enoch George, and others were the preachers traveling this charge. In 1796 Jenkins and Thomas Humphries were on Great Pee Dee. It was a year of trial, the junior preacher helping only at Quarterly Conferences; yet a year of revival, the Jeffrey's Creek Church sharing largely.

The old Neck Church must have been organized in 1786. It was here that James Jenkins joined in 1789. The society seems to have declined, for in 1800 he writes of "a second society raised here." Out of it in after years came John L. Greaves,

13

who died in 1826, William H. Ellison and Richardson (James J.), who died in 1833.

In 1802 Mr. Jenkins, being presiding elder, held a Quarterly Conference at Harleeville. Jonathan Jackson preached on "the little stone cut out of the mountain," and Mr. Jenkins on being "weighed in the balances." Daniel Asbury used to tell humorously of a Dutchman's account of that sermon. He said: "I wents to de camp meetin', and one Schenkins breached. His tex' vas, 'You's veighed in de palance and found vantin'.' He vent on veighin' many beeples, an' at las' throwed ole Fisher into de palance, an' ole Fisher did come out jes' noting at all." But he weighed something afterwards—adorned the gospel, and died in the faith.

About this time Mr. Jenkins preached the funeral sermon of Moses Wilson. He was admitted in 1795, died in 1803, and was buried at James Skinner's, on Little Lynch's Creek. A more pious or upright man has rarely been seen. He left his property to the Conference; but upon Bishop Asbury saying, "The kings of Israel are merciful men," the Conference sent it to some of his friends who were needy. This same year (1803) Mr. Jenkins visited Fayetteville, N. C. There was a small society under the care of a colored man named Evans. He had leased a lot for seven years, and commenced building a church twenty by thirty feet out of rough-edge materials. This was the first Methodist church in the place. In a short time an addition of ten feet was made to it.

In the fall of 1805 Mr. Jenkins attended a camp meeting at the noted old Gully Camp Ground, in Darlington county. Here, amid much opposition, they had a gracious time. George Dougherty, the presiding elder, reproved from the stand certain outlaws, and called on the congregation to notice if the judgments of Heaven did not overtake them. This was the time when Dougherty gave that discourse on "the swine choked in the sea," so graphically described by Dr. Lovick Pierce in "Sprague's Annals": "His remarkable skill as an impromptu preacher was strikingly displayed at a camp meeting in Darlington Circuit in 1805. At this meeting the assembled rowdies hallooed, cursed, drank, and fought. Preaching they would not hear, but if at any time there was a shout raised this tumultuous crowd would come rushing to the altar of prayer like cattle to a salt-lick, laughing and profanely ridiculing the work of God. On Sunday, under the preaching of James Jenkins—famous through all that country for having a stir and a shout—a lady began praising God aloud. The rowdies broke from every point of the compass and came thundering into the camp like a herd of buffaloes. Mr. Dougherty prepared to launch a thunderbolt at them. He announced his text: 'And the herd ran violently down a steep place into the lake, and were choked.' He commented upon the generous policy of Satan, showing that he cared nothing as to the means used for the accomplishment of an object, success only being aimed at. If dislodged from a man, he was well satisfied to enter swine, so as to prejudice men against Christ. Then he noticed, first, the herd into which the devil entered; secondly, the drivers employed; and, thirdly, the market to which they were going. And then he began an *exposé* of the infernal entrances into men—the agencies employed, under the figure of drivers, in the establishment of brothels, saloons, gambling hells, and other auxiliaries of ruin. It was pertinent, awful, loving, scathing, and unique. He swept along his pathway like a blazing comet, drawing such pictures of vice and diabolical intrigue that the miserable creatures before him seemed spellbound. Though they were all standing, scarcely a man among them broke ranks. When he reached his imaginary market with them—the end of an abandoned life—the picture took on such an appalling hue that an involuntary shudder seized the audience. The most stout-hearted sinners present seemed to be overwhelmed with amazement. As the preacher began to draw in his lines upon them they left in wild confusion, and were soon *en route* for home."

A year after, and it may have been at this very Gully camp meeting, as we learn from Travis, "he was too far spent to attempt preaching; but on the Sabbath, after another had preached, he arose, and propping himself against the bookstand, said: 'Brethren, this is the last time you will ever recognize my presence among you; but next year, when you have a camp meeting here, I will ask my heavenly Father to permit my mingling with you around that altar; and although in person you will not see me, I expect to be with you in spirit, rejoicing and praising God.' For a time a deathlike silence of weeping prevailed, broken by a loud burst of 'Glory to God!' From this meeting he went to Wilmington, N. C., and in a few weeks died."

The next record concerning the Great Pee Dee Circuit was in 1814. Joseph Travis had located, and for that and the two following years had opened an academy at Marion Courthouse. There being no church in the village, the courthouse was used for religious services. Mr. Travis preached here every Wednesday night. Regular appointments were kept up in the country, and two or three days' meetings were frequently held; two excellent local preachers, the Rev. Jesse Le Gett and the Rev. Jesse Wood, living near. Ebenezer Le Gett—afterwards of the South Carolina Conference, admitted in 1827 and located in 1838 —was the son of Jesse Le Gett. Le Gett and Woods were good preachers, and great lovers of primitive Methodism. The first named was somewhat of a censor, reproving Travis for a rather metaphysical sermon he had preached that not ten persons out of hundreds attending understood. The reproof was well received by Mr. Travis, and he greatly profited by it.

Immediately after the war of 1812 land and cotton rose in value. A gentleman sold land at twenty dollars an acre which shortly before would not have brought five dollars. Fearing that he had sold too hastily, he wished the purchaser to rue the bargain; and failing in this, he went out and hanged himself.

In 1816 Bishop Asbury passed through Marion for the last time, stopping several days and nights with Mr. Travis. He was on his way to the General Conference in Baltimore, but he never reached it. Patience and entire resignation to the will of God were manifested by him from day to day. On recovering often from paroxysms of pain he would shout, "Halleluiah! halleluiah!" On his long and arduous life being referred to, he declared: "My only hope of heaven is in the merits and righteousness of the Lord Jesus Christ."

James Jenkins having located in 1813, although compelled to labor from day to day for bread, would often take his horse out of the plow to serve the Church. Much of his time was devoted to two days' meetings in Sumter and Darlington counties, portions of which were embraced in the old Great Pee Dee Circuit. About this time he preached the funeral sermon of a woman whose husband, a Mr. Meeks, kept a tippling shop at Cootersboro (?). He became awakened, converted, and was long after a class leader in the circuit. The next year Mr. Jenkins settled near Bishopville. The country at that time, with a few worthy exceptions, was close akin to heathendom. Bishopville was then called the Cross Roads, and was owned by an old woman named Singleton. Sodom was not much worse. Whisky and whisky shops abounded. Here men would get drunk, quarrel, fight, dance, and murder. Several persons killed themselves drinking at this place; and the old woman's two sons murdered a man and had to flee for their lives. Bishopville is quite another sort of place to-day.

In 1820 District Conferences for local preachers principally were instituted, and in the fall of 1821 one was held at Catfish, in the Pee Dee Circuit; Joseph Travis, presiding elder, presiding.

During 1830 the first Methodist church in Darlington was completed, and was dedicated by the Revs. Joseph Moore, Turrentine, and Jenkins. At this place were several conversions, among them Horatio McClenagan, who for many years was an esteemed local preacher, dying in the faith. There had been preaching there before, but no society had been formed until this time. In 1831 Noah Laney and A. Hamby were on the Darlington Circuit, and there was a second revival in the village. William M. Wightman, who was on the Santee Circuit that year, attended this meeting. Two of the principal men of this neighborhood, Gibson and Saunders, had been at variance for years. They were awakened, and meeting at the chancel faced each other and electrified the audience by their reconciliation. At this meeting many came weeping to the chancel for prayers without any invitation. All of the churches in Darlington shared in the fruits of this revival.

The forty-sixth session of the Conference—Bishop Hedding, presiding; William M. Wightman, secretary—was held in Darlington, January 26, 1832. It was very harmonious and well entertained. There was not another session held here until sixty years afterwards, the one hundred and sixth—Bishop Granbery, presiding; H. F. Chreitzberg, secretary. This Conference was also handsomely entertained.

In 1832 J. J. Allison and A. McCorquodale, the preachers, aided by James Jenkins, held a meeting continuing for near three weeks. Over fifty joined the different churches. It was a deep, genuine, glorious work.

In 1825 the church in Cheraw was organized by the Rev. Charles Betts. Colonel David Harlee was for many years one of its chief supporters.

In 1840 the preachers on the Pee Dee Circuit were Bond English, presiding elder; John R. Pickett and A. M. Chreitzberg. The circuit extended from Parnassus in Marlboro county to the Ark in Britton's Neck, and from the Warhees on the Big to Little Pee Dee River. The church structures, save at Marion Courthouse, were quite ordinary, some twenty-four being served every two weeks. There were no parsonages, the wives traveling around with their husbands. The amount collected for the support of the two preachers and presiding elder was seven hundred dollars.

Of the Little Pee Dee Circuit there is but little on record. To merely enumerate the names of the preachers would be of no profit. So, closing up the record of the eastern half of the state, attention is called to the third circuit formed, namely, Edisto, bringing the western section into view.

CHAPTER XXIII.

THE old Congaree Circuit was first named in the General Minutes in 1809. William Scott was the preacher in charge, and reported four hundred and forty-six white and one hundred and one colored members in 1810. Lexington and a part of Richland county was the field of operation; the Congaree River running between gave the name. In 1834 it was changed into Columbia Circuit; in 1850 divided into Lexington and Columbia circuits; in 1868 the Lexington Mission was formed, and is now incorporated with Lexington Circuit; and in 1872 the Leesville Circuit was set off. At the time of which I write the Saluda River was the northern boundary, but how far above and to the east of Columbia the circuit extended I have no certain knowledge.

The names of the preaching places in 1830 were as follows: Laurel Chapel (in Orangeburg county), Crim's, Sandy Run, Niece's, Boiling Springs, Poindexter's, Ralls's, Halfway House, Granby, Mill Creek, Livingston's, Justice's, Dry Creek, Brown's Chapel, Mt. Zion, Donnovan's, Smyrna, Sharp's, Longtown, Ebenezer, Rabb's, Rollinson's, English's, Rock Spring, Platt's Springs, Logue's, Lexington Courthouse, and New Hope, twenty-eight in all—one for each day in the four weeks' round; enough, one would think, to occupy the time of any slow preacher, or indeed any fast one as well. In 1831 Long's Schoolhouse was added, and possibly some other dropped. In 1832 Bethel and Cureton's, Hopkins's, and Heal All Springs appear; in 1833, Chestnut Grove; in 1834 Davis's is set down. Methodist preachers, especially the early ones, were rarely known to refuse appointments—"at it, and all at it, and always at it," seemed to be the rule. So accommodating were they that they seemed inclined to give every man a church at his own door. With some this is just as it should be, but may it not

(199)

militate against the sociality of our natures, which religion is intended to foster? and may it not make the service so cheap as to become almost worthless? In the round of near sixty years' ministry, the writer has been thrown into connection with some of the above preaching places, and the memory thereof is not altogether refreshing. Good people, and I don't know but that the bad alike, desire to see things *couleur de rose;* but this is not a rose-colored world, alas! Who that ever preached at Lexington Courthouse, in the old battered hull of a house, doorless and shutterless, can forget it? It may be better now, but I do not know that it is. And Dry Creek, was it not appropriately named, for was it not exceedingly dry? Laurel Chapel and Sandy Run have more pleasant memories. Who that ever knew them does not recall the Colclasures and Louis Pou? And there was old Uncle Peter Buyck, whose laugh was so like a cry that when he prayed it puzzled you to tell which he was doing; and when either was up, you wished it *vice versâ,* and was glad when both were ended. Good old man, he wanted ordination when a licentiate, and his brethren would not recommend him, and so he left us. But who knowing him would have supposed that his grandfather was once a wealthy merchant, and that the last named Peter was the owner of and resided on what was once a fine estate? And who, indeed, that traveled that old state road (remembering that long, lonely reach of sand), and turned off to Laurel Chapel, would have supposed himself near Commodore Gillon's fine estate, the Retreat? He was the commodore of Revolutionary fame. In fitting out privateers in the war he obtained loans from Peter Buyck, a wealthy merchant of Amsterdam, but he, not receiving the prizes captured, became a bankrupt. After the Revolution he went to Charleston to prosecute his claims, and was reduced to penury, and supported himself by dealing in empty bottles. Commodore Gillon left the city and settled on the Congaree River, three or four miles above Totness, embellishing his residence with taste and elegance. Johnson, in his traditions of the Revolution, states: "A son of Peter Buyck came forward about 1794 with claims against the estate, and produced a mortgage of the elegant place, the Retreat. He certainly became the owner of it, and a grandson of Peter Buyck is still the proprietor and resident at Gillon's Retreat."

Louis Pou worshiped at Sandy Run, and not far away was his home; the home of the itinerant preacher likewise, where his devoted wife and daughters cheered him with their kind attentions. Brother Pou was a faithful official of the church, always in his place as recording steward. Clarence A. Graeser was another who, as long as he represented Granby, made it the foremost charge in the circuit.

Platt Springs was the seat of an academy of high order in the past. Here Lucius Bellinger was inducted into the mysteries of Cæsar, and learned something, doubtless, of the *pons assinorum*. I wish the old veteran had given us some of his knowledge of men and things hereabout at that time. This is as far as my own personal knowledge of the same concerning the old Congaree Circuit goes. Anything further must be wrought out of the old records before me.

The Quarterly Conference for 1830 was of the following order: William M. Kennedy, presiding elder; Frederick Rush and R. N. Kelly (a supply), circuit preachers; John D. Sharp and Samuel Smoke, local preachers; A. S. Edgeworth and William C. Bell, exhorters and stewards; Louis Pou, steward; Pressly Garner, Jacob C. Slappy, C. Murph, J. D. Brown, A. Elkins, D. Stivender, T. Parrot, J. Livingston, Martin Baker, class leaders.

In after years, up to 1836, as far as the present records run, the following are set down as members: John N. Kennedy, Benjamin Tradewell, N. D. C. Colclasure, and Christian Mood, local preachers; C. A. Graesar and Thomas Starke, stewards; G. Godbold, William F. Snead, John Sewell, William Watson, John Donnovan, Moses Duke, Henry Niece, William Miles, James Loreman, William Purse, John Rowan, J. Graham, and David Davis, class leaders; and Joab Cotton, steward.

The last name recalls an incident. The Rev. J. R. Pickett meeting one on the road within these boundaries, inquired his name. "*Cotton*," was the reply. "And mine," said the preacher, blandly, "is *Pickett*." The other became very much excited, and, beginning to pull off his coat, demanded if he meant to insult him. The preacher had much trouble to show that he did not intend to *pick him*.

The Edisto Circuit is said to have been formed by Isaac Smith. It is not named in the General Minutes for 1786, and that year Henry Willis and Smith were in Charleston, Smith extending his labors in the country; but in 1787 it is named, with Edward West as preacher in charge. It is said to have extended from the Savannah River to within thirty miles of Charleston, and from Coosawhatchie Swamp to Santee River. The Edisto River empties into the Atlantic about midway between Charleston and Beaufort, running up into Lexington county. Thus this early circuit took in all the lower part of the state. In 1788 Henry Bingham and William Gassaway, and in 1789 Isaac Smith and Lemuel Andrews, were the preachers. Thus was Isaac Smith on his old mission ground. It was a year of trial, dissensions abounding, and some of his own particular friends becoming opposed to him, but before the close of the year all was healed.

It must have been in 1786 that Henry Willis visited the Cattle Creek section of Edisto Circuit, for the next year he was in New York, and never again in Carolina, dying triumphantly in 1808. So it was in 1786 that Willis preached in a Lutheran church on Cattle Creek. Jacob Barr was an old Continental officer, and at the investment of Charleston was on duty at Sullivan's Island. After the war he married and settled in Orangeburg county. On Willis's visit he, with others, attended, strongly prejudiced against Methodist preachers. As money was said to be their object, Mr. Barr took care to leave his purse at home. He was deeply affected by the service, concluding that the man must be a god, or else the servant of God. He united himself with Methodism. A storm of persecution arose, and the infant society was compelled to leave the Lutheran meetinghouse; but they soon built a neat house of worship. Its site is now within the lines of the old Cattle Creek Camp Ground. Mr. Barr became a local preacher, and on the 15th of June, 1823, died in his seventieth year. His last words were, "I am going to glory." His son, grandson, and great-grandson were all Methodist preachers.

The metes and bounds of Broad River Circuit are now indefinable. It extended—that is, the river—northwestwardly above Columbia into North Carolina, having the counties of Newberry, Union, and Spartanburg on the west, and Fairfield, Chester, and York on the east; Bush River emptying into Saluda and Saluda into Broad River, Enoree and Tiger rivers emptying into Broad just above. In 1786 Stephen Johnson was on the Broad River Circuit; in 1787, John Mason and Thomas Davis; in 1788, William Partridge. This year Saluda Circuit appears—Lemuel Andrews, preacher; in 1789 Cherokee Circuit, already noticed—John Andrews and Philip Mathews, preachers; also Bush River (Newberry)—William Gassaway, preacher. In 1790 Catawba first appears—Jonathan Jackson, preacher in charge; and in 1791 Union, afterwards Enoree, already noted. In 1794 Black Swamp appears—Jonathan Jackson, preacher in charge. In 1801 the entire state was in one district; James Jenkins, presiding elder, with ten charges. In 1802 there were two districts: Saluda, seven charges, under George Doughler, presiding elder; and Camden, eight charges, under James Jenkins, presiding elder. In 1803 Sandy River was set off; Coleman Carlisle, preacher in charge. In 1804 Union was changed to Enoree and Sandy River, and Bush River and Keowee united. In 1805 Columbia was first named, with Bennett Kendrick, preacher in charge.

It is absolutely impossible to be minute and correct in noting all changes of the charges; only a general outline can be given, and our object is to set down all now known of the prominent charges in our Conference.

The old Keowee Circuit lies within the boundaries of Anderson county. In the General Minutes it is first mentioned as separate from other charges in 1802. Its name was changed to Pendleton in 1833, then to Anderson Circuit in 1835; and nearly within the same boundaries are now the Anderson and Williamston stations, Walhalla and Pendleton, Anderson and Sandy Springs circuits.

Division and subdivision, and division again, have long been the order of Conference action, sought to be retarded often by some croaking cry of ruin. Yet the ruin is hard to be discovered, unless the multiplication of churches, members, preachers, and charges betokens it. A short-sighted policy would have held on to the old four and six weeks' circuits, if for no other reason, that large families might be supported; but results prove that better work gives better pay, and greater stability and force to all religious action. This old circuit is a proof in point, as may likely be seen before this present reading is ended.

The old journal in my possession extends from 1833 to 1844. There is little of interest in it, save in the exhibit of finances in completeness rarely equaled. So exact was the recording steward (I knew him well) that an error of half a cent in a balance-sheet would have caused him trouble until rectified. Most Conference journals lack in this important feature. It is rarely the case that the proceedings of the "fifth quarter"—a technicality well understood by Methodist preachers—are put on record, and the charge thereby often loses its credit. By the way, ought not this to be incorporated in the order of business of a Quarterly Conference? And will not those having charge of the matter insert another question, to this effect: What was collected, and how expended, in closing the business of the past year?* It would hurt nobody, and in case there had been a heavy deficiency, it would be a gentle reminder to all to do better. Loss lies often in a slovenly way of doing business.

But to take up the old Keowee records. The Quarterly Conference for 1833, sixty-three years ago, had Malcolm McPherson for presiding elder, and John W. McCall as preacher in charge. Local preachers: Levi Garrison, Robert Gaines, R. Shockley, William G. Mullinax, Philip Elrod, Willis Dickerson. Exhorters: William Rhodes, Samuel Hamby, James Shockley, Basil Smith. Class leaders: Lawson Mullinax, John Golden, Thomas Gassaway, Anderson Smith, Thomas Evatt, William Fleming, Robert Pickins, Joel Ledbetter, John Ledbetter, Wesley Earp, John Morris, Hugh H. Whittecur, Sidney Smith, Allen Harbin, John Adams, James Holland, Thomas Carpenter, Dugal McKellar, James B. Clark, Washington Clark; and Garrison Linn, steward.

The churches forming the circuit were Anderson Courthouse, Ebenezer, Mount Zion, Sharon, Sword's, Wesley Chapel, Shiloh, Snow Hill, Lynn's, Bethel, Sandy Springs, Bethesda, Cooper's Chapel, Rhuhama, Siler's, Providence, Asbury, Smith's Chapel, Pendleton; nineteen in all.

The sums collected at these churches for the year 1833 ranged from $19.95, the highest, to 50 cents, the lowest amount contributed, making an aggregate of $105.39. The traveling expenses paid amounted to $11.68¾, leaving $93.70½, of which the presiding elder received $21, leaving to the preacher in

---

*This was done at the Atlanta General Conference.

charge $72.70¼. White members in the circuit, 754; an average per member of 12½ cents—not an excessive amount, one would think, allowing that the laborer was at all worthy of his hire.

In 1834 James Stacy was the preacher in charge. Finances were better, $156.87½ cents being collected. After deducting $13.86 for traveling expenses, $148.01½ was left, of which the presiding elder received $43, leaving to the preacher more than his full claim, $100.01½. Membership, 792; an average of 18 cents per member—an improvement certainly. One still greater is seen in 1835, but then there were three preachers to pay instead of two. The presiding elder received $55.75, the preacher in charge $100, and the junior preacher $49.50, aggregating $205.25. Membership, 783; an average per member of 26 cents.

This improvement doubtless led to the appointment of a man of family in 1836, and $100 was allowed for his family expenses. But alas for the vanity of human hopes! only $165.61 was raised, paying the presiding elder $28, the balance, all told, to the preacher in charge. Membership, 615; an average per member of 25 cents.

The returns for 1837, 1838, and 1839 are imperfect, some vandal having defaced them. The record for 1840, however, is complete. The Rev. William M. Wightman was the presiding elder, and John H. Zimmerman the preacher in charge. This year there was a surplus sent to Conference. The following are the collections in detail:

Anderson Courthouse	$27 75
Smith's Chapel	16 00
Bethel	6 62½
Bethesda	9 00
Rhuhama	13 25
Asbury Chapel	10 25
Sandy Springs	14 94
Sword's	1 25
Pendleton	13 25
Mount Zion	10 50
Sharon	7 00
Wesley Chapel	6 25
Lynn's	1 00
Siler's	8 25
Providence	21 25 =$ 166 56½

Presiding elder..................................	$35 50		
Traveling expenses.........................	3 50	=$ 39 00	
Preacher in charge, quarterage...............	100 00		
Traveling expenses........................	16 00	= 116 00	
Shoeing horse.............................		1 31¼	
Sent to Conference........................		10 25	
Total		$166 56½	

The reader will find that the account does not balance by one quarter of a cent; but put the Sandy Springs collection at $14.93¾ (doubtless the correct amount, which an exuberant liberality made $14.94), and the discrepancy at once disappears.

In 1841 the whole amount collected was $204.75; in 1842, to pay three preachers, $253.92; and in 1843, $303.69.

This closes the record, and is sufficient to show that the ministry, at this time at least, was not burdensome; and most of all, that these servants of the Church were certainly not lovers of filthy lucre. St. Peter says: " Feed the flock of God which is among you, taking the oversight thereof not by constraint, but willingly; not for filthy lucre, but of a ready mind." So did these men, undoubtedly. If not, there is no such virtue on the earth. Just consider that for an entire decade, from 1833 to 1843, the total amount contributed (from twenty churches) for their support was $1,685.62, giving an average for each year of $168.56; averaging to the twenty-five preachers, fifteen of whom were men of family, $67.42, an average per member for ten years' service of $2.60. Is it possible for economy of expenditure to go farther? If love of filthy lucre moved them, it is very clear that the appetite grew not on what it fed upon. I am well aware that an average is not a standard of Christian liberality, yet it cannot be denied that it forcibly brings out the lack of that quality and the ridiculously low value put by many on the gospel. The poverty of the Church is the usual excuse for failure in supporting the gospel, so that it might readily be concluded that the half, or nearly the whole, of one's income was necessary to that end; but if it can be shown that there is no such requisition, but that in fact the gospel has been preached for a long series of years at a little cost—we will not say at what to the preachers themselves, but most certainly at a very ridiculously low cost to the aggregate membership— then assuredly the averages are useful.

At no time within the period named did the collections reach three hundred dollars, two hundred and fifty-three dollars being the highest amount any one year, and ninety-four dollars and twenty-five cents the lowest. For the next decade there was not much improvement; the writer knows whereof he affirms, the figures only lacking to confirm the fact. But what good comes of this raking up the past, and the portrayal of the poverty of the Church, and the poor pay of its preachers? Just this, if no more, that men may understand that the ministry are not so mercenary as many suppose. The world is fully agreed that the laborer is worthy of his hire, and sees no difficulty in the abandonment of the work, if the hire be withheld; but here are instances of the one not forthcoming and the other still going on. Nor is this a solitary case. All over a widespread connection this has been going on, and is still going on to this hour.

Methodism has never yet recognized the ministerial life as professional merely; it requires a divine call; it is a vocation emphatically. All that is proffered is a support; but that this ought to be given, no sane mind doubts. Many have prayed fervently, and often, "Give him souls for his hire," but all know that he cannot eat, drink, or wear them; and however excellent they are in the currency of heaven, payable at the great judgment day, what in the name of common sense is the man to do until pay-day comes round? There must be an inconceivable littleness of soul about one who insists on this as the only mode of payment; and we are not surprised at a preacher's rejoinder to one urging it: "Souls! A thousand such as yours would make a very poor meal."

Deficiency in payments of salary was not unfrequent in the annals of Methodism in Carolina. But matters were not so to remain in this old Keowee Circuit. The large four weeks' circuit of twenty-four appointments, mostly served on week days, was to give place to smaller fields and better culture. And in the year 1875, when this calculation was first made—where twenty years before scarcely three hundred dollars per annum could be raised for ministerial support, and where thirty years before, for ten consecutive years, only $1,600 was raised—within the same boundaries $1,880.94 was contributed for the support of five families, besides $381.10 for the general collections of the Church; and the singularity is that two weak stations paid double the amount of the two strong circuits.   The statement is as follows:

	Average per Member.	
	For Salary.	Gen. Col.
Anderson Station......................	$5 12	$1 01
Williamston Station..................	4 35	1 18
Anderson Circuit	75	16
Pendleton Circuit	72	09

Anyone desiring to see the advance over 1875 in this year 1896 has but to refer to our Conference Minutes for the facts.   At a rough calculation over $4,000 was collected for salaries alone.

Newberry county is celebrated as containing a population noted for industry and good morals.   It lies between the Enoree and Saluda rivers, with a corner of Lexington and the whole of Laurens, and parts of Fairfield and Union counties forming the other boundaries, with an average extent of country of about twenty-four square miles; within it was Bush River, which gave name to the original circuit.   The Bush River (Newberry) Circuit is first named in the General Minutes in 1789, with William Gassaway, preacher in charge.   In 1801 it was called Bush River and Cherokee, a mistake likely, as the numbers are given for Bush River and Keowee, and so called until 1805; Keowee being separate in 1806, and so remaining until 1820, when it was changed to Newberry, with Coleman Carlisle and J. L. Jerry, preachers.

The Bush River Baptist Church, near the river and twelve miles southwest from Newberry Courthouse, was constituted in 1771 by elders Philip Mulkey and Samuel Newman.   In 1773 Elder Thomas Norries, a Primitive, practicing feet washing, and who died in 1780, was the pastor.   The Dunkards were there anterior to the Revolution, and the Universalists, under Giles Chapman, highly esteemed according to O'Neal's Annals, began to preach in 1782.   Their faith had but limited influence, and there is no church organization to-day.   In 1802 there was a great revival of religion in the Baptist Church; the "jerks" troubling them as it troubled all religious bodies of that time.

The first Methodist church is supposed to be at Ebenezer, but Bethel (Finch's) may have been before it.   If George Clark, formerly an itinerant, was admitted in 1792 and located in 1802, this is hardly likely; for Finch's is mentioned in 1794, and Lemuel Andrews was on Saluda Circuit in 1788.

The very last record of the Newberry Circuit, within a late period, is from the Rev. J. B. Traywick's account in the "Newberry Annals," to which we are indebted for the following:

"The first Methodist church in Newberry county may have been at Mt. Bethel Academy, a Quarterly Conference being held at Mr. Finch's house in 1788. Mt. Pleasant was built about 1822. The first structure was plain; the present one was erected about 1862. A gift of about one thousand dollars was left by Micajah Suber toward its erection. It is now in the Prosperity Circuit. Among the first members were the Goodwins, Oxnears, Lyleses, Gilliams, and Hattons. The Grahams, Eptings, Adamses, Cromers, and Willinghams were among the officials. It is about five or six miles from the site of old Mt. Bethel. New Hope, organized in 1795, had Salem added in 1835. The church was built in 1831. New Chapel, an old log house, stood one mile from the present building, and gave way in 1830 to a neat frame building, when in 1879 the present structure was erected, Isaac Herbert being foremost in that good work. Zion was organized and the first church built in 1813; Tranquil in 1799, Tabernacle in 1842, Mt. Tabor in 1820, and Ebenezer in 1814. The Kilgores have been associated with it for sixty years, and the Slighs for more than forty."

Newberry Station was organized in 1833. Newberry rejoiced in a great revival in 1831, which resulted in the building up of both the Baptist and Methodist churches. It remained in the circuit until 1854, when it was set off as a station; John R. Pickett, preacher in charge. The present church structure has been in use over sixty years, but is expected soon to give place to a more modern building, in keeping with the wealth and respectability of the congregation.

14

CHAPTER XXIV.

IT is exceedingly difficult to get the exact metes and bounds of the earlier circuits, the names as well as territory constantly changing. The first mention in the General Minutes of the territory covered by the old Winnsboro Circuit is in 1803, then called Sandy River, with Coleman Carlisle the preacher. In 1804 it was called Enoree and Sandy River. In 1805 Sandy River was dropped and the circuit continued as Enoree until 1812, when it was again called Sandy River—William Gassaway and John Bunch the preachers—so continuing for twenty-two years, to 1833. In 1834 it was changed to Winnsboro Circuit, with Joseph Holmes and J. H. Wheeler the preachers, and in 1835 Joel W. Townsend and Samuel Leard. In 1853 Winnsboro and Chester Station, Chester Circuit, and Fairfield Circuit were formed, so remaining until 1858, when Rocky Mount was set off. In 1859 Sandy River Mission was added, and it so remained during the civil war. Now there are nine separate charges—Chester Station, Chester Circuit, Winnsboro Station, East Chester Circuit, Richburg, Blackstock's, Ridgeway, Fairfield, Monticello, and Cedar Creek circuits—within the old boundary. We can go no farther back than to 1803, unless Saluda Circuit or Bush River held a portion of this territory. From 1804 to 1833 it was served by such men as Daniel Asbury, William M. Kennedy, Griffin Christopher, John Howard, Samuel Dunwody, and Charles Betts, closing in 1833 with Whitefoord Smith as junior preacher, in 1834 with Holmes and Wheeler, and in 1835 with Joel W. Townsend and Samuel Leard. To Brother Leard we are under obligations for his memorial address in Chester in 1886, from which we gather matters of interest as here presented.

The circuit in 1835 embraced the counties of Fairfield, Chester, a small part of Richland, and a corner of York—twenty-four appointments, filled in twenty-eight days, leaving two days

(210)

to ride between distant points, and two for rest. With preaching, meeting classes, and other pastoral duties, to say nothing of the travel the preacher's time was fully employed. His hours for study were on horseback and occasionally in afternoons or evenings. The churches were Monticello, Shiloh, Bethel, Cedar Creek, Mount Pleasant, Pine Grove, Winnsboro, Gladden's Grove, Bethesda, Ebenezer, Mount Moriah, Union, Liberty, Chesterville, Smith's Chapel, Armenia, New Hope, Flat Rock, Zion, Cove, Branch, Bethlehem or Stockdale's, and some other points, names forgotten or ceasing as places of worship.

Monticello held the parsonage—a small building, needing repairs badly, and but half furnished. Much of the aristocratic element in Fairfield county, both as to wealth and position, was here. Dr. Pierson and his cultured and fashionable wife lived here. He was a gentleman of the old school, and to the end of his life maintained an elegant hospitality. The Rev. Joseph Holmes, once an acceptable member of the Conference, who located, exerted a fine influence. He was of solid intellect, well informed; a devout man, fully exemplifying the doctrine of holiness. His brother William, a local preacher, lived near Shiloh: he was rather superior in intellect to Joseph, and a man of wealth and good business qualifications; also an excellent preacher, with a very worthy family. They were the sons of a pious Associate Reformed elder, whose habit was often to seek out retirement in the field for prayer with his boys.

Near Shiloh lived the Cooks, the Robinsons, the Ruffs, and many others deserving record.

Cedar Creek was a point where Methodism made some of her finest triumphs. The church structure itself was of the very humblest appearance—a long, low building of wood, and, when seen by the writer, was in the very last stages of decay. But the "living stones" were "elect and precious." The Rev. J. P. Cook, a local preacher from the North, of rare intellect and eloquent speech, exerted a fine influence; Nathan Center, an old patriarch of much intelligence and devotion to the Church; Dr. Thomas R. Center, his son, a graduate of the South Carolina College, an excellent physician and kind neighbor, dying some time after the civil war at the advanced age of seventy-five years; Colonel D. D. Finley, still older, who after great affliction passed to his reward. Adam Du Bard, at

Mt. Pleasant, an efficient steward and devotedly pious, was murdered while on his way to Columbia. Daniel Ruff was for many years a steward at Pine Grove, and dying, left many tokens of piety and devotion to Christ.

In Winnsboro were many fine representatives of olden time Methodism, among them John R. Buchanan and his excellent wife. Mr. Buchanan was a county officer and a steward, and of great influence civilly and religiously. He and his wife were converted under the ministry of James Jenkins in 1808, and for years were interested in all the movements of the Church. One of Mr. Buchanan's sisters married the Rev. Mr. Carlisle, and became the mother of James H. Carlisle, of Wofford College. Mrs. Carlisle was a true Buchanan, possessing the mental and moral characteristics of the old Scotch-Irish, a noble basis for the upbuilding of religious character. Mrs. Means, mother of Governor Means, of South Carolina, with her daughter, once the widow of Hilliard Judge, were all their lives fine exponents of earnest Christian experience. Thomas Jordan, at that time a mere youth, but lately deceased at a good old age, was a leading spirit in our Church at Winnsboro. Near Bethesda was a Brother Lewis. Bishop Asbury says of him in 1809, "but late emerging into light." He was the grandfather of John R. and Philip Pickett, both famous in the Methodist ministry. Philip Pickett's body rests in Bethesda; John's in the Winnsboro cemetery, as also does the dust of Hilliard Judge.

Methodism was introduced into Winnsboro in 1808 by the Rev. James Jenkins. After many changes we hold our own, and though as far as wealth and numbers go the charge may not be considered eminently strong, yet if the past could be minutely recorded it would be seen that Methodism has largely influenced religious life and thought.

Near the church is the house where President Carlisle, of Wofford College, was born, and the graveyard adjoining contains the dust of many of his ancestry. Certainly upon their minds and his the Methodism of the early day wrought its influences. Around Winnsboro and old Bethesda, some dozen miles away, cluster memories of Robert Jones Boyd and Hugh Andrew Crawford Walker. Estimating all wrought through their agency—not written mayhap on earth, but certainly not unknown in heaven—the profit must exceed all computation.

A few years ago Brother Carlisle invited Brother Walker to a review of the past at old Bethesda Church (once Mount Moriah, now in the East Chester Circuit). Alas! this cannot be; and it is not to be regretted, for while the old house is gone, it has given place to a modern brick structure far in advance of the old. While they may call up the strong sermons, the shouts of praise, and the "still small voice" resounding through the humbler temple, they cannot but be thankful that a larger and better one occupies its site.

The writer was talking not long since with the Rev. L. A. Johnson—not a fast man, it is true; rather slow, but exceedingly sure, in building churches especially. "Brother Johnson," said I, "do you remember the old Bethesda church?" "Yes, sir, I do. When on the Sandford Mission, I remember that in preaching one could have slung a buzzard through the roof." "A buzzard through the roof! Why, how could you think of such a thing?" "Very easily," was the reply. "While preaching, I could see them flying overhead." "Ah! yes, I see; time enough, indeed, to think of getting a new church." "But that was not all, sir," he continued. "During service I saw the carriages [this was before the war, and the country surrounding was exceedingly rich] rolling by to another church beyond, and I thought it time to stop that going by." And so, as in many other things competitive, the new brick church was the result of that thought. Constituted as men are, there must be competition, civilly and religiously as well; and the energizing influences of Methodism are much indebted to the aphorism, "As much as in me is." In all matters relating to the extension of Christ's kingdom it can never be a matter of mere living. That is very good in its place, but "man shall not live by bread alone" supersedes all other considerations; so that when James Jenkins began preaching at Winnsboro and a brother minister took it as an act of unkindness, as "taking the bread out of his mouth," all knowing the old veteran and the animus inspiring him are not surprised at his answer: "If bread was all he was after, it made no matter how soon he lost it." A living, and how to obtain it, was the very last consideration of that old prophet. His one business was to preach, whether they would hear or forbear.

The first members at Winnsboro were Captain Buchanan and wife, Captain Harris and wife, and Major Moore. After reading the "rules" in the courthouse, Mr. Jenkins invited attendance at a class meeting. Some twenty-five were present, and they had a "solemn and profitable time." Soon after a church was built, and dedicated in 1800 by Reddick Pierce, the presiding elder. This venerable structure we saw just before its removal. It was square in form, high-roofed, and resounded often with prayer and praise conducted by the fathers. Under date of December 26, 1809, Bishop Asbury writes: "I made an acquaintance with a venerable pair, Mr. Buchanan and wife, Presbyterians, and happy in the experience of religion. A brick chapel is building at Winnsboro for the Methodists." Second Sabbath in December, 1810: "At Winnsboro I preached to a few people." December 9, 1812: "I came to Winnsboro late at night." November 13, 1814: "I preached at Winnsboro a long discourse on 1 Peter iv. 17, 'For the time is come that judgment must begin at the house of God,' etc. Monday at the widow Means's."

A bell (now cracked and long laid aside) adorned this structure. Bishop Asbury, under date of Augusta, November 16, 1786, writes: "And behold, here is a bell over the gallery—and cracked, too; may it break! It is the first I ever saw in a house of ours in America; I hope it may be the last." Good old man! Doubtless he thought, with many of the early Methodists, that it was best to have the bell in the pulpit.

A neat wooden church, the outcome of the energetic action of Brother Thomas Jordan and a few others, is now our place of worship. A parsonage alone is wanting to render complete a monument to zeal and liberality that shall be enduring. The ladies of the church are looking and laboring to this end, and I would by no means be surprised if Brother Jordan, after awhile, impatient at the delay, should come to their help in pretty much the same way as the church was built. "So mote it be."

Near where the old church stood Hilliard Judge is buried. His tomb has the following inscription: "Sacred to the memory of Rev. Hilliard Judge, who was born in Halifax county, N. C., on the 6th of March, 1787; and ended his labors, life, and afflictions in triumph, March, 1817, aged near thirty. He was early converted to God, and labored an ambassador of his for more than fourteen years, with fidelity, zeal, approbation, and success; of which many in Virginia, the two Carolinas, and Georgia are witnesses. This stone is erected at the request of his surviving bosom friend, left to mourn her loss with their child." Near by is another monument to the memory of "Rev. John Raidford Pickett, born April 2d, 1814. He was baptized by the Rev Hilliard Judge in 1817, assuming this consecration personally in the year 1834. He was immediately sent into the itinerancy by his presiding elder, Rev. Bond English, and continued to his death, which was March 15, 1870."

From Winnsboro the travel, after a day's riding, took the preachers to the old Union Church, between Fisher's Creek and Catawba River. This was among the first Methodist churches organized in the country Two other churches were colonized from it, namely, Mount Prospect and El Bethel. Farther away are the remains of one of the earliest structures, where in 1809 Bishop Asbury preached, saying it was "a log cabin scarcely fit for a stable." In this country and attendant on these churches were the Hardins, Hicksons, Howzes, Heaths, McCullys, and others well worthy of mention. Gladden's Grove and Mount Moriah, although noted in their day, have now disappeared. Pleasant Grove, erected mainly through the efforts of W. T. D. Cousar, where the Keys worship, and Richburg later still, are choice exponents of Methodism to-day.

Chester, once called Chester Hill and Chesterville, ably represents Methodism now. In the early days all denominations worshiped in the courthouse. Judges, lawyers, lecturers, showmen, ministers, all occupied it. Then there was no house of worship in the town. The Baptists were the first to build. The Presbyterians worshiped at Purity, two miles away. The Methodists had a church at Smith's Chapel, five miles from Chester. Mrs. Terry was the first and only member in Chester. Her house was the preachers' home. James Graham subsequently became a leading and influential member. Until 1837 there was no organization, when T. R. Lipsey, James Graham, Robert Walker Thomas Terry, Mrs. Terry, and Adelaide Stokes, together with Isaac McDonald, colored, were organized into a church, and a site was selected for building. Smith's Chapel (now Capers Chapel, near its site) was a small building of hewed pine timber, on Sandy River. It is now extinct, but was then of much importance, the Smiths and Hardins worshiping there.

Armenia was at this time small and feeble, but has much increased in strength. The Presslys and Davises were noted members. Near by was the Bonnet Rock Camp Ground, so called from
a conglomerate formation in the shape of a country bonnet, still
extant. The site of the camp ground is now planted in cotton. New Hope was not far away, where worshiped the Cassels,
Hardins, and Atkinsons. Baton Rouge and Flat Rock were appointments at which there are now no Methodist Church structures.

In 1830, in Columbia, S. C., under Joshua Soule, president,
at the forty-fourth session, the Georgia Conference was set off.
There were reported that year 40,335 white and 24,544 colored
members. At the forty-fifth session but 20,513 white and
19,144 colored members remained in the South Carolina Conference. There were but five districts: Charleston, W. Capers,
presiding elder; Saluda, Robert Adams, presiding elder; Columbia, William M. Kennedy, presiding elder; Fayetteville,
Charles Betts, presiding elder; Lincolnton, H. Spain, presiding elder. The whole number of effective men was sixty-eight.
A decade after, in 1839, the numbers reported were whites,
24,756; colored, 24,822; preachers, 106.

At this time a large part of North Carolina was in the South
Carolina Conference, but at the sixty-fourth session, at Camden, in December, 1849, a goodly part was taken off. At that
Conference the numbers were whites, 34,477; colored, 41,617.
At the sixty-fifth session there were whites, 31,143; colored,
37,840. At the eighty-fourth session, at Cheraw, in December,
1869, the numbers were 42,926 whites; colored not estimated—
such was the disintegration by the war. In 1870 there were reported whites, 32,371—a loss of over 10,000 members, transferred
to the North Carolina Conference; so that from 1870 dates all the
numbers in the South Carolina Conference now. In twenty-
five years, in 1895, were reported 72,651, showing a goodly increase of members. In 1839 there were five districts; in 1849,
six; in 1859, eight; in 1869, nine; in 1879, nine; and in 1889 ten
districts, so remaining until 1895. Owing to the scarcity of
material in relation to the territory of the Conference—for
very few records remain—we turn our annals to the men who
wrought the field, and, in addition to those already named, refer to others more in detail.

Joseph Moore (admitted 1791, died 1851) was a Virginian, born in 1767, and died at the age of eighty-five. For sixty-seven years he was a member of the Church, and a preacher for sixty-five years. His labors in the early years were mostly in the North Carolina and Virginia Conferences, locating in the latter Conference in 1806. In 1826 he entered the South Carolina Conference, laboring eight years; the next year he was made a supernumerary; in 1835 he was without appointment, at his own request, and in 1836 was superannuated, and so continued to the end. His preaching was largely controversial, ever combating doctrinal error. He lived respected, and died beloved in the community around Edgefield. Of large body and of great strength of mind, both failed at the last under protracted years of toil and of disease. His portrait (would there were more portraits of the fathers!) adorns the parsonage at Edgefield.

In 1792, among others admitted were James Jenkins, Tobias Gibson, Coleman Carlisle, and George Clark. Of the first three our annals are full; of the last it may be said that he had quite respectable preaching talents, was always highly esteemed, and very social and pleasant in his manners. Although a man of much wealth, he was very plain in his apparel. On his location in 1801 he resided on Enoree River, Union county. He lived to an advanced age, and the Church in that section was much aided by his influence and talents.

John Harper was from England, and held his authority to preach from Mr. Wesley himself. In 1795 his name appears as stationed in Boston, Mass.; in 1799 in Charleston, S. C., remaining there in 1800 and 1801. In 1803 he located, and settled in Columbia, S. C., when he was eminently useful in building up the Church in that city. Mr. Travis speaks of him in the highest terms—of his "superior intellect," "universal popularity," his affectionate manner toward himself, correcting instead of upbraiding him for any errors. He speaks of his "lucid and well-balanced mind," even in age extreme. He was the first Methodist preacher that ever got any foothold in Columbia, S. C. He was indeed one of the fathers, and in connection with Bishop Asbury, George Dougherty, and Mark Moore, established the Mount Bethel Academy, afterwards transferred to Columbia as the nucleus of what expanded into the South Carolina College. Professor Hammond, from Mount Bethel, was afterwards elected to a chair in the college. Mr. Harper's son William was the first graduate from the college, and afterwards chancellor of the state. John Harper died in the faith. His dust rests in the cemetery at Mount Bethel, and stones marked "J. H." are his only monument.

Lewis Myers was admitted on trial in 1799, and, although in 1830 he transferred to the Georgia Conference, was long a leading and influential member of the South Carolina Conference. For many years he served the Church in the most responsible positions. Of German descent, and not entirely free in the pronunciation of English, it served somewhat in rendering his speech peculiar. In personal appearance he was not attractive; not tall, but rather rotund. He was an earnest, holy, devoted minister of Christ. His mind, plain in order, was by diligence and fervor able to make up what he lacked in genius and culture. He traveled and worked for twenty-eight years, one of the hardest workers in the Church. Often on the Conference floor he was opposed to marriage, and many a speech called the young preacher to reflection before entering on matrimony. His speech was often sententious, one word thrice repeated— " punctuality "—being its entire burden. Tradition states that he went farther even than that, with no word at all—a motion of his forefinger under his chin indicating the propriety of a preacher's shaving clean. What would he say now to see nearly all of them " bearded like the pard? " He, like many others then, was opposed to the needless (?) suspenders. But marrying himself at last, he would turn away the raillery of the younger men by raising his vest a little, saying: " Look here, boys; I have been married but six months, and you see my wife has brought me to the ' gallows ' already. " His life was marked by close economy, and his will revealed the fact that the widows and orphans were his beneficiaries. He died in the faith on the 16th of November, 1851.

CHAPTER XXV.

Pen Pictures—Bishop Roberts: His *Incognito*—Amusing Mistakes Engendered—The Young Preacher—The Class Leader—The Young Lawyer—John Gamewell—Reddick Pierce—James Russell—William M. Kennedy—Samuel Dunwody—Hilliard Judge—Joseph Travis.

BEFORE continuing in chronological order the portraiture of our preachers, as nearly a dozen pages in Dr. Shipp's "Methodism" have been given to a sketch of Bishop George, it may be well to note in these annals another of our early bishops, Robert R. Roberts. He presided at three Conferences in Carolina, namely: the thirty-third, at Camden in 1818; the thirty-seventh, at Savannah, Ga., in 1823; and the thirty-ninth, at Wilmington, N. C., in 1825. Bishop Morris, in Sprague's Annals, gives a full portraiture, from which, as also from other sources, we condense as follows:

Robert Richeford Roberts was born in Maryland, August 2, 1778. His father was a plain farmer, in moderate worldly circumstances. He had no early literary advantages beyond those furnished by the common school. He was pious from early childhood, but not decidedly religious until his fourteenth year. He possessed by nature the elements of an orator—an imposing person, a clear and logical mind, a ready utterance, a full-toned, melodious voice—and to all added an ardent love for souls and an unction from above. He of course became a powerful preacher. He was elected to the episcopacy in 1816. In person he was not above the ordinary height, but broad set and of corpulent habit; so that in full vigor of life his weight was not far from two hundred and fifty pounds. His features were large and manly rather than elegant, and the general expression of his countenance was frank and agreeable. His commanding person and forcible utterance were of service to him as a presiding officer, but he possessed other qualifications—a well-developed common sense, tempered by mildness of disposition. His usual manner in the chair indicated more of the patriarch than of the prelate, more of the friend than of the officer; and yet if on the Conference floor any excited floods of passion were exhibited, he has been known to assume as much authority as would suffice to command any warship engaged in battle, until order was restored—calming all agitation by a few gentle remarks, or by some amusing incident giving a pleasant direction to their thoughts. His most prominently developed trait of character was meekness. He never thought more highly of himself than he should have done; on the contrary, all his movements indicated that he placed too low an estimate upon his own character. He seemed to prefer everyone to himself. He studied the accommodation of others, even at the expense of his own. In 1836, when he had exercised his office twenty years, and was then senior bishop, he tendered his resignation, simply because in his own estimate of himself his powers would be so diminished by the infirmities of age that he could not be safely intrusted with the duties of the position. No one entertained the same opinion, and he was greatly disappointed when no one moved to accept his resignation; and he bore his official honors as a cross to the end of his life. His death was calm and peaceful. His body was deposited in a lonely cornfield on his own farm, but in the year 1844 it was removed to the seat of the Asbury University, by order of the Indiana Conference, and reinterred with appropriate ceremonies. The Rev. Joseph Travis, who was intimately associated with him, gives several relations concerning him, indicative of the correctness of Bishop Morris's estimate of his meekness and humility. Mr. Travis states: "Bishop Roberts was very reluctant to make himself known as a bishop, or even as a minister. He was modest to a fault. He gave me an example of the fact, wherein he was at a certain time truly mortified by keeping *incognito*. It was at a tavern, when he neither asked a blessing at the table nor proposed prayer in the family. Next morning, when he went to pay his bill, the tavern-keeper very mildly replied: 'I never charge Methodist preachers.' On another occasion, calling at a land office to hand in some papers for a friend—the day being cold and disagreeable—the clerk in a polite way asked him " if he would not take a dram." " No, sir, not any," was the reply. The cold winds had considerably reddened the bishop's nose. The clerk looked at him curiously, and then remarked: " Sir, from your looks, I should judge that you were fond of the creature."

Another incident erroneously attributed to Bishop George actually occurred with Bishop Roberts. Traveling through

South Carolina on his way to Augusta, Ga., he sought lodging at Dr. Moore's, a local preacher, in Newberry county. A young traveling preacher was there. The night advanced; supper and prayers were over. The host, having no idea of the character of his guest, did not even ask if he desired supper — expecting that if he did he would call for it. The young preacher and the bishop were to occupy the same bed. They both knelt for prayer at the bedside. Arising, the preacher said: "Sir, if you have no objection I will take the front side of the bed." "None at all," replied the stranger. After getting in bed, the preacher asked the stranger: "Sir, are you a professor of religion?" "I am." "To what Church do you belong?" "To the Methodist." "Do you ever exercise in public?" "I try to do so occasionally." "Where are you going, sir?" "To Augusta." "To the Conference, sir?" "Yes." "What might be your name, sir?" "Roberts." "Ah! we are looking for a bishop of that name to be at our Conference. Are you a relative of his?" "My name is Robert R. Roberts." With that the young preacher gave a leap forward and out of the bed, and for awhile remained silent. At length he replied: "Why, bishop, did you serve us thus? I must rouse the family and let you have supper." "No, no," was the reply, "by no means. I am not hungry." "Well, then, bishop, do take the fore side of the bed." "By no means; I am comfortably situated. Now, my dear brother, let us go to sleep." I rather opine the preacher did not suffer loss: the good bishop put him in charge, in his second year, over a very good circuit, Oakmulgee, Ga.

On another occasion, as related by Mr. Travis, the bishop, traveling in Alabama, stopped at the house of a Methodist. At the table the host asked a blessing, and one of the boarders returned thanks. After rising from the table, he said to the stranger: "Sir, that is your room; you will excuse us, as we are going to meeting to-night." "What meeting?" queried the stranger. "It is what we Methodists call a class meeting." "Well," said the stranger, "if you have no objection, I will walk with you." "None at all; come along." A young man led the class, and after getting through he asked the stranger "if he had a desire to serve God and get to heaven." The reply was, "Yes." "But do you, my strange friend, try to put these good desires into practice?" "I do," was the emphatic answer. "Do you think," my dear sir, "that you enjoy religion?" "I do," was the unhesitating reply. "How long, sir, since you professed religion?" "Upward of thirty years," was the prompt answer. The leader exhorted him to fidelity, watchfulness, and perseverance. Returning home, he was asked to join in family worship. His prayer was so full of heavenly influence that they were surprised. On rising, he bade them good-night and retired. After a little wondering silence, his host said, "I must find out who that stranger is"; and entering the room without any ceremony, he said, "Sir, who are you?" He answered, "My name is Roberts." "Not our Bishop Roberts?" said the man. "I pass for him." "Well, sir," said the brother, "you don't go to bed yet. Come out, come out of this room." And immediately he sent for the leader and introduced the bishop. The young man soon began to apologize for so plain a talk, but was interrupted by the bishop's saying that "he had given him most excellent advice, and that he was determined to practice upon it."

At another time, when he was on a steamboat, a respectable young lawyer, judging that he was some old Methodist preacher, concluded to have some chat with him. He stated that "he had heard Bishops Soule and Emory preach, but was informed that there was another bishop by the name of Roberts, and, although he had never seen or heard him, understood that he was a man of only moderate talents, yet of undoubted goodness, and that he would like to see and hear him." Bishop Roberts permitted the young lawyer to go ahead with all his remarks about the bishop, the Church, etc. On retiring to where his wife was he told her of a long conversation with an old Methodist preacher on deck, pointing him out to her; whereupon she said: "My dear, that is Bishop Roberts, and he baptized me." "Oh, hush!" said the young man; "then I am ruined! I must hasten to apologize to him." But the bishop quickly calmed his feelings, and by his good sense and profound humility raised the young man's esteem to love for him as a man of God truly worthy of his high calling.

Mr. Travis remarks on one special trait in the bishop's character—his entire freedom from partiality in his episcopal administration. He "knew no man after the flesh." Neither talent, influence, nor wealth could warp his mind; justice and equity to all, he ever aimed at.

John Gamewell was born in North Carolina, and was received on trial in 1800. For several years he traveled within that state, and the remainder of his itinerant life in South Carolina. In 1820 he was superannuated, retaining that relation until his death in 1828. During its continuance he traveled and preached as far as he was able. The Rev. Joseph Travis, who was presiding elder on the Pee Dee District, writes of him as traveling with him from point to point—"good company, a good man, and a very acceptable preacher; much given to prayer in private, in the family, and in public.'' His family was admirably reared in the ''nurture and admonition of the Lord." He ever advocated whatsoever was excellent, lovely, and of good report. He especially regarded "cleanliness as next to godliness," and doubtless as he moved among the people had occasion to recommend that virtue. He is said to have once startled his hostess, when he heard her calling to the maid for a "dirty towel to wipe Brother Gamewell's feet," by asking "if a clean one would not do as well." After a laborious and successful ministry and eight years of superannuation, filled up with such labor as he could give the Church he loved, he ceased at once to work and live, dying in peace, October 7, 1828. His dust rests near Conwayboro, S. C.

Reddick Pierce was born in Halifax county, S. C., September 26, 1782, and died in Barnwell county, S. C., July 24, 1860, at the age of seventy-eight years. In 1799 he began a life of prayer on the Three Runs, under the ministry of the Rev. James Jenkins. In 1801 he and his brother, Lovick Pierce, joined the Church. In 1802 he began exhorting sinners to repentance. "A purer Christian never lived. His whole religious life was a rich development of the most guileless devotion to God, his cause and kingdom." It is related of him that attending a Baptist meeting where, after the pastor had preached, the way was opened for religious experiences, Mr. Pierce arose and began one of his soul-stirring exhortations, and in half an hour the floor was nearly covered with the fallen. Many obtained peace. He began his itinerant ministry in 1805. In 1810 he was presiding elder on Saluda District. This year, his health failing, he was superannuated; in 1811 and in 1812 he located, settling in Fairfield county, where he did much in building up the Church. His next removal was to Mount Ariel

to educate his children. His deafness increasing, he became
unable to perform the regular duties of the pastorate, and was
used only as a helper, or as a supply. For many years he never
heard anything that was said in preaching, but always attended.
When asked why he did so, under such circumstances, he replied: " I go to fill my place, as every good man ought." The
judgment of all who ever heard him was that by nature he was
great, and in his own way a powerful preacher. All that was
needed for an intellectual treat was to give him a subject, and
he would discourse on it for hours, with infinitely more of light
and heat and devotion than ever did Coleridge in his celebrated
monologues. The writer, when on the Barnwell Circuit in 1845,
was often privileged to hear him thus discourse at the hospitable home of Mr. Jacob Stroman. Here he spent the last
twelve years of his godly life, and in the ample mansion and
ampler heart of his friend found all that life needed, and all
that kindness could bestow. After the stormy passage over
life's ocean, he entered safely the final port. His dust is at rest
in the Rocky Swamp graveyard.

James Russell entered the Conference with the two Pierces
and nine others in 1805. Born in North Carolina in 1786, he
was about nineteen years of age when he began to preach. At
the time he was scarcely able to spell or read, tradition stating
that at the Waxhaws he was indebted to the children at school
for teaching him his letters. His after circumstances were not
favorable to intellectual culture, but it is very certain that he
lost no opportunity for attaining it. It is said of him " that he
copied no man, was perfectly original, and was preëminently a
Holy Ghost preacher." It is also said of him that not only
the uneducated, but persons of the highest culture, were carried away by his matchless proclamations of the gospel. Thousands were converted under his ministry. Dr. Olin said, " It
was only eighteen months before his dissolution that I became
acquainted with him, and occasionally had the happiness to
hear him preach," and expresses the highest admiration of
" his original genius and irresistibly powerful preaching." In
1815 he located on account of impaired health, and engaged in
merchandising, and became involved in financial embarrass-
ments, from which he was extricated only by death. In person
he was said to be of ordinary stature, perfectly symmetrical in

form, with a well-developed head, keen blue eyes, dark hair, prominent cheek bones, a nose slightly aquiline, and a rather large and handsome mouth. A most admirable analysis of his character, from Dr. Olin's pen, is given in Sprague's "Annals of the American Pulpit," and copied freely, with full acknowledgment from whence derived, by the Rev. William M. Wightman, who closes his record as follows: "During his last illness it was thought by his friends that he was better, and the hope was expressed that he might be able to preach on the next Sunday. 'Before next Sabbath,' said Russell, 'I shall be in paradise.' His words were prophetic." He died at Dr. Meredith Moon's, in Newberry county, on the 16th of January, 1825. Having located, his name, however worthy, does not appear in the necrological record of the South Carolina Conference.

William M. Kennedy was born in North Carolina January 13, 1783. He was converted to God in 1803; admitted on trial in 1805. On circuits he spent three years, on stations fifteen years, on districts fifteen years, and as agent two years—thirty-five years in all. For fourteen years he served the Conference as secretary, and all the while may have been said to be the business agent of the Conference. He was distinguished for soundness of judgment, fine taste, and great tenderness of feeling. He was a manager of men as well as of affairs, preëminent as a peacemaker, and of great personal influence both with preachers and people. In stature he was rather below the medium height, but well proportioned, inclined to corpulence. With an active, nervous temperament, he was always in movement. His face was the very index of kindness and brotherly love. He possessed a voice of remarkable compass and sweetness, which made him the Asaph of the Conference. His preaching was hortatory, full of zeal and love for souls. He was known preëminently as a peacemaker, showing forth his love to God in his love for his fellow-men, and, like Ben Adhem, "his name led all the rest." In 1840 he was reluctantly compelled to take a superannuated relation, and while on a journey, stopping at Dr. Moon's in Newberry county, he died from a stroke of apoplexy.

Samuel Dunwody was born in Pennsylvania, August 3, 1780; was converted in his twenty-second year; admitted to Conference in 1806, and served effectively forty years. He was on

15

circuits twenty-two years, on stations sixteen years, on districts one year, and non-effective nine years, making forty-eight years in all. As a preacher he was original, both as to matter and manner, and his sermons were scriptural and great. He combined the intellectual greatness of the theologian with the simplicity of the child. His manner in the pulpit was unique, scarcely describable. In many respects he was one of the most remarkable men ever connected with our Conference. Ill shaped in body, careless in his attire, with little refinement in manner or attractiveness of style; with a rough voice, monotonous and rapid utterance, awkward gesticulation; with an abstracted, almost idiotic, expression of countenance—he was certainly the most logical and most scriptural preacher in the body. It has often been affirmed that if the Bible were lost he could reproduce it from memory. To the young and old alike possibly, his reading of a hymn was unique, if not amusing, apparently with the endeavor to repeat the entire stanza at a single breath. He seemed to live mentally and religiously in a world of God's special creation. The basis of his philosophy and theology was the Bible, which he seemed to have committed to memory. In the Calvinistic controversy of years past he was the champion of Arminianism, and one sermon was of great force, on the text, "Every plant that my Father hath not planted shall be rooted up." His arguments were scripturally unanswerable, and remain so. At a General Conference, on the great slavery debate the cry was made, "Can't hear you." "You'll hear me presently," he responded; and certainly they did. Mrs. Young, the excellent wife of an Episcopal rector in one of the parishes, writes in Sprague's Annals an admirable sketch. In preaching at a schoolhouse one night, candles had to be provided, and out of the usual order these were used. On seeing them Mr. Dunwody ejaculated: "Spermacity! spermacity! I do believe you want to make an Episcopalian of me." Simplicity and innocence were marked features in his character, and however many might have been amused by his idiosyncrasies, none doubted his sincerity or his ability as a minister of God. The end came as usual to all over threescore and ten—the inevitable retirement and surcease of active labor. It was exceeding pitiful to witness his struggle against it: the worn-out laborer pleading for work, and the stern behest of his brethren refusing it. The thought of location, superannuation, or cessation from a loved employ never entered his mind. He was amazed and confounded when it was realized, and he was told by his loving brethren that he was actually an *old, worn-out man.* The free spirit refused to succumb, but the flesh was weak. Blessed change awaiting us all when the cumbrous flesh shall drop, and we be clothed with the immortality that God giveth! His dust was interred at old Tabernacle, near Cokesbury.

Hilliard Judge was admitted on trial in Virginia in 1806. For eight years he was connected with the South Carolina Conference. His active itinerant life covered eleven years. He located at the close of 1816. From Joseph Travis we learn that he was a preacher of no ordinary talents, and of good report everywhere. He was very pleasant in his manners, never sour or morose. He was equally at home in the palace or the hut. No company, however grand, discomposed him. He was invited to preach before the legislature in Columbia, S. C., and discoursed from, " Except ye repent, ye shall all likewise perish." His discourse was just as plain and emphatic it was as on all occasions elsewhere. He married a lady of Fairfield county, of great personal worth, and of a family distinguished for wealth and intelligence. Mr. Judge died in the faith, and his body rests in the Winnsboro cemetery.

Joseph Travis was born in 1786, in Maryland. When an infant he narrowly escaped death in the burning of his father's house, and by an accident, when three years old, was lamed for life. On the removal of his parents to South Carolina, he was happily converted to God. Hearing the eccentric Lorenzo Dow preach, he resolved to devote himself to the ministry. He was admitted into the Conference in 1807, locating in 1825, but was readmitted into other Conferences. His life extended beyond 1855, but the date of his death is unknown to the writer. He filled important stations and districts, and represented the South Carolina Conference more than once in the General Conference. He located to take charge of the Mount Ariel Academy, and after awhile went West. He has left an autobiography, full of interest concerning the early Church in Carolina, and to which the writer is much indebted in compiling these annals. He died in peace.

CHAPTER XXVI.

The Abbeville Circuit—Mount Ariel—Stephen Olin—James E. Glenn—Joseph Travis—Mrs. Ann Moore—Cokesbury School—Sketch of Preachers—William Capers—Henry Bass—N. Talley—J. L. Belin—J. O. Andrew—H. Spain—C. Betts—James Dannelly—Bond English—M. McPherson—William Crook—George W. Moore—Jacky M. Bradley—David Derrick—William M. Wightman—S. W. Capers—William Martin—John R. Coburn—James Stacy.

LEAVING for awhile the portraiture of our older preachers, we would turn attention to some old circuits, and first among them Abbeville. To find their metes and bounds in the early days, we go by conjecture only. There are no records, and all capable of giving them correctly are now dead. We are inclined to think that the old Saluda, Bush River, and Keewee circuits to some extent covered the territory. In the General Minutes Bush River is first mentioned in 1789, with William Gassaway as preacher in charge. In 1790 Saluda is first named, and in 1803 it is Bush River and Keewee. In 1806 they were separated, and so remained until 1820, when Bush River disappears. In 1821 the record is Saluda, Abbeville, and Keewee, all separate, with Robert L. Edwards on Abbeville Circuit. In 1822 Barnett Smith and Abner P. Many, and in 1823 James Dannelly and Elisha Askew, were the preachers in charge. It remained a separate circuit until, in 1857, it was divided into Abbeville and Cokesbury circuits. In 1839 William M. Wightman was the presiding elder, and Samuel Dunwody and A. M. Chreitzberg the preachers in charge; and at the time of division, sixteen years after, Colin Murchison was on Abbeville and A. M. Chreitzberg on Cokesbury Circuit. The later divisions are in the memory of all, so we need not particularize.

Its earlier history, so far as the meager records exist, is that Cokesbury, formerly called Mount Ariel, was known as connected with the second enterprise of the Church anent education, being the successor of the Mount Bethel Academy, which was founded in 1792 or 1794, and ran successfully until 1800, 1803, or 1806, about which time the South Carolina College was es-

(228)

tablished. Elijah Hammond, teaching at Mount Bethel, was transferred to the college as a professor. Alas! that so many years—some twenty or thirty—should elapse before any steps were taken by the Methodists to secure high schools or colleges. What has been lost to the Church can hardly be estimated. About 1820—the date is not exact—some effort was made for a high school at Tabernacle, near the present Cokesbury. In 1822 the Ogeechee District, extending across the Savannah River, took in Abbeville, Edgefield, and old Pendleton circuits. Joseph Travis was the presiding elder. A school was under way at Tabernacle, under the mastership of Stephen Olin. In 1825 Joseph Travis was induced to locate, in order to take charge of it, and removed to Mount Ariel, afterwards Cokesbury.

It was on this district that a great camp meeting was held in 1822 at Tabernacle. There were over one hundred and fifty conversions. It was here that Stephen Olin began his religious career. From a late article in the New York *Christian Advocate* we gather, as given in his own words, incidents connected therewith. He met a trustee of the institution of which he had come to take charge, and inquiring where it was, he was pointed "to a log cabin, the door hung on a couple of sticks, and the windows miserable." Mr. Olin boarded in the family of a local preacher, James E. Glenn. One day he overheard the mother of the family ask if the teacher opened his school with prayer. This induced him to begin, and it resulted in his conversion. Among his manuscripts was found the following:

ABBEVILLE, S. C., September 21, 1821.

Yesterday, after a long season of darkness and sorrow, it pleased God to manifest his pardoning mercy to my soul. O Lord, the riches of thy goodness are unsearchable! Accept me as one of thy hired servants. Lead me in the way everlasting, and keep my feet from falling. Oh, bring me to see thy face in peace!   STEPHEN OLIN.

Applying for license to preach some little time after, the presiding elder, Mr. Travis, was not favorably affected toward him, and stated his doubts to Mr. Glenn, who replied: "Brother Travis, you don't know the man." Mr. Travis, trusting in Mr. Glenn's good judgment, thereupon ceased opposing him. He was put up to preach, and his sermon was so excellent that Mr. Travis judged it a plagiarism. He was again put up and preached, and that sermon surpassed the first. A third time he was tried, and his effort excelled both of the others. Finally, on Sunday, before an immense congregation, he preached on the daughter of Herodias dancing before Herod. Then he swept the field; and the presiding elder had to conclude that if ever St. Paul was called to the ministry so was Stephen Olin, in which judgment many thousands have since agreed.

Near here James E. Glenn, afterwards the founder of Glennville, Alabama, lived; indeed, it was he who first employed Dr. Olin to teach. Mr. Glenn was a man of no ordinary ability. His polemic gifts were unequaled; his zeal, purity, and knowledge made him a very acceptable minister. As a trustee of Mount Ariel Academy, he had much to do in securing the services of Mr. Travis to teach. Both of them frequently preached in all the surrounding country. In it there was a neighborhood of Hardshells, "great advocates for water, but liking it still better if well mixed with whisky." They were much opposed to the Methodists, and especially to Mr. Glenn. They believed in folklore and witches. Mr. Glenn put up a notice that on a certain day he intended to *kill witches*. The news spread from Dan to Beersheba. The day came, and the crowd was great. The text was, "Thou shalt not suffer a witch to live." He said: "There are witches in this neighborhood; yea, and I believe it. There are at least three: one is called Calvinism; the second, Universalism; and the third, Infidelity." He understood that the best way to kill witches was to draw their pictures and then shoot at them. He drew the picture of Geneva Calvinism, descanting on the horrible decrees, etc., for some time. "Now," said he, "just look at her! What a haggard, frightful old wretch she is!" It was thought *silver* bullets were best to shoot at them with, but he would shoot *golden* balls. You will find the first load in such a book, such a chapter, such a verse. "Now, make ready! Take aim! Fire!" He would then roll out the text loudly and distinctly. And thus on for hours. After this, when he preached the house was always crowded.

Mr. Travis frequently visited Abbeville, the county seat. Having no church, the courthouse was used for divine service. There were but two members there, James Moore and his excellent wife, Ann, of whom too much cannot be said as founders of Methodism in Abbeville. She had been brought up a Roman

Catholic, but, under conviction from the ministry of the Methodists, was in doubt about joining them. Once, after earnest prayer, her eyes fell on these lines:

> I the chief of sinners am,
> But Jesus died for me.

Immediately she exclaimed, "If that is Mr. Wesley's language, I shall be a Methodist!" She joined at once, and was one of the most zealous members. She was foremost in procuring a church. Her perseverance in this good work soon resulted in a very respectable church structure for those days. Well does the writer remember that house, and his attempts at preaching in it fourteen years after its erection, in 1839; well does he remember, also, kind Sister Moore, and her motherly care of his youth. Her house was ever the young preacher's home. Dr. Henry D. Moore, now at Louisville, is her son. He was admitted into the South Carolina Conference in 1857. He has been a member of the Florida, South Georgia, and Alabama Conferences, and now belongs to the Kentucky Conference—having fully experienced the power of transfer, through no fault of his own. He is a worthy son of most excellent parentage.

The portraits of these venerable pioneers in Abbeville are herewith given, together with their son, Dr. Moore, of Louisville, Ky.; and also of William Bird, of Bethel Church, Charleston, S. C., and A. E. Williams, of Round O, S. C., with two elect ladies of Charleston—Mrs. Margaret Just and Mrs. Jackson, long known as zealous workers for God in that city.

Lewis H. Davis, the blind preacher, resided in Abbeville, loved by all. By an accident in his youth he became blind, but that did not hinder his usefulness as a preacher. He joined the Methodists soon after the erection of the church.

The Rev. George Moore and his excellent family resided for a time in Abbeville. His house was likewise the young preacher's home.

The brothers John and Franklin Branch were firm supporters of Methodism in 1839. Two sons of Franklin Branch are esteemed ministers in the Georgia Conference.

The Rev. James Dannelly was often appointed to this circuit, and in 1839, then superannuated, resided at Smyrna, but made frequent preaching tours into Georgia and preached often at Abbeville. The appointments were some twenty or twenty-four, covering the entire county. The houses of worship were ordinary structures, Cokesbury having the only painted house of any architectural shape. The contrast after nearly sixty years is of course exceedingly great.

Cokesbury, as the seat of the Conference school, was the headquarters. Here the presiding elder of the district and the preacher in charge of the circuit resided. Thomas Williams, famed as one of the best stewards of the time, with his devoted household, were strong supporters of the Church. So were James Shackelford, Dr. Francis Connor, Dr. Thomas Cottrell, and Brother Marion devoted Christian men in their day. With the exception of Dr. Cottrell, all were there in 1839. A more lovely or well-regulated community existed nowhere. Many members of the South Carolina Conference received their academical training at this school, and the only regret can be that our Church did not sooner begin the great work of the education of her youth.

In 1839 the Conference had upon its roll 106 effective preachers and superannuates, 111 in all. In 1895 there were but three surviving—William Patterson, Simpson Jones, and the writer.

We resume the pen portraiture of the preachers. It will be seen that priority of record is owing to the date of admission on trial, and but one or two of each class can be given; and while we aim at chronological order, some years will necessarily be omitted. Of fifteen admissions into the Conference in 1809, but one or two will here be named.

The name of William Capers appears frequently in these annals, and his fame is known so well that mention here must necessarily be brief. He was born in St. Thomas Parish, S. C., January 26, 1790. He was admitted into the Conference in 1809, and for forty-six years (except one or two local) served the Church on circuits, stations, districts, and as an editor; and closed up his earthly career in the episcopacy in 1855, at the age of sixty-five. Tradition states that at his birth, like Philip Doddridge, he was seemingly dead, and the doctor said that he would soon die; but the attendants, thinking differently, labored for his resuscitation, the nurse declaring that "he would yet be a bishop." As to person, he was shaped most faultlessly in form and feature; of medium height, with a voice of wonderful sweetness and power; a keen black eye, and, as his portraits show, all in all most beautiful. His influence on Methodism was world-wide, and in the Carolinas and Georgia will be enduring. We are not surprised that so large a space is given in Dr. Shipp's "Methodism in South Carolina" to his life and labors, with such large extracts from his excellent autobiography. To that we would refer all readers who appreciate beauty of style, with true simplicity and godly sincerity. The end came, as we poor mortals judge, all too soon. He died as he had lived, an earnest man and minister, and a most decided Methodist. In his last illness, after a paroxysm of pain, he asked the hour, and when the answer was given, he said: " What! only three hours since I have been suffering such torture! Only three hours! What then must be the voice of the bird that cries, 'Eternity! eternity!' Three hours have taken away all but my religion." Not long after, he sank back upon his bed and breathed his last. His sacred dust is interred in the Washington street cemetery, Columbia, S. C.

One other name connected with this class of fifteen who were admitted on trial in 1809 was the very antipodes of William Capers, and only serves to show the propriety of the year's trial before one can become a member of the Conference; and likewise the further propriety that when one is found wanting he is speedily dismissed. The contrary course of action, to our certain knowledge, has burdened the Conference with men who could not teach, and who were too dull to learn. In this case the Conference promptly discontinued the applicant after one year's trial. Dr. G. G. Smith, in his " Methodism in Georgia," thus discourses concerning William Redwine: " Dr. Pierce says he once called on Redwine to exhort after him. He took a text: ' Behold, ye despisers, and wonder and perish.' The first of the despisers was the deist. ' He stands,' said the preacher, ' with his legs as wide apart as if he was the empire of France, and he won't hear any man preach who can't speak romatically and explay oratory.'" Clearly, it is not every good man that is called to preach.

Henry Bass was born in Connecticut, December 9, 1786. He removed to Fayetteville, N. C., and was converted and joined the Church in 1807. He was admitted into the Conference in 1812, and was on circuits and stations nineteen years, on districts eighteen years, and superannuated eleven years—forty-

eight years in all. He was not over tall in person, but of medium size, with an apparent sternness of mein. His gravity,
good common sense, and conscientiousness obtained for him
position and influence for many years. Such was his gravity
that he never relished any lightness of spirit. No one could
think for a moment of taking liberties with him, and yet all
were ready to go to him for counsel or sympathy. He had
much of the New England puritan, combined with the true joy
of the Christian. He was without blame and reproach—the good
pastor, safe counselor, and steadfast friend. In the close of his
life he was a great sufferer from cancer, and from which he died
May 13, 1860, at Cokesbury. His mortal remains were buried
at Tabernacle Church. In his protracted sufferings he was steadfast in the faith, giving glory to God, and frequently exclaiming, " How good the Lord is! I trust in him above all."

Nicholas Talley was born in Virginia, May 2, 1791; converted to God in 1810; admitted into the Conference in 1812. He
effectively served the Church on circuits, stations, and districts
for fifty-three years, and was superannuated a little over seven
years—thus being for more than sixty years a member of the body.
This is the longest record of effective service in the Conference
with the exception of one other, who received fifty-four appointments and has been a superannuate for five years. Mr. Talley
was above the common height, and of great physical endurance;
his face was expressive of intelligence and benevolence; his voice
was not musical, but rather nasal, and his delivery somewhat
monotonous; yet, in all his ministry, he was self-possessed,
dignified, and refined. His preaching was hortatory in character and often powerful in effect, his ministry popular and successful. He lived to the age of eighty-two years, and his death
was peaceful. His last uttered words were: " Calm, calm."
His dust rests in the Washington street cemetery, Columbia,
S. C.

James L. Belin was born in All Saints' Parish, S. C., in 1788;
admitted into the Conference in 1812; and, after forty-seven
years' connection with the Conference, died May 19, 1859,
and was buried on the mission premises, on Waccamaw Neck.
He was staid in manner, and would not impress one as being
very genial in temperament, and yet he was always most benevolent and kind. He was slow of speech, deliberate in all his

ABBEVILLE METHODIST CHURCH; REV. J. A. CLIFTON, D.D., PASTOR.

movements, and as steady as the needle to the pole in all that was pure and of good report. During all his life he was much concerned for the cause of missions to the slaves, and was among the very first to serve them as early as 1819, and in 1836 formed the Waccamaw Mission, to which he bequeathed his entire estate. His death was caused by a fall from his buggy, and the testimony of a holy life shows that his end was peace.

James O. Andrew (Bishop Andrew), although transferred to Georgia in 1830, when the South Carolina Conference was divided, passed a large part of his life in Carolina. Some memorial of him should be placed in these annals. He entered on trial in the South Carolina Conference in 1813, was transferred to Georgia in 1830, and in 1832 was elected to the episcopacy. Seventeen years of his earlier ministry were in connection with the South Carolina Conference. In personal appearance he, in his early days, was leonine, to the writer seeming to resemble that prince of men, Oliver Cromwell. He was not tall, but stout, with a wealth of curly hair, and features expressive of great self-reliance and determination of will; his manner simple and entirely natural. His under lip protruded, giving expression to his various moods, with no approach to self-conceit. In speech he was quick, somewhat brusque, but not crabbed. He seemingly would have grappled with a giant, but never harming a pigmy. His style in the pulpit was discursive, never apparently following any well-arranged plan; but his grasp of thought was gigantic, his sermons clear, forcible, and convincing, and full of unction, amply attesting his spiritual power. In a word, he was the Boanerges of the Conference in that early day. Under complete control himself, he always had his audience entirely at his command. The chair of any Conference was to him a throne of power, his decisions being quickly made, kindly expressed, and rarely called in question. Like many great men, he was careless as to dress, but by no means slovenly. It was inquired in parliament of Cromwell once, "Who is that sloven?" "That sloven," said Hampden, "if we ever come to an issue with the king, will be the greatest man in England." James O. Andrew, though never called to kingly rule, stood in his lot heroically to the end of his days.

Hartwell Spain was born in Wake county, N. C., February 10, 1795; converted to God in 1810; admitted into the Conference in 1817. His connection with the Conference in the active ministry, with the exception of six years' local work, embraced twenty-five years. Owing to feeble health he was, from time to time, superannuated about twenty-six years. In person he was tall, slender, and graceful; his face expressive of intelligence and amiability. In preaching he was at first very deliberate —indeed, slow. A stranger would predict failure, but as he warmed with his subject great would be the change, his tones louder, utterances quickened, and his face very expressive. After awhile his whole nature seemed aglow, a transformation such as Patrick Henry's had occurred; his face shone with an unearthly radiance, an entire cessation of self was apparent, and he seemed aflame with God. His audience caught the influence, and, borne along on the stream of his eloquence, felt that truly God was with him, and high religious enthusiasm was always aroused. His efficient ministry was sadly hindered by inefficient health. His old age was protracted beyond the usual length of time. He died at Summerton, S. C., fully attesting his joy in the Lord.

Charles Betts was born in North Carolina in 1800; converted in his sixteenth year, and for fifty-two years itinerated in our Conference. One year he was local, and one superannuated, but for all the rest was entirely zealous in the work of the ministry. His consistent piety, vigorous intellect, and untiring energy gave him a leading position in the Conference. In personal appearance he was compact, rotund, strong, almost fierce at times. In the pulpit he was something like Richard Watson, interminable in the construction of his sentences, but as a platform preacher he swept the field. He was a man of affairs, and largely useful in all the business of the Church. His brethren honored him with eight returns to the General Conference. His end was peace. Dying in Marion county, his body was buried at the county seat. Taken all in all, he was a remarkable man and minister. Ardent and firm in his attachments, and courageous in the advocacy of the right, he made many friends, being popular both with preachers and people. He had a powerful physical frame, and his severe labors taxed it to the uttermost. After fifty-two years of toil, he rests from his labors.

James Dannelly was born in Columbus county, Ga., February 4, 1786; converted in 1816, in his thirtieth year; admitted into the Conference in 1819. Being a man of great affliction, he traveled but fourteen years; during the remainder of the time he was superannuated. He was one of the most eccentric, and yet ranked among the ablest, preachers of his day. By a scrofulous taint from birth, and on that account in boyhood, he lost a limb, and never knew a well day during his life. He was a heavy man, and moved about with difficulty. His eyes were expressive, and shone at times fearfully. His manner in the pulpit was peculiar: he used to stand balancing himself, looking deliberately on his congregation, panting for breath, snapping his gray, twinkling eyes; and then in a fine, almost squeaking voice he would announce his text, giving utterance to some simple truth or illustrative anecdote, and gained the attention of his audience, then in his simple, monosyllabic style held his hearers spellbound to the end. On some occasions he was grand in thought beyond description; at other times he was cynical, sharp, even snappish. He lashed the popular vices unsparingly. He was fearless, bold, and direct to an amazing degree. One who knew him well would often say of him: "If he did not edify, he would be sure to scarify." Sinners gnashed upon him with their teeth, cursed him, and swore that they would never hear him again, and yet be the first at his next appointment. On the authority of Bishop Wightman it is stated: "Mr. McDuffie, then a senator in congress, heard his withering denunciations of vice in high and low places, his graphic delineations of the modes in which the vulgar undertake to imitate the fashionable follies of high life. The statesman, himself an orator of celebrity, and famous for the vigor of his onslaughts, was so struck with the pungency of the discourse that, on retiring, he said to a friend: 'This is certainly one of the ablest sermons I have ever heard; it told the truth, the whole truth, and nothing but the truth, though in the roughest possible manner.' So strong was the impression made upon Mr. McDuffie that he solicited Mr. Dannelly to visit Washington City, and preach the same sermon before congress, offering to pay his expenses." With all this, it must not be supposed that Mr. Dannelly was destitute of the finer feelings of our nature. He had a heart as tender as a woman's, and was often affected to tears. As a husband and father he was most indulgent. In 1839 the writer, as junior preacher on the circuit where he lived, without knowing him, dreaded his acquaintance; but this fear proved groundless when the old preacher took him to his home and heart. His soul was purified by suffering and pain. He loved Methodism as the very best expression of the truth of God, and he fairly wore himself out in the service of the Church. His record is with God, and his reward on high. He died at his residence, at Lowndesville, Abbeville county, and was buried at old Smyrna Church.

Bond English was born in Kershaw county, S. C., January 31, 1797. He was converted in 1817, admitted in 1821, and died March 4, 1868, in the seventy-first year of his age. For nearly forty-seven years he was an honored minister in the South Carolina Conference—modest, retiring, self-depreciating, clear-headed, warm-hearted, and eloquent. In person he was small of stature, inclined to be corpulent, lame from an accident, and blind in one of his eyes. He was quick and impulsive in all his movements, and diffident almost to a fault. He read men intuitively, and was rarely mistaken in judging character, but was not born to control by inflexible will. He was well fitted for any kind of ministerial work, but, yielding to discouragements, located in the prime of life. Readmitted, increasing infirmities placed him among the superannuated. His manner in the pulpit was ardent, and not unfrequently caused stirring emotion. His sermons were deeply spiritual, simple, natural, and, best of all, full of the divine Spirit. He was greatly beloved wherever he labored, and was successful in his ministry. He died in peace near Sumter, S. C., and his dust rests in the cemetery there.

Malcolm McPherson, a native of North Carolina, was connected with the South Carolina Conference eighteen years, for ten of which he was presiding elder. The Rev. Samuel Leard pronounces him a master in Israel. Before his conversion he was a terror to the bullies of his native county. His was the true Scotch type of manliness, shrewdness, and soundness of judgment. Stern in manner, slow of speech, exacting in duty, he was always solemn and decorous in all things relating to the worship of God. His sermons were clear and simple in arrangement, with an earnestness and unction at times overwhelming. As a preacher he was not always equal to himself; if he failed, he failed; but when he succeeded, he passed beyond the limit of ordinary men. To those knowing him well he was as open and gentle as a child; but woe to the sinner who provoked his rebuke in the congregation! What he said in public he was ready to maintain in private, and the sight of his broad shoulders, heavy hands, and determined face has made more than one pause before seeking a personal encounter. The impress of his clear intellect, sound judgment, deep-toned piety, and his unwavering faith in God, is well remembered even to this day. Much to the regret of the Conference, he emigrated to the West. In 1840 he served, with great acceptability, the Holly Springs District, and was appointed the next year to the same work, but died before the year closed. Joseph Travis, whom he claimed as his spiritual father, preached his funeral sermon at the Memphis Conference in 1842.

William Cook was born in Chester county, S. C., in 1805. He was converted in early life, and admitted in 1825. He traveled extensively in North Carolina and South Carolina; was frequently on stations, and served eight years as presiding elder. He was noted as an excellent singer, and was greatly beloved as a pastor and Christian. After traveling thirty-six years, and being superannuated six years, he died in the triumphs of faith, in York county, November 25, 1867.

George W. Moore was born in Charleston, S. C., September 27, 1799. He was converted in 1819, admitted on trial in 1825, filled various appointments until 1837, located in 1838, and was readmitted in 1839. He was one of the first missionaries to the slaves. He ceased at once to work and live, at a camp ground in Anderson county, S. C., August 16, 1863. He was well known as a zealous and faithful minister of Christ. His ashes lie in Bethel cemetery, Charleston, S. C.

Jacky M. Bradley was admitted in 1826, and traveled regularly until 1860, when he removed to the West, and died during the civil war. He was a remarkable man, physically, spiritually, and mentally—tall and loosely built, with large head and long, bony arms and hands. Of his personal courage none doubted who glanced at his stalwart body. He cared little for dress, and was always unclerical in appearance. His mind was seemingly in unison with the leading traits of his body. He was always fearless and independent; was never governed by any of the laws of elocution. He copied no man either in subject-matter

16

or in manner of delivery. With a mind of great native strength, he was sound in doctrine, clear in his own religious experience, and utterly fearless; he was indeed a giant in the pulpit. His independence in feeling often gave offense, but he never cherished malice against any. His voice was harsh and his utterance rapid, often elevated almost to a scream, accompanied by a habit of expectoration by no means graceful; and yet, withal, he was most powerful in debate and in the pulpit. His was evidently a hard lot in life. He was a diligent worker, and but poorly recompensed as to this world's goods. His record is with God, and his reward is on high.

David Derrick was born July 28, 1800. He was admitted on trial in 1827. After long years of superannuation, he died in 1883. Reared as a Lutheran, under Methodist preaching he was awakened and converted, and faithfully served the Church until failing vigor caused his retirement; but all those years of feebleness only made his godly life more conspicuous. Having a voice of power and sweetness, he excelled in song, and was gifted in prayer. Faithful and true as a pastor, he was eminently useful in the Church. His body rests in Columbia cemetery.

William M. Wightman was born in Charleston, January 29, 1808. He was admitted on trial in 1828, and died in Charleston, February 15, 1882. His name stands last in a class of twenty admitted at the forty-second session of the South Carolina Conference, held at Camden in 1828—Joshua Soule, presiding; but from the beginning he was always first on the roll of the Conference until his election to the episcopacy in 1866. In 1828 he traveled the Pee Dee Circuit with Philip Groover and William Culverhouse; in 1829, Orangeburg Circuit, with Elisha Callaway; in 1830, stationed in Charleston; in 1831, preacher in charge on Santee Circuit; in 1832, Camden; in 1833, Abbeville Circuit; 1834–38, agent for Randolph-Macon College; in 1839–40, presiding elder of Cokesbury District; in 1841, editor of the *Southern Christian Advocate*, so remaining until 1854; in 1855, president of Wofford College, and was connected with colleges and universities until elected to the episcopacy in 1866. For many years he was the *Magnus Apollo* of our Conference, and it is marvelous that one who wrought so long for the Church, and so well, should lack a proper biography. An article in the *Review* for 1896 indicates clearly that a proper biographer can easily be found. His memory is honored by a tablet on the walls of Trinity Church, Charleston, and his body rests in Magnolia cemetery.

Samuel Wragg Capers was born in Georgetown, S. C., March 5, 1797. He was admitted into the Conference in 1828. He was a half-brother of Bishop Capers. He was a large man, above medium size, with full, round face, short neck, fine head firmly set on ample shoulders, and a face expressive of much intelligence and good humor. His voice was like a trumpet, clear, loud, and commanding. He filled well the offices of presiding elder, college agent, and circuit preacher. He was superannuated in 1855, and died the same year. His dust rests in the Camden cemetery.

William Martin was born in North Carolina, March 9, 1870. He was admitted on trial in 1828. He died in Columbia, S. C., January 10, 1889. For sixty-one years he was a member of the South Carolina Conference, serving on circuits, stations, and districts, in agencies, and as president of the Columbia Female College. During the civil war he was superintendent of the bureau of relief for the soldiers. His preaching was expository, his style simple and fervent, and his illustrations plain and pointed. His death was eminently calm and peaceful. His body sleeps in Washington street cemetery, Columbia, S. C.

John R. Coburn was born in Charleston county, September 18, 1799. He died in Florence, S. C., September 29, 1880, in the eighty-second year of his age. He was long a laborious and successful missionary to the slaves, having the full confidence of the planters and the ardent affection of those to whom he ministered. His end was peace.

James Stacy was a native of Burke county, N. C., and was born November 18, 1807. He was admitted into the Conference in 1830, and served the Church thirty-eight years, dying at Sumter in 1868. "Called, chosen, and faithful" may well be said of him. To a sound religious experience he added abilities of a high order. He was a student all his life, and showed his profiting by constant study in his ministrations in the pulpit. Of an extremely nervous temperament, he was often a great sufferer mentally as well as bodily; but he never failed to meet the full demands of his ministry. About his last words were, "Harvest home."

CHAPTER XXVII.

TO the antiquarian old journals are valuable. I have been favored with a sight of the journal of the old Orangeburg Circuit. The first record is dated Cattle Creek, August 7, 1819 —seventy-eight years ago—closing April 2, 1870. There is very little of historical interest in these old journals save the routine business of a Quarterly Conference; yet the names recorded call up the fathers of many now foremost in the good work of the Church, the records also showing great advancement in temporal interests at least, while we sincerely hope that the spiritual interests are not one jot abated.

It is hard to make out the boundaries of our ever-changing circuits, widening as to religious influence, and yet contracting as to territorial limits. The writer well remembers the great opposition to the cutting-up process by which circuits of from twenty-four to thirty-five appointments were brought down to eight and four, giving better service to the people and far better support to the preachers concerned. In the beginning many presaged ruin, but results show the reverse.

The old Edisto Circuit, which embraced Orangeburg, was formed in 1787. The record in the General Minutes for 1787 is, Beverly Allen, presiding elder; Edisto, Edward West; Charleston, Lemuel Green. The returns of membership for Edisto were 340 whites and 25 colored. The next year, 1788, for Edisto, Henry Bingham and William Gassaway were the preachers. The circuit so remained as to territory until 1800, when Orangeburg is mentioned, with Lewis Myers preacher in charge. In 1801 the record is Orangeburg and Edisto; the next year the names were reversed to Edisto and Orangeburg; in 1804 they were reversed again; in 1806 the name was changed to Edisto and Cypress; in 1807 the two were separate, and so remained up to 1812, when Edisto disappears, leaving Cypress, Saltketcher (Salkehatchie), Black Swamp, and Orangeburg, with William Capers preacher in charge. Its boundaries as already given by Bishop Capers are on record. These boundaries must have been afterwards enlarged, inasmuch as Green Pond Camp Ground is often a place of Quarterly Conference meetings, and there is record in 1832 of a building committee for a church to be built at Walterboro. But here we would place on record the names of members of this third Quarterly Conference held at Cattle Creek, August 7, 1819. They were James Norton, presiding elder; John Schreble, Matthew Raiford, and George Hill, circuit preachers; James Koger, Henry Seagrist, Joseph Howell, and Joseph Winningham, local deacons; Andrew Inabinet, John McCormick, and John Jeffcoat, licentiates; Martin Gramling, Christian Gramling, and David Riley, exhorters; Thomas Simpson, George Pooser, Lewis Bryant, George A. Campbell, Thomas Cliffts, John Staley, and Andrew H. Jones, class leaders. Other names appearing at other early Quarterly Conferences are Jacob Barr, Gideon Hutto, Richard Bryant, Peter Hyatt, James Crosby, Benjamin Tarrant, Jacob Whetstone, Robert Robinson, Thomas McAdams, and William Dickenson, local preachers; Stephen Ackerman, David Felder, Daniel Herlong, Benjamin Jeffcoat, John Chreitzberg (an uncle of the writer, and who died in Alabama a local preacher), and Jacob Jeffcoat, class leaders. In addition to the foregoing, from a full list under date of October 7, 1826, we gather the names of Daniel F. Wade, John Murrow, and Wilson Langley; and Samuel Inabinet, Jacob Doremus, John Wannamaker, Calvin Hyden, Benjamin Culler, Jacob Wannamaker, and Samuel Smoak, exhorters; John Golson, Edward Bolen, Christian Riley, John Staley, John Rhode, Gotleib Zeigler, James A. Williams, and Jacob Hook, class leaders; Thomas Raysor and Jacob Inabinet, stewards. Other stewards named in 1829 are Andrew Inabinet, David Dannelly, William Pou, Charles V. Stewart, and Isham Lowery; as exhorters, Jacob S. Linder and Robert J. Boyd; as class leaders, William Varn, Henry Ulmer, Thomas O'Bryan, John L. Golson, and Joseph McAlhany.

This is a large array of names, but useful to call up some memories of the past. Farther on we reach the names of the Dantz-

lers, Keitts, Klecklys, and others; but for the present let us
glance at financial matters. These were the old days of traveling expenses, quarterage, and family expenses. The quarterage rarely reached $300, and the family expenses from $200 to
$300. In 1829 the committee reports that they "find the sum
of $175 needful for that purpose." This was not likely paid, as
it is provided that the trustees of the parsonage, from its sale,
pay over to the stewards enough to pay the rent of the house
occupied by the preacher; a measure, we fancy, not likely to
obtain now. In 1834 Benjamin H. Capers, preacher in charge,
was allowed:

For corn...	$125 00
For fodder.......	25 00
For bacon	50 00
For sugar..	20 00
For coffee.....	14 00
For tea..	2 50
For beef...	10 00
For flour....	18 00
For lard...	12 50
For soap...	5 00
For candles..	5 00
For butter.	10 00
For salt...	3 00
For freight, extras, and servant hire..................	100 00
Total..	$400 00

Those dear old brethren closely scanned the dietary ability
of their preacher.

After Matthias Pooser was elected secretary the records are
fine, especially the financial statements, two of which we give.
The recapitulation is as follows:

FOR 1840.

		Receipts.	Deficit.
For presiding elder...........$	152 50	$100 15	$ 52 35
For preacher in charge	500 00	327 08	172 92
For junior preacher...........	548 00	358 26	187 74
Total....................$	1,200 50	$785 49	$413 01

FOR 1841.

		Receipts.	Deficit.
For presiding elder. ....$	154 00	$ 89 94	$ 64 06
For preacher in charge........	525 00	343 50	181 50
For junior preacher...........	525 00	343 50	181 50
Total....................$	1,204 00	$776 94	$427 06

For 1852 there is the most complete record of all amounts collected and paid out. The entire collection was:

Paid the presiding elder	$115 00
Paid the preacher in charge	609 37
Paid the junior preacher	100 00
Traveling expenses	83 38
Total	$907 45

This was collected from the following churches: Wesley Chapel, $120; Asbury Chapel, $100; Tabernacle, $100.50; Shady Grove, $100; New Hope, $52; Orangeburg, $45; Cattle Creek, $40; Prospect, $43; Laurel Chapel, $50; Bethel, $23; Calvary, $23; Andrew Chapel, $39.75; Bethlehem, $30.50; Zion, $34.50; Sardis, $28.75; Ebenezer, $15; Trinity, $26; Kedron, $20; Gethsemane, $10; Humility, $8. In a little over forty years there has been much of an advance. There are now eight or nine preachers within the same boundary at a cost of some $5,000, to say nothing of amounts raised for benevolent purposes.

In 1841 the Orangeburg preachers were Henry Bass, presiding elder; Allen McCorquodale, preacher in charge; and A. M. Chreitzberg, junior preacher. Fifty-five years of time's annals seem prodigious. Many with whom we were then associated have crossed the flood. The appointments were eighteen, to wit: Asbury Chapel, Shady Grove, Tabernacle, Orangeburg, New Hope, Cattle Creek, Sardis, Humility, Bethlehem, Zion, Limestone, Gethsemane, Jeffcoat's, Trinity, Calvary, Pizgah, Wesley Chapel, and Prospect. No one church gave much over $100. Salaries were settled in 1841 at a discount of 41.59 per cent for presiding elder; and for the preachers, each of whom was allowed $525, at 34.57 per cent. Meager as were these returns they were a tremendous advance over earlier years, and many a preacher in that age rejoiced when read out for Orangeburg Circuit. There were received into the Church during the year 145; expelled, 31; Sunday schools, 4; teachers, 16; scholars, 88. The local preachers were John Wannamaker, Samuel Smoak, John S. Gray, L. J. Crum, and John Law; exhorters, John Hooker, Samuel Inabinet, Calvin Hoger, and Francis Baxter; stewards and leaders, George H. Pooser, D. R. Barton, Jacob H. Pooser, Lewis Zeigler, John L. Golson, M. H. Pooser, James Berry, John Fairy, Daniel Funches, James Cox, E. T. Pooser, Peter Oliver, A. Pooser, A. Whetstone, A. Inabinet, W. Jeff-

coat, John J. Salley, Thomas Tatum, Henry Moorer, Adam
Holman, and Lewis Rast. The four principal churches were
Asbury Chapel, Tabernacle, Wesley Chapel, and Shady Grove.
Of Orangeburg, more in the sequel. Contrasted with others
they may have been regarded as being on the cathedral order.
They were usually assessed $100 each, which large sum for the
times was usually paid without discount. Asbury Chapel had
been built for an academy, and afterwards used as a chapel.
The Keitts, Dantzlers, and Wannamakers worshiped there. Tabernacle was more in churchly shape. It is now abandoned, and
fast going to ruin. Thomas Zimmerman and the Dantzlers are
kindly remembered. Shady Grove was but ordinary, yet well
represented by Adam Holman and Morgan Keller. But what
shall we say of Wesley Chapel? The long, low, time-worn
structure was in use close up to the nineties, and has since, we
hope, given place to a better building. That good man John
Riley was a power there. Asbury Chapel has vanished, and is
superseded by St. Paul's at St. Matthew's City, an improvement
in every way over the Asbury of the olden times. To Dr. Pou,
the Wannamakers, and others this is certainly due, and St.
Paul's stands out upon the record in St. Matthew's Circuit.
With mournful interest we visited old Tabernacle in 1888. The
lines of desolation were there—the old graveyard overgrown
with weeds. Here reposes the dust of the noble rivals, Dantzler
and Keitt. Memory ran back to half a century and more, when
many came here to worship. The gospel of the blessed God has
been sounded out from that old pulpit for many years by men not
taught in the schools, it is true, but who were full of faith and
the Holy Ghost, and of whom the world was not worthy. Glance
at the record, will you? Isaac Smith, Enoch George, Tobias
Gibson, James Jenkins, Lewis Myers, George Dougherty, William Gassaway, Richmond Nolley, Samuel Dunwody, William
Capers, William M. Kennedy, Samuel K. Hodges, and James
O. Andrew. The lesser lights are not here set down, but are
not forgotten in heavenly archives. All these were on this
work previous to 1830. After that time there were William M.
Wightman, Bond English, William H. Ellison, J. C. Postell,
R. J. Boyd, and others.

A portion of the circuit about Trinity, Calvary, etc., was under culture with indigo. Well do we remember the vats of

Lewis Zeigler, the Whetstones, the Cullers, and others. The other sections were devoted to the culture of cotton. Many of the people of that section were well off, but their contributions to religious purposes, as the assessments on the entire number of churches show, must have been exceedingly meager. There were no other collections, except at long intervals, and yet only a few hundred dollars were raised from twenty churches, from year to year, for the support of three preachers. The extent of the work and a lack of knowledge on the part of the people, together with a delicacy on the part of the preachers in insisting on a better support, account for it. Besides, with the great mass of the people, money was rarely seen. To have one or two hundred dollars for division on a Quarterly Conference table was a sight indeed. Some used to wonder what a preacher could do with a hundred dollars. They saw him once a month, hale and hearty, always cheerful, with store clothes on, and always driving a fat horse, with the very best things most cheerfully given him when entertained by them. What was the use of money to men of his class? Is it any wonder that with them the technical "quarterage" meant anything more than twenty-five cents a quarter? The preachers in 1829 were William Capers, presiding elder; Elisha Callaway, preacher in charge; and William M. Wightman, junior preacher. For the support of the three but a little over six hundred dollars was assessed, and yet the final settlement was made at a heavy discount. We are glad to say that the junior preacher got his hundred dollars in full, he having but a little while before refused a thousand-dollar salary in another employment. Was it money that moved these men? The idea is preposterous.

In 1863 the circuit contained twelve appointments, namely: Orangeburg, Bethel, Cattle Creek, Humility, Sardis, Prospect, Asbury Chapel, Tabernacle, Shady Grove, New Hope, Bethlehem, Zion, with the Rev. John W. Kelly as preacher in charge. The collections were better, the four Quarterly Conferences showing a total of $1,321.45, the stewards' meeting (not recorded) rendering possibly about as much. But you will remember that those were the flush times of Confederate money.

Suffer a word or two as to the Orangeburg church. The contrast between then and now is striking. In 1871 Orangeburg was set off as a station, F. Auld being the preacher in charge. The years from 1865 to 1870, the earliest after the war, were the most trying. The writer was the presiding elder, and William G. Connor the preacher in charge. The churches were Orangeburg, Zion, and Prospect. They were evidently languishing and ready to die. The preachers' reports as to the state of the church were, "No religious influence"; "A general coldness." In 1868 it was asked, " What is the state of the church?" and the answer was, " No report "; in 1869, " Rather encouraging "; in 1870 F. Auld was the preacher in charge. And here the old record book ends. In 1868 the presiding elder was paid $25, the preacher in charge $211; in 1869 the presiding elder received $49.65, the preacher in charge $508; in 1870 $497.70 was shared between the presiding elder and the preacher in charge. In 1871 Orangeburg was set off as a station, and paid $600; in 1872 it paid $700, and the rise has been gradual, with increasing prosperity up to date. They had had for years a very creditable church structure, but the papers say that just the other day it had been rolled back with the intention of erecting a still better one on the site.

A rapid review of the increase of the Methodist Episcopal Church is not out of place. In 1787, two years after their entrance into the state, there were 595 white and 43 colored members; in 1800, thirteen years later, the whites numbered 3,399, and the colored members 1,283. In 1825, thirty-eight years afterwards, Mr. Mills, the statistician of the state, makes the Methodists within it " the most numerous of all the religious denominations." In the light of contrast, as to the early triumphs of Methodism, and because we have documentary evidence of the period, 1793, and of this very section of country, there will be seen the difference of operation in church organization, and be shown clearly the worth of an itinerant ministry. The scope of country extends somewhat above Orangeburg City, embracing the territory between the Edisto and Santee rivers, and extending within twenty miles of the city of Charleston, a scope of country some fifty or sixty miles in length by about twenty or thirty in breadth. The documentary evidence consists of the report of the Rev. Robert Wilson, the missionary of a sister communion, and is published at length in Dr. Howe's " History of the Presbyterian Church." Being ordered by the synod to spend three months in the lower part of South Carolina, on the

6th of December, 1793, he started from Long Cane, Abbeville county, to Columbia, his field of operation lying below that place. On reaching it, he tells of the country as thickly settled; but the opinions of the inhabitants concerning religion were so unsettled and various that no one denomination could obtain a settled pastor. He laments the great and marked profanation of the Sabbath, hunting and all kinds of diversions being indulged in. Baptists and Methodists abounded, the former the most numerous. He states: "The most of the preachers of that denomination who have frequented this section are men of infamous character, such as are an indignity to human nature—much more, a disgrace to the Christian name. No man of the smallest discernment can possibly become one of their party." This is certainly very severe, but something must be allowed for his great desire for the people to have a settled ministry. His route led to Turkey Hill (Prospect), Orangeburg, Cattle Creek, Indian Fields, Four Holes, Wasmasaw, and Beech Hill; and he writes of the people as having encouraged since the war "almost every man who came unto them calling himself a preacher, and therefore have been supplied by a great number in succession who have been invariably addicted to vice, most commonly drunkenness. Hence, with the idea of a minister here is always associated the idea of a mercenary creature, unworthy of the attention of gentlemen; and truly it has been too much the case." After a detail of travel throughout these boundaries, in which the object of his mission received but little encouragement, he concludes as follows:

The people among whom I have spent three months as a missionary have indeed been needy, and their situation must be acknowledged one of the most solemn lessons to ministers that can possibly be given. Thousands of poor, ignorant creatures have, by the unholy lives of ministers, been made to believe there is no reality in religion, and therefore the most affectionate efforts appear to be in a great measure lost. They are like the deaf adder who stoppeth her ear, and will not hearken to the voice of charmers, charming never so wisely. The lower parts of South Carolina, in general, appear to be in some measure sensible of the necessity of religion, even for the good of civil society; but in order to general usefulness, a minister would be under the necessity of tarrying so long in one place that the people would be convinced of his sincerity by his Christian walk and conversation. The practice of traveling from place to place in quick succession is in many places unpopular, and, as has been hinted, probably not the most profitable.

Now be it remembered that within these boundaries in 1793

Isaac Smith, whose record is beyond reproach, was a presiding elder, and that anterior to that time, and after, such men as Francis Asbury, Reuben Ellis, Henry Bingham (buried at Cattle Creek Camp Ground), William Gassaway, Enoch George, Jonathan Jackson, James Jenkins, Benjamin Blanton, Lewis Myers, men who "jeoparded their lives unto the death," and whose records are unstained, served in that section. It follows clearly that the ill-living ministers referred to in the above report were not of the Methodist order or persuasion, and we are in doubt if there were many of any other "religious persuasion."

The practice of ministers "traveling from place to place in quick succession," and regarded as "so unpopular and unprofitable," finds its answer in the contrasted statistics of both the religious denominations concerned. There was reported at the Conference of 1794 but one preacher, with 452 church members; while in 1876, at the time the compilation was made, there were 12 separate charges, served by 13 traveling and 12 local preachers, 11 parsonages, 63 churches, 52 Sunday schools, 307 officers and teachers, 1,689 pupils, 4,036 church members, and $47,770 worth of church property—with some 20,000 or 30,000 people under Methodist influence. And within the twenty years since, up to 1896, all this has been largely increased. Now, to say nothing of the garnered sheaves in heaven, this "traveling from place to place in quick succession" looks reasonably profitable; and the more so, when it is remembered that this is but a small portion of the territory of the entire state, as well as the fact that the "settled pastors" of the Church chiefly concerned in the above report are few and far between. Assuredly, Methodism was a most important factor in the great revival in the eastern and western continents; and what a reversal of men's judgments, when he who was its chief instrument was cast out of the Establishment, and it would have been deemed an indignity to enshrine his dust in Westminster, has to-day his appropriate niche in Britain's noblest Pantheon! And more: what though in aristocratic old Charleston, when thousands hung entranced on the ministry of Capers, Anderson, Olin, the Pierces, Wightman, Smith, and others, but few of "the rulers" believed in it, and only "the common people" received it gladly? Heaven knows where to bestow the plaudit, and the conventionalities of this world pale before the coronations of that other.

CHAPTER XXVIII.

THE old Black Swamp Circuit and the Walterboro Circuit that adjoined it greatly deserve notice. This, with the Barnwell Circuit noticed farther on, will complete the survey of the state as far as these annals can do so. Black Swamp is first noted in 1811, and was then in Ogeechee District. Lewis Meyers was presiding elder, and John S. Capers preacher in charge. The membership reported in 1812 was 96 whites and 55 colored. In 1813 it was transferred to Edisto District, and numbered 213 whites and 112 colored; and that year Thomas Mason was the preacher in charge. Up to 1830 it was served by such men as J. C. Belin, Freeman, Hill, McDaniel, Callaway, Laney, Watts, and Crook. From that time to 1850 it was served by Bond English, King, T. Huggins, M. C. Turrentine, William Martin, H. A. C. Walker, R. J. Boyd, Bass, Durant, and McSwain. Its early boundaries are not now definable. In 1851 and 1852 the parsonage was at Brighton's Cross Roads. The circuit swept on down to Robertsville and Purisburg, then on to Ebenezer and Kadesh, and up to Cave's and Gillette's, then turning to Swallow Savannah, then down toward the Bluff and on down to Union and Brighton. There were some twenty appointments. It was always regarded as a choice charge in the Conference. Here were the Manors, Martins, Lawtons, Bosticks, Solomons, and Davises, most of them men of wealth and deeply pious; with many who, if not so well off in this world's goods, held to the true riches. The people were universally kind, and unexcelled in attention to their preachers. Union Church at that time was at the head of all. Manor Lawton, one of the chief stewards, used to say to the preachers: "We keep no books; get all you can from the others, and Union will make up deficiencies." And on this being reported, in less than half an hour a deficit often amounting to hundreds of dollars was made up. Swallow Savannah came next in liberality. The younger Bosticks and Martins were there, and their training at Union was not forgotten. One member now at Black Swamp Church, well known as "Old Bill," still survives, and may he long do so. We would like to put on record all who helped to make this so pleasant a charge, but this cannot be done. The civil war spread desolation over this fine country, swept away its wealth by emancipation, and many a palatial mansion was given to the flames. Several charges have been made out of this grand old circuit, and since railroads have invaded its quiet, towns and villages have sprung up, and Methodism is still on the advance.

The Walterboro Circuit was another of those famous old charges of the past. Long incorporated with Edisto and Orangeburg, it was not known as Walterboro until 1834. T. E. Ledbetter and George Wright were the preachers. The churches at that time and afterwards were Pine Grove, Green Pond, Ebenezer, Carmel, St. John's, Little Swamp, Mizpah, Rehoboth, Sheridan's Chapel, Island Creek, Buckhead, Cross Swamp, Shiloh, Bethel, Antioch, Salem, Peniel, Sandy Dam, Walterboro, and Tabernacle. Among the chief stewards was Thomas Raysor, famous in his day for liberality rather beyond what was common then. He was always attendant on Quarterly Conference, ever exerting a most healthful influence in supporting religion. Within its boundaries lived the Rev. Lucius Bellenger, remarkable for his zeal and long travel, far and wide. He was noted for eccentricity, not by any means harmful, but always attracting attention. This good man, without fee or reward of earthly nature, long preached the gospel of Jesus, and now rests from his labors. Aaron Smith was noted as a class leader at Pine Grove. Brother Steadly was another, as also was Allen Williams. At Ebenezer were Alfred Raysor, B. Risher, Stevens, and Martin Jacques. At Rehoboth were Philip Jacques, Ackerman, and Dandridge. At Sheridan Chapel were the Johnsons, Willises, and, though not a member, Dr. Shendon, who has left an admirable son, Hugo, who is doing good service educationally for the Church. At Island Creek Louis O'Brien can never be forgotten. This was one of the first charges, as to time, in the old Edisto Circuit. At Mount Carmel were the Robinsons, Bloxes, and Blockers; and the good man Linden must not be forgotten. The Rishers, Stewarts, Stevenses, Varns, Sniders, Ulmers, Campbells, Pages, Hendersons, Lowrys, Larasys, Fulkses, Kirklands, Muses, Brabhams, and many more, have left descendants who are an honor to our Church. Benjamin Stokes, at old Sandy Dam, still survives; as also Col. William Stokes, often representing his circuit at Conference. Dr. A. E. Williams still lives, and has done yeoman service for the cause. The old Green Pond Camp Ground was long a rallying point for the hosts of Methodism, with old Binnaker's in Barnwell Circuit, both gone into desuetude. At the latter place in the early days may have been seen a man not especially remarkable then, but developing finally into H. N. McTyeire, one of our bishops. Joseph Moore and Reddick Pierce were often at Binnaker's, preaching with power to delighted thousands.

We have said little, and only incidentally, concerning our missions to the slaves. This lower part of the state was covered over by them. They were once our chief joy; but since the civil war has swept them out of existence, and since the whole body of colored people have gone into other communions, we can look alone to heaven for the reward due for the labor expended on them. From the very beginning attention was given to these poor beings; and not only sermons, prayers, and tears were freely bestowed upon them, but the record from 1830, when $201.33, an average of $1\frac{1}{4}$ cents per member, up to 1864, when $63,813.70, an average of $1.77, was given, together with the full yearly exhibit as seen in the Appendix, will prove clearly that much had been done for them. The Methodist Church was the first to care for the slaves, beginning with the very advent of Asbury, and for years trained the best instructed of the African race. And it is well known that when emancipation came— to say nothing of their behavior during the war—because of this they quietly adjusted themselves to their new relations. And yet how absurd is the northern sentiment on the religious condition of the negro in slavery! To show this convincingly we quote from an address delivered by the Rev. Charles Cuthbert Hall, D.D., at Norlan, Mass., June 28, 1893, and published in the *Outlook* for September 16:

Character is invisible thought translated into visibility, and fixed before the eye, cut on life. And the nature of character is affected—yes, is determined—by that whereon the mind principally dwells, by the tools principally used. To an astonishing extent this can be verified by the observation of human life. Even upon so broad a scale as a comparison of nations it is possible to make this verification. Take the African race, while still in slavery, in our southern states, and contrast it with the New England

communities of the same period. As a comparative study of racial character the contrast is appalling. On the one hand, servile dejection, laziness,
impurity, and an intellectual life not many removes from imbecility; on
the other hand, proud consciousness of liberty, intellectual vigor, industry,
social cleanness. What determined this contrast? The respective range of
thought. I thank God that thirty years of free thought under the direction
of schools like Hampton and of saints like Armstrong have made that African race almost as wondrous a contrast to its former self as New England
to the slaves.

With this address on "The Mystery of Worship, and Its Effect upon Character," we have no quarrel, and have none especially with the statement copied above, save in one particular,
which is this: the attributing *all* advancement in religious culture of the negro *"to schools like Hampton, and saints like Armstrong," and that within the last thirty years.* One would think
from these last words, emphasized by us, that the negro religiously was utterly uncared for in all the South under slavery;
that with the interdict on letters, no man cared for his soul;
when the fact is that all Christian denominations gave special
care to the negro, while the Methodist missions to slaves on the
plantations for more than thirty years gave the benefit to thousands. The self-complacency is enormous that attributes the
advancement of the negro religiously to the efforts of northern
saints within the space of thirty years just past.

In the year 1865, in the rear of the Federal army, came chaplains whose sole aim was to disintegrate and absorb. They
found thousands under religious culture, and many of them
saintly, and after a short space worthy of the highest positions
in Church and State, the North being the judge. Some of
these chaplains, well known to the writer, like St. Paul, "very
crafty, caught them with guile." Of course not the guile St.
Paul gloried in, for under cover of the truth they lied most
egregiously, and sought to appropriate southern church property, and did, until compelled to restore it by Federal law.
Were these men saints, too? In contrast with "the servility,
laziness, and impurity" of the African, was this good Christian
conduct typical of the racial instinct of New England character?

As to the "proud consciousness of liberty," is pride of any
sort consistent with the humility taught by Jesus? And as to
"intellectual" culture, can the knowledge of letters alone puri-
fy the heart? As to "industry," did not, or does not, much of

it find place in getting the most money for the least value, even to the manufacture of wooden hams and nutmegs? And for "social cleanness," my! what about divorce, unknown in South Carolina until attempted to be introduced by northern sentiment? Is it any better, is it as good as the polygamy of Mormonism? Say what you will of the hardness of men's hearts, there is the law divine, as unchangeable as God himself. Then how about prenatal infanticide, limitation of offspring by human will, antenatal murder against God's and nature's laws, so common even in godly New England? I would as soon not believe at all as to believe Jesus false, and imbecile in issuing commands that cannot be obeyed. Then what say you to the rampant lust, awakening most fearful retribution and contempt of law throughout the South, *utterly unknown under slavery,* when the tender innocence of childhood is not safe from the bestial proclivities of black brutes? Is this the product of a "proud consciousness of liberty, intellectual vigor, industry, social cleanness," of which, in the judgment of the lecturer, the unfortunate South knows nothing?

Many instances of the very highest religious character, all trained under slavery, might be given. Some yet live who remember Castile Selby, known to the writer and the children then as old "Daddy Castile." He was one of the very best specimens of honesty and Christian gentleness. He was, with his black face and patched clothing, much more a true gentleman than many a bedizened rascal—white or black—covered with broadcloth and decked with jewels, who looted the treasury of South Carolina in the sad days of reconstruction. Then old Maum Clarinda, true type of many a colored "mammy," the trusted nurse and foster mother in many a southern household. Then John Boquet, who when dying, and William Capers told his wife that he must want for nothing, exclaimed: "Want! want! I'm done with want forever! I want nothing but heaven, and I'm almost there by the blood of Jesus!" Could "saints like Armstrong" say more? Were such as these, and thousands more in our happy Southland, made so by the prevalence of "free thought, schools like Hampton, and saints like Armstrong"? By no means. They had learned in the school of Christ, fully equal to the Hampton school or any other.

It is fully time this northern conceit should be rebuked; and though it is hard to get into the northern mind that "any good can come out of Nazareth," it may, in the language of Burns,

> From many a blunder free them,
> And foolish notion.

We close this chapter by giving the Rev. F. A. Mood's testimony to the character of the Christianized negro. He says:

It would hardly be in keeping with the plan hitherto followed in these articles to pass over in utter silence the names of the many worthy and excellent people who, among the colored Methodists in the city, have vindicated the truth and power of godliness. Much might be written about them that would be appropriate and profitable as well as interesting. A mention of a few of the names conspicuous in former days must suffice. Among the early colored members remarkable for their intelligence and business traits were Harry Bull, Quaminy Jones, Peter Simpson, Abraham Jacobs, Ben McNeil, Smart Simpson, Aleck Harleston, Amos Baxter, Morris Brown, Richard Holloway, Castile Selby, and John Boquet. Harry Bull and Morris Brown went off in the African schism; the latter moved to Pennsylvania, where he afterwards was known as Bishop Brown, of the African Church in that state. Castile Selby was eminent for his humility, holiness, and unbending integrity. Though a black man, an humble carter, moving in the humblest position in life, he was eminently a good and, no doubt in the sight of God, a great man. But I will give his character as summed up by Bishop Capers, in a private letter to a friend, the use of which has been granted me. The bishop says: "The weight and force of his character were made up of humility, sincerity, simplicity, integrity, and consistency, for all of which he was remarkable, not only among his fellows of the colored society of Charleston, but I might say among all whom I have ever known. He was one of those honest men who need no proof of it. No one who ever saw him would suspect him. Disguise or equivocation lurked nowhere about him. Just what he seemed to be, that he invariably was, neither less nor more. Add to this a thorough piety—which was the root and stock of his virtues—and you find elements enough for the character of no common man; and such was Castile Selby." As early as 1801 he is on record as a leader, and he held the office untarnished for over half a century.

John Boquet, a slave, was very intelligent and deeply pious, and in consideration of his virtue and good services was set free by his owner. The following affecting occurrence was related of him by Bishop Capers in the letter referred to: "Visiting him on his deathbed, I found him unspeakably happy in the love of God, but not as well provided as I thought he ought to be with little comforts and refreshments which his wasted body might require. I noticed it, and told his wife of several things which he might take for nourishment, and which she must procure. 'He wants them,' said I, 'and he must have them. The expense is nothing, and he must want for nothing.' 'Want! want!' exclaimed the dying man. 'Glory be to God! I am done with want forever! Want! want! I know no want but heaven, and I am almost there by the blood of Jesus!'"

Richard Holloway was also conspicuous for his intelligence and zeal. His zeal, however, was sometimes intemperate and ill-judged, but he died much beloved and respected.

There are two or three names among the females which must not pass unnoticed. Mary Ann Berry will be long remembered as the tender, careful, ladylike nurse and humble saint. Bishop Capers says of her: "I never knew a female in any circumstances in life who better deserved the appellation of 'deaconess' than Mary Ann Berry; one who seemed to live only to be useful, and who, to the utmost of her ability, and beyond her ability, served the Church and the poor; and I might say, too, that what she did was always exceedingly well done, directed by an intelligent mind as well as a sanctified spirit; so that, humble as was her position in common society, she was really a mother in Israel. Her meekness, her humility, and a peculiar gentleness and softness of spirit which distinguished her at all times, might have done honor to a Christian lady of any rank." Rachel Wells, too, was remarkable for her humility and piety, and in most respects was the counterpart of Mary Ann, except in personal appearance. Of her the bishop in his letter also speaks in high terms. He states that not long before her death he called to see her after she had received a severe contusion which prevented her going to church, at which a protracted meeting was then in progress. When sympathized with upon the unfortunate accident which prevented her getting to church, she replied: "Ah, Mr. Capers, since this occurred to me, which you call an unfortunate accident, God has found a much nearer way to my heart than by Trinity Church." Nanny Coates also was a colored woman of marked piety and generosity. And here again let Bishop Capers speak: "Did I mention Maum Nanny Coates? Bless old Maum Nanny! If I had been a painter going to represent meekness personified, I should have gotten her to sit for the picture. It was shortly after I had been appointed secretary for the missions, that being in Charleston at the house of my brother, as we were sitting together in the parlor one evening, Maum Nanny entered. I wish I could show her to you just as she presented herself, in her long-eared white cap, kerchief, and apron of the olden time, with her eyes on the floor, her arms slightly folded before her, stepping softly toward me. She held between her finger and thumb a dollar bill, and courtesying as she approached, she extended her hand with the money. 'Will you please, sir,' said she, in subdued accents, and a happy countenance, 'take this little mite for the blessed missionaries?' I took it, pronounced that it was a dollar, and said: 'Maum Nanny, can you afford to give as much as this?' 'Oh! yes, sir,' she replied, lifting her eyes which till then had been on the floor. 'It is only a trifle, sir. I could afford to give a great deal more—if—I—had—it.'"

The three last mentioned were all freed by their owners for their faithfulness and virtue. But these are but a few of the many souls and many interesting facts identified with the colored membership of the Charleston churches. They are not enrolled among the great and mighty of the earth, but what is far better, their names and deeds have honorable mention in the Lamb's book of life.

CHAPTER XXIX.

Necrology from 1830 to 1850: H. A. C. Walker, A. B. McGilvray, Whitefoord Smith, R. I. Boyd, W. A. Gamewell, H. A. Durant, Samuel Leard, J. R. Pickett, W. A. McKibben, William C. Kirkland, William P. Mouzon, William A. McSwain, L. M. Little, C. H. Pritchard, A. M. Shipp, D. I. Simmons, William A. Fleming, R. P. Franks, John W. Kelly, William T. Capers, H. C. Parsons, A. H. Harmon, William Hutto—Benevolent Organizations in Connection with the Conference—Same in Charleston, S. C.

UP to 1830 we gave in chronological order short memoirs of prominent members of the Conference from the beginning. The space remaining will only allow brief mention of one or two in each class from 1830 to 1850, and of those only who have closed up life and labor on earth. With regard to all the rest the reader will consult the record in the Appendix, where every name is set down.

Hugh A. C. Walker was admitted in 1831, and died in 1886. He was born in Antrim county, Ireland, coming in early life to America, and remaining here until, at the age of seventy-seven, he was removed by death, in the fifty-sixth year of his ministry. He was meek, gentle, patient, persevering, sincere, honest, and accurate; calm, dignified, prompt, and punctual; a clear, sound, logical, instructive preacher, and a fine administrator in all Church affairs. His end, as might well be expected, was eminently peaceful.

Archibald B. McGilvray was admitted in 1832, and died in 1863. He was born in the Isle of Skye, coast of Scotland, and arrived in America in 1806. He was a modest, cheerful man, and a devoted friend. As a minister he was faithful, holy, laborious, and useful. In view of death he praised God aloud, and so passed away.

Whitefoord Smith (1833) was born in Charleston, S. C., November 7, 1812, and died at Spartanburg, April 27, 1893. Long connected with the educational interests of the Church, and a most eloquent preacher, he well merited the title of "the golden-mouthed." His oratory was unique, his voice clear and sweet, his taste faultless, and his style pure. He was sound in theology, and devoted in seeking the salvation of souls. He was loy-

(260)

al to his Church, refusing offers that weaker men might have accepted. Fully conscious of the approach of death, he met it calmly, trustfully, and triumphantly.

Henry H. Durant (1834) was born in Horry county, S. C., April 3, 1814, and died at Spartanburg, S. C., December 3, 1861. Noted as a revivalist, he was no doubt instrumental in the conversion of thousands. The charm of oratory was added to his pulpit efforts. His sermons were strong, cogent, and spiritual; in exhortation he was powerful and prevailing; in prayer, remarkably gifted. His sickness was borne with Christian confidence and resignation, and of course his end was peace.

Robert J. Boyd (1834) was born in Chester county, S. C., November 24, 1805, and died at Marion, S. C., September 3, 1869, being nearly sixty-four years of age. He was one of the best, wisest, and most trusted men in our Conference. However elevated in position, his humility was prominent. In every position he evinced dignity and simplicity of character, and was seemingly unconscious of his real ability and worth. His end was peaceful.

Whatcoat Asbury Gamewell (1834) was the son of a pioneer preacher; born in Darlington county, May 6, 1814, and died at Spartanburg, S. C., October 13, 1869. He was a man very much beloved. He was tall and commanding in appearance; always serious, and yet never tinctured with a sour godliness, never given to railing, and so free himself from the faults common to humanity as to bear patiently the failings of others. His voice was deep and sonorous; and being of an easy elocution both in the pulpit and at the fireside, he effectively preached and practiced. He was much distinguished as a pastor, and his pulpit efforts were persuasive and sincere. His character was of unusual beauty, symmetry, and completeness. His last days were in perfect harmony with his precious life, and his victory over death and the grave was signally triumphant.

John R. Pickett (1835) was born in Fairfield county, S. C., April 2, 1814, and died at Chester March 15, 1870. His dust rests in the Winnsboro graveyard. With all the simplicity of a child, he was fearless in his pulpit utterances, and was self-possessed and deliberate. He had unusual facility in acquiring languages; was an earnest student, and frequently excelled oratorically. He was instrumental in the conversion of hun-

dreds, if not thousands. He devoted his entire estate to Wofford College. In the hour of death, his submission to God's will
was clearly evident.

Samuel Leard (1835) was born in Abbeville county, S. C., and
died at Raleigh, N. C., March 9, 1896, in his eighty-second year.
Of unusual amiability of character, he won the approval of all
associated with him. In the pulpit he was strong, convincing,
and useful; unexcelled as a pastor, and a good writer. In his
last illness he gave evidence that all was well, and but a little
while before his departure he was aroused by the repetition
of the Lord's Prayer so as faintly to follow its petitions to the
close, and then whispered, " Let us pray." But faith was rapidly
giving way to sight, and prayer to endless praise.

Marcus A. McKibben (1836) is the most fitting of his class for
record here. He was born in Mecklenburg county, N. C., in
1804, and died at Barnwell Courthouse, S. C., January 23, 1887, in
the eighty-third year of his age. He was quite original, his
mind logical, and he reasoned well. For forty-one years he was
effective, and the last eight years superannuated. His end was
peaceful.

William C. Kirkland (1837) was born in Barnwell county, S.
C., January 6, 1814, and died in Greenville county, S. C., March
29, 1864. He was remarkable for his sweetness of spirit, and
in all graces of character resembled the beloved disciple. He
was a good man and a successful laborer in the gospel. In the
end he found the Good Shepherd in the valley of the shadow of
death.

William P. Mouzon (1838) was born in Charleston, S. C., January 16, 1819, and died at Bamberg on the 28th of January, 1885.
He was an able minister of the New Testament, and as a preacher
earnest, instructive, and impressive. He served on missions,
circuits, stations, and districts, and was acceptable and useful
in all. He died in great peace.

William A. McSwain (1839) was born in Stanly county, N. C.,
and died January 1, 1866. A self-made man, gifted with a vigorous mind, by diligence in study he rapidly rose in the Conference.
He was deservedly popular both with preachers and people. His
comparatively early death ended too soon a career promising
so much more than even that which he had attained. In his
removal from the earth he triumphed in the grace of Jesus.

Lewis M. Little (1840), of a class of six admitted, is noticed here, because of the early retirement of the others. He was born in Lincoln county, N. C., July 12, 1815, and died at Sumter, December 5, 1888, in the seventy-fourth year of his age. While not eminently great as a preacher, he was certainly useful as a pastor, diligent and sympathetic. His was an active ministry of forty-eight years. He was "called, chosen, and faithful."

The class of 1841 was an unusually strong one, and four of them are eminently worthy of mention here.

Albert M. Shipp was born in Stokes county, N. C., June 15, 1819, and died on the 27th of June, 1887. As a preacher he occupied the first rank both as to matter and manner in the pulpit. He was esteemed highly as an educator of youth, and for years was the leader in his Conference. Asserting to the end his faith in Jesus, his last utterance was, " It is all right."

Dennis J. Simmons was born near Charleston, March 22, 1818, and died January 5, 1887, aged nearly sixty-nine years. Of very staid demeanor, some would have thought him morose, but this was only outward; within, he was genial and kind. Of Spartan bravery, he would have defended a Thermopylæ. He was modest in life, and well beloved. His trust was in Him who had redeemed him from sin and death.

William H. Fleming was born in Charleston, S. C., January 1, 1821, and died April 16, 1877. He was buried in Bethel cemetery, of which church he was then pastor. In disposition he was genial and kind; in judgment, clear, judicious, and safe; in all intercourse with men, frank and honorable. He was one of the leading men of his Conference, and his death was considered all too early for his promised usefulness. He died in the faith.

Claudius H. Pritchard was born in Charleston, S. C., and died at Abbeville, S. C., March 5, 1896. He was preëminently saintly. Early in his religious experience he was given full consecration, and was long a witness of the power of holiness. He was scriptural in his preaching, unwearying as a pastor, visiting from house to house, and eminently useful for over fifty-five years' connection with his Conference. None doubted the integrity of his character or the depth of his piety. Such a life could not be otherwise than triumphant in its ending.

Of the class of nine in 1842, one was transferred, three discontinued, and three located. There are but two surviving in connection with the Conference, and may it be long before any necrological record is made of them.

The class of 1843 is nearly like the one of 1842. It numbered seven members. Two were transferred, three located, and three discontinued.

John W. Kelly (1845) was born in Union county, S. C., January 29, 1825, and died February 18, 1885. He was a large man physically, and of great mental strength, quick of apprehension, and never at any loss in expressing his ideas. His preaching was often in demonstration of the Spirit and with power. His manner was simple and natural, often carrying away his hearers by a tide of unaffected eloquence. He was always inclined to take the weaker side, and none doubted his proffer of friendship. Suddenly he was called, and his dust rests in hope at Providence Church in Berkley county.

Robert P. Franks (1844) was born in Laurens county, S. C., September 19, 1818, and died at Lowndesville, S. C., January 25, 1895. He was remarkably clear in his judgment as to men and measures, firm in his decisions, and well calculated to guide or govern in all affairs. As a preacher, he was spiritual and always interesting in the pulpit. Genial and kind, he was highly regarded by his brethren. He had no long illness, but passed suddenly away to his rest.

William T. Capers (1845) was born in Milledgeville, Ga., January 20, 1825, and died at Greenville, S. C., September 10, 1894. He was the second son of the venerated Bishop Capers. Perhaps no family anywhere had such a number of the same name and lineage devoted to the ministry. " In the pulpit the love of the Father, the sympathy of Jesus, and the comfort of the Spirit were the themes he delighted to dwell on. These he preached with a naturalness so perfect that to some it seemed affected, with the graces of oratory as unstudied as if he knew nothing of elocution, and with an enthusiasm and pathos that frequently carried him to the height of eloquence." His end was peace.

Hilliard C. Parsons (1846) was born in Sumter county, S. C., February 28, 1824, and died at Wadesboro, N. C., January 29, 1866. The son of a preacher formerly connected with the Conference, he had all the advantages of religious training. He was a man of remarkable talent, and early took a commanding position in the Conference. He was amiable in spirit, possessed of fine conversational powers, while his intelligent and exalted Christian virtues made him influential everywhere. His counsel to his family, when dying, was all a Christian father's should be, and he left as his testimony that he had trusted in Christ and had not trusted him in vain.

The class for 1847 numbers eight: four discontinued, two located, and two living—may they long survive!

The class for 1848 numbers seven: two transferred, two located, one dead, and two still living—we would keep them so.

Allison H. Harmon (1849) was born in Cleveland county, N. C., and died August 29, 1861, in his thirty-ninth year, and was buried near one of the churches in Lancaster Circuit. Although not the most noted in this class, he deserves a record, if for no more than his dying message to his brethren. He was fully consecrated to the ministry, laborious and useful. "Tell my brethren," he said, "that my work is done, and that I shall rest now." He could truly say, "For me to live is Christ, to die is gain."

William Hutto (1850) was born in Orangeburg county, January 24, 1828, and died at Williamston, S. C., January 19, 1892. He was a most devoted and uncomplaining minister of the cross; during forty-two years of service he was truly acceptable as such, showing himself an earnest, humble, and devoted Christian. As a preacher he was sound, instructive, and edifying; as a pastor, kind, attentive, and sympathetic. In his last sickness he was patient, gentle, and of unswerving faith and hope in Jesus. He died in great peace.

As we had determined not to go beyond 1850, this finishes the necrological record so far as these annals are concerned. In the summing up of the last chapter matters may be brought down to the present date, but others must write of events occurring after the fearful civil war ended. We close this chapter with a brief review of the benevolent organizations connected with the Conference.

First and chief is the Missionary Society of the Conference, auxiliary to the Society of the Church, South. Strange to say, its constitution does not appear in the published Minutes of the Conference until 1835. The first collection for missions, published in 1831, amounted to $261.33, at an average cost per member of one and one-quarter cents. The amounts collected each year, up to 1896, may be seen in the Appendix, under the exhibit there set forth, and also full amounts, with deficits, per cent discounts, and averages per member for the Conference collection; in which it will be seen that the averages were often as low as three cents, rarely exceeding fourteen cents, per member.

Next in order is the Woman's Missionary Society of the Methodist Episcopal Church, South, South Carolina Conference, organized at Newberry, S. C., in December, 1878; Bishop William M. Wightman, presiding. The officers elected were: Mrs. W. M. Wightman, President; Mrs. G. W. Williams, Mrs. William Martin, Mrs. W. K. Blake, Mrs. J. L. Breeden, Vice Presidents; Mrs. J. W. Humbert, Corresponding Secretary; Mrs. A. M. Chreitzberg, Recording Secretary; Mrs. F. J. Pelzer, Treasurer. In the first annual report, in 1879, there were 44 auxiliary societies, 1,069 members, and $223.30 collected. At the seventeenth annual meeting, held at Abbeville, S. C., there were reported 265 auxiliary societies, 5,286 members, and $5,922.49 collected during the year; grand total collected, from December, 1878, to March, 1896, $76,758.48. The following are the present officers: Mrs. M. D. Wightman, President; Mrs. E. S. Herbert, Vice President; Mrs. J. W. Humbert, Corresponding Secretary; Miss I. D. Martin, Recording Secretary; Miss Josie B. Chapman, Juvenile Secretary, with ten district secretaries; Mr. J. T. Medlock, Auditor. Three missionaries have gone out from this South Carolina Conference Society, namely: to Brazil, Miss Susan Littlejohn; to China, Miss Sallie B. Reynolds and Miss Johnnie Sanders.

In the Minutes of 1835 appears the constitution of each of the following four trusts of the Conference. The full history of each cannot now be written. It may be in the coming years, but now the names alone are set down:

1. Trust for the relief of superannuated or worn-out preachers and the widows and orphans of preachers.

2. The society of the South Carolina Conference for the relief of the children of its members.

3. The Fund of Special Relief.

4. The Rutledge Trust Fund.

These are all under the administration of the legal Conference, and the interest accruing is distributed annually.

MRS. E. S. HERBERT,
VICE PRESIDENT.

MRS. J. W. GREENE,
TREASURER.

MRS. M. D. WIGHTMAN,
PRESIDENT.

MISS ISABEL D. MARTIN,
RECORDING SECRETARY

MRS. J. W. HUMBERT,
CORRESPONDING SECRETARY

OFFICERS OF THE SOUTH CAROLINA CONFERENCE W. F. M. S.

The South Carolina Brotherhood was organized in 1885, and up to 1895 has paid to its beneficiaries, numbering thirty-five, $21,662.85.

All these are connected with the Conference. In the city of Charleston, S. C., the following charitable trusts are connected with the Church:

1. The Methodist Charitable Society was organized in 1808, and incorporated three years afterwards. Members and their families are regular pensioners. No one is a beneficiary under seven years, or until he has paid dues equal to seven years' membership. The aged and indigent members are entitled to benefits. Entrance fee, $10; annual dues, $2.

2. The Methodist Female Friendly Association was founded in 1810, and incorporated in 1819. Invested fund, $6,000; annual charity, $400. There are five regular pensioners. One-third the interest and donations is reserved to increase the capital.

3. The Cumberland Benevolent Society was founded in 1845, and incorporated in 1847. Fund invested, $2,500, of which $1,000 was from a legacy of Mrs. Sarah Hewie. The society has sixty-five members.

CHAPTER XXX.

ALLEGORICALLY, two men once became neighbors. The
first settler—none near him for a long time—conceived
that he had the right to the whole demesne, though owning really
no more than his title covered, that covering, however, the rich-
est alluvial spots. The second, coming after, had to be content
with barrens and waste places. It seemed as if he really preferred these, though preference had little to do with it, his indomitable pluck determining him to make the bad good, and
the good the best that could be. The first settler, from some
cause or other, did not like the newcomer; whether from personal habits or fear of encroachment, or what not, he evidently
wished to make him travel—*beyond*. And travel he did, into
every nook and corner of what the first settler deemed his own
domain. This certainly ought not to have worried him; for,
according to his cherished theory, all happening being decreed,
this actually happened; then why find fault?

Another peculiarity was that the opinions held by the one,
while especially soothing to himself and his immediate family,
were terribly repulsive to all outside; as a consequence, his
hand was against every man not of his own way of thinking,
and every man's hand against him. It is not at all surprising
that, holding such opinions, he should be so inclined to melancholy, and always stern and unbending in demeanor. His very
religion was of a gloomy cast; considered, like medicine, the
more bitter the better. Song he could not abide; and no wonder, for one believing as he did, so far from singing, would find
it a heavy task even to smile. Though rich, he was exceedingly
plain in his attire, abominating flowing robes and flowers, seemingly thinking sackcloth and ashes the best array for this poor,
forsaken world; yet, because of something happening before

the foundation of the world, in which he was *favorably* concerned—whatever might become of the outside crowd—he conceived that his safety was secured both for this world and the next. Having gotten a goodly number of sheep, well pastured and walled in, neither to be added to nor diminished, he became careless as to the employment of shepherds, and in many places the sheep were left to take care of themselves, which they might very well do, seeing that their safety was perfectly secured long before they were born.

Now all this had a tendency to produce somnolency; and it is not surprising, on the newcomer's entrance, to find all like the Ephesian sleepers. This other was by no means a rollicking blade; far from being wickedly hilarious, he was yet so happy and so sunshiny in heart and soul that he couldn't help making a noise, even shouting aloud sometimes. This worried the other exceedingly, keeping him awake o' nights, and it must be stopped if remonstrance could do it. But, that failing, the conclusion was to let him desperately alone. And so matters have moved on: every time one seems falling asleep the other nudges him, until at this present writing he is fully awake; and may the Lord keep him so!

The moral is: If Methodism has done no more than to wake up Calvinism, and to keep it awake, that much at least will be set down to its credit by the recording angel in heaven's high chancery.

The date of the entrance of Methodism into York county can only be approximated. Mr. Robert Love, near King's Mountain, remembers, when a boy, the entertainment of the early preachers at his father's house; and I think they were so entertained before he was born. He is now nearly eighty years of age. The earliest mention of York in the Minutes is 1828, namely: "Lincolnton District, Malcolm McPherson, presiding elder; Joseph Holmes, preacher in charge." But, inasmuch as the two states were ecclesiastically connected, the circuits in North Carolina, no doubt, reached down to York county, giving a much earlier entrance than the Minutes state.

I doubt if the statement that William Gassaway and Joseph Holmes organized the first Methodist church in the county at Yorkville is entered correctly. Gassaway may have had, in 1824, something to do with the organization of the church in

Yorkville, but Joseph Holmes was not stationed in York until 1828. In 1824 and 1825 he was on Newberry Circuit, and in 1826 and 1827 stationed in Columbia. Old Zion, or a church near that, existed before the church in Yorkville. Brother Patterson, the son-in-law, states that Brother John Chambers, then living below Yorkville, near Philadelphia Church, under deep conviction, had gone away up to Zion seeking peace. On his arrival he entered the humble structure, and saw the young preacher come in with his saddlebags on his arm. He saw him reverently kneel on entrance, and thought that *good;* heard him preach, and thought *that good;* and was so impressed that he, with a daughter, returned four weeks after, and they were converted and joined the Church. This daughter afterwards married the Rev. Hartwell Spain. This places it beyond conjecture that Methodism entered York county previous to the organization at Yorkville in 1824. In 1828 the Minutes placed Joseph Holmes in York, and he returned one hundred and fifty white members in 1829. The record thereafter for preachers in charge is as follows, giving the return of members by each:

		No. Members.
1828.	Joseph Holmes	150
1829.	Whitman C. Hill	185
1830.	Benjamin Bell	220
1831.	Stephen Williams	221
1833.	James J. Richardson	296
1834.	Josiah Freeman	208
1835.	D. G. McDaniel	238
1836.	John Watts	259
1837.	A. M. Forster	297
1838–39.	James W. Wellborn	304
1840.	J. G. Postell	391
1841.	S. Townsend	341
1842.	C. S. Walker	341
1843.	P. G. Bowman	372
1844–45.	M. A. McKibben	416
1846.	John A. Porter	355
1847.	William C. Clark	408
1848.	Abraham Nettles	382
1849.	P. R. Hoyle	387
1850.	(Not on Minutes)	398
1851.	L. M. Little	377
1852.	E. J. Meynardie (Station)	89
1853.	William E. Boone "	95
1854.	J. W. North "	75

1855.   G. W. M. Creighton (Station)...................... 87
1856–57. A. H. Lester   " 123
1858.   O. A. Darby   " 116
1859–60. L. A. Johnson....................... 136
1861.   L. C. Weaver..... 137
1862.   William S. Black..... ....
1863.   J. W. Humbert. ....
1864.   E. G. Gage...
1865.   L. A. Johnson........................... ....
1866.   W. T. Capers...................................... 87
1867–68. J. S. Nelson, M. E. Hoyle (Circuit)................
1869.   J. A. Wood (Station. No report).................
1870.   R. L. Harper " 94
1871.   G. M. Boyd   " ....
1872–73. A. W. Walker.....................................185
1874.   D. D. Dantzler....................................167
1875.   J. W. Dickson....................................185
1876.   J. E. Carlisle.....................................171
1877.   W. S. Martin........................ 177
1878–80. T. E. Gilbert......................................116
1881.   M. Dargan.......................................120
1882–83. R. P. Franks......................................103
1884.   John A. Mood (Circuit)........................... 96
1885.   J. T. Pate.......................................109
1886–89. W. W. Daniel....................... 120
1890.   G. H. Waddell.....................................

Thus it will be seen that Yorkville was connected with the circuit for a long time, the figures of membership indicating this clearly. It 1852 it was set apart as a station, so continuing —occasionally united with Philadelphia or King's Mountain Chapel—until 1886; since then it has stood alone. The handsome structure now erected shows very clearly the status of Methodists in Yorkville. But the numbers as given above indicate not very clearly its progression in the county. In 1828 the number of Methodists in York county was but one hundred and fifty. In 1889 the Minutes, after taking off two churches in Lancaster county connected with the Fort Mill Circuit, gave over 2,200—2,473 being the grand total; a very good percentage of increase. And where there were in the beginning but two or three churches, the number now is eighteen, valued at over $21,-000, with parsonages valued at over $7,000. We need say but little concerning the beautiful structure in Yorkville; the picture speaks for itself. It is in contemplation to place a memorial window in the Sunday-school department of the building to

18

the memory of Mr. James Jeffries, one of the first Sunday-school workers in the state; a memorial most assuredly well deserved.

The presiding elders having supervision over York county from 1828 are as follows:

1828–29	Malcolm McPherson.	1860	F. A. Mood.
1830–31	William M. Kennedy.	1861	John T. Wightman.
1832–33	Hartwell Spain.	1862–64	R. P. Franks.
1834	Charles Betts.	1865–68	J. W. North.
1835	Benjamin Bell.	1869–70	E. J. Meynardie.
1836–37	Henry Bass.	1871	T. G. Herbert.
1838–40	William M. Wightman.	1872	O. A. Darby.
1841–43	William Crook.	1873	William Martin.
1844–46	W. A. Gamewell.	1874–75	William H. Fleming.
1847	A. M. Shipp.	1876–79	E. J. Meynardie.
1848–50	A. M. Forster.	1880–83	A. M. Chreitzberg.
1851–53	H. H. Durant.	1884–87	A. J. Cauthen.
1854–57	John W. Kelly.	1888–90	A. M. Chreitzberg.
1858–59	H. C. Parsons.		

Not long since the author received information concerning William Gassaway, to wit: A certain Mr. Fulton, owning a large body of land near Tirza Church, York county, S. C., wishing, like Micah, to have a priest of his own, did not, like Micah, stipulate with the priest to give him "ten shekels of silver by the year, a suit of apparel, and his victuals," but did better. Finding Gassaway in the low country, about starved out in the itinerant ministry, he gave him one hundred and fifty acres, on which he built and settled, and where his dust now reposes. That Gassaway was fully worthy of the gift no one doubts—Heaven foreseeing the necessity of some provision for the apostle of Upper Carolina, not obtainable otherwise just then, as the present financial records fully show. To give an idea of the same, glance over this record. The first Quarterly Conference was held in Yorkville, April 30, 1831. Members present: William M. Kennedy, presiding elder; Stephen Williams, preacher in charge; William Gassaway, local elder; James B. Fulton, exhorter; Alexander Hill, Sr., exhorter; John Chambers, class leader; William Rowell, exhorter; James Jeffries, law secretary. To these, added at other Conferences were Charles Willson, Sr., Thomas Williams, Jr., James Farley, William Nance, J. Dawson, and Payton B. Darwin.

The following churches and preaching places composed the circuit, with the payments each quarter:

1831.

Churches.	First Quarter.	Second Quarter.	Third Quarter.	Fourth Quarter.	Total.
Yorkville........................	$ 6 75	$ 4 62½	$ 3 12½	$12 43¾	$ 26 93¾
Zion............................	1 87½	2 50	4 50	1 25	10 12½
Bethel..........................	......	1 12½	1 00	1 37½	3 50
Walnut Grove....	3 00	2 75	2 00	2 00	9 75
Schoolhouse.....................	......	......	......	1 00	1 00
Unity...........................	3 75	3 50	3 50	......	10 75
Siloam..........................	......	6 00	......	6 00	12 00
Sardis..........................	......	......	2 00	......	2 00
Prospect........................	2 00	......	......	......	2 00
Mrs. Howell's...................	......	......	......	......	......
Captain Jameson's...............	......	......	......	......	......
Ed Feamster's...................	......	......	......	......	......
Cove Spring.....................	......	......	......	3 00	3 00
Mount Hebron....................	......	......	......	......	......
Cross Roads.....................	......	......	......	......	......
Public Collection...............	3 93	10 18	10 62	......	24 73
	$21 30	$30 68	$26 74	$27 06	$105 78

Disbursed thus: Traveling expenses...........................$ 10 12
Presiding elder 38 00
Preacher in charge.......................... 57 66

$105 78

In 1832, $244.78; 1833, $73.80; 1834, $299.75; 1835, $258.92; 1836, $208.21; 1837, $63.18; 1838, $61.11; 1839, $197.05; 1840, $264.12; 1841, $393.91; 1842, $230.99.

Thus it will be seen that the expenditure for religion was not burdensome in those days, proving clearly that it was not the fleece but the flock cared for by these men. Other men have labored, and we have entered into their labor. The Lord make us as faithful!

At this time a preacher's stipend was not known as salary, but divided into *traveling expenses, family expenses, and quarterage;* the first seen at once, the second far off, and the third only in rarest instances seen at all. It is not surprising, therefore, to find in this journal but few payments on the last account. That word *quarterage* has had a most withering effect on Methodist finance (church). Some minds even now cannot rid themselves of the idea that it means *quarter of a dollar a quarter.* And so for years and years we dragged on in this Upper Carolina, not stimulated or rebuked by our Presbyterian brethren, who always provide well for their ministry.   But within late years great improvement has been made, and some generous men have led the way in bringing the Church up to a proper standard of support. May their tribe increase!   In 1832—Joseph Holmes, preacher in charge—Chesterville, now Chester, was added to the circuit, contributing $27, and disappearing in 1833.   James J. Richardson was the preacher in charge, and died that year.   His obituary in the Minutes states: " He was a very amiable man, a highly gifted preacher, and a faithful and successful laborer.   In him genius was blended with sweetness of spirit, and uncommon ability with an humble mind.   He seemed to die almost literally in sight of heaven."   They paid the widow $10.62.   Richardson was aged twenty-eight years.

An extract from a report on Church property states: "For the church in York J. M. Harris gave half an acre of land, and the house built since 1825 or 1826.   The land was sold by the sheriff of York district, but the half acre was excepted.   Zion Church has five acres reserved, the title in Samuel Burns, Sr. The camp ground called Siloam and the land on which Hebron Church now stands have title vested in Thomas Williams, Jr. Walnut Grove is held jointly by William Rowell and R. Sadler, Esq."

In 1834 Charles Betts was the presiding elder, and Josiah Freeman the preacher in charge.   At the third Quarterly Conference two hundred and sixteen dollars were paid for boarding the preacher's family, and the significant "No funds to pay quarterage" closes the report of stewards for that year.   It seems that Freeman did not serve the fourth quarter, Jacob B. Anthony appearing as preacher in charge, and Freeman retiring to die.   He kept on his appointment until August, and left his circuit for Columbia, S. C., where he died November 27, 1834. The affliction was painful, but he was patient, resigned, and happy; he often said, "All is well."   His dust lies in Washington street graveyard.   Thus two preachers of the South Carolina Conference ceased their labors on the York Circuit.

As an evidence of improvement within the decade, we give the financial return of the fourth Quarterly Conference, held at Unity Church (Where was Unity?   Is it the present Mount Vernon?), October 30, 1841: Yorkville, $54.61; Feamster's,

$10; Postell's, $9; Prospect, $17.37; Unity, $16; Philadelphia, $14.93; Concord, $30; Walnut Grove, $33.50; Canaan, $6; Zion, $24.56; Sitgreave's, $35.25; society not known, $8.50; public collection, $28.62. Total, $288.36. Where was Feamster's? (Is this Shady Grove?) Where was Unity, Hebron, Postell's, Prospect, Walnut Grove, Sitgreave's? Where was Siloam Camp Ground? Can anyone tell?

We now call attention to the new church lately erected at Yorkville. This splendid structure is a decided ornament to the town, and none the less a shining testimonial to the earnest zeal of the denomination by which it was erected; and representing the present condition of Methodism in Yorkville, after seventy years of existence, it stands forth as a prominent example of renewed growth and prosperity.

The Methodist Episcopal Church (now the Methodist Episcopal Church, South) was organized in this place in the year 1824, by two ministers, the Rev. William Gassaway and the Rev. Joseph Holmes, and was the first denominational organization to occupy this field, as well as the first Methodist church in the county. The little band originally commenced its labors with only nine members, as follows: James Jeffries, Mrs. Elizabeth H. Jeffries, Colonel Thomas W. Williams, Dr. John E. Jennings, John Chambers, Mrs. Margaret Chambers, Mrs. Sarah Beaty, and Mrs. Tabitha Wilkerson. Of the original members, one—Mrs. Elizabeth Jeffries—has been permitted to watch the progress of the work until the present. All were earnest workers, and as the result of their efforts the church rapidly grew in numbers and strength. Two years afterwards, in 1826, the congregation built the first house of worship erected in Yorkville. It was a plain wooden structure, and stood in College street, nearly opposite the graded school building, until some fifteen years ago, when it was torn down, the congregation having purchased the building it is now leaving. Until 1852 this and two other congregations constituted the only Methodist churches in the county, and, as York Circuit, were served by the same pastor. In 1852, however, the progress of the Yorkville Church had been so rapid as to justify its becoming a separate station, which, with eighty members, it was accordingly made. From this time on the church continued to prosper until interrupted by the war, when the membership became scattered and reduced. The close of the war found the congregation too weak to continue as a separate charge, and uniting with King's Mountain Chapel, then very weak, but now numbering five hundred members, and Philadelphia Church, it once more became a part of Yorkville Circuit. Continuing thus until 1885, the church again felt strong enough to stand alone, and, resolutely making the effort, has continued to progress rapidly until it now has a membership of one hundred and thirty—some fifty more than at the breaking out of the war—while the denomination in the county has grown to be nearly two thousand five hundred strong.

The idea of building a new church in Yorkville originated about nine years ago, the first meeting having been held on the 6th of April, 1887. Over two thousand five hundred dollars were raised among the members by subscription before the meeting adjourned, and the project never once lost the impetus thus given, the amount continuing to swell until sufficiently large to justify the commencement of the work of erection. This was placed in charge of a building committee consisting of T. S. Jeffries, chairman; F. Happerfield, H. C. Strauss, Dr. John May, Jr., and J. W. Dobson, who let out the contract on the 15th of September, 1890. Under the faithful superintendence of this committee every detail of the work has been looked after with the most scrupulous care, and although the building, fixtures, and furniture have cost only about six thousand dollars, it looks as though a much greater sum had been expended.

The church is constructed of brick, with granite trimmings, and in the Gothic style of architecture. The main auditorium is to the left of the tower, and the Sunday-school room to the right, and entrance is made by means of two sets of stone steps, which are approached from East Liberty street, and lead into the building through a nicely arranged vestibule. This vestibule occupies the base of the tower. It is twelve feet square, and the floor is laid with alternate squares of black and white marble. Including the spire, the tower is seventy-eight feet high. The auditorium is thirty by fifty-eight, not including a recess four feet deep which contains the pulpit. Overhead the woodwork is left open between the girders, and, alike with the walls, is ceiled with cherry and yellow pine panel work, finished in oil, and giving the whole interior a decidedly pleasing and artis-

TRINITY CHURCH, YORKVILLE, S. C.

tic appearance. The floor and rostrum are to be covered with a rich crimson carpet, and the pews, which are most comfortably arranged, are made of yellow pine, cherry, ash, and walnut, also finished in oil, and are capable of accommodating four hundred people. The windows, of which there are ten to the auditorium and three to the Sunday-school room, are highly ornamental— ground glass center panes, surrounded by a four-inch border of cathedral glass—and present a very pretty appearance, thoroughly in keeping with the general handsome finish. The pulpit is made of walnut and ash in the highest perfection of the cabinet-maker's art, and has inlaid in the center a dainty little cross made from a piece of oak which the architect, Mr. Bonnewell, sawed from the timbers of Independence Hall, Philadelphia.

The building is lighted by two French bronze chandeliers, each holding twelve lamps, and all having duplex burners. In addition to these, there are two lamps for the pulpit and another suspended in the vestibule. A powerful furnace has been placed in the cellar underneath, and so arranged as to heat comfortably the entire building.

A handsome and costly church clock is a present from Mr. Joseph W. Neil, of Yorkville; and among the other presents is a large marble tablet, containing the Decalogue, from the Sheldon Marble Company. Two other tablets, containing the Creed and the Lord's Prayer, will be placed on either side of it.

The grounds of the church, which are very level, have been sown with grass. Shade trees have been planted, and the whole surroundings are already beginning to present a pretty and refreshing appearance.

CHAPTER XXXI.

Early Reminiscences—Old Cumberland—Ancient Worthies—Mrs. Matilda Wightman—Preachers of the Period—Worship Devotional, Often Demonstratively Emotional—A Successful Period Followed by Declension—Early Religious Impressions—Old-time Love Feasts—Names of Early Members—Personal Experience—Examination of Character as Seen in the Forty-eighth Session—Fifty-fourth Session—Chief Ministers—Some Retired—Protest Against Religious Formalism.

MY first recollections are associated with Methodism in Charleston, from 1825. Born and reared in a city of no mean reputation, my religious advantages were many. Methodism flourished amid revilings and scorn; and though not many wise or noble were among its adherents, the power of the Holy Ghost was clearly manifest. The first church I ever entered was old Cumberland, erected by Asbury. It was a long, low, wooden structure, with its straight-backed benches and well-sanded floor. Part of the lower floor was reserved for the free colored people, and the galleries, entirely for the slave population, were always filled. The "service of song," both by white and colored, was far beyond the usual orchestral service; not so artistic, maybe, but full of devotion, lifting the soul right up to God. Anything less in worship ought to be driven out of Christendom.

In this humble place of worship in his youth year by year sat the writer, with his back to the wall and his feet dangling from the hard bench; or while all were in prayer, kneeling devoutly, he—shame on him—was engaged in tracing figures on that well-sanded floor. When again seated, with all the deep thought of youth his eyes wandered over an always large and seriously attentive congregation. Memory brings up some of these worthies of more than seventy years ago. To my left sat Abel McKee, the very synonym of fidelity, unalterably firm in duty; next to him, George Just, a kind-hearted German, godly and zealous; next, Samuel J. Wagner, steward, class leader, trustee, and chorister; next, William White, a dapper little man, always happy, and true-hearted to the end. The Rev. John Mood, for a while an itinerant preacher, a pattern of faith and patience,

(282)

the worthy sire of a noble family—four sons, preachers—was often there. Henry Muckenfuss, a glorious old veteran, then and for long the standard-bearer of the Charleston artillery, sometimes worshiped there when he could be induced to leave Trinity. William Bird, a fixture in Bethel, was rarely at old Cumberland; for how could the former exist without him? To our right sat George Chreitzberg, steward and leader, "called, chosen, and faithful." Next, good old Brother Prince, familiarly known as the lamplighter, because of his contract with the city. Few live who remember the men with torches and ladders, and oil-begrimed, who kept the lamps alight in the godly city then. Old Parson Munds, one of Hammet's followers, must not be forgotten. His attentive, smiling face and rapidly-turning head, to see how others enjoyed the sermon, are fully impressed on my memory. He wore the clerical garb of the olden time—knee breeches, buckles, and all. Dear, kindly old man, a constant visitor at my father's house, how I often wished to hear him preach, but never did; that function of his ministry had ceased, only prayer and a holy life remaining. A thin, spare, and exceedingly quiet worshiper was the aged Brother Wightman, father of the bishop; and seated near the center of the church was a lady of calm exterior and plain apparel, nearly Quakerish, always with her children around her. As a child she had been caressed by John Wesley in England, often sitting upon his knee, and well beloved by Adam Clarke. Little did that good woman think then that an embryo bishop formed one of the group of children, and that all of them by her example and counsel would be a credit to Methodism. Her sacred dust rests in the old Limestone cemetery, Orangeburg county, and her spirit has been long with God.

Each of the devout worshipers on entrance knelt in silent prayer, with countenances settled to a rapt devotion. There was no simply bending the head, or the face hidden behind a fan, and no after "nods and becks and wreathed smiles" so much more becoming a theater than the house of God. Oh no; these simple people came for communion with a King.

The preachers of the period were Lewis Myers, N. Talley, William M. Kennedy, S. Dunwody, Henry Bass, Daniel Hall, John Howard, Charles Bell, Bond English, and, hardly yet in the meridian of their fame, William Capers, James O. Andrew, and S.

Olin. Among the lesser lights, yet somewhat brilliant, were James Norton, Thomas L. Wynn, Elijah Sinclair, J. Murrow, R. Flournoy, James W. Wellborn, Robert Adams, Noah Laney, B. L. Hoskins, and others. Under their ministrations, especially during prayer, many "amens" were uttered and deep groanings audible. Wrong, you say? Of course it was wrong. Where now, in any refined, intellectual, respectable congregation, do you find anything like it? So in the strength of our wisdom we pronounced it, resolving that if ever we became religious it should be after a different fashion. Why groan at all? We knew not the reason, but the fact, to our supreme disgust, was patent. We know now that persons getting a glimpse of their own hearts and a sense of the divine purity, and any longing for that, will groan too, and will be glad of the intercession of the divine Spirit, with "groanings that cannot be uttered." If any are right in thus toning down the emotional, St. Paul was certainly wrong in patronizing the "amen" of the unlearned; and worse, the falling down of the worshiper, and reporting "that God is in you of a truth."

A religion of tinsel and drapery, of forms and frippery, whether Romanist or Protestant, may demand a staidness that never utters a cry or lets fall a tear, but such was not the Methodism of that early day; and may she never abandon her rich experimental knowledge of God! "God in you of a truth" comes down from the early Church, and if this be evidenced by an "amen," or even falling down on one's face, what matter even though vanity's sons and daughters be grieved thereat?

The preachers of the period were earnest men, evidenced by the *abandon* and *unction* of their ministry. Clearly they had but little thought concerning literary reputation. Precision in utterance and well-rounded periods were lost sight of in the higher enterprise of saving souls. Intellectuality and refinement did not round off the rough edges of transgression; both were in danger of ruin, and they were plainly told so. They spoke as the Holy Ghost gave them utterance, and many asked, "What shall we do to be saved?"

Amid all the opposition that Methodism encountered from the beginning, it was during the period from 1818 to 1833 that statistics show the membership nearly doubled in the half cycle of a generation. The same ratio of increase for the next sixty-three years ought to have run over two thousand, when the fact is, notwithstanding the large increase of population, the numbers are but a fraction over the returns of 1833. There were 650 white members then, and but 680 now. At other points in the state there has been unmistakable increase, with districts and circuits multiplied, divided and subdivided. At this point we barely hold our own.

The old opprobrium, as set forth by Dr. Capers, in the inter-meddling with slavery had much to do in keeping Methodism under the ban in Charleston. This, together with the attach-ment to aristocratic Church-of-England forms, has influenced many who, while charmed with the ministry of Capers, Olin, Andrew, Wightman, and Whitefoord Smith, gave in their adher-ence to other Churches. And more, a truly religious life de-mands " the putting off the old man and his deeds, and the put-ting on the new man, which after God is created in righteousness and true holiness." No putting on the new man over the old is in any degree tolerated. The true religion ever demands the sep-aration of the sinner from his sins. Sinner he might feel himself to be—yea, the very chief—but not now lying with his sin and dreaming of heaven, but by grace divine freed from its domin-ion and seeking its extirpation. Its ministry had but little to do with oppositions of science falsely so called, but very much to do with "Christ in you the hope of glory." Now if the ad-vocacy of the like impedes numerical strength, we are willing that it should be ever impeded.

The preaching of that early day was in demonstration of the Spirit and with power. A childish reminiscence records: Long ago in old Cumberland our first remembrance of any preacher is connected with John Howard, a man of no mean fame and power. We remember his warm, earnest, animated manner, tempered with a divine love, melting all hearts; his coming down out of the pulpit with streaming eyes and impassioned utterance, and the burst of feeling filling the entire church. The thought uppermost in our mind was that the preacher had said "bad words"—"devil" and the like, and even worse. "How silly!" you say, and "What ignorance!" Very true, maybe; but better that than hardened iniquity. St. Paul says, " I would have you wise unto that which is good, and simple con-cerning evil." There have been great changes since then; many young gentlemen now of the sober age of five and six are not squeamish as to using bad words themselves. We were not particularly good as a child, but we are astonished at our ignorance of evil as contrasted with the knowledge of evil in the young to-day. But the pictured sheets of sin so attractive to youth now were not then in vogue. There was the same devil, but he had not got so far along in the education of the young. At the early age of five, suffering the pain of a burned finger, we connected with it thoughts of eternal burning. Where was learned anything like that but in that old house of God? Will any dare say how soon the divine Spirit moves the soul? Thoughts concerning *predestination* were troublesome; a wise mother cut the Gordian knot by assuring us that that matter "had puzzled wiser brains than ours was or ever would be." How often did the writer hang entranced on Dr. Capers's ministry! George F. Pierce thrilled his audiences with his sunny eloquence. One day how he did preach! Our hair fairly stood on end under that sermon. And so with many others already named.

The great fire of 1861 that swept diagonally across the city removed the solid brick structure occupying the site of the old wooden Cumberland church. We looked upon the *débris* then covering the ground to find any remains of the tablet to Mr. Joshua Wells, one of the first Methodists of Charleston, but the last vestige was gone. The sweet chimes of old St. Michael's bells still ring out upon the air, and they are yet as sweet as when falling upon childhood's ear; yet sweeter still were the high hymns of praise filling that humble church, from voices now still in death, or—why not?—now swelling the nobler anthems of the skies.

Would that there could be given an exact transcript of the old-time love feast! Alas! this cannot be. There rises up reminiscently the well-filled church, the gathering of the elect from all the churches in the city, the warm, devotional tone, the spirited singing, the tears and joy beyond counterfeiting. The fathers are all gone; their streaming tears and burning words are forgotten, or remembered only by Him who hearkened and heard, and declared they should be his in the day when he should make up his jewels. All are gone. Long lingered old " Brother I-too-for-one," a *sobriquet* earned by his invariably beginning his talks as a witness for our Lord with "*I, too, for one, dear brethren."* This man was perfectly consistent in his loyalty to Christ, surrendering cheerfully his means of livelihood rather than to offend his conscience. An indelible picture in that old church was a plain little man, known by a peculiar, rusty hat. He was as simple and as loving as a child, found at one or other of the churches three times on Sunday, and at every other meeting during the week. Possibly but few, except the angels, missed him out of that " amen corner." It was plain Tommy C——. If they watched closely, the profane would think he always had a refreshing time—asleep. Don't you believe it; his devotions were aided by his closed eyelids, that's all. Talk with him and he would tell you of his rich enjoyment of the manna of the word. He would tell you that he joined the Church only because his wife was a member, thinking the whole of religion consisted only in going to church, but soon found out his error. In great darkness, he held to one simple promise: "A bruised reed shall he not break, and smoking flax shall he not quench." "That was me!" he exclaimed; "and it brought me to the Saviour." Could ye have said more, ye doctors of the law? Could ye have said as much? Alas! how often little esteemed are these rich in faith, giving glory to God! Beware, ye pastors of the Lord's heritage, how ye slight these poor; "they are the children of a King, and the coming day shall so declare it."

Some of the names of the earlier Methodists are on record. Alex. McFarlain (who took the place of Edgar Wells), A. Sevier, J. McDowell, W. Adams, J. Milnor, G. Milnor, W. Smith, J. Hughes, M. Moore, B. Lukeson, J. Cox, and J. Gordon are all of the earlier days; George Airs, Philip Reader, Eliab Kingman, Amos Pilsbury, John Kugley, and Robert Riley are later; and still later are Abel McKee, Jacob Miller, Henry Muckenfuss, George Just, George Chreitzberg, John Mood, John Honor, Duke Goodman, Joseph Galluchat, and Urban Cooper (the last five were preachers), William Wightman, Samuel J. Wagner, William Bird, and many others. A few names among the godly women are still remembered: Mrs. Catharine McFarlain, the hostess of Bishop Asbury; Mrs. Kugley, the rescuer of Dougherty from a mob; Mrs. Selena Smith, the kind housekeeper of the bachelor preachers; Mrs. Agnes Ledbetter, Mrs. Ann Vaughan, Mrs. Matilda Wightman, Mrs. Margaret Just, Mrs.

Susannah Sayle, Mrs. Catharine Mood, Mrs. Susannah Bird, Mrs. Charlotte Will, Mrs. Magdalene Brown, and Mrs. Mary Chreitzberg. Among the early colored members remarkable for intelligence and piety were Harry Bull, Quamby Jones, Peter Simpson, Abraham Jacobs, Ben McNeil, Smart Simpson, Aleck Harleston, Amos Baxter, Morris Brown, Richard Holloway, Castile Selby, John Boquet, Mary Ann Berry, Rachel Wells, and Nanny Coates.

"These all died in the faith, not having received the promises, but having seen them afar off, and were persuaded of them, embraced them, and confessed that they were strangers and pilgrims on the earth." They were diligent in business, fervent in spirit, serving the Lord. Many were toiling in humble occupations, as their Master did before them. As aforetime, so now many a disciple is found among the lowly; but if not ennobled now, then there is no truth upon the earth, and never has been.

In the year 1836 the preachers in Charleston, S. C., were N. Talley, presiding elder; William Capers, preacher in charge; James Sewell, J. W. McCall, and W. A. Gamewell. That year a meeting was held at Goose Creek Camp Ground, at which the writer was converted. In the ministry of these men, an experimental knowledge of God was always insisted upon. Said Dr. Capers on receiving us into the Church in 1836: " Do you know God as a sin-pardoning God? " We did not, and shall never forget his earnest advice never to rest satisfied without it. If any were disposed to forget the question, its constant recurrence in the class meeting would have prevented. The only alternative was to get this knowledge or to retire from the Church. The fidelity of the leaders and constant oversight of the preachers gave no rest to any disposed to rest in their sins. Alas! these old class meetings have gone into desuetude, and vital godliness has been sadly injured.

This close examination into personal experience and building up a Christian character was pursued in the Conferences as well as in the societies. An old letter from Dr. Wynn, in the *Advocate*, gives a graphic picture of this examination of character at the forty-third session of the Conference held in Charleston, S. C., January 28, 1829. Dr. Wynn says: "There were in 1827 twenty-seven inexperienced, uneducated, and unmarried young men entered as probationers in the South

Carolina Conference.* Out of that number I reckon but three are left: Dr. Murrah, of Mississippi; Dr. Boring, of Georgia; and myself." All have since gone. He continues: "Dr. Emory, book agent, two years thereafter at Charleston, asked and was granted the privilege of addressing that class of young men, which he said was the largest that he had ever known to be admitted at one time into any Conference. That speech was made in connection with the trial of one of the members of the Conference for immoral conduct. The charge was, having broken a marriage engagement with one young lady and married another. That day I matriculated in the school of common sense, by listening to the speeches and witnessing the voting. Never before did I know the sacredness and sanctity of woman's person and character. Of the fathers present in the ministry that day, I remember Lewis Myers, Dr. Pierce, S. Dunwody, J. Dannelly, William Arnold, S. K. Hodges, William M. Kennedy, J. Howard, Bond English, C. Betts, J. O. Andrew, N. Tally, J. L. Wynn, and William Capers, besides others not now remembered. These holy men unitedly portrayed the enormity of this offense in such glowing terms as to preclude all hope of keeping him from being thrown overboard; and but for J. O. Andrew, who pleaded that the Conference hold him by at least a slack-twisted cord lest he sink never more to rise, he would have been cast into the open sea, across the bar, where he had been driven by the speeches made against him. Do not we of this day need more admonitions from such holy men as these were?"

This young man had been admitted on trial in 1828, in a class of twenty, among whom were Samuel W. Capers, William M. Wightman, and William Martin, and in that year and in 1829 he traveled with the Rev. John Mood on Cypress Circuit. He was discontinued in 1830, and his course afterwards abounded in shallows to the very end of his life.

We wish that those speeches could have been fully reported. What admirable lectures on ministerial character and conduct! We several times heard the like in our earlier Conferences. Alas! they have gone into desuetude since Conference doors have been thrown open in the examination of character. It is very doubtful if we have been gainers thereby.

The portraiture of another Conference, the first the writer

---

19   * See class in Appendix.

ever attended, may here be given. It was the fifty-fourth session of the South Carolina Conference, held January 8, 1840. Thomas A. Morris was the presiding bishop, and William M. Wightman the secretary. The membership in the Conference was 24,016 whites and 27,630 colored. It was held in the somber basement of Trinity Church, still intact, only divided and subdivided into different rooms, and more dark than then, seemingly waiting until some of our millionaires give us a modern structure more in keeping with their wealth and the demands of our improving city, and of His glory who of old said by his prophets, "Ye dwell in your ceiled houses, while the house of the Lord lieth waste." That this will come eventually, is true; but the pity of it is that some of us will not live to see it, and will lose the prestige of making it monumental, and, alas! miss the "well done" of the final day.

The author was then a youth of nineteen, fresh from Cokesbury, his first circuit, having been under the colleagueship of the Rev. Samuel Dunwody. Of the bishop very little is remembered save the admirable sermon he preached in old Cumberland Church from the text, "Ye must through much tribulation enter into the kingdom of God." The number of preachers in connection with this Conference receiving appointments was just one hundred. Of supernumeraries there were none, and of superannuates thirteen. Of this total, to-day there are but four survivors, namely: J. W. Wellborn, of Mississippi, now in his eighty-eighth year; Simpson Jones, William C. Patterson, and the writer. There were five districts: Charleston, Henry Bass, presiding elder; Cokesbury, William M. Wightman, presiding elder; Columbia, Hartwell Spain, presiding elder; Wilmington, Bond English, presiding elder; Lincolnton, William Crook, presiding elder.

A passing glance at some of the leaders, as well as of the rank and file, is in order; and if of no other use it may show how youthful opinion has been confirmed by the experience of age. If the roll were called to-day the response in nearly every case might not be in the grandiloquent style of Napoleon's veterans, "Dead upon the field of honor," but, which is far better, "Died in the faith." By all odds the *Magnus Apollo* of the body was William Capers, then editor of the *Southern Christian Advocate*. He long held this position, and for six quadrenniums, from

REV. BOND ENGLISH.

1828 to 1846, led the Conference delegation until elected to the episcopacy. His influence on the Church at home and abroad is well known, and need not be enlarged upon here. It was quite apparent even then who would be his successor, and upon whom his mantle would fall.

William M. Wightman was coming largely into prominence, closing up a well-ordered life in 1882. We regret that his is the only name not on the list of the dead of the South Carolina Conference, for, though in the episcopacy, he is still "ours." This list was originally prepared by the writer, but the preparation of the Conference Minutes passing out of his hands, he is not responsible for the omission. We trust that it will be remedied.

Whitefoord Smith, "the golden-mouthed," as he was called, was following after. These two were the young men of promise in the body. If such were permissible, they might have been considered rivals. Each has filled his allotted space and work, and gone to his reward.

Among the elder men of influence was Charles Betts. In person he was compact, rotund, strong, almost fierce at times. In the pulpit his sentences were so involved as not to show to advantage, but he was argumentative and strong in debate. He was the very personification of energy on a district, and in business matters of the Conference an adept. His popularity with the brethren placed him near the head of the delegation to the General Conference for years.

William M. Kennedy, as one of the pioneers, was much beloved in the Conference, and was soon to close up his earthly career; while Samuel Dunwody, his classmate (both entering in 1806), was to linger until 1854, dying at the age of seventy-three years.

Bond English, in 1840, was fifth in the election to the General Conference, the others being Capers, Betts, Wightman, and Kennedy. Mr. English was modest, retiring, self-depreciating to a fault, but clear-headed, warm-hearted, and eloquent. He was small of stature, inclined to corpulence; lame from an accident; with the loss of an eye, his somewhat oval face was marred; quick, impulsive in his movements; an excellent judge of character, but so diffident in nature that he was not born to control. His sermons were deeply spiritual, ardent, simple, natural, and best of all, full of the divine Spirit. We did not know it then, but he was destined to be our presiding elder in 1840; and such was our estimate of the man that we named our first-born for him.

The sober, staid, wise H. A. C. Walker was coming up among the younger men. In 1844 he was fifth on the list for the General Conference, and for a long series of years was foremost in every good word and work.

It was not until 1850 that W. A. Gamewell became prominent. He was admitted into the Conference in 1834, and held on in his quiet way. Tall and commanding in appearance, he was always serious, and preached effectively.

James Stacy had been connected with the Conference for ten years. His personal appearance was neat, his face pale, his eyes bright, his speech intense. Being of an extremely nervous temperament, of course he was a sufferer, but always to the full measure of his strength he labored until called to his reward.

Albert M. Shipp was admitted into the Conference in 1841. It was not until 1862 that he led the General Conference delegation. But we are approaching too nearly the time of living men, and must restrain our pen.

A glance at the subalterns of this mighty host may be indulged in. A class of twelve had been admitted at the previous Conference, the writer being one of them, and came up for review at this session. Would you believe it? decidedly the foremost man of the class was discontinued, a very small jealousy inducing it, and only continued by a reconsideration of the vote. W. A. McSwain was the man. He died all too soon, both for his fame and the good work he might have done. Examinations of character were then held with closed doors, and were minute and severe. "They order this matter better now." We beg leave to differ; for if a good university be a bench with a proper teacher at one end and a pupil at the other, we cannot despise the training these good men put their pupils through. "Too severe!" you say. Was it? Yet it put some sense into skulls that "could not teach and would not learn." For example, one of this very class was excoriated—well, just awfully. He wanted to marry, and didn't, but got it—the excoriation—all the same. Mercy! thought the writer, if that comes of only wanting to marry, what will become of one who has actually done so? He found out afterwards that in this case all proprieties had been observed; in the other they had not, one objection being that the brother seemingly wanted more wives than one. That cannot be thought of in our country, however much some find that one wife is too many for them. The truth may be that in that early day a man had to marry to get an increase of salary, in that event it always being doubled; the Discipline saying $100 for himself, the same for his wife, and $16 to $24 for each child under sixteen years of age. Now this was undoubtedly "poor pay," and yet in one case we know it was decidedly "*poor preach.*"

At this Conference, the fifty-fourth session, there were stationed one hundred preachers. At the one hundred and tenth session two hundred and sixteen received appointments— very evident signs of growth. At this fifty-fourth session there were but five preachers on the retired list, among them James Jenkins, Joseph Moore, and James Dannelly. These three men were the connecting links between that generation of preachers and the pioneers of old. They had been in labors abundant, with the very poorest of earthly recompense, and were now in receipt of the very smallest stipends allotted by the Church; but however small, it was fully in keeping with the allowances of the active ministry. For fifteen years of active service James Jenkins received $1,623, a little over $100 per annum. During his superannuation he received from $110, the highest, to $8, the lowest, per annum. His obituary, evidently by Bishop Wightman, states: "When the time of his departure came, he hailed the approach of death not only with composure but with the gusto of indescribable joy. The conqueror's shout, so familiar to his lips when in health, lingered upon those lips now fast losing the power of utterance. Along with this triumphant mood he maintained and manifested to the last a remarkable degree of that profound self-abasement so often observed in the dying moments of the most eminently useful men. His language was: 'I have never done anything; don't mention these things to me; I am nothing, nothing but a poor, unworthy sinner, saved by grace. Christ is all; to him be all the praise.' Without a struggle or a groan, he fell asleep in Jesus. His witness is with God, and his record on high." He was the first of the three to die, closing his life on earth June 24, 1847, aged eighty-three years. Joseph Moore followed, February 14, 1850, aged eighty-four years; and James Dannelly, April 28, 1855, aged sixty-nine years.

From the fifty-fourth Conference, held in 1840, to the one hundred and tenth session, held at Abbeville in 1896, is a long interval, more than half a century. We are glad to testify that whatever may have been time's changes, improvements, and what not, Methodism still maintains its integrity in doctrine and its great business to spread scriptural holiness over the earth. Fashionable formalism is seen in Jenny June's whilom fashion letter. She says:

Easter should be a pleasant month this year, for it gives us, with its first incoming, Easter flowers, Easter festivity, and Easter fashions. Not that Lent has been dull by any means, for, since religion is fashionable, even a Lenten season has its bright side, and we have had Nilsson to give it additional attraction. But fashion does not take naturally to penitence, though softened by manifold indulgences; and therefore the advent of Easter, with its gayety and fresh toilets, is heartily welcomed, and one can be as fashionable and as pious as one pleases. In fact, you cannot be fashionable without being pious.

The whole letter might be considered dreadfully satirical, but alas! the depth of its satire is in its awful truthfulness. The celebration of Easter, as set forth in Acts ii. 32, is strikingly in contrast—"This Jesus hath God raised up, whereof we are all witnesses"—magnified especially in the conversion of the three thousand souls.

Methodism in the olden time ever entered its protest against mere formalism in religion, and labored with a self-sacrificing energy to promote the soul's peace with God. God's prediction concerning his Church is that "his righteousness shall go forth as brightness, and his salvation as a lamp that burneth." "Among whom ye shine as lights in the world," says St. Paul. If there be any darkness, lack, or failure now, the only safety is in a return to the old paths.

ST. JOHN'S CHURCH, ROCK HILL, S. C.; H. B. BROWNE, PASTOR.

CHAPTER XXXII.

A Summing Up—First Period—The O'Kelly Schism—Second Period—Third Period—Cokesbury, Pee Dee, Orangeburg, and Barnwell Circuits—Methodist Journalism—Sunday Schools—Education—William Capers—Fourth Period—Fifth and Last Period.

NOW to sum up the whole, we present in a more condensed form the results of Methodism in South Carolina. What if there be somewhat of repetition? If needful to a proper insight into the work, surely it can be condoned.

A Romanist once asked a Protestant, "Where was your religion before Luther?" The answer, scathingly satirical, was, "Where was your face before it was washed?" The rejoinder would have been equally forcible if it had been, "Where was *your* Church before Luther?" True, there was the papacy, the holy Roman empire, much of royal rule, Latin Christianity, and crime; but certainly not the Catholic Church as it is to-day. Orthodoxy was at a discount; bulls were contradictory; doctrine unsettled. A reformation like that in Germany was needed, and history records that, "from the halls of the Vatican to the most secluded hermitage of the Apennines, the great revival was everywhere felt and seen."

So with the Church of England. What was she before Wesley? More pure than Rome, it is true, yet an offshoot; and with all her grand cathedrals, orders, royal patronage and power, how little of the divine Spirit! Rigidly holding to the divine right of kings, like Festus she lightly esteemed "one Jesus, who was dead, whom Paul affirmed to be alive," and who truly is "God over all, blessed for evermore." In her blinded rage she cast forth her sons, who, actuated by that faith, would have made her incorporate with life, and they went forth triumphing everywhere; "so mightily grew the word of God and prevailed."

The people called Methodists were never troubled by the arrogant claims of the Anglican or Roman Church, but, building upon the prophets, apostles, and martyrs, "Jesus Christ himself being the chief corner stone," have wrought mightily through God unto this hour. Not caring an iota for the dogma of apostolical succession, they held firmly to the succession of

(299)

the truth as taught by Him, first bearing witness to it, and running down through Paul, the martyrs, Wyclif, Huss, Luther, and Wesley, as the only anchor for eternal hope; and persecution, rack and gibbet, faggot and flame cannot harm it. Down to the judgment trump shall this succession of the truth run on. For

> Truth forever on the scaffold,
> Wrong forever on the throne,
> Yet that scaffold sways the future,
> And, behind the dim unknown,
> Standeth God within the shadow,
> Keeping watch above his own.

I shall divide the century of our existence as a Conference into *five* unequal periods of fifteen, thirty, then again thirty, then five, and lastly twenty years, each forming an epoch in our history.

Our first period begins at the close of the war of the Revolution. The English Church existed with the first settlement of Carolina; the Presbyterians had an early existence; the Congregationalists in 1682, the Baptists in 1685, the French Protestants in 1700, the Lutherans in 1750, and the Methodists in 1785.

The war had wrought great changes in the country; the parish churches were closed, for the clergy of the Church of England had fled from the state. At the peace, religion had sadly declined. Churches had been reopened, but, because of the lax morality of the clergy, were closed again. Great religious destitution prevailed everywhere. In many populous sections of the country months and even years elapsed, and a minister of religion was never seen. Only here and there throughout the state was found a Presbyterian or Baptist congregation.

As late as 1790 ministers were disciplined for drunkenness, and at funerals often the living were not sufficiently sober to bury the dead. Tradition asserts that in one of the upper counties of the state a minister was so far gone as to fall asleep in the pulpit during the singing of the hymn, and when aroused by the precentors telling him "*it was out,*" he drowsily told them to "*fill her up agin.*" Such being the morality of the shepherd, to what sort of pastures must the flock have been led?

In the General Minutes of our connection for 1795 the Church is called to a fast with sabbatical strictness, to bewail such sins

as covetousness, superstition (in trusting to ceremonial and
legal righteousness), profanity, Sabbath-breaking, making con-
tracts without the intention of honest heathen to fulfill them,
various debaucheries, drunkenness, and such like. What need
just then for a cry like John's in the wilderness, "Repent, for
the kingdom of heaven is at hand"; and faithfully did Asbury
and his coadjutors sound it forth.

At first Georgia and South Carolina were united. Two years
after, Georgia was separate, until 1794; then included again in
the South Carolina Conference, so remaining until 1830. The
historic circuits took the names of the broad streams flowing
through the state. Wherever the people were, there were the
preachers found. These had not entered on lives of ease or
fruition; they were in labors most abundant, wrestling with
floods of great waters; and floods of ungodly men made them
not afraid. They met with no favor from coreligionists, were
rather considered weak and unlettered men, poor enthusiasts,
disturbers of the quiet order of things, wandering stars emitting
a baleful light, and dealing in magic even to effect base ends.
They were put down in church reports as men of "infamous
character," an "indignity to human nature," "a disgrace to the
Christian name." Their rapid movements, "traveling from place
to place in quick succession," were highly censurable: how
could men be "convinced of their sincerity" when they had
"no settled abiding place"? And it is gravely written down
in Church history, "*This* is not most profitable." Profitable,
forsooth! Nay, verily; profit in that sense these preachers
never thought of. They sought no chapels of ease, nor thrones
of power; never thought solely of wealthy neighborhoods, or
ran lines of circumvallation around rich alluvial sites, but
went anywhere and everywhere on their grand mission. The
fact is, such objection grew out of the apprehension that the
objectors' craft was in danger; but the cry, "Great is Diana
of the Ephesians!" had no more effect upon these men than
on the first apostles: they kept on turning the world down-
side up, it having been in their judgment "upside down" long
enough. And so "they went forth and preached everywhere,
the Lord working with them and confirming the word with signs
following."

In the "Dialogues of Devils," in the council held in Pandemonium, when the question is up, "How to stop the revival under John Wesley?" a sleek, knowing little devil, with a piping voice, ventures the advice: "Make John a bishop." We wish it had been done; then the grand old Church of England might have been most gloriously leavened at a much earlier date.

The line of travel marked by Asbury and his coadjutors, from Cheraw down the Pee Dees, and down the coast to Georgetown, thence to Charleston, then throughout the lower part of the state, then up on both sides of the Santee, and only occasionally up to King's Mountain as the place of exit, gave the section, favored yearly with the bishop's visits, a very great advantage, even the greater preponderance of Methodism. It is in the memory of living men that much of the territory above Columbia has only within the last half century been fruitful for Methodism. Indeed, it is but of recent date that in Chester, Yorkville, and Lancaster our Church is becoming formidable. True, the upper country at this early day was more sparsely settled, and ancient Calvinism had been long intrenched; but who can tell if these giants of the olden time, whose forte was strong assaults along the line of doctrine, might not have earlier achieved greater results? These preachers were of a *sui generis* race. Said ex-Governor W——, a strong Universalist, to a friend in Charleston once: "I went into a barroom lately, and who should I see there but our own dear little parson. We took a drink together; *it was a very great comfort!*" These gave no such comfort to parishioners; it was ever "woe to the wicked," whether men would bear or whether they would forbear. The authoritative tone and dogmatic utterance were there because God put them there; they spake with authority, and not as the scribes. The lower counties of our Conference hardly realize how much they are indebted for the line of travel adopted by our early bishops, leading on the fiery cohorts of Methodism to the battle; their pathway one of consuming flame, for cloven tongues as of fire sat upon each as of old at Pentecost, and they spake as the Spirit gave them utterance. Thanks be unto God, the gift of the Holy Ghost is still with the Church!

The first convert to God, in Charleston, at least (who can make the record of the many, many thousands since?), was Mr. Edgar Wells, who became the Gaius of the apostles of Methodism. He died in 1797, and two bishops officiated at his funeral.

His remains lie under the foundation of the once Cumberland Church. Often when a child has the writer looked upon the marble covering his dust. Many other converts rapidly succeeded, the statistics showing great progression in five years. In Carolina proper in 1786 the membership reported was 595 whites and 43 colored; in 1790, five years after, they numbered 2,768 whites and 488 colored. Ratio of increase for whites, 365.21; for colored, 1,034.88 per cent.

The preachers of eminence during these fifteen years were James Foster (probably the first Methodist in Carolina, antedating even Asbury's arrival), Henry Willis, Reuben Ellis, Isaac Smith, Hope Hull, Jonathan Jackson, Thomas Humphries, Tobias Gibson, Enoch George, James Jenkins, William McKendree, Benjamin Blanton, Alexander McCain, Nicholas Snethen (both of the latter afterwards in the Methodist Protestant Church), and John Harper—historic worthies, of whom much might be written.

As regards the rapid growth marking the first five years of our history, the same was not borne out in the decade closing in the year 1800. All over the connection there was a decrease during that period. In our Conference, even with Georgia added, the numbers in 1791 were 5,731 whites, 848 colored. Then began an unusual but steady decrease, the returns being, in 1792, 5,619 whites, 964 colored; 1793, 5,265 white, 882 colored; 1794, 5,172 whites, 1,221 colored; 1795, 4,428 whites, 1,126 colored; 1796, 3,862 whites, 971 colored; 1797, 3,715 whites, 1,038 colored. A decrease in six years of whites 35.17 per cent, the colored having a small increase. This is worth considering, and the causes ought to be inquired into.

Great as were the self-sacrifice and zeal of these preachers, it was not always the joyful song of "harvest home" that greeted their ears. They must often have been sad; "for the divisions of Reuben there were great searchings of heart." "All they in Asia have turned away from me," once wrote Paul; and these had need of a like lamentation. The reasons for this are not hard to seek. The O'Kelly schism was one, and, though not to the same degree affecting the work here as elsewhere, doubtless had its influence. But good came out of the evil, settling for once and all the great question of appeal from the appointing power; such appeal involving endless difficulty, often provoking vain jangling for change. If any fear, in the many and wondrous changes in our day, that episcopal prerogative is too great, it might be met by more fully defining the prerogatives of the bishop's counselors; the impartial decree of ten men being as worthy of confidence as that of one hundred.

Another and chief disturbing cause at this period, as well as for the disruption of the Church in after years, was the vexed question of slavery. The early journals of the Conference are full of it, and as early as 1789 Dr. Coke, with all his prestige for piety and zeal, greatly erred in his ill-judged and persistent interference with matters under Cæsar's jurisdiction. It is hardly possible to estimate the loss to Methodism by such action. For long years the struggle went on, and all might have been avoided if good men could but have risen to the altitude of Pauline precept and example.

Another disturbing cause appeared in the right assumed by some of choosing their pastors, induced by the appearance of an exceedingly popular preacher in Charleston, culminating finally in the Hammet schism, shaking the Church in that city to its very foundations and threatening its entire overthrow, resulting in a short time in a loss of membership of 27.27 per cent. Bishop Asbury writes in 1791: "Charleston.—I went to church under awful distress of heart. . . . . The people claim a right to choose their own preachers—a thing quite new among Methodists. None but Mr. Hammet will do for them. We shall see how it will end." So he did, and we all see it. Doubtless he loved the people, loved his own peace, but he stood firmly because he loved the cause of God more.

These were all causes enough for the declension in numbers alluded to, but there was yet another—the apostasy of Beverly Allen, a man of great popularity, brilliant parts, and widespread reputation as a preacher; but he fell, and foully, and much injury was done the Church by his fall.

Thus outward persecution, intestine disputes, and apostasy at this early period threatened ruin to the cause. Assuredly, if it were not of God it must have come to naught, instead of reaching the grand proportions over which we rejoice to-day. Notwithstanding these hindrances, however, in the first fifteen years of our history the increase was great. Numbers in Carolina and Georgia in 1786, 673 whites and 43 colored; in

1800 there were 4,802 whites, 1,535 colored; in 1785, preachers 3; in 1800, 33—ratio of increase, 1,000 per cent; ratio of increase in white members, 628.38, and in colored members over 3,000 per cent.

Our second period extends from 1800 to 1830, an epoch marking the more regular development of Conference boundaries, districts, circuits, and stations, and showing a more steady increase in membership. Paradoxical as it may seem, divisions but increased our strength. We divided but to conquer, and this has been characteristic of Methodism throughout its history.

In 1800 the South Carolina Conference was composed of Georgia, South Carolina, and a small part of North Carolina, forming but one ecclesiastical district, presided over by Benjamin Blanton, in which boundaries there are now several Annual Conferences. It had 16 charges, 32 preachers; white membership, 4,802; colored, 1,535. In 1801 it was divided into two districts: Georgia—Stith Mead, presiding elder; and South Carolina—James Jenkins, presiding elder. In 1802 Saluda District was formed. In 1805 five districts made up the Conference, so remaining until 1810, when there were six, and continuing thus until 1818, when there were seven. In 1825 there were eight districts, and in 1830 ten, when Georgia was made a separate Conference.

An increasing membership, while not the best test of spirituality, evidently marks material progression; and while we would not, in King David's spirit, "number Israel," may we not, attributing all to the Divine favor, say with exultant Jacob: " I am not worthy of the least of all the mercies, and of all the truth, which thou hast shewed unto thy servant; for with my staff I passed over this Jordan; and now I am become two bands."

This increase from 1800 to 1818 was regular, and from one to three thousand yearly; but in 1818 there was a loss of nearly 1,500 whites, and the heavier decrease of over 5,000 colored. For the decrease of the whites we cannot account, but the loss of the latter was because of the dreadful schism occurring that year in Charleston. From 1810, when the colored members numbered 8,202, to 1817, their numbers increased to 16,789, thus in seven years more than doubling their numbers—a ratio

20

of increase of 104.95 per cent. But in 1818 they fell to 11,587, 30.99 per cent of loss. This schism originated in a stricter exercise of Church discipline among them, giving great offense to their leaders. The agitation was secret for a time, but culminated in the withdrawal at one fell swoop of 4;367 members in Charleston alone. The loss was seen and felt, the empty galleries of the city churches proclaimed it, and the volume of song of thousands of the most musical voices of the earth was sadly missed in the praise of God. They set up for themselves, even building a church, but soon came to naught, the discovery of the intended insurrection in 1822 destroying their hopes of separate existence as a Church.

But the Conference, like some gallant ship, weathered the storm, and with the freshening gales of grace, and steady hands at the helm, kept on in the open sea until, in 1830, only twelve years after, she had nearly more than doubled her numbers, both of whites and blacks. In 1818 there were 20,965 whites and 11,714 blacks; in 1830, 40,335 whites and 24,538 colored; a ratio of increase among the whites of 92.39, and colored 109.47 per cent.

The ratio of increase for this first period of thirty years, notwithstanding all the losses, was certainly great:

Year.	Districts.	Preachers.	Charges.	White.	Colored.
In 1800.	1	33	16	4,802	1,535
In 1830.	10	158	97	40,335	24,538

Increase—Districts, 900; preachers, 393.75; charges, 818.75; whites, 739.96; colored, near 1,500 per cent.

On this review, well may we exclaim, "What hath God wrought!" And how were these glorious results achieved? By agents, the counterpart of him "that goeth forth and weepeth, bearing precious seed"; and undoubtedly they returned with rejoicing, bringing their sheaves with them. How they were sustained is fully known only to Him who "feedeth the young ravens when they cry." The sending forth was much on the same plan as by the Lord himself: "Save a staff only, no scrip, no bread, no money in their purse." The yearly stipend for years on years reached but from one to two hundred dollars, and that rarely paid in full, as the Conference records abundantly testify. How like Elijah the prophet, at the brook Cherith! Ahab's princes and Ahab himself may have rejoiced in being the

GREENWOOD METHODIST CHURCH; REV. MARION DARGAN, PASTOR.

prophet's benefactors; but God gave the honor to the ravens, and relieving them of the burden, sent him to Sarepta, saying: "I have commanded a widow woman there to sustain thee." "Hear now, O princes, and be instructed, ye judges in the earth." If divine Almightiness goes with the handful of meal, it outweighs all your power and wealth; and to be helpers with God, men may well struggle for preëminence in any field. No wonder these men, with all their self-sacrifice and toil, were so deeply in love with their work; and if they had been asked by the Master, as of old, "Lacked ye anything?" with the rich recompense of present joy would they not have answered, "Nothing, Lord "?

Our third period runs from 1830 (when Georgia was set off) to 1860, and comes more nearly within the memory of living men, who are too near the events recorded to see them in the heroic lights of the past; but time will mellow and sanctify them in the eyes of coming generations.

The South Carolina Conference, in 1831, consisted of the state, with the lower part of North Carolina attached. It was composed of five ecclesiastical districts: Charleston, Saluda, Columbia, Fayetteville, and Lincolnton. The presiding elders were Henry Bass, Malcolm McPherson, William M. Kennedy, Nicholas Talley, and Hartwell Spain. The districts, with some changes of territory and name, continued five in number until 1841, when six were formed; so remaining until 1850, when they were reduced to five, because of the transfer of territory to the North Carolina Conference; and in 1853 six were formed, so remaining until 1859, when eight districts composed the Conference.

The crowning glory of this period, and one peculiarly marked in the history of our Conference, was its care for, and religious culture of, the slave. One attestation of the divine mission of our Lord was, "The poor have the gospel preached unto them." From 1812 the General Minutes bear witness to the precedence of the Conference in this matter; from that time till 1840 (the latest date of connectional Minutes consulted) our returns of colored members numbered five units, and all the other Conferences but four. As early as 1809 this good work was begun. For that year among the appointments stand: "From Ashley to Savannah River, James H. Mellard, missionary;

from Santee to Cooper River, James E. Glenn, missionary."
But there were hindrances for next year, and long afterwards
the record disappears. It was not until 1829, twenty years after,
that negro missions proper were formed. The first missionaries
appointed that year were the Rev. John Honor and John H.
Massey. The former died the following year, a martyr to his
work. The writer remembers well, when a boy, the solemn burial in Trinity churchyard, Charleston, where a cenotaph marks
the grave of the first missionary to the slaves in Carolina.

Our grand old Conference was the first to enter this field.
No sickly sentiment moved her, but only the love of souls; and
money and human life were freely expended in behalf of the
spiritual interests of the slave. She may well have borne the
cognomen of the Missionary Conference. The contributions
for missions in 1831 were but $261.33, at the rate of but 1¼ cents
per member, increasing in amount yearly, until in 1858 they
reached $28,138.03, or at the rate of 75 cents per member. In
1860, thirty years from the beginning, $3,853,596.06 had been
expended for missions. Will any ask, "Why was this waste of
the ointment made?" The answer is, The light of eternity will
reveal that a good work was wrought by the expenditure.

Prosperity attended the work until 1862, when the significant
words in the Minutes, "Broken up by the abolitionists," and
later on, "In the enemy's line," told the tale of disaster. The
numbers returned in 1830 were 657 members, served exclusively by the missionaries. In 1861, at the beginning of the war,
there were 32 missions, served by 37 missionaries; over 200
plantations; over 12,000 members, including probationers; and
over 4,000 catechumens. When the war closed, or shortly afterwards, there was not one remaining.

In 1830 the membership returned was 19,750 whites and
18,422 colored—glorious old Georgia carrying off more than
half. But steadily the preachers wrought, increasing the number
year by year until 1835, when a decrease of 1,347 whites appears,
caused greatly by the schism in Charleston. Would that that
could have been prevented. No great principle was involved
requiring the sacrifice, but it was a little spark that kindled the
flame, causing the severest disaster that has ever happened to
Methodism in Charleston; not only sweeping off many of the
younger members of the Church, but seriously injuring its

spirituality for a time. It resulted in the formation of the Methodist Protestant Church, not long since merged into the Lutheran. Notwithstanding this severe loss, however, the increase for the decade was good, the ratio of increase being for the whites 26.51, and for the colored 35.28 per cent. From 1840 to 1859 it was still better—36.35 for whites, and 67.66 per cent for the colored; but from 1850 to 1859 the ratio of increase was much reduced, being 10.11 for whites, and 11.93 per cent for the colored. This was caused by the transfer of 3,926 whites and 3,757 colored members to the North Carolina Conference. But for the entire period of thirty years, from 1830 to 1860, progression was well marked, the ratio of increase being for the whites 103.36 and 170.18 per cent for the colored. An increase of over 100 per cent in a generation is certainly no bad showing.

The financial matters of the period, from the lack of systematic fullness now obtaining, must be left entirely to conjecture. Except the Conference collections and money for missions, there are no records in the Minutes, and even these were not on record until 1831. In the matter of salaries, however, it is very certain that, as from the beginning, they were on the most economical basis. The quarterage of a man of family rarely exceeded $300, and family expenses, in favored cases, as much, but more frequently much less. The writer feelingly knows of a case in the decade from 1840 to 1850 where the average of a preacher's salary for ten years, with a family to support, was but little over $300 per annum. Buckle and tongue were made to meet, but it required a very heavy strain. The average payment for ministerial support in 1884, in the South Carolina Conference, was $595. It is very certain that the average payments of the period under review did not reach the half of that sum.

The circuits of that day were large, with two preachers, having from twenty to twenty-four appointments. Those of the present time know but little of territorial extent. They are like Canon Farrar, who, accustomed to the narrow confines of old England, was amazed at the vast distances of our Western world, and was obliged to cancel engagements on that account. We can speak feelingly of some of those vast areas.

The Cokesbury Circuit in 1839 covered nearly the whole of Abbeville county, and the lower part of Anderson, with some twenty appointments, served every fortnight by two preachers.

The junior preacher received $100, every dollar of it; for Thomas Williams, of precious memory, was one of the stewards, and he never permitted anything like discount in settling with the pastors. Will any say, "That was certainly *mighty poor pay*"? The preacher can very truthfully assert that "it was certainly *mighty poor preach*." The wonder to this day is how the people could have put up with it. The numbers returned for that year were 888 whites and 631 colored, 3 Sunday schools, 30 teachers, and 216 children. In 1884 there were in the same boundaries six separate charges, 1,634 members, 28 Sunday schools, 141 teachers, 1,060 pupils, with near $4,000 raised for salaries, and $26,550 value of Church property.

The Pee Dee Circuit in 1840 began at Parnassus, in Marlboro county, thence to Brownsville, across to Harleeville and Little Rock, then on to Marion Courthouse, taking in nearly all the country between the two Pee Dees, down through Britton's Neck at the confluence of the two rivers to a church appropriately called the Ark, for the flood would come often and take them all away. There were some twenty-four appointments, occasionally twenty-seven for good measure, filled every two weeks. The aggregate of salaries for two preachers and presiding elder was $700, not fully paid. For that year were returned 1,034 white and 876 colored members, and $43 collected for missions. No parsonage nor Sunday schools were reported. Within the same territory there are now 6 charges, 5 parsonages, 33 Sunday schools, 1,758 pupils, over $5,000 for ministerial support, more than $700 contributed for missions alone, near 3,500 members, and $43,000 worth of Church property.

The Orangeburg Circuit in 1841 extended from Jeffcoat's over to St. Matthews', down to the courthouse, and then some six miles below Branchville. There were twenty-four appointments. The salary for three preachers was $700, not all paid that year. Now there are seven separate charges, all doing well.

The Barnwell Circuit, the last we shall mention, was said, in terms of hyperbole, to contain as much territory as the kingdom of Great Britain. Starting from Blackville, it ran across the Edisto, taking in all the country around Boiling Springs Camp Ground; on to Rocky Swamp, Pine Grove; on to Jordan's Mills; then some forty miles above to Nazareth; then across to Vaucluse, Aiken, Beech Island; down to six miles below Barnwell

Courthouse; thence to Graham's, Union, and back to Blackville again. There were over thirty appointments, filled in five weeks by two preachers—on one Sunday preaching four times in order to get a little rest. To the preacher appointed in 1844, good Dr. Capers said: "Get married to your circuit, my young brother; take it for better or worse." "The banns are forbidden, Doctor," said the preacher; "for they say it is the fag end of creation." "Who says so?" indignantly exclaimed the Doctor. It was not so, certainly; many of the best men that ever adorned the earth were there, and are now denizens of the city of God in heaven. The membership returned was 1,026 whites, with 9 Sunday schools, 33 teachers, 202 pupils. The salary for two preachers was $600, all paid. In the same boundaries now there are eight separate charges, 2,312 members, 25 Sunday schools, 154 teachers, 876 children, near $5,000 for salaries and $40,000 worth of Church property. Pretty good, one would think, for what some considered the frazzle end of creation only forty years ago.

METHODIST JOURNALISM.

Methodist journalism is worthy of notice, and the South Carolina Conference was one of the first to invoke the power of the press. As early as 1825 James O. Andrew, Samuel Dunwody, and Lewis Myers were appointed a committee "to inquire into the expediency of establishing within the bounds of this Conference a religious newspaper," resulting in the publication, the same year, of the *Wesleyan Journal*, afterwards incorporated with the *Advocate* in New York, becoming thus the *Advocate and Journal* of Northern Methodism. In 1837 was begun the publication of the *Southern Christian Advocate*, removed to Georgia in 1862, brought back to South Carolina in 1878, and now published in Greenville, S. C.

SUNDAY SCHOOLS.

Our Church in this good old Conference was foremost in the care of its children. As early as 1779 Methodist preachers were required to meet the children once a fortnight, and to examine the parents in reference to their conduct toward them. This was some time before the movement of Robert Raikes in behalf of "neglected street children" in England. It was at the South Carolina Conference, held in Charleston, February,

1790, that the term Sunday schools first appears in the official records of Methodism. The Journal for that year contains the following:

Question. What can be done in order to instruct poor children, white and black, to read?

Answer. Let us labor, as the heart and soul of one man, to establish Sunday schools in or near the place of public worship. Let persons be appointed by the bishops, elders, deacons, or preachers to teach, *gratis,* all that will attend, and have a capacity to learn, from six o'clock in the morning until ten, and from two o'clock in the afternoon till six, when it does not interfere with public worship.

Although thus early at this important work, singularly it was not until 1828 that it was made the duty of the preachers to form Sunday schools within their respective charges; and it was not until 1835 that the schools were reported in Conference Minutes, the returns for that year being 185 schools, 3,885 officers and teachers, 6,028 scholars, and $1,014.78 collected for their support. In 1884, fifty years after, the returns were 591 schools, 3,885 officers and teachers, 29,362 scholars, $5,370.15 collected. Ratio of increase: schools, 220; officers and teachers, 250; children, 400; money collected, 430 per cent.

EDUCATION.

Our other educational institutions demand mention. The stigma of being unlettered and ignorant men long attached to Methodist preachers. Whether well or ill deserved, it is certainly singular that they have left such records behind them attesting their zeal for literature, far exceeding others making larger pretensions. As early as 1793 Bishop Asbury projected the Mount Bethel Academy, in Newberry county. He was well sustained by his able lieutenant, Dougherty, who was incessantly engaged in getting the Church awake to denominational education. To him the Church owes its first inspiration of educational ambition. To Mount Bethel succeeded Tabernacle Academy, so gloriously connected with Dr. Olin's conversion; then Mount Ariel, then Cokesbury, and finally Wofford College. Methodism in Carolina has the honor of one of her adherents bestowing one of the largest individual gifts—one hundred thousand dollars—for educational purposes ever bestowed in the state since its foundation. Would that others might imitate the example, and let this cherished institution go free on its high mission. It should not be forgotten that our grand old Conference was once copartner in Randolph-Macon with Virginia.

WILLIAM CAPERS.

The necrology of the period numbers some fifty-one, among them men of mark. One, William Capers, for long years considered the *Magnus Apollo* of the Conference, is thus sketched by our venerable brother, Samuel Leard:

An ancient lady of Georgetown told me that she was present at his birth, when the physician directed all his attention to the mother, whose case was critical, and told the attendants to lay aside the newborn infant, as it was dead or would soon die. They thought differently, and soon succeeded in restoring the child to life, and then said to the doctor: "He will be a Methodist bishop some day." He laughed at their prediction, but all know that it was fulfilled. As to his person he was shaped in nature's most exquisite mold. In youth he must have been eminently beautiful for a man. In middle life he was faultless as to form and feature, of medium height, graceful in person, with a voice of wonderful sweetness and power, keen, penetrating black eyes, seemingly searching your thoughts, and yet glowing with the warmth of the most intense feeling. He was the orator *par excellence* of our Conference, and did more than any other man to give his beloved Methodism caste and power among the wealthy and refined classes of South Carolina. He sat mentally at the feet of Asbury and Lee and others of lesser note, and drank in the very spirit of the martyrs until he was prepared to sacrifice all he held dear in life for the cause of spiritual religion. The chaste monument in Washington street churchyard marks his grave.

Our fourth period is memorably epochal, taking in the dreadful civil war, from the close of 1860 to the end in 1865. Amid its fearful ravages, while there was much foreboding, our territory was saved from the tread of hostile armies until near its close. Many of our bravest were at the front, many of our preachers served as chaplains, yet the exercises of religion were sacredly kept up throughout. Conferences met, appointments were made, and preachers traveled as usual; but from the pressure upon the country, religious progression was much stayed.

Starvation threatened, but did not come; articles of food became very scarce; poor substitutes for coffee and sugar abounded; every expedient was adopted to "make old clo' look maist as well as new"; and yet salaries were enormous as to amount—$5,000, $10,000, $15,000, and $20,000 were apportioned, but being in depreciated currency, when scaled down the amounts were not larger than usual. "Tax in kind" was far more preferable. A juicy ham or fat middling was considered far greater riches than all the treasures of our Confederate currency. Yet, notwithstanding, the Angel of the covenant was near and delivered us.

The year 1860 closed with an enumeration of 40,165 white members, including probationers, and 49,774 colored. At the close of 1865 there were 40,296 white and 26,884 colored members, a gain of 131 whites and a loss of 22,890 colored. Yankee chaplains of the Union army hovered about camp grounds and everywhere else, showing great sympathy for the colored race and inviting them into the Northern Church. Disintegration and absorption was the cry. Churches and parsonages were seized, and strange bishops were parceling our circuits and stations. It was pitiable that human nature should sink so low, but erelong it all ceased. Our chief pastors were soon in labors most abundant, and rank and file hastened to the rescue. The war cloud passing, South Carolina Methodism was again on rising ground. Our white membership did not disintegrate, and were not absorbed in the least.

Our fifth and last period dates from the close of 1865, and ends with 1896. As there are men living who were witnesses as well as workers in these last twenty years of our centennial existence, we need not go into details. A few statistical notations, and we close. The white membership enrolled at the close of 1866 was 39,601, with 648 probationers; these last were soon eliminated from the record. The colored membership was reduced to 15,718, and in a year or two ceased to be reported at all, for the very good reason that there were none to report. In 1869 the members enrolled were 42,926, but in 1870 the number was reduced to 32,240, a decrease of 10,686, caused by the transfer of over 10,000 to the North Carolina Conference; so that when the decade ended in 1875 there were reported but 40,568—the ratio of increase, because of the transfer, being only 2.47 per cent, when, if not for that, it would have been 8.49 per cent. For the decade there was collected for superannuated preachers $33,040.18, and for missions $30,516.84. The number of church structures in 1875 was 550; number of parsonages, 68; value of Church property, $706.791. The ratio of increase for these ten years cannot be given, as there are no data upon which to base calculations; but from the end of 1875 to the close of the decade in 1884, there was unexampled prosperity, both spiritually and temporally, as the percentage of increase clearly shows. From 1875 to the close of 1884 there was paid on Conference collections, $47,434.02; for missions, $87,637.53; for education, $22,556.22. For all purposes, save ministerial support, there was collected these last ten years, $170,206.60. In 1884 the membership was 52,443; Sunday schools, 591; officers and teachers, 3,885; pupils, 29,362; church structures, 611; parsonages, 114; value of Church property, $801,850. The ratio of increased numbers was 29.29; Sunday schools, 26.76; officers and teachers, 41.05; pupils, 63.29; churches, 11.09; parsonages, 67.64; and Church property, 3,000 per cent.

The next decade, from 1885 to 1894, shows a still greater increase: For ministerial support, $1,137,033.26; for Conference collections, $76,902.49; for missions, $182,974.94; for education, $24,075.66; for Church extension, $23,646.35; for building and repairing, $508,416.06; for Sunday school literature, $7,343.26; for other benevolent purposes, $16,677.73. To recapitulate:

For salaries...	$1,137,033 26
For Conference collections......................	76,902 49
For missions..................................	182,974 94
For education	24,075 66
For Church extension...........................	23,646 35
For Sunday schools and other objects............	532,437 05
Total...	$1,977,069 75

FROM 1884 TO 1895.

Year.	Members.	Sunday Schools.	Officers and Teachers.	Pupils.	Churches.	Parsonages.	Value.
1895	72,711	702	4,912	40,197	717	164	$1,084,519 50
1884	52,443	591	3,885	29,362	611	114	801,850 00
Increase	20,268	111	1,027	10,385	106	50	$282,669 50

INCREASE FROM 1831 TO 1896.

Year.	Districts.	Charges.	Preachers.	Numbers.
1896	10	204	250	72,651
1831	5	41	62	20,513
Increase	5	163	188	52,138

And now, in closing, let us briefly note the causes of the success of Methodism, in so far as the ministry was concerned.

I. FIDELITY.

In that little word how much is bound up—faithfulness, a careful and exact observance of duty, or performance of obligation, especially expected by all in a minister of religion; strict honesty, uncompromising veracity.

Fidelity to God. "Called, chosen, and faithful."

Fidelity to each other. The early journals of the Church are covered all over with evidences of this virtue.

Fidelity to the world. No softening truth for advantage.

II. THEIR AGGRESSIVENESS.

They did not wait for attack; they were always the assailants of hell's strongholds—never satisfied until success crowned their efforts. Enduring hardness as good soldiers of Jesus Christ, campaigns were planned, battles fought, and victories achieved by full obedience to the command of our risen and ascended Lord: "Go."

III. PRAYERFULNESS.

Praying fervently, praying in faith, brought down the Holy Spirit to give the word success. Let us emulate them, and generations yet unborn "shall see Jerusalem a quiet habitation, a tabernacle that shall not be taken down; not one of the stakes thereof shall ever be removed; neither shall any of the cords be broken."

METHODIST EPISCOPAL CHURCH, SOUTH, MARION, S. C.

APPENDIX.

All of this tabulated matter was with much labor prepared and published from time to time in our Annual Minutes, during the decade from 1870 to 1880, by the author while editor of the same. The tables may be useful for ready reference in this volume.

21 (321)

I.

PREACHERS CONNECTED WITH THE SOUTH CAROLINA ANNUAL CONFERENCE FROM 1776 TO 1896.

ABBREVIATIONS, ETC.

Numerals indicate the years they entered and left the connection. D., deceased. L., located. Disap., disappeared from the minutes. Disct., discontinued. W., withdrawn. T., transferred. Ex., expelled. Epis., made bishop. Some transfers do not appear. An asterisk (*) denotes living members.

1776.		
Nicholas Watters,	D	1804
James Forster,	L	1787

1777.		
Henry Willis,	L	1790
John Tunnell,	D	1790
Reuben Ellis,	D	1796
Richard Ivy,	D	1795

1781.		
William Partridge,	D	1817

1782.		
Woolman Hickson,	D	1787
Beverly Allen,	Ex	1792

1783.		
John Major,	D	1788
Richard Swift,	T Va	1790
Thomas Humphries,	L	1799
Philip Bruce,	T Va	1796
William Phoebus,	T N Y	1809
Lemuel Green,	T Va	1800
Ira Ellis,	T Va	1797
Jesse Lee,	T Va	1800

1784.		
Isaac Smith,	D	1834
John Smith,	Disap	1789

1785.		
Jeremiah Mastin,	L	1790
Hope Hull,	L	1795
George Norsworthy,	Disct	1786
Henry Bingham,	D	1788
Stephen Johnson,	Disap	1788
Mark Whittaker,	L	1793

1786.		
Daniel Asbury,	D	1825
Robert J. Miller,	Disct	1787
Michael Gilbert,	Disct	1787
John Simmons,	Disap	1789
John Mason,	Disct	1787
Mark Moore,	L	1799
Thomas Williamson,	T West	1791

1787.		
Lemuel Andrews,	D	1790
Henry Ledbetter,	L	1806
Barnabas McHenry,	L	1795
Benjamin Carter,	D	1792
James Connor,	D	1789

1788.		
Hardy Herbert,	D	1794

Michael Burge,	T Ga	1830
William Gassaway,	L	1814
Bennett Maxey,	L	1797
James Parks,	L	1795
Aquilla Sugg,	L	1797
John Ellis,	L	1794
Jesse Richardson,	T Ga	1830
Josiah Askew,	L	1798
William McKendree,	T West Epis	1808

1789.		
Wyatt Andrews,	D	1790
C. S. Mooring,	T Va	1795
Jonathan Jackson,	L	1815
Wheeler Grissom,	L	1792
John Andrew,	L	1792
Philip Mathews,	Disap	1792
John Crawford,	L	1794
William McDowell,	L	1795
John Russell,	L	1799
Lemuel Moore,	L	1791
Daniel Smith,	L	1794
Joshua Cannon,	Disct	1790

1790.		
Hubbard Saunders,	L	1793
William A. Lilly,	L	1797
John Bonner,	Disap	1802
James Powell,	Disct	1791
Arthur Lipsey,	L	1795
Francis Parker,	Disap	1796
John Halliday,	L	1793
Hezekiah Arnold,	L	1797
Enoch George,	T Va Epis	1816
Samuel Cowles,	L	1806
Benjamin Blanton,	L	1800
John N. Jones,	D	1798
Rufus Wiley,	L	1801

1791.		
Samuel Ansley,	L	1810
James Tolleson,	D	1800
John Wood,	Disct	1793
Josias Randall,	L	1809
R. Lipsey,	Disct	1793
John Clark,	Disap	1796
James Holly,	Disct	1792
A. Henley,	L	1796
Joseph Moore,	D	1851

(323)

James Rogers,	T Va	1798	Britton Capel,	L		1810
Henry Hill,	L	1797	Lewis Myers,	T Ga		1830
Jeremiah Norman,	L	1821	**1800.**			
William Ormand,	T Va	1801	John Gamewell,	D		1828
1792.			Moses Floyd,	L		1805
Benjamin Tarrant,	L	1796	Buddy W. Wheeler,	L		1806
Tobias Gibson,	D	1804	Jeremiah Russell,	L		1806
William Fullwood,	L	1796	Levi Garrison,	L		1807
Stith Mead,	T Va	1805	Ezekiel Burdine,	L		1804
James Jenkins,	D	1847	John Campbell,	L		1809
Coleman Carlisle,	L	1823	**1801.**			
George Clarke,	L	1801	Isaac Cook,	L		1806
1793.			Benjamin Jones,	D		1804
J. Johnson,	Dist	1794	William Jones,	Disap		1805
S. Risher,	T Va	1796	James H. Mellard,	L		1810
James Douthet,	L	1806	Thomas Darley,	L		1806
Anthony Sale,	L	1799	**1802**			
1794.			Meshac Boyce,	L		1807
Richard Posey,	L	1799	James Hill,	L		1806
James King,	D	1797	Hugh Porter,	L		1807
David Thompson,	L	1797	Samuel Mills,	D		1811
John King,	L	1803	**1803.**			
Charles Ledbetter,	L	1799	John McVean,	Disap		1811
N. Snethen,	T N Y	1804	James Crowder,	L		1806
1795.			James Taylor,	Dist		1805
James Patterson,	L	1804	**1804.**			
William Guiry,	Dist	1797	Benjamin Watts,	Dist		1805
N. Norwood,	Dist	1797	Eppes Tucker,	L		1819
Moses Wilson,	Disap	1802	J. Lumsden,	L		1809
Charles Tankerly,	Dist	1796	William McKenny,	Dist		1807
Nathan Williamson,	Dist	1797	David Dannelly,	Dist		1807
Josiah Cole,	L	1801	Gabriel Christian,	Dist		1807
Henry M. Gaines,	L	1806	Wiley Warwick,	T Ga		1830
John Harper,	L	1803	Joseph Tarply,	L		1821
1796.			**1805.**			
Moses Black,	T West	1805	Reddick Pierce,	D		1860
1797.			Lovick Pierce,	T Ga		1830
Alexander McCain,	T Va	1803	John Porter,	L		1813
William West,	L	1805	William Hardwick,	Dist		1806
Robert Gaines,	L	1801	Benjamin Treadwell,	L		1808
James Floyd,	L	1800	John Hill,	L		1815
Laomi Floyd,	W	1800	James Boykin,	Dist		1806
Thomas Nelson,	L	1803	James Russell,	L		1815
Samuel Douthet,	L	1805	Francis Bird,	L		1809
Lewellen Evans,	L	1804	Amos Curtis,	L		1809
John Watson,	Disap	1808	W. W. Shepard,	Dist		1806
1798.			M. P. Sturdivant,	L		1812
Hanover Donnan,	L	1808	**1806.**			
Samuel Hooser,	L	1801	William M. Kennedy,	D		1840
Thomas Shaw,	L	1806	Robert Porter,	L		1816
T. Milligan,	T West	1803	Samuel Dunwody,	D		1854
George Dougherty,	D	1807	Abda Christian,	L		1811
1799.			Benjamin Gordon,	L		1810
Moses Mathews,	L	1809	Jesse Stancel,	L		1814
William Avant,	L	1805	George Fletcher,	Dist		1808
J. Dillard,	Dist	1801	Thomas Paine,	Dist		1807
Z. Maddox,	T Miss	1821	George Philips,	Dist		1807
B. Kendrick,	D	1807	Hilliard Judge,	L		1816
John Garvin,	L	1804	Stephen Thompson,	L		1808
			John Brockington,	L		1808

Thomas Hearthcock,   L   1811
James E. Glenn,   L   1814

1807.

Osborn Rogers,   L   1814
John W. Kennon,   Disap   1813
John Hunter,   L   1811
Solomon Bryan,   L   1819
Charles Fisher,   Disap   1812
Joseph Harley,   Disct   1809
William Scott,   L   1813
Elias Stone,   Disct   1808
Joseph Travis,   L   1825
John Collinsworth,   T Ga   1830
Robert L. Edwards,   T Ga   1830
Angus McDonald,   Disct   1809
Leven Sellers,   Disct   1809
James Norton,   D   1825
William Arnold,   Disct   1808
John Pinner,   L   1809

1808.

Richmond Nolley,   D   1815
Charles L. Kennon,   L   1812
Eli Wheat,   Disct   1809
Coleman Harwell,   L   1812
Samuel Harrison,   L   1811
Benjamin Dulany,   L   1815
Christian Rumph,   Disap   1811
Thomas Herne,   Disct   1809
Thomas D. Glenn,   L   1813
Thomas Mason,   L   1812

1809.

Moses Andrew,   L   1813
Robert L. Kennon,   L   1813
William S. Talley,   L   1814
M. Kimball,   Disct   1811
Lewis Hobbs,   T Tenn   1813
William Redwine,   Disct   1810
Anthony Senter,   D   1817
Nicholas Power,   L   1818
Jacob Rumph,   D   1812
Lewis Pickins,   Disct   1810
John Henning,   Disct   1811
Joseph Saltonstall,   L   1813
William Capers,   Epis 1846 D   1855
John Rye,   Disct   1811
Urban Cooper,   L   1812

1810.

F. D. Wimberly,   L   1814
Alexander Talley,   L   1820
Alexander McEwen,   L   1813
Thomas Griffin,   L   1812
John Jennings,   Disct   1812
A. Jones,   Disct   1812
John B. Glenn,   L   1819
Andrew Gramling,   L   1813
John Tarrant,   D   1849
M. Durr,   L   1813
John S. Ford,   Disct   1812
John Webb,   Disct   1812
John S. Capers,   L   1814

James Capers,   L   1814
Henry D. Green,   L   1815
Duncan King,   Disct   1811
Drury Powell,   L   1815
Whitman C. Hill,   T Ga   1830

1811.

John J. E. Bird,   Disct   1813
John Postell,   Disct   1813
Lewis Hatten,   Disct   1813
John Boswell,   L   1817
Daniel Brown,   D   1816
Samuel Jenkins,   Disct   1813
John Sewell,   L   1818
Reuben Tucker,   L   1825
Aaron Maddux,   Disct   1812
James Hutto,   L   1821
Samuel L. Meek,   L   1814
Thomas Dickenson,   Dis   1812
A. Pickins,   L   1816
Elias Stone,   Disct   1812
John Mullinax,   L   1823
Ashley Hewett,   T Miss   1817
James Hays,   Disct   1813
John Shrock,   Disct   1813

1812.

Griffin Christopher,   L   1821
T. W. Stanley,   L   1818
Benjamin C. Scott,   L   1818
Allen Turner,   T Ga   1830
N. Talley,   D   1873
James C. Sharp,   L   1816
Benjamin S. Ogletree,   L   1816
John Freeman,   Disct   1813
Henry Bass,   D   1860
Nicholas Punch,   L   1815
L. Q. C. De Yampert,   L   1816
James C. Koger,   L   1815
Britton Bunch,   Disct   1813
John Bunch,   D   1838
Jacob Hill,   D   1855
H. McPhail,   T Tenn   1817
A. Brown,   L   1817
James L. Belin,   D   1859
Alexander H. Saunders,   L   1816
B. R. Brown,   L   1815
Charles Dickenson,   D   1820

1813.

Anderson Ray,   L   1817
Allen Bass,   Disct   1814
Samuel K. Hodges,   T Ga   1830
Daniel McPhail,   L   1817
James Parsons,   Disap   1818
William Harris,   L   1817
West Harris,   L   1817
Dabney P. Jones,   L   1817
William Collinsworth,   L   1818
John Wright,   L   1817
James O. Andrew,   T Ga   1830
    Epis 1832   D   1871
William B. Barnett,   L   1821

D. S. McBride,	L	1819	John L. Greaves,	Disap	1826
Samuel Johnson,	L	1819	Thomas A. Smith,	L	1822
James B. Turner,	L	1819	A. Simmons,	Disct	1819
P. Ogletree,	L	1820	John L. Jerry,	L	1830
Elijah Bird,	L	1822	John Dix,	D	1823
Samuel T. Elder,	Disct	1814	William Connell,	Disct	1820
James M. Sharp,	Disct	1814	H. T. Fitzgerald,	D	1819
1814.			Charles Betts,	D	1872
David Hilliard,	L	1823	**1819.**		
John Lane,	Disct	1816	James Dannelly,	D	1855
John Scott,	L	1819	B. Pipkin,	T Miss	1822
Ransom Adkins,	Disct	1816	M. Raiford,	T Ga	1830
W. F. Easter,	Disct	1816	Levi Stancel,	Disct	1820
D. Monagon,	L	1819	John Schroble,	Disct	1820
N. McIntire,	T Miss	1820	John B. Chappel,	T Ga	1830
John Murrow,	L	1825	Peter Duff,	Disct	1820
West Williams,	L	1818	C. G. Hill,	D	1840
John McClendon,	Disap	1819	John Howard,	T Ga	1830
W. L. Winningham,	L	1818	Thomas Gardner,	Disct	1823
Travis Owen,	L	1825	**1820.**		
A. Leatherwood,	L	1818	Thomas Sanford,	T Ga	1830
1815.			B. Gordon,	Disct	1821
John W. Norton,	L	1819	Jesse Wall,	Disct	1821
William Palmer,	Disct	1816	Thomas Clinton,	T Miss	1821
John Simmons,	L	1820	Barnett Smith,	L	1831
William Kennedy,	L	1836	Robert Adams,	L	1836
John Mote,	L	1821	N. H. Rhodes,	T Ga	1830
Bryan Gause,	L	1819	Aquila Norman,	Disct	1823
1816.			Stephen Bass,	Disct	1821
Zaccheus Dowling,	T Ga	1830	B. L. Hoskins,	L	1830
Z. Williams,	T Miss	1822	A. T. Simmons,	Disct	1821
Daniel Gartman,	Disct	1817	John H. Treadwell,	L	1824
James Bella,	T Ga	1830	Thomas Mabry,	L	1830
Samuel Harrison,	Disct	1817	Robert Wilkinson,	Disct	1821
Jesse Sinclair,	T Ga	1830	**1821.**		
D. F. Christenberry,	Ex	1829	David Riley,	Disct	1823
Andrew Hamill,	T Ga	1830	Henry Seagrist,	Disct	1823
Tilman Snead,	T Ga	1830	A. Purifoy,	L	1827
David Garrison,	T Ga	1830	Thomas Thweat,	Disct	1822
1817.			J. N. Glenn,	T Ga	1830
Josiah Evans,	T Ga	1830	John H. Robinson,	L	1858
John Taylor,	L	1827	Daniel G. McDaniel,	D	1833
T. A. Rosamond,	L	1823	Elias Sinclair,	L	1828
Benjamin Wofford,	L	1820	R. T. Ward,	Disct	1822
William Hankins,	L	1824	Elijah Sinclair,	T Ga	1830
Benjamin Green,	Disct	1818	John J. Triggs,	L	1828
Hartwell Spain,	D	1868	Noah Laney,	T Ala	1833
1818.			Bond English,	D	1868
James Dunwody,	T Ga	1830	M. McPherson,	L	1839
Elisha Calloway,	T Ala	1835	John Reynolds,	L	1826
Raleigh Green,	L	1821	**1822.**		
Robert Flournoy,	L	1827	M. Westmoreland,	L	1826
J. Freeman,	L	1825	A. P. Manley,	L	1827
Thomas L. Wynn,	D	1830	P. L. Wade,	Disct	1824
Hugh Hamill,	L	1822	Josiah Freeman,	D	1834
J. Moser,	Disct	1819	William J. Parks,	T Ga	1830
N. Ware,	L	1826	Gideon Mason,	Disct	1823
A. Morgan,	D	1828	M. C. Turrentine,	T Ala	1851
Benjamin Rhodes,	D	1826	John Bigby,	L	1826
A. W. Philips,	Disct	1819	George White,	Disct	1823

John Covington,	L	1825
Ed J. Fitzgerald,	Disct	1824
William Knight,	Disct	1824
H. W. Ledbetter,	L	1828
Peyton Graves,	Disct	1823

1823.

Alexander F. Edward,	Ex	1826
Benjamin Crane,	Disct	1824
James Tabor,	L	1828
Philip Groover,	L	18_9
Isaac Sewell,	L	1826
Samuel Sewell,	L	1827
McC. Purifoy,	L	1828
John Slade,	L	1830
Elisha Askew,	L	1827
Charles Hardy,	T Ga	1830
D. N. Burkhalter,	L	1826
Benjamin Gaines,	Disct	1826
Ewell Petty,	L	1827
P. N. Maddux,	L	1830
N. P. Cook,	L	1826
S. B. Abbott,	Disct	1825
Adam Wyrick,	T Ga	1830
G. W. Huckabee,	L	1830
Joel W. Townsend,	D	1880

1824.

John C. Wright,	L	1829
Isaac Oslin,	Disct	1826
John H. Massey,	L	1833
Stephen Olin,	L	1828
John Mood,	L	1830
Joseph Galuchat,	Disct	1825
Daniel F. Wade,	L	1830
Washington Mason,	Disct	1825.
Reuben Mason,	L	1828
Joseph Holmes,	L	1829
James Stockdale,	L	1832
James Hitchner,	L	1830

1825.

Isaac Boring,	T Ga	1830
John Hunter,	T Ga	1830
W. W. King,	L	1836
George W. Moore,	D	1863
Isaac Hartley,	D	1826
Jeremiah Norman, Jr.,	T Ga	1830
William Crook,	D	1867
John Watts,	D	1886

1826.

F. P. Norsworthy,	T Ga	1830
Benjamin H. Capers,	L	1836
Angus McPherson,	D	1836
Jacob Ozler,	L	1837
William Gassaway,	T Ga	1830
Thomas D. Howell,	D	1828
John M. Tatum,	Disct	1827
David Lowe,	Disct	1828
Benjamin Bell,	D	1838
Jacky M. Bradley,	L	1860
William H. Mabry,	T Ga	1830

1827.

Robert Rogers,	Disct	1830
William Williams,	Disct	1829
George W. Parnell,	T Ga	1830
John L. Oliver,	T Ga	1830
Joseph B. Andrew,	T Ga	1830
John Simmonds,	Disct	1828
Joab M. Mershon,	Disct	1828
Wesley P. Arnold,	T Ga	1830
John Honor,	D	1830
John Coleman,	Disct	1828
E. Le Gett,	L	1838
K. Murchison,	L	1843
David Ballew,	L	1833
Robert Williams,	T Ga	1830
Jesse Boring,	T Ga	1830
R. J. Wynn,	T Ga	1830
J. S. P. Powell,	L	1831
William Steagall,	T Ga	1830
John M. Dorris,	T Ga	1830
Lewis Miller,	L	1830
F. C. Spraggins,	L	1834
Vardy Wooley,	T Ga	1830
D. F. Wade,	L	1830
William T. Smith,	L	1836
William J. Jackson,	D	1859
Malon Bedell,	T Ga	1830
David Derrick,	D	1883

1828.

Benjamin Pope,	T Ga	1830
Tilman Douglas,	T Ga	1830
J. T. Weatherly,	T Ga	1830
S. L. Stephens,	T Ga	1830
John Wimbush,	T Ga	1830
George W. Davis,	T Ga	1830
Ignatius A. Few,	T Ga	1830
John W. Tally,	T Ga	1830
William B. Smith,	T Ga	1830
William Culverhouse,	T Ga	1830
Daniel McDonald,	T Ga	1830
Samuel W. Capers,	D	1855
M. Bythewood,	Disct	1830
William H. Ellison,	T Ala	1833
John M. Kelly,	L	1833
Absalom Brown,	D	1833
Ed McNair,	L	1831
Thomas C. Smith,	D	1838
William M. Wightman,	Epis	1866
	D	1882
William Martin,	D	1889

1829.

Vernal Mahaffy,	T Ga	1830
William Young,	T Ga	1830
George A. Chappel,	T Ga	1830
Appleton Haygood,	T Ga	1830
Thomas H. Capers,	T Ga	1830
W. R. H. Moseley,	T Ga	1830
John C. Carter,	T Ga	1830
William N. Sears,	T Ga	1830
John Sale,	T Ga	1830

John D. Bowen,	Disct	1830	Alexander W. Walker,	D	1870
Thomas D. Turpin,	D	1838	C. S. Walker,	D	1857
John G. Humbert,	Disct	1830	Samuel Armstrong,	T West	1842
William Murrah,	T Ala	1835	S. D. Laney,	L	1853
F. Rush,	D	1858	Harris Starnes,	Disct	1835
David J. Allen,	L	1836	Joseph H. Wheeler,	T N C	1850
William Howie,	Disct	1830	William Brockington,	Disct	1835
C. A. Crowell,	T Ga	1850	P. G. Bowman,	Ex	1870
James J. Richardson,	D	1833	W. A. Gamewell,	D	1869
J. J. Allison,	L	1837	Campbell Smith,	D	1854
William Lackey,	Disct	1830	J. C. Coggeshell,	Disap	1837
John R. Coburn,	D	1880	H. H. Durant,	D	1861
1830.			Hope H. Parnell,	Disct	1835
Henry W. Hilliard,	Disct	1831	William C. Ferrill,	L	1843
C. A. Brown,	T Ga	1830	Willis Halton,	T N C	1870
A. H. Palmer,	T Ga	1830	J. W. Wellborn,	T West	1842
T. D. Purifoy,	T Ga	1830	John N. Davis,	D	1844
T. P. C. Shelman,	T Ga	1830	**1835.**		
George W. Carter,	T Ga	1830	Ira L. Potter,	T Fla	1847
George Collier,	T Ga	1830	T. L. Young,	Disap	1841
R. H. Jones,	T Ga	1830	Samuel Leard,	D	1896
Joseph L. Moultry,	T Ga	1830	T. S. Daniels,	D	1877
J. D. Chappel,	T Ga	1830	A. Nettles,	D	1889
Z. Brown,	T Ga	1830	P. H. Pickett,	T Miss	1837
R. J. Richardson,	T Ga	1830	J. R. Pickett,	D	1870
Henry Heath,	Disct	1832	David Seal,	D	1895
Samuel Boseman,	L	1834	James C. Postell,	L	1841
John W. McCall,	L	1842	W. T. Harrison,	L	1845
T. R. Walsh,	D	1867	**1836.**		
Allen Hamby,	L	1840	R. J. Limehouse,	L	1847
T. Stackhouse,	D	1831	William Holliday,	L	1842
Thomas Herne,	Disct	1832	John A. Minnick,	D	1858
James Stacy,	D	1868	Samuel Townsend,	D	1865
Allen McCorquodale	D	1875	Joseph P. Kirton,	L	1844
1831.			Jehu G. Postell,	D	1840
Charles Wilson,	D	1873	Archibald Kelly,	Disct	1837
S. Williams,	Disct	1832	Neil Monroe,	Disct	1838
L. Rush,	L	1840	William Patterson.*		
Thomas Neil,	D	1833	M. A. McKibben,	D	1887
William Whitby,	L	1840	**1837.**		
H. A. C. Walker,	D	1886	Andrew J. Green,	L	1847
1832.			P. A. M. Williams,	D	1863
William M. D. Moore,	L	1843	Alexius M. Foster,	D	1868
John K. Morse,	L	1838	William C. Kirkland,	D	1864
J. B. Anthony,	W	1845	C. Murchison,	T Ill	1869
A. B. McGilvray,	D	1863	James H. Chandler,	L	1850
Mark Russell,	L	1842	D. Le Gett,	Disct	1838
P. W. Clenny,	D	1838	James Collins,	Disct	1838
W. C. McNabb,	Disct	1834	C. McLeod,	D	1866
1833.			George R. Talley,	L	1845
B. Thomason,	D	1841	William M. Kerr,	L	1847
H. McLenaghan,	Disct	1834	William C. Clark,	L	1855
William R. Smith,	L	1838	John McMakin,	D	1846
George W. Huggins	D	1835	Abel Hoyle,	D	1844
T. Huggins,	L	1849	Lewis Scarboro,	D	1884
John L. Smith,	L	1837	**1838.**		
Whitefoord Smith,	D	1893	Lewis J. Crum,	Disct	1840
1834.			John M. Deas,	L	1842
George Wright,	Disct	1836	H. E. Ogburn,	D	1860
R. J. Boyd,	D	1869	Sherrod Owens,	Disct	1840

A. B. Kelly,	Disct	1840	P. R. Hoyle,	L	1850	
B. Hamilton,	L	1844	Stephen Miller,	L	1847	
M. P. Myers,	L	1841	John W. Kelly,	D	1885	
W. E. Collier,	L	1842	R. P. Franks,	D	1895	
William P. Mouzon,	D	1885		**1845.**		
John H. Zimmerman,	D	1889	William T. Capers,	D	1894	
Simpson Jones.*			John M. Carlisle.*			
	1839.		Charles Taylor,	T Ky	1866	
Lark O'Neal,	L	1848	Peter W. McDaniel,	L	1850	
Z. W. Barnes,	L	1853	William M. Lee,	L	1852	
A. M. Chrietzberg.*			T. M. Farrow,	L	1850	
John S. Thomason,	L	1843	A. P. Avant,	D	1889	
E. L. King,	D	1875	Joseph Warnock,	L	1851	
Jacob Nipper,	D	1844	William Barringer,	T N C	1850	
Wesley L. Pegues,	D	1894	Daniel McDonald,	T Miss	1855	
Martin Eaddy,	Ex	1862	R. S. Ledbetter,	Disct	1847	
Alfred Richardson,	L	1846	T. W. Postell,	Disct	1847	
William A. McSwain,	D	1866	Jacob L. Shuford,	D	1892	
Samuel Smoke,	Disct	1840		**1846.**		
	1840.		John S. Capers,	Disct	1847	
John R. Locke,	T Ala	1843	John A. Mood,	D	1896	
Michel Robbins,	L	1849	William A. Robinson,	Disct	1847	
Allen Huckabee,	L	1845	A. P. Martin,	D	1862	
Williamson Smith,	L	1855	O. A. Chrietzberg,	Ex	1861	
Sherod Kennerly,	Disct	1842	H. C. Parsons,	D	1866	
Lewis M. Little,	D	1888	Abner Ervine,	D	1886	
	1841.		A. L. Smith,	D	1872	
C. H. Pritchard.			A. G. Stacy,	T Mo	1869	
D. D. Cox,	L	1851	F. X. Forster,	Disct	1848	
Samuel M. Green,	L	1852		**1847.**		
Nathan Byrd,	L	1844	U. S. Bird,	Disct	1848	
S. P. Taylor,	Ex	1851		Re	1873	
Solomon W. Daves,	T Cal	1851	J. O. A. Conner,	L	1850	
Wade H. Bettis,	Disct	1842	Joseph Galluchat,	Disct	1848	
Thomas Hutchins,	Disct	1842	Hugh F. Porter,	L	1849	
A. M. Shipp,	D	1887	Robert Taylor,	Disct	1848	
D. J. Simmons,	D	1887	J M. Richardson,	Disct	1848	
William H. Fleming,	D	1887	Sidi H. Browne.*			
John A. Porter.*			Paul F. Kistler.*			
	1842.			**1848.**		
William Carson.*			John T. Wightman,	T Balt	1885	
Henry M. Mood,	D	1897	Lewis A. Johnson.*			
James W. Wightman,	T Ky	1866	M. L. Banks.*			
John C. McDaniel,	L	1848	Benjamin Jenkins,	D	1870	
Henry Cloy,	Disct	1843	James T. Munds,	L	1859	
M. Michan,	L	1847	S. H. Dunwody,	L	1851	
William H. Brunson,	Disct	1844	J. W. J. Harris,	D	1855	
James F. Smith,	L	1848		**1849.**		
William H. Smith,	Disct	1844	E. J. Meynardie,	D	1890	
	1843.		John Finger,	D	1884	
James E. Davis,	Disct	1844	A. J. Cauthen.*			
William G. Conner,	T Tex	1868	Thomas Mitchell,	L	1881	
Henry A. Bass,	L	1854	J. P. Hughes,	L	1866	
Joseph Parker,	T Tex	1869	A. H. Harmon,	D	1861	
N. Goudelock,	D	1848		**1850.**		
John W. Vandiver,	Disct	1845	Reddick Bunch,	D	1851	
Daniel Boyd,	Disct	1844	W. W. Jones.*			
	1844.		William Hutto,	D	1892	
H. Judge Glenn,	L	1847	J. J. Fleming,	Ex	1852	
Miles Puckett,	L	1864	E. J. Pennington,	D	1877	

James N. Bouchell,	Disct	1852
John W. North,	T N C	1870
William B. Currie,	L	1860
A. M. Rush,	Disct	1852
R. Washburn,	Disct	1852
D. D. Byars,	D	1887
1851.		
F. A. Mood,	T Tex	1869
J. Wesley Miller,	D	1866
C. O. Lamotte,	W	1854
W. E. Boone,	D	1858
George W. Ivy,	T N C	1870
J. W. Faulkner,	L	1853
Daniel May,	T N C	1870
W. W. Mood,	D	1897
T. Raysor,	D	1896
W. A. Clarke.*		
James T. Kilgo,	D	1888
1852.		
O. A. Darby.*		
William M. Easterling,	D	1855
A. H. Lester,	D	1897
R. L. Abernathy,	L	1855
James L. Palmer,	Disct	1854
J. D. W. Crook,	D	1866
1853.		
George W. Stokes,	L	1860
James S. Ervine,	T N C	1870
E. A. Price,	L	1865
G. W. M. Creighton,	L	1873
William H. Lawton,	D	1893
1854.		
E. D. Boyden,	D	1856
J. S. Conner,	L	1873
Joseph T. Du Bose,	D	1859
R. W. Burgess,	L	1859
R. Thornton Capers,	Disct	1856
Daniel A. Ogburn,	D	1865
Lewis M. Hamer.*		
Basil G. Jones,	D	1891
1855.		
George K. Andrews,	L	1858
C. E. Wiggins.*		
A. B. Stephens,	Ex	1873
E. W. Thompson,	T N C	1870
John W. Crider,	T Va	
W. A. Hemingway,	D	1867
Jesse S. Nelson,	T N C	1870
Landy Wood,	D	1892
S. B. Jones,	D	1894
F. Milton Kennedy,	D	1880
M. A. Connolly,	D	1894
1856.		
John W. Murray,	D	1891
R. R. Pegues,	D	1877
A. J. Evans,	L	1860
James M. Cline,	L	1869
Samuel J. Hill,	D	1884
W. J. Black,	T N C	1870
John W. Puett,	T N C	1870

1857		
W. J. E. Fripp,	L	1855
E. G. Gage,	D	1870
J. E. Gleason,	Disct	1858
E. A. Lemmond,	D	1870
F M. Morgan,	L	1881
J. L. McGregor,	D	1862
1858.		
A. R. Bennick,	T Hol	1868
W. W. Graham,	L	1855
H. D. Moore,	T Fla	1864
O. A. Sharp,	T N C	1870
Abram N. Wells,	L	1869
Manning Brown,	D	1892
William C. Power.*		
Augustine W. Walker.*		
R. R. Dagnall.*		
1859.		
George H. Wells,	D	1886
James C. Stoll.*		
J. B. Massebeau,	D	1884
T. G. Herbert.*		
F. Auld.*		
William Bowman,	L	1875
O. Eaddy,	T Fla	1870
C. E. Land,	T N C	1870
R. B. Allston,	T L R	1871
1860.		
E. T. R. Fripp,	T Balt	1871
T. F. Barton,	Disct	1861
C. F. Campbell,	D	1860
John Lee Dixon,	D	1873
T. H. Edwards,	L	1869
James W. Coward,	L	1868
John Hutchinson,	L	1863
P. L. Herman,	T N C	1870
A. S. Link,	D	1864
T. W. Munnerlyn.*		
James B. Campbell.*		
J. W. McRoy,	D	1893
T. J. Clyde.*		
J. W. Humbert.*		
A. J. Stokes.*		
L. C. Weaver,	D	1863
G. W. Du Pree,	D	1861
1861.		
John L. Sifley.*		
D. J. McMillan,	D	1881
James H. Tart,	L	1870
James J. Workman.*		
J. P. De Pass,	T Fla	1866
R. B. Tarrant,	L	1875
William M. Wilson,	D	1864
J. E. Penny,	L	1872
H. J. Morgan,	D	1884
William A. Hodges,	L	
J. L. Stoudemyer,	L	1869
J. F. Wilson,	D	1864
J. W. Raby,	Disct	1862
J. Hoover,	Disct	1862

S. A. Roper,	Disct	1862
J. D. Carpenter,	L	1871
N. K. Melton.*		
John A. Wood.*		
J. H. C. McKinney,	Ex	1873

1862.

None.

1863.

J. J. Snow,	L	1869
J. C. Hartsell,	T N C	1870
R. C. Oliver,	D	1897
S. A. Weber.*		

1864.

G. W. Bird,	L	1867
T. A. Boone,	T N C	1870
J. R. Little,	L	
George F. Round,	T N C	1877
A. J. Stafford.*		
C. Thomason,	D	1872
J. E. Watson,	D	1889

1865.

J. C. Crisp,	T N C	1873
J. K. Tucker,	Disct	1867
M. C. Davis,	Disct	1867
James H. Sturtevant,	Disct	1867
John C. Randal,	T Tex	1866
John Attaway.*		
Samuel Lander.*		

1866.

J. B. Traywick.*		
J. B. Platt,	D	1893

1867.

J. B. Griffith,	T N C	1870
R. L. Duffie.*		
R. Lee Harper,	D	1884
R. M. Harrison,	L	1871
J. P. Morris,	D	1868

1868.

S. P. H. Elwell.*		
J. J. Prather,	T N C	1870
S. M. Davis,	T N C	1870
M. H. Hoyle,	T N C	1870

1869.

T. E. Wannamaker.*		
L. C. Loyal.*		
William Thomas,	D	1890
M. G. Tuttle,	D	1869

1870.

J. A. Clifton.*		
George T. Harmon.*		
C. V. Barnes,	L	
J. Marion Boyd,	D	1894
William D. Lee,	T N C	1870
T. P. England,	T N C	1870
W. T. McClelion,	T N C	1870
B. F. Dixon,	T N C	1870
James T. McElheny,	T N C	1870
J. F. England,	T N C	1880
A. G. Gantt,	T N C	1880

1871.

J. Claudius Miller,	D	1875
J. S. Beasley.*		
G. M. Boyd.*		
E. T. Hodges.*		
R. N. Wells,	D	1895
W. D. Kirkland,	D	1896
G. W. Gatlin.*		
R. D. Smart,	T Mem	1892

1872.

A. R. Danner,	D	1878
D. D. Dantzler.*		
Dove Tiller.*		
T. W. Smith,	L	1873
J. K. McCain.*		
H. W. Whitaker.*		
C. C. Fishburn,	D	1885
O. L. Durant.		
J. B. Wilson.		

1873.

H. Bass Green,	D	1874
W. A. Rogers.*		
John C. Russell,	L	1880
A. Coke Smith,	T Va	1891
C. D. Mann.		
J. Walter Dickson.*		
M. V. Wood,	D	1874
George H. Pooser.*		
R. W. Barber.*		
James C. Davis.*		

1874.

W. S. F. Wightman,	W	1893
M. H. Pooser.*		
H. F. Chrietzberg,	T W N C	1893
J. W. Whitman,	Ex	1882
C. H. Pritchard, Jr.,	D	1874
E. L. Archer.*		
William H. Kirton.*		
C. D. Rowell,	D	1887
Le Roy F. Beaty.*		
J. O. Willson.*		
James C. Bissell.*		
John E. Carlisle.*		
John Q. Stockman,	Ex	1876
George W. Walker.*		

1875.

John L. Stokes.*		
Felix Hartin,	T Ark	1879
W. W. Williams.*		
M. M. Ferguson.*		
A. W. Jackson.*		
James W. Wolling,	T Brazil.	
O. N. Rountree.*		
J. C. Counts.*		
E. M. Merritt,	T N C	1894
J. J. Neville.*		
William H. Ariail.*		
S. D. Vaughn.*		
W. W. Duncan,	T Va	
	Epis	1887

1876.

B. M. Boozer,	D	1882
D. Z. Dantzler.*		
A. C. Walker.*		
W. S. Martin.*		
James W. Ariail.*		
T. P. Phillips.*		

1877.

A. C. Le Gett,	T Fla.	
Joseph F. Mozingo,	Disct	1878
Thomas E. Gilbert,	L	1881
Le Grand G. Walker,	Disct	1878
R. H. Jones.*		
E. G. Price.*		
A. B. Lee,	D	1886
H. B. Browne.*		
William P. Meadors.*		

1878.

J. S. Meynardie,	Disct	1880
J. W. Tarbourx,	T Brazil.	
J. S. Porter.*		

1879.

J. T. Pate.*		
W. R. Richardson.*		
J. W. Koger,	D	1886
J. Ware Brown,	T Ga	1891

1880.

J. Walter Daniel.*	
J. M. Fridy.*	
T. E. Morris.*	
P. A. Murray.*	
W. H. Wroton.*	

1881.

Thomas B. Boyd,	D	1884
N. B. Clarkson.*		
A. A. Gilbert,	D	1891
W. M. Hardin.*		
J. W. Neeley.*		

1882.

M. M. Brabham.*		
J. E. Rushton.*		
J. E. Beard.*		
J. C. Chandler.*		
William A. Betts.*		
P. B. Jackson,	T West.	

1883.

T. H. Wannamaker,	Disct	1884
William H. Hodges,	Disct	1884
B. J. Guess,	T Tex.	
J. W. Elkins.*		
C. B. Smith.*		
J. D. Frierson.*		
J. C. Kilgo,	T N C	1894
David R. Brown,	W	1895

1884.

James E. Grier.*		
B. M. Grier.*		
S. J. Bethea.*		
H. C. Bethea,	L	1892

D. P. Boyd.*		
G. P. Watson.*		
J. A. Harmon.*	T Tex.	
W. W. Daniel.*		
G. R. Whitaker.*		

1885.

J. S. Mattison,	T Brazil.	
J. C. Young.*		
W. C. Gleaton.*		
M. Dargan.*		
G. H. Waddell.*		
W. M. Duncan.*		
W. B. Baker.*		

1886.

E. B. Loyless.*		
L. S. Bellenger.	D	1897
A. F. Berry.*		
E. O. Watson.*		
J. M. Steadman.*		
T. C. O'Dell.*		
J. F. Anderson.*		
A. M. Attaway.*		
M. H. Major.*		
T. C. Ligon.*		
W. I. Herbert.*		
John Owen.*		
D. A. Calhoun.*		

1887.

A. W. Attaway.*	
P. L. Kirton.*	
J. A. Rice.*	
C. W. Creighton.*	
M. W. Hook.*	
M. L. Carlisle.*	

1888.

J. P. Attaway.*		
S. S. Blanchard,	W	1895
S. T. Blackman.*		
W. E. Barr.*		
W. B. Duncan.*		
A. B. Earle.*		
J. L. Harley.*		
R. L. Holroyd.*		
J. W. Kilgo.*		
J. E. Mahaffey.*		
H. G. Scudday,	D	1889
W. L. Waite.*		
R. A. Yongue.*		
W. Mc. Zimmerman.*		

1889.

N. G. Ballenger.*		
B. O. Berry,	Ex	1895
T. M. Dent.*		
W. B. Ford,	D	1895
P. F. Kilgo.*		
B. T. Lucas.	T China.	
A. Macfarlain.*		
H. C. Mouzon.*		
G. R. Shaffer.*		
R. E. Stackhouse.*		

E. P. Taylor.*
E. A. Wilkes.*
W. A. Wright.*
1890.
J. F. Abercrombie.*
A. H. Best.*
R. A. Child.*
J. R. Copeland.*
G. W. Davis.*
W. H. Hodges.*
M. B. Kelly.*
J. Manning.*
E. D. Mouzon.*
J. M. Rogers.*
J. W. Shell.*
W. S. Stokes.*
A. B. Watson.*
J. A. White.*
1891
David Hucks.*
E. W. Mason.*
D. A. Phillips.*
J. H. Noland.*
S. H. Zimmerman.*
1892.
A. J. Cauthen, Jr.*
J. C. Spann,   L   1895
C. H. Clyde.*
D. H. Thacker.*
J. D. Crout.*
W. C. Wynn.*
A. N. Brunson.*
1893.
E. H. Beckham.*
G. F. Clarkson.*
J. L. Daniel.*
R. M. Du Bose.*
O. L. Durant.*
S. W. Henry.*
J. B. Ingram.*
J. N. Isom.*
W. B. Justus.*
A. S. Leslie.*
W. H. Miller.*
R. C. McRoy.*

D. M. McLeod.*
A. B. Phillips.*
A. Q. Rice.*
J. J. Stevenson.*
R. W. Spigner.*
T. J. White,   D   1894
W. B. Wharton.*
W. E. Wiggers.*
J. D. Major,   D   1894
E. K. Moore.*
1894.
L. L. Bedenbaugh.*
James A. Campbell.*
R. A. Few.*
T. G. Herbert, Jr.*
J. B. Holly,   W   1895
J. B. Harris.*
R. E. Mood.*
W. A. Massebeau.*
Peter Stokes.*
G. Edwin Stokes.*
1895.
M. L. Banks, Jr.*
R. C. Boulware.*
C. B. Burns.*
H. J. Cauthen.*
W. T. Duncan.*
W. S. Goodwin.*
E. S. Jones.*
W. A. Kelly, Jr.*
S. A. Nettles.*
W. A. Pitts.*
J. R. Sojourner.*
W. J. Snyder.*
J. B. Wells.*
1896.
J. G. Beckwith.*
A. V. Harbin.*
E. C. Herbert.*
L. L. Inabinet.*
G. C. Leonard.*
B. M. Robertson.
H. V. Stokes.*
W. B. Verdin.*
J. F. Way.*

II.

SOUTH CAROLINA GENERAL CONFERENCE DELEGATIONS, FROM THE FIRST DELEGATED GENERAL CONFERENCE TO THE PRESENT TIME.

The record of the South Carolina Conference Journal for the year 1808 is as follows: "The following brethren purpose to attend the ensuing General Conference: Lewis Myers, Britton Capel, Josias Randall, Wiley Warwick, John McVean, Daniel Asbury, James H. Mellard, William Gassaway, John Gamewell, Samuel Mills, Joseph Tarpley, and Moses Matthews." After that time they were elected, as follows:

1812.

Lewis Myers,	William M. Kennedy,	Hilliard Judge,
Daniel Asbury,	James Russell,	Samuel Dunwody.
Lovick Pierce,	James E. Glenn,	*No reserves.*
Joseph Tarpley,	Joseph Travis,	

1816.

Lewis Myers,	Hilliard Judge.	James Norton,
Daniel Asbury,	Samuel Dunwody,	Henry Bass,
Joseph Tarpley,	Anthony Senter,	Reuben Tucker,
William M. Kennedy,	John B. Glenn,	Alexander Talley.
Thomas Mason,	Solomon Bryan,	*No reserves.*

1820.

Joseph Tarpley,	James Norton,	S. K. Hodges,
Joseph Travis,	Lewis Myers,	Samuel Dunwody,
William Capers,	Daniel Asbury,	William M. Kennedy.

Reserve—J. O. Andrew.

1824.

James O. Andrew,	James Norton,	Lovick Pierce,
Lewis Myers,	Henry Bass,	Nicholas Talley,
William M. Kennedy,	William Capers,	Joseph Travis.
S. K. Hodges,	Samuel Dunwody,	

Reserve—Andrew Hamill.

1828.

J. O. Andrew,	Samuel Dunwody,	M. McPherson,
William Capers,	S. K. Hodges,	Robert Adams,
William M. Kennedy,	George Hill,	Elijah Sinclair.
Lovick Pierce,	William Arnold,	*No reserves.*
Henry Bass,	Andrew Hamill,	

1832.

William Capers,	Henry Bass,	Hartwell Spain,
Malcolm McPherson,	Samuel Dunwody,	Charles Betts,
William M. Kennedy,	Nicholas Talley,	Bond English.

Reserves.

Robert Adams,	Daniel G. McDaniel,	Joseph Holmes.

1836.

William Capers,   William M. Kennedy,   Malcolm McPherson,
Samuel Dunwody,   Nicholas Talley,   Charles Betts.

Reserves.

Henry Bass,   William M. Wightman, Hartwell Spain.

1840.

William Capers,   William M. Wightman, Bond English.
Charles Betts,   William M. Kennedy,

Reserves.

Hartwell Spain,   H. A. C. Walker,   Nicholas Talley.

1844.

William Capers,   Charles Betts,   H. A. C. Walker.
William M. Wightman,   Samuel Dunwody,

Reserves.

Whitefoord Smith,   Bond English.

DELEGATES TO CONVENTION, 1845.

William Capers,   H. A. C. Walker,   Whitefoord Smith,
William M. Wightman,   Samuel Dunwody,   Samuel W. Capers,
Charles Betts,   Bond English,   Robert J. Boyd.

1846.

William Capers,   H. A. C. Walker,   Nicholas Talley,
William M. Wightman,   Charles Betts,   Bond English.

Reserves.

Whitefoord Smith,   Samuel Dunwody,   Samuel W. Capers.

1850.

William M. Wightman,   Charles Betts,   W. A. Gamewell,
Whitefoord Smith,   A. M. Shipp,   Nicholas Talley,
H. A. C. Walker,   James Stacy,   Samuel W. Capers.

Reserves.

Robert J. Boyd,   Hartwell Spain.

1854.

William M. Wightman,   Whitefoord Smith,   Robert J. Boyd,
A. M. Shipp,   H. A. C. Walker,   James Stacy.
W. A. Gamewell,   William A. McSwain,

Reserves.

T. R. Walsh,   H. H. Durant.

1858.

William M. Wightman,   Robert J. Boyd,   J. W. Kelly,
W. A. Gamewell,   W. A. McSwain,   James Stacy,
A. M. Shipp,   Nicholas Talley,   Charles Betts.
H. A. C. Walker,

Reserves.

William P. Mouzon,   H. C. Parsons.

1862.

A. M. Shipp,   Robert J. Boyd,   William P. Mouzon,
W. A. Gamewell,   W. A. McSwain,   James Stacy,
H. A. C. Walker,   S. H. Browne,   H. C. Parsons.

Reserves.

Charles Betts,   C. H. Pritchard,   H. M. Mood.
J. T. Wightman,

1866.

Whitefoord Smith,
A. M. Shipp,
W. A. Gamewell,

H. A. C. Walker,
S. H. Browne,
Robert J. Boyd,

James Stacy.
William H. Fleming,
Charles Betts.

Reserves.

J. W. Kelly,

J. R. Pickett,

William P. Mouzon.

1870.

A. M. Shipp,
H. A. C. Walker,

W. Smith,
W. P. Mouzon,

William H. Fleming,
F. M. Kennedy.

Reserves.

S. H. Browne,

A. M. Chrietzberg,

J. W. Kelly.

Lay Delegates.

W. J. Montgomery,
G. W. Williams,

A. A. Gilbert,
H. J. Wright,

J. H. Carlisle,
S. Bobo.

Lay Reserves.

J. V. Moore,
B. Stokes,

E. T. Rembert,
R. F. Simpson,

T. S. Moorman,
D. R. Barton.

1874.

A. M. Shipp,
F. M. Kennedy,

H. A. C. Walker,
William H. Fleming,

J. W. Kelly,
S. H. Browne.

Reserves.

A. M. Chrietzberg,
S. B. Jones,

H. M. Mood,

J. T. Wightman.

Lay Delegates.

S. Bobo,
J. H. Kinsler,

A. A. Gilbert,
F. A. Connor,

A. E. Williams,
S. A. Nelson.

Lay Reserves.

L Bellenger,
W. C. McMillan,

S. M. Rice,
W. W. Pemberton,

S. C. Clyde,
R. H. Yeargin.

1878.

A. M. Shipp,
W. W. Duncan,
F. M. Kennedy,

H. A. C. Walker,
A. M. Chrietzberg,

S. B. Jones,
O. A. Darby.

Reserves.

Sidi H. Browne,
J. W. Kelly,

J. T. Wightman,

W. C. Power.

Lay Delegates.

J. H. Carlisle,
T. S. Moorman,
W. C. McMillan.

William Stokes,
F. A. Connor,

Dr. H. Baer,
G. J. Patterson.

Lay Reserves.

W. K. Blake,
John A. Elkin,

J. R. Mood,

W. H. Smith (L. P.).

1882.
Clerical.

A. M. Shipp,
S. B. Jones,

W. W. Duncan,
O. A. Darby,

W. P. Mouzon.

Alternates.

Sidi H. Browne,

S. A. Weber,

J. M. Carlisle.

Lay Delegates.

J. H. Carlisle,	W. T. D. Cousar,	H. H. Newton.
F. A. Connor,	William Stokes,	

Alternates.

W. K. Blake,	T. W. Stanland,	J. F. Carraway.
R. Y. McLeod,	W. S. Morrison,	

1886.
Clerical.

W. W. Duncan,	S. A. Weber,	W. D. Kirkland,
S. B. Jones,	A. M. Chrietzberg,	A. M. Shipp.

Alternates.

J. M. Boyd,   A. Coke Smith.

Lay Delegates.

James H. Carlisle,	J. F. Lyon,	R. H. Jennings,
Dr. H. Baer,	W. T. D. Cousar,	I. G. Clinkscales.

Alternates.

George E. Prince,   W. L. Gray.

1890.
Clerical.

A. Coke Smith,	S. B. Jones,	R. D. Smart,
W. D. Kirkland,	J. O. Willson,	S. Lander.

Alternates.

J. M. Boyd,   W. C. Power.

Lay Delegates.

J. H. Carlisle,	J. W. Quillian,	L. D. Childs,
William M. Connor,	A. C. Dibble,	W. L. Gray.

Alternates.

W. B. Stuckey,   J. Y. Westendorp.

1894.
Clerical.

W. D. Kirkland,	J. O. Willson,	S. Lander,
R. N. Wells,	J. C. Kilgo,	J. A. Clifton.
S. B. Jones,		

Alternates.

S. A. Weber,	T. G. Herbert,	T. J. Clyde.
J. W. Dickson,		

Lay Delegates.

J. H. Carlisle,	L. B. Haynes,	R. O. Purdy,
Dr. H. Baer,	H. H. Newton,	E. B. Craighead.
D. R. Duncan,		

Alternates.

R. W. Major,	H. J. Judy,	William M. Connor.
J. F. Lyon,	J. D. Eidson,	

22

III.

EXHIBIT OF NUMBERS, CONFERENCE COLLECTIONS FOR SUPER-
ANNUATES, WIDOWS AND ORPHANS, MISSIONS, AND AVERAGE
PAID PER MEMBER, FROM 1831 TO 1896, A PERIOD OF SIXTY-
FIVE YEARS.

Year.	Numbers.	Increase.	Decrease.	Conference Collections. Amount Assessed.	Conference Collections. Amount Collected.	Deficiency Per Cent.	Average Paid Per Member.	Collected for Missions.	Average Paid Per Member.
1831	20,513							$ 261 33	$0 01¼
1832	21,731							727 66	03
1833	24,773							1,519 45	06
1834	25,186			$ 2,362 41	$ 1,548 91	34	.06	1,119 34	04
1835	23,789							2,621 42	11
1836	24,110			2,799 12	2,427 68	13	.10	3,789 79	11
1837	23,615			2,859 63	1,990 82	30	.08	3,551 23	15
1838	24,016			2,333 71	1,783 92	23	.07	7,780 55	28
1839	24,986			2,037 50	2,074 60	....	.08	6,649 08	26
1840	27,338			2,774 55	1,755 75	36	.06	7,163 58	26
1841	27,188			3,841 32	1,621 40	57	.05	7,420 25	27
1842	27,491			4,659 72	1,934 85	54	.07	9,943 23	36
1843	29,887			3,780 13	1,455 94	61	.04	10,155 77	33
1844	32,306			3,935 09	1,853 21	52	.05	14,097 36	43
1845	33,387			3,747 45	1,708 19	54	.05	14,362 58	43
1846									
1847	32,371			4,032 69	1,397 84	65	.04	17,805 39	54
1848	33,313			4,937 00	1,624 87	67	.04	14,118 53	42
1849									
1850	30,906			5,410 60	2,462 99	54	.07	17,713 76	57
1851	32,390			5,799 00	2,644 89	54	.08	18,398 00	56
1852	32,828			4,995 00	3,413 14	31	.10	22,361 50	68
1853	33,214			4,369 00	3,993 46	8	.10	25,049 12	75
1854	34,621			4,052 00	3,873 21	4	.11	22,766 12	65
1855	35,028			7,859 50	4,092 74	47	.11	26,070 61	74
1856	35,297			7,764 16	4,205 44	45	.11	27,321 17	77
1857	35,733			7,715 00	4,313 05	44	.12	24,035 28	67
1858	37,095			8,711 00	4,732 75	45	.12	28,138 03	75
1859	38.294			8,000 00	5,299 93	33	.13	27,192 59	71
1860	39,935			8,830 00	5,381 73	41	.13	24,463 34	61
1861	37,986			6,979 00	2,700 31	38	.07	14,538 93	38
1862	38,161			6,935 00	5,020 00	27	.13	15,438 22	40
1863	39,288			8,420 00	10,772 00	....	.27	*40,500 29	1 03
1864	41,272			7,900 00	18,068 92	....	.43	*63,813 70	1 54
1865	40,296							302 80	¾
1866	40,059			7,344 10	1,401 65	81	.03	2,636 39	06
1867	38,467			8,540 00	1,369 40	82	.03	1,892 10	04
1868	40,395			5,875 00	3,290 00	44	.08	2,996 11	07
1869	42,752			6,450 00	4,357 00	32	.10	2,828 91	06
1870	32,240			7,125 00	3,791 85	46	.11	2,909 68	09
1871	34,737			7,000 00	3,951 88	43	.11	2,670 70	07
1872	36,041			7,000 00	4,717 20	32	.13	4,480 29	12
1873	36,432			7,175 00	4,745 50	34	.13	4,632 38	12
1874	28,954			6,944 45	5,415 30	22	.13⅔	5,167 48	13⅓

* Confederate currency.

Year.	Numbers.	Increase.	Decrease.	Conference Collections. Amount Assessed.	Conference Collections. Amount Collected.	Deficiency Per Cent.	Average Paid Per Member.	Collected for Missions.	Average Paid Per Member.
1875	40,568	......	......	$ 7,791 00	$ 5,424 16	30	.13	$ 7,003 45	$0 17
1876	41,770	1,202	......	8,000 00	4,948 00	38	.04	6,052 21	14
1877	43,701	1,931	......	5,655 25	4,950 15	12	.11	6,841 21	15
1878	44,513	812	......	5,000 00	3,775 36	34	.08	7,640 49	17
1879	44,701	218	......	6,013 37	4,868 50	19	.10	7,919 14	18
1880	46,619	1,918	......	5,993 50	5,144 31	14	.11	8,529 27	18
1881	48,191	1,572	......	6,000 00	4,679 24	22	.09	10,277 00	21
1882	49,280	1,084	......	6,000 00	5,654 35	5	.11	13,939 76	28
1883	50,831	1,551	......	6,000 00	5,207 90	11	.10	13,126 94	25
1884	52,433	1,612	......	6,000 00	5,217 08	13	.09	13.126 94	25
1885	54,469	2,026	......	6,500 00	4,922 12	24	.09	14,905 06	27
1886	62,142	7,673	......	7,000 00	5,190 05	25	.08	16,469 56	26
1887	63,122	980	......	11,000 00	7,985 00	27	.12	15,693 93	24
1888	65,415	3,293	......	11,050 00	8,343 22	24	.12	19,167 33	29
1889	67,906	2,491	......	11,000 00	8,436 56	23	.12	19,252 66	28
1890	67,091	......	815	11,000 00	9,409 06	23	.14	22,147 29	33
1891	69,315	2,224	......	11,000 00	8,833 86	19	.12	22,917 77	33
1892	69,861	546	......	11,000 00	7,549 38	31	.10	20,449 23	29
1893	71,791	1,930	....	14,631 38	8,593 85	47	.11	16,365 13	22
1894	71,535	.....	256	14,578 70	7,986 86	45	.11	16,759 12	23
1895	72,651	.....	1,116	15,000 00	8,729 87	41	.12	19,234 02	26
1896	72,665	14	......	15,000 00	10,086 86	32	.13½	20,197 17	27

IV.

CHRONOLOGICAL ROLL OF THE CLERICAL MEMBERS OF THE SOUTH CAROLINA CONFERENCE, FROM 1836 TO 1896.

February, 1836. William C. Patterson.
January, 1838. S. Jones.
January, 1839. A. M. Chreitzberg.
February, 1841. John A. Porter.
January, 1842. William Carson, H. M. Mood, and James F. Smith.
December, 1844. John M. Carlisle.
December, 1845. Sidi H. Browne and P. F. Kistler.
January, 1848. M. L. Banks and L. A. Johnson.
December, 1848. A. J. Cauthen.
December, 1849. W. W. Jones.
December, 1850. W. A. Clarke, W. W. Mood, and Thomas Raysor.
December, 1851. O. A. Darby and A. H. Lester.
November, 1853. L. M. Hamer.
November, 1854. C. E. Wiggins.
November, 1857. R. R. Dagnall, William C. Power, and A. W. Walker.
December, 1858. F. Auld, T. G. Herbert, and James C. Stoll.
November, 1859. J. B. Campbell, T. J. Clyde, J. W. Humbert, Thomas W. Munnerlyn, and A. J. Stokes.
December, 1860. N. K. Melton, J. L. Sifly, J. A. Wood, and J. J. Workman.
December, 1862. S. A. Weber.
December, 1863. A. J. Stafford.
November, 1864. John Attaway and S. Lander.
November, 1865. J. B. Traywick.
December, 1866. Reuben L. Duffie.
December, 1867. Silas P. H. Elwell.
December, 1868. L. C. Loyal and T. E. Wannamaker.
December, 1869. J. A. Clifton and G. T. Harmon.
December, 1870. J S. Beasley, George M. Boyd, G. W. Gatlin, and E. Toland Hodges.
December, 1871. D. D. Dantzler, J. K. McCain, D. Tiller, and J. B. Wilson, W. D. Kirkland.
December, 1872. R. W. Barber, J. C. Davis, J. Walter Dickson, C. D. Mann, G. H. Pooser, and William A. Rogers.
December, 1873. L. F. Beaty, James C. Bissell, J. E. Carlisle, William H. Kirton, I. J. Newberry, M. H. Pooser, John O. Willson, and George W. Walker.
December, 1874. William H. Ariail, J. C. Counts, M. M. Ferguson, A. W. Jackson, J. J. Neville, J. L. Stokes, S. D. Vaughn, W. W. Williams, and O. N. Rountree.
December, 1875. J. W. Ariail, D. Z. Dantzler, W. S. Martin, T. P. Phillips, and A. C. Walker.
December, 1876. H. B. Browne, R. H. Jones, W. P. Meadors, and E. G. Price.
December, 1877. J. Thomas Pate and James S. Porter.
December, 1878. William R. Richardson.

December, 1879. J. Walter Daniel, J. M. Fridy, T. E. Morris, P. A. Murray, and William H. Wroton.

December, 1880. N. B. Clarkson, William H. Harden, and J. W. Neeley.

December, 1881. M. M. Brabham, J. E. Rushton, J. E. Beard, J. C. Chandler, and William A. Betts.

December, 1882. J. W. Elkins, C. B. Smith, and J. D. Frierson.

December, 1883. James E. Grier, B. M. Grier, S. J. Bethea, D. P. Boyd, G. P. Watson, W. W. Daniel, and G. R. Whitaker.

December, 1884. J. C. Yongue, W. C. Gleaton, M. Dargan, G. H. Waddell, W. M. Duncan, and William B. Baker.

December, 1885. E. B. Loyless, L. S. Bellenger, A. F. Berry, E. O. Watson, J. M. Steadman, T. C. O'Dell, J. F. Anderson, A. M. Attaway, T. C. Ligon, W. I. Herbert, John Owen, and D. A. Calhoun.

December, 1886. A. W. Attaway, J. A. Rice, C. W. Creighton, M. L. Carlisle, M. W. Hook, and P. L. Kirton.

December, 1887. R. L. Holroyd, A. B. Earle, W. E. Barre, James W. Kilgo, W. B. Duncan, John L. Harley, R. A. Yongue, S. T. Blackman, J. P. Attaway, W. L. Wait, James E. Mahaffey.

November, 1888. Nicholas G. Ballenger, Thomas M. Dent, Pierce F. Kilgo, Henry C. Mouzon, John L. Ray, George R. Shaffer, Robert E. Stackhouse, Ellie P. Taylor, E. Alston Wilkes, and W. Asbury Wright.

November, 1889. Jefferson S. Abercrombie, Albert H. Best. Rufus A. Child, J. R. Copeland, George W. Davis, Melvin B. Kelly, J. Marion Rogers, John William Shell, Whitefoord S. Stokes, Artemus B. Watson, W. H. Hodges, J. Manning, and J. A. White.

December, 1890. David Hucks, Edward W. Mason, J. Hubert Noland, David A. Phillips, and Samuel H. Zimmerman.

December, 1891. Alexander N. Brunson, A. J. Cauthen, Jr., C. Hovey Clyde, John D. Crout, James H. Thacker, William C. Wynn; and Eli M. McKissick, from Protestant Methodist Church.

November, 1892. E. Palmer Hutson, from Presbyterian Church; H. W. Bays, from Western North Carolina Conference; J. A. White, from Florida Conference. Admitted on trial: E. H. Beckham, G. F. Clarkson, J. L. Daniel, R. M. Du Bose, O. L. Durant, S. W. Henry, P. B. Ingraham, J. N. Isom, W. B. Justus, A. S. Lesley, W. H. Miller, E. K. Moore, R. C. McRoy, D. M. McLeod, J. J. Stevenson, R. W. Spigner, T. J. White, W. B. Wharton, and W. E. Wiggins.

December, 1893. L. L. Bedenbaugh, J. A. Campbell, R. A. Few, T. G. Herbert, Jr., Barr Harris, R. E. Mood, W. A. Massebeau, Peter Stokes, and G. Edwin Stokes.

November, 1894. Martin L. Banks, Jr., Waddy T. Duncan, William S. Goodwin, E. S. Jones, W. A. Kelly, Jr., S. A. Nettles, W. A. Pitts, W. I. Snyder, and P. B. Wells.

V.

CONFERENCE REGISTER AND DIRECTORY FOR 1896.

E. Elder; D. Deacon; S'y, Supernumerary; S'd, Superannuated; P. E. Presiding Elder.

NAMES.	POST OFFICE ADDRESS.	Year Entered the Conference.	Years on Districts.	Years on Stations.	Years on Circuits.	Years on Missions.	In Colleges, Army, Local, or Transferred.	Supernumerary.	Superannuated.	Years in All.	Present Relation
Abercrombie, J. S.	Salter's	Nov., 1889	..	..	..	6	..	..	..	6	E
Anderson, J. F.	Easley	Dec., 1895	..	10	..	..	..	..	10	E
Archer, E. L.	Spartanburg	Dec., 1873	..	..	5	..	11	6	..	21	S'y
Ariail, W. H.	Abbeville	Dec., 1874	..	2	18	1	..	..	..	21	E
Ariail, J. W.	Mullins	Dec., 1875	..	..	20	..	..	..	..	20	E
Attaway, John	Williamston	Nov., 1864	..	..	31	..	..	..	..	31	E
Attaway, A. McS.	Williamston	Dec., 1885	..	..	8	..	..	..	2	10	S'd
Attaway, A. W.	Williamston	Dec., 1886	..	..	6	..	..	3	..	9	S'y
Attaway, J. P.	Tiller's Ferry	Nov., 1887	..	..	8	..	..	..	..	8	E
Auld, F.	Williamston	Nov., 1858	..	9	22	1	..	..	5	37	S'd
Baker, W. B.	Columbia	Nov., 1884	..	..	11	..	..	..	..	11	E
Ballenger, N. G.	Leesville	Nov., 1888	..	..	7	..	..	..	..	7	E
Banks, M. L.	St. Matthew's	Nov., 1847	..	6	28	8	..	1	5	48	S'd
Barber, R. W.	Branchville	Nov., 1874	..	..	14	..	..	7	..	21	E
Barre, R. W.	Kinard's	Nov., 1887	..	..	7	..	..	..	1	8	E
Bays, H. W.	Charleston	Nov., 1892	..	3	..	..	..	..	..	3	E
Beard, I. E.	Graniteville	Dec., 1881	..	3	6	5	..	..	..	14	E
Beasley, J. S.	McColl	Dec., 1870	4	4	17	..	..	..	..	25	E
Beaty, L. F.	Nashville, Tenn.	Dec., 1873	..	4	15	..	3	..	..	22	E
Beckham, E. H.	Foreston	Nov., 1892	..	..	3	..	..	..	..	3	D
Bedenbaugh, L. L.	Tradesville	Dec., 1893	..	..	2	..	..	..	..	2	D
Bellinger, L. S.	Woodford	Dec., 1885	..	..	10	..	..	..	..	10	E
Berry, A. F.	Livingston	Dec., 1885	..	..	10	..	..	..	..	10	E
Best, A. H.	Sumter	Nov., 1889	..	..	6	..	..	..	..	6	E
Bethea, S. J.	Lake City	Dec., 1883	..	..	7	5	..	..	..	11	E
Betts, W. A.	Richburg	Dec., 1881	..	5	9	..	..	..	..	14	E
Bissell, J. C.	Cherokee	Dec., 1873	..	..	18	..	..	..	4	22	S'd
Blackman, S. T.	Whitmire	Nov., 1887	..	..	8	..	..	..	..	8	E
Boyd, G. M.	Trough Shoals	Dec., 1870	..	..	25	..	..	..	..	25	E
Boyd, D. P.	Gray Court	Dec., 1882	..	..	13	..	..	..	..	13	E
Brabham, M. M.	Edgefield	Dec., 1882	..	..	13	..	..	..	..	13	E
Browne, H. B.	Rock Hill	Dec., 1876	..	10	9	..	..	..	..	19	E
Browne, Sidi H.	Columbia	Dec., 1845	16	6	14	4	2	..	8	50	S'd
Brunson, A. N.	Yorkville	Dec., 1891	..	..	4	..	..	..	..	4	E
Calhoun, D. A.	Laurel	Dec., 1885	..	..	10	..	..	..	..	10	E
Campbell, J. A.	Waterloo	Dec., 1893	..	..	2	..	..	..	..	2	D
Campbell, J. B.	Rock Hill	Nov., 1859	4	16	12	3	1	..	..	36	P. E
Carlisle, John E.	Union	Dec., 1873	..	22	..	..	..	..	..	22	E
Carlisle, John M.	Spartanburg	Dec., 1844	4	11	16	..	11	..	9	51	S'd
Carlisle, M. L.	Chester	Dec., 1886	..	5	4	..	..	..	..	9	E
Carson, William	Foreston	Jan., 1842	..	..	32	12	2	..	7	53	S'd
Cauthen, A. J.	Spartanburg	Dec., 1848	9	5	25	..	8	..	..	47	P. E
Cauthen, A. J., Jr.	Little Rock	Dec., 1891	..	..	4	..	..	..	..	4	E
Chandler, J. C.	Cokesbury	Dec., 1881	..	..	13	..	1	..	..	14	E
Child, R. A.	Darlington	Nov., 1889	..	2	4	..	..	..	..	6	E

CONFERENCE REGISTER AND DIRECTORY FOR 1896.—*Continued.*

Name.	Post Office Address.	Year Entered the Conference.	Years on Districts.	Years on Stations.	Years on Circuits.	Years on Missions.	In Colleges, Army, Local, or Transferred.	Supernumerary.	Superannuated.	Years in All.	Present Relation.
Chreitzberg, A. M.	Moultrieville ...	Jan., 1839	23	10	19	2			3	57	S'd
Clarke, W. A	Laurens.........	Dec., 1850			32	5		5	3	45	S'd
Clarkson, G. F....	Nashville, Tenn.	Nov., 1892			3					3	D
Clarkson, N. B....	Clinton.........	Dec., 1880			15					15	E
Clifton, J. A......	Abbeville.......	Dec., 1869		13	13					26	E
Clyde, C. Hovey...	Williston	Dec., 1891			3	1				4	E
Clyde, T. J........	Anderson.......	Nov., 1859	9	3	24					36	P. E
Copeland, J. R....	Loris...........	Nov., 1889			6					6	D
Counts, J. C	Clyde...........	Dec., 1874			20		1			21	E
Creighton, C. W...	Newberry.......	Dec., 1886		2	7					9	E
Crout, J. D........	Gaffney	Dec., 1891		2	2					4	E
Dagnall, R. R.....	Gibson	Nov., 1857			32	2	4			38	E
Daniel, J. L.......	Walhalla	Nov., 1892			3					3	D
Daniel, J. W......	Sumter	Dec., 1879		9	7					16	E
Daniel, W. W.....	Columbia.......	Dec., 1883		10	2					12	E
Dantzler, D. D....	St. Matthew's ...	Dec., 1874		2	19					21	E
Danztler, D. Z.....	Reidville.......	Dec., 1875		2	18					20	E
Darby, O. A.......	Kingstree.......	Dec., 1851	5	17	13		9			44	E
Dargan, Marion...	Greenwood	Dec., 1884		5	3		3			11	E
Davis, George W..	Rome...........	Nov., 1889			6					6	E
Davis, J. C........	Lake City	Dec., 1872			19	2	2			23	E
Dent, Thomas M..	Winnsboro......	Nov., 1888		3	4					7	E
Dickson, J. Walter.	Columbia.......	Dec., 1872	9	4	6		4			23	P. E
Du Bose, R. M.....	Lexington	Nov., 1892			3					3	D
Duffie, R. L.......	Westminster....	Dec., 1866			20				9	29	S'd
Duncan, W. B.....	Allendale.	Nov., 1887		2	6					8	E
Duncan, W. M.....	Summerville....	Dec., 1884		11						11	E
Dowell, W. J......	Wedgefield.....	Dec., 1893			2					2	E
Dunlop, A. T......	Piedmont	Dec., 1893		2						2	E
Durant, O. L......	Reedy Creek....	Nov., 1892			3					3	E
Earle, A. B	Williamston	Nov., 1887			8					8	E
Elkins, J. W......	Bishopville	Dec., 1882		6	7					13	E
Elwell, S. P. H....	Bamberg........	Dec., 1867		7	21					28	E
Ferguson, M. M...	Sally	Dec., 1874			9	10		2		21	S'y
Few, R. A	Swansea	Dec., 1893			2					2	D
Fridy, J. M	Cherokee.......	Dec., 1879		1	11				4	16	E
Frierson, J. D.....	Jefferson........	Dec., 1882			13					13	E
Gatlin, G. W	Kollock	Dec., 1870			23				2	25	E
Gleaton, W. C.....	Kelton..	Dec., 1884			10	1				11	E
Grier, B. M	Gibson Sta., N. C.	Dec., 1883			12					12	E
Grier, J. E........	Greenville......	Dec., 1883		2	10					12	E
Hamer, L. M......	Bennettsville....	Dec., 1853		1	21		5	4	11	42	S'd
Harden, W. M....	Pickens	Dec., 1880			15					15	E
Harley, J. L.......	Clifton..	Dec., 1887			8					8	E
Harmon, G. T.....	Cokesbury......	Dec., 1869	4	8	12		2			26	P. E
Harris, J. Barr....	Rock Hill.......	Dec., 1893			2					2	D
Henry, S. W......	Heath Spring...	Nov., 1892			3					3	D
Herbert, Thomas G.	Batesburg	Dec., 1858	16		21					37	E

CONFERENCE REGISTER AND DIRECTORY FOR 1896.—*Continued.*

NAMES.	POST OFFICE ADDRESS.	Year Entered the Conference.	Years on Districts.	Years on Stations.	Years on Circuits.	Years on Missions.	In Colleges,Army,Local,or Transferred.	Supernumerary.	Superannuated.	Years in All.	Present Relation.
Herbert,T.Grigsby.	Sumter	Dec., 1893	..	..	2	..	..	..	..	2	D
Herbert, W. I.	Florence	Dec., 1885	..	10	.	..	..	..	..	10	E
Hodges, E. T	Florence	Dec., 1870	5	3	16	..	1	..	..	25	P. E
Hodges, W. H.	Manning	Nov., 1889	..	3	2	..	1	..	..	6	E
Holroyd, R. L.	Scotia	Nov., 1887	..	..	8	..	..	..	..	8	E
Hook, M. W	Horeb	Dec., 1886	..	..	9	..	..	..	..	9	E
Hucks, David	Hendersonville	Nov., 1890	..	..	5	..	..	..	..	5	E
Humbert, J. W	Fort Mill	Nov., 1859	..	16	20	..	..	..	..	36	E
Hutson, E. Palmer	Holly Hill	Nov., 1892	..	..	3	..	..	..	..	3	E
Ingraham, P. B.	Mt. Carmel	Nov., 1892	..	..	3	..	..	..	..	3	D
Isom, J. N	Chesterfield	Nov., 1892	..	..	3	..	..	..	..	3	D
Jackson, A. W.	Rome	Dec., 1874	..	1	15	..	..	3	2	21	S'd
Johnson, L. A.	Yorkville	Dec., 1847	..	10	16	9	3	10	..	48	E
Jones, R. H.	Walterboro	Dec., 1876	..	9	10	..	..	..	..	19	E
Jones, Simpson	Darlington	Jan., 1838	..	..	40	1	..	6	10	57	S'd
Jones, W. W	Butler	Dec., 1849	..	..	46	..	..	..	..	46	E
Justus, W. B	Phœnix	Nov., 1892	..	..	3	..	..	..	..	3	D
Kelly, M. B.	Denmark	Nov., 1889	..	..	6	..	..	..	..	6	E
Kilgo, James W.	Greenville	Nov., 1887	..	5	3	..	..	..	..	8	E
Kilgo, Pierce F.	Lydia	Nov., 1888	..	5	2	..	..	..	..	7	E
Kirton, P. L	Columbia	Dec., 1886	..	4	3	..	2	..	..	9	E
Kirton, W. H	Hartsville	Dec., 1873	..	2	18	2	..	..	..	22	E
Kistler, Paul F.	Denmark	Jan., 1846	..	..	49	..	..	..	..	49	S'd
Lander, Samuel	Williamston	Nov., 1864	..	3	2	..	26	..	..	31	E
Leard, Samuel	Raleigh, N. C	Feb., 1835	5	9	22	13	3	..	8	60	S'd
Lesley, A. S	Cross Keys	Nov., 1892	..	..	3	..	..	..	..	3	D
Lester, A. H	Spartanburg	Dec., 1851	..	21	7	..	7	3	6	44	S'd
Ligon, T. C	Rock Hill	Dec., 1885	..	..	10	..	..	..	..	10	E
Loyal, L. C	Luray	Dec., 1868	..	2	16	3	..	..	6	27	S'd
Loyless, E. B.	Spartanburg	Dec., 1885	..	..	7	3	..	..	..	10	E
Macfarlan, Allan	Santuc	Dec., 1894	..	..	1	..	..	..	..	1	E
Mahaffey, J. E.	Lowrysville	Nov., 1887	..	..	8	..	..	..	..	8	E
Mann, Coke D.	Timmonsville	Dec., 1872	..	..	23	..	..	..	..	23	E
Manning, John.	Columbia	 1889	..	..	6	..	..	..	..	6	D
Martin, W. S	Marion	Dec., 1875	..	10	10	..	..	..	..	20	E
Massebeau, W. A.	Ridgeville	Dec., 1893	..	..	2	..	..	..	..	2	D
Mason, E. W	Lowndesville	Nov., 1890	..	..	5	..	..	..	..	5	E
McCain, J. K.	Fork	Dec., 1871	..	..	24	..	..	..	..	24	E
McKissick, E. M.	Summerville	Dec., 1891	..	..	4	..	..	..	..	4	E
McLeod, D. M	Aiken	Nov., 1892	..	1	2	..	..	..	..	3	D
McRoy, R. C	Donald's	Nov., 1892	..	..	3	..	..	..	..	3	D
Meadors, W. P.	Charleston	Dec., 1876	1	1	16	1	..	..	..	19	P. E
Melton, N. K.	Sampit	Dec., 1860	..	3	31	1	..	..	..	35	E
Miller, W. H	Enoree	Nov., 1892	..	..	3	..	..	..	..	3	D
Moore, E. K	Macbeth	Nov., 1892	..	..	3	..	..	..	..	3	D
Mood, H. M	Sumter	Dec., 1842	8	20	14	2	9	..	..	53	S'd
Mood, J. A.	Spartanburg	Jan., 1847	..	11	23	10	1	..	3	48	S'd
Mood, W. W	Sumter	Dec., 1850	..	10	20	5	..	..	10	45	S'd

CONFERENCE REGISTER AND DIRECTORY FOR 1896.—*Continued.*

Names.	Post Office Address.	Year Entered the Conference.	Years on Districts.	Years on Stations.	Years on Circuits.	Years on Missions.	In Colleges Army, Local, or Tran-ferred.	Supernumerary.	Superannuated.	Years in All.	Present Relation.
Mood, R. E	Indiantown	Dec., 1893			2					2	D
Morris T. E	Charleston	Dec., 1879		11	5					16	E
Mouzon, H. C	Ridgeland	Nov., 1888			7					7	E
Munnerlyn, T. W.	Smithville	Nov., 1859			18	3	4		11	36	S'd
Murray, P. A	Beaufort	Dec., 1878		5	12					17	E
Neeley, J. W	Columbia	Dec., 1880			15					15	S'y
Neville, J. J	Anderson	Dec., 1874			11			1	9	21	S'd
Newberry, I. J	Gaffney	Dec., 1873			7			1	14	22	S'd
Noland, J. H	Gourdin	Dec., 1890		2	2		1			5	E
Odell, T. C	Georgetown	Dec., 1885		3	7					10	E
Owen, John	Orangeburg	Dec., 1885		1	9					10	P. E
Pate, J. Thomas	Camden	Dec., 1877		12	6					18	E
Patterson, W. C	Cureton's Store	Feb., 1836			18				39	57	S'd
Phillips, A. R	Lewiedale	Nov., 1892			3					3	D
Phillips, D. Arthur	Landrum's	Nov., 1890			5					5	E
Phillips, T. P	Greer's	Dec., 1874			21					21	E
Pooser, George H.	Branchville	Dec., 1872			21	2				23	E
Pooser, M. H	Westminster	Dec., 1873			22					22	E
Porter, James S	Lynchburg	Dec., 1877		1	16					17	E
Porter, John A	Marion	Feb., 1841	1	19	28	3			3	54	S'd
Power, W. C	Sumter	Nov., 1857	14	10	8		6			38	P. E
Price, E. G	Prosperity	Dec., 1876		3	15	1				19	E
Pritchard, C. H	Abbeville	Feb., 1841	9	28	14	1			2	54	S'd
Ray, J. L	Pacolet	Nov., 1888			7					7	E
Raysor, Thomas	Lyons	Dec., 1850	10		33	2				45	E
Rice, John A	Columbia	Dec., 1886		6	2		1			9	E
Richardson, W. R.	Charleston	Dec., 1878		15	2					17	E
Rogers, J. Marion	Mullins	Nov., 1889		1	1		2	2		6	D
Rogers, W. A	Spartanburg	Dec., 1872		13	10					23	E
Rountree, O. N	Parksville	Dec., 1874			9		12			21	E
Rushton, J. E	Oswego	Dec., 1881			14					14	E
Shaffer, G. R	Princeton	Nov., 1888			7					7	E
Shell, John W	Fountain Inn	Nov., 1889			6					6	E
Sifly, J. L	Irmo	Dec., 1860			35					35	E
Smith, Charles B.	Spartanburg	Dec., 1882		9	3		1			13	E
Smith, James F	Spartanburg	Jan., 1842			18	2	21	12		53	S'd
Stackhouse, R. E.	Johnston	Nov., 1888		5	2					7	E
Stafford, A. J	Cheraw	Dec., 1863		22	7	3				32	E
Steadman, J. M	Charleston	Dec., 1885		3	5	2				10	E
Stevenson, J. J	Blackstock	Nov., 1892			3					3	D
Spigner, R. W	Jonesville	Nov., 1892			3					3	D
Stokes, A. J	Laurens	Nov., 1859	8	20	8					36	E
Stokes, G. Edwin.	Springfield	Dec., 1893			2					2	D
Stokes, J. L.	Bennettsville	Dec., 1874		13	8					21	E
Stokes, Peter	Rembert	Dec., 1893			2					2	D
Stokes, W. S	Conway	Nov., 1889		5	1					6	E
Stoll, J. C	Ninety-six	Dec., 1858	4		31	1				36	E
Taylor, E. P.	McCormick	Nov., 1888			7					7	E

CONFERENCE REGISTER AND DIRECTORY FOR 1896.—*Continued.*

Names.	Post Office Address.	Year Entered the Conference.	Years on Districts.	Years on Stations.	Years on Circuits.	Years on Missions.	In Colleges, Army Local, or Transferred.	Supernumerary.	Superannuated.	Years in All.	Present Relation.
Thacker, J. H.....	Hickory Grove..	Dec., 1891	..	...	4	..	..	..	...	4	E
Tiller, Dove	Newberry	Nov., 1871	..	3	21	..	..	..	...	24	E
Traywick, J. B....	Clio...	Nov., 1865	..	...	30	..	..	..	...	30	E
Vaughn, S. D.....	Denny'sX Roads.	Dec., 1874	..	...	16	5	..	..	...	21	E
Waddell, G. H....	Columbia.......	Dec., 1884	..	3	7	1	..	..	...	11	E
Wait, W. L.......	Barnwell........	Nov., 1887	..	...	7	1	..	..	...	8	E
Walker, Arthur C.	St. George's.....	Dec., 1875	..	2	18	..	..	..	...	20	E
Walker, A. W.....	Pickens	Nov., 1857	..	7	15	1	....	1	4	38	S'd
Walker, George W.	Augusta, Ga	Dec., 1873	..	9	2	..	11	..	..	22	E
Wannamaker, T. E.	Orangeburg.....	Dec., 1868	4	6	11	..	..	6	..	27	S'y
Watson, Artemas B.	Summerton.....	Nov., 1889	..	2	4	..	..	..	...	6	E
Watson, E. O.... .	Orangeburg.....	Dec., 1885	..	5	5	..	..	..	...	10	E
Watson, G. Pierce.	Anderson........	Dec., 1883	..	7	5	..	..	..	...	12	E
Weber, S. A.......	Lancaster	Dec., 1862	..	18	5	..	10	..	...	33	E
Wharton, W. B ...	Greenwood	Nov., 1892	..	...	3	..	..	..	...	3	D
Whittaker, G. R...	Centenary	Dec., 1883	..	...	12	..	..	..	...	12	E
White, J. A.......	Savage..........	Nov., 1892	..	...	3	..	..	..	...	3	D
White, T. J.......	Columbia.......	Nov., 1892	..	...	3	..	..	..	...	3	D
Wiggins, C. E.....	Ehrhardt.......	Nov., 1854	..	...	12	3	26	..	...	41	E
Wiggins, W. E ...	Orangeburg. ...	Nov., 1892	..	...	3	..	..	..	...	3	D
Wilkes, E. Alston.	Lamar..........	Nov., 1888	..	...	7	..	..	..	...	7	E
Williams, W. W...	Latta	Dec., 1874	..	1	20	..	..	..	...	21	E
Willson, John O ..	Greenville......	Dec., 1873	5	16	..	..	..	1	...	22	E
Wilson, J. B	Marion.........	Dec., 1871	5	..	19	..	..	..	...	24	P. E
Winn, W. C.......	Ridgeway	Dec., 1891	..	...	4	..	..	..	...	4	E
Wood, John A....	Fairview........	Dec., 1860	..	1	11	3	....	16	4	35	S'd
Workman, J. J...	Lancaster.......	Dec., 1860	..	2	28	..	..	..	5	35	S'd
Wright, W. A.....	New Zion	Nov., 1888	..	...	7	..	..	..	...	7	E
Wroton, W. H....	Hampton	Dec., 1879	..	...	16	..	..	..	...	16	E
Yongue, J. C.....	Bowman	Dec., 1884	..	...	7	4	..	..	...	11	E
Yongue, R. A.....	Rocky Mount ...	Nov., 1887	..	...	8	..	..	..	...	8	E
Zimmerman, S. H	Pendleton.......	Nov., 1890	..	1	4	..	..	..	...	5	E

PREACHERS ON TRIAL.

First Year.—Sidi B. Harper, L. Inabinet, D. W. Keller, W. C. Kirkland, John C. Roper, F. H. Shuler, Foster Speer, W. H. Thrower.

Second Year.—J. G. Beckwith, R. C. Boulware, C. B. Burns, H. J. Cauthen, C. C. Herbert, G. C. Leonard, B. M. Robertson, J. R. Sojourner, Henry Stokes, W. B. Verdin, J. F. Way.

SUPPLIES.

J. C. Abney, S. D. Bailey, T. L. Belvin, W. R. Buchanan, W. A. Faerey, J. T. McFarlane, J. R. F. Monts, J. L. Mullinix, J. M. Shell, I. E. Smith, J. C. Welch, J. N. Wright.

LAY MEMBERS.

Charleston District.—William Stokes, B. Greig, M. H. Carter, J. S. Wimberly.

Cokesbury District.—Thomas W. Keitt, J. B. Humbert, J. G. Jenkins, R. W. Major.

Columbia District.—R. H. Jennings, J. C. Abney, L. B. Haynes, A. M. Boozer.

Florence District.—G. H. Hoffmeyer, G. A. Perritt, J. G. McCall, J. A. Kelly.

Greenville District.—G. E. Prince, J. G. Clinkscales, B. F. Few, R. Abercrombie.

Marion District.—L. H. Little, C. N. Rogers, J. Smith, W. J. Adams.

Orangeburg District.—H. I. Judy, A. C. Dibble, J. B. Guess, J. E. Smook.

Rock Hill District.—I. M. Yoder, F. M. Hicklin, J. M. Riddle, W. S. Hall, Jr.

VI.

SOUTH CAROLINA CONFERENCE BROTHERHOOD—NET PROCEEDS OF ASSESSMENTS.

No.	Date	Name	Clerical	Lay	Special	Total	Expense	Net
1	Dec. 10, 1885	C. C. Fishburn	$ 381 00	$ 42 00	$ 18 20	$ 441 20	$ 6 20	$ 435 00
2	Feb. 14, 1886	George H. Wells	272 00	42 00	1 00	415 00	4 55	410 45
3	May 22, 188	H. A. C. Walker	363 00	50 00	......	413 00	5 00	408 00
4	Jun. 5, 1887	D. J. Simmons	477 00	88 00	......	565 00	2 00	562 10
5	Jun. 23, 1887	M. A. McKibben	474 00	87 00	......	561 00	4 15	553 85
6	May 2, 1887	C. D. Rowell	459 00	79 00	......	538 00	3 48	534 52
7	June 16, 1887	A. M. Shipp	456 00	78 00	......	534 00	1 67	532 33
8	Jan. 4, 1888	James T. Kilgo	489 00	88 00	8 00	585 00	2 00	583 00
9	Dec. 15, 188	Lewis M. Little	525 00	112 00	11 00	648 00	2 27	645 73
10	Jan. 10, 1889	William Martin	522 00	123 00	4 00	649 00	4 05	644 95
11	Mar. 24, 1889	J. P. Zimmerman	516 00	123 00	......	645 00	1 29	643 71
12	June 10, 1889	J. Emory Watson	513 00	129 00	6 25	648 25	75	647 50
13	July 13, 1889	Abram P. Avant	510 00	131 00	15 75	656 75	89	655 86
14	Nov. 6, 1889	Abram Nettles	498 00	153 00	5 65	656 65	1 62	655 03
15	Dec. 4, 1890	William Thomas	516 00	153 00	......	639 00	5 00	664 00
16	Feb. 6, 1891	B. G. Jones	546 00	146 00	5 00	697 00	5 00	692 00
17	Aug. 2, 1891	R. C. Oliver	537 00	128 00	......	655 00	5 15	659 85
18	Aug. 27, 1891	A. A. Gilbert	534 00	139 00	5 00	678 00	3 20	674 80
19	Dec. 2, 1891	J. W. Murray	525 00	132 00	......	657 00	5 06	651 94
20	Jan. 19, 1892	William Hutto	537 00	128 00	......	665 00	5 16	659 84
21	Mar. 10, 1892	J. L. Shuford	534 00	130 00	......	634 00	5 42	658 58
22	July 29, 1892	Manning Brown	525 00	127 00	6 00	658 00	4 35	653 65
23	Sept. 5, 1892	Landy Wood	522 00	123 00	......	645 00	4 03	640 97
24	Jan. 17, 1893	J. B. Platt	588 00	124 00	1 00	713 00	4 64	708 83
25	Apr. 27, 1893	Whiteford Smith	582 00	116 00	2 00	700 00	4 87	695 13
26	Aug. 15, 1893	J. W. McRoy	567 00	102 00	5 00	674 00	4 71	639 20
27	Nov. 3, 1893	W. H. Lawton	552 00	102 00	8 00	662 00	4 61	657 39
28	Jan. 28, 1894	M. A. Connolly	561 00	96 00	9 00	666 00	3 72	662 28
29	Feb. 25, 1894	J. Marion Boyd	555 00	100 00	2 00	657 00	3 51	653 49
30	July 17, 1894	W. L. Pegues	531 00	85 00	......	616 00	3 27	612 73
31	Sept. 8, 1894	S. B. Jones	522 00	77 00	......	599 00	3 37	595 63
32	Sept. 10, 1894	W. T. Capers	519 00	78 00	3 00	600 00	3 35	595 65
33	Dec. 11, 1894	R. N. Wells	519 00	68 00	99 00	633 00	3 54	682 46
34	Jan. 25, 1895	R. P. Franks	504 00	70 00	3 00	577 00	3 45	573 55
35	Apr. 6, 1895	W. D. Seale	489 00	70 00	......	559 00	3 94	555 06
		Total	$17,820 00	$3,619 00	$223 85	$21,662 85	$130 17	$21,532 68

December 23, 1895.

S. LANDER, *Treasurer.*

Seven more assessments, with two unfinished, nine in all, up to August, 1897, give $4,427; making an aggregate of $25,959.68 for the eleven years' operation.—AUTHOR.

BISHOP AND CABINET.

1. Bishop Charles B. Galloway, D.D. 2. John B. Wilson. 3. E. T. Hodges. 4. G. T. Harmon. 5. J. Walter Dickson. 6. J. B. Campbell.
7. W. P. Meadors. 8. John Owen. 9. T. J. Clyde. 10. A. J. Cauthen. 11. William C. Power.

VII.

SESSIONS OF THE SOUTH CAROLINA CONFERENCE.

Number.	Place.	Date.	President.	Secretary.	White Members.	Colored Members.
1	Charleston, S. C	Mch. 22, 1787	Coke and Asbury............	Not known............	2,075	141
2	Charleston, S. C	Mch. 12, 1788	Francis Asbury............	Not known............	2,246	224
3	Charleston, S. C	Mch. 17, 1789	Coke and Asbury............	Not known............	3,087	290
4	Charleston, S. C	Feb. 15, 1790	Francis Asbury............	Not known............	2,962	496
5	Charleston, S. C	Feb. 22, 1791	Coke and Asbury	Not known............	3,830	699
6	Charleston, S. C	Feb. 14, 1792	Francis Asbury............	Not known............	3,655	742
7	Charleston, S. C	Dec. 24, 1792	Francis Asbury............	Not known............	3,371	826
8	Finch's, in fork of Saluda and Broad rivers..................	Jan. 1, 1794	Francis Asbury............	Not known............	5,192	1,220
9	Charleston, S. C	Jan. 1, 1795	Francis Asbury............	Not known............	4,428	1,116
10	Charleston, S. C	Jan. 1, 1796	Francis Asbury............	Not known............	3,862	971
11	Charleston, S. C	Jan. 5, 1797	Coke and Asbury............	Not known............	3,715	1,038
12	Charleston, S. C	Jan. 1, 1798	Jonathan Jackson............	Not known............	4,457	1,381
13	Charleston, S. C	Jan. 1, 1799	Francis Asbury............	Jesse Lee............	4,806	1,385
14	Charleston, S. C	Jan. 1, 1800	Francis Asbury............	Jesse Lee............	4,802	1.535
15	Camden, S. C	Jan. 1, 1801	Asbury and Whatcoat ...	Jeremiah Norman	4,745	1,562
16	Camden, S. C..........	Jan. 1, 1802	Francis Asbury............	N. Snethen............	5,663	1,780
17	Camden, S. C..........	Jan. 1, 1803	Francis Asbury............	N. Snethen............	9,256	2,815
18	Augusta, Ga...	Jan. 2, 1804	Coke and Asbury............	N. Snethen............	11,064	3,456
19	Charleston, S. C	Jan. 1, 1805	Asbury and Whatcoat....	John McVean............	12,258	3,831
20	Camden, S. C..........	Dec. 30, 1805	Asbury and Whatcoat....	James Hill............	12,665	4,387
21	Sparta, Ga..............	Dec. 29, 1806	Francis Asbury............	Lewis Myers.........	12,484	4,432
22	Charleston, S. C	Dec. 28, 1807	Francis Asbury...	Lewis Myers.........	14,417	5,111
23	Liberty Chapel, Ga..	Dec. 26, 1808	Asbury and McKendree..	W. M. Kennedy....	16,344	6,284
24	Charleston, S. C	Dec. 23, 1809	Asbury and McKendree..	W. M. Kennedy....	17,788	8,202
25	Columbia, S. C	Dec. 22, 1810	Asbury and McKendree..	W. M. Kennedy....	19,404	9,129
26	Camden, S. C..........	Dec. 21, 1811	Asbury and McKendree..	W. M. Kennedy....	20,863	11,063
27	Charleston, S. C	Dec. 19, 1812	Asbury and McKendree..	W. M. Kennedy....	23,966	13,771
28	Fayetteville, N. C ...	Jan. 14, 1814	Asbury and McKendree..	W. M. Kennedy....	23,711	14,348
29	Milledgeville, Ga.....	Dec. 21, 1814	Asbury and McKendree..	A. Talley............	23,240	14,527
30	Charleston, S. C	Dec. 23, 1815	William McKendree......	A. Talley............	25,065	16,429
31	Columbia, S. C........	Dec. 25, 1816	McKendree and George..	A. Talley............	22,383	16,789
32	*Augusta, Ga..........	Jan. 27, 1818	William McKendree...... ...	S. K. Hodges........	20,905	11,714
33	Camden, S. C..........	Dec. 24, 1818	R. R. Roberts	S. K. Hodges........	21,059	11,587
34	Charleston, S. C......	Jan. 20, 1820	Enoch George............	W. M. Kennedy....	21,221	11,748
35	Columbia, S. C........	Jan. 11, 1821	Enoch George............	W. M. Kennedy....	22,105	12,485
36	Augusta, Ga..........	Feb. 21, 1822	McKendree and George ..	W. M. Kennedy....	21,290	12,906
37	Savannah, Ga	Feb. 20, 1823	R. R. Roberts.......	W. M. Kennedy....	23,121	13,895
38	Charleston, S. C	Feb. 19, 1824	Enoch George............	W. M. Kennedy....	24,909	14,766
39	†Wilmington, N. C..	Feb. 16, 1825	R. R. Roberts............	W. M. Kennedy....	27,756	15,293
40	Milledgeville, Ga....	Jan. 12, 1826	Joshua Soule............	W. M. Kennedy....	28,405	15,708
41	Augusta, Ga	Jan. 11, 1827	McKendree,Roberts, and Soule..................	S. K. Hodges........	29,419	16,552
42	Camden, S. C..........	Feb. 6, 1828	Joshua Soule............	S. K Hodges........	35,173	18,475
43	Charleston, S. C......	Jan. 28, 1829	William McKendree......	W. M. Kennedy....	38,708	21,300
44	‡Columbia, S. C ...	Jan. 27, 1830	Joshua Soule............	John Howard........	40,335	24,554
45	Fayetteville, N. C ...	Jan. 26, 1831	W. M. Kennedy............	S. W. Capers........	20,513	19,144
46	Darlington, S. C......	Jan. 26, 1832	Elijah Hedding............	W. M. Wightman.	21,731	20,197
47	Lincolnton, N. C......	Jan. 30, 1833	J. O. Andrew............	W. M. Wightman.	24,772	22,336
48	Charleston, S. C	Feb. 5, 1834	Emory and Andrew........	W. M. Wightman.	25,186	22,788
49	Columbia, S. C........	Feb. 11, 1835	J. O. Andrew............	W. M. Wightman.	23,789	22,737
50	Charleston, S. C	Feb. 10, 1836	J. O. Andrew............	W. M. Wightman.	24,110	23,643
51	Wilmington, N. C ...	Jan. 4, 1837	Malcolm McPherson......	W. M. Wightman.	23,615	23,166
52	Columbia, S. C........	Jan. 10, 1838	Thomas A. Morris........	William Capers....	24,016	23,498
53	Cheraw, S. C..........	Jan. 9, 1839	J O. Andrew............	W. M. Wightman.	24,756	24,822
54	Charleston, S. C	Jan. 8, 1840	Thomas A. Morris........	W. M. Wightman.	26,974	27,630
55	Camden, S. C	Feb. 10, 1841	J. O. Andrew............	J. H. Wheeler......	26,945	30,481
56	Charlotte, N. C........	Jan. 26, 1842	B. Waugh..................	J. H. Wheeler......	27,475	30,850
57	Cokesbury, S. C......	Feb. 8, 1843	J. O. Andrew............	J. H. Wheeler......	30,540	33,375
58	Georgetown, S. C....	Feb. 7, 1844	Joshua Soule............	J. H. Wheeler......	31,568	37.952
59	Columbia, S. C........	Dec. 25, 1844	Joshua Soule............	J. H. Wheeler......	32,306	39,495
60	Fayetteville, N. C ...	Dec. 10, 1845	J. O. Andrew............	P. A. M. Williams.	33,387	41.074

* Removed from Louisville, Ga.   † Removed from Fayetteville, N. C.   ‡ Georgia Conference set off.

SESSIONS OF THE SOUTH CAROLINA CONFERENCE.—*Continued.*

Number.	Place.	Date.	President.	Secretary.	White Members.	Colored Members.
61	Charleston, S. C	Jan. 13, 1847	William Capers.................	P. A. M. Williams	32,699	40,975
62	Wilmington, N. C....	Jan. 12, 1848	J. O. Andrew....................	P. A. M. Williams	33,023	40,988
63	Spartanburg, S. C ...	Dec. 26, 1848	William Capers.................	P. A. M. Williams	33,589	41,888
64	Camden, S. C	Dec. 19, 1849	J. O. Andrew....................	P. A. M. Williams	34,477	41,617
65	Wadesboro, N. C......	Dec. 18, 1850	R. Paine	P. A. M. Williams	31,143	37,840
66	Georgetown, S. C....	Dec. 10, 1851	J. O. Andrew....................	P. A. M. Williams	32,629	37,481
67	Sumter, S. C.............	Jan. 5, 1853	William Capers.................	P. A. M. Williams	33,054	40,350
68	Newberry, S. C	Nov. 23, 1853	R. Paine	P. A. M. Williams	33,213	42,280
69	Columbia, S. C	Nov. 15, 1854	G. F. Pierce....................	P. A. M. Williams	34,621	45,261
70	Marion, S. C	Nov. 28, 1855	John Early	P. A. M. Williams	34,938	43,688
71	Yorkville, S. C.........	Nov. 16, 1856	J. O. Andrew....................	P. A. M. Williams	35,277	43,356
72	Charlotte, N. C.........	Nov. 25, 1857	R. Paine	P. A. M. Williams	35,733	45,190
73	Charleston, S. C	Dec. 1, 1858	J. O. Andrew....................	F. A. Mood	37,095	46,740
74	Greenville, S. C.......	Dec. 30, 1859	John Early	F. A. Mood............	38,294	48,583
75	Columbia, S. C.........	Dec. 13, 1860	R. Paine	F. A. Mood............	39,935	49,774
76	Chester, S. C	Dec. 12, 1861	J. O. Andrew....................	F. A. Mood............	38,018	48,759
77	Spartanburg, S. C ...	Dec. 11, 1862	John Early........................	F. A. Mood............	37,686	45,767
78	Sumter, S. C.............	Dec. 10, 1863	G. F. Pierce....................	F. A. Mood............	39,304	42,400
79	Newberry, S. C	Nov. 16, 1864	G. F. Pierce....................	F. A. Mood............	40,920	47,461
80	Charlotte, N. C........	Nov. 1, 1865	G. F. Pierce....................	F. A. Mood............	40,593	29,283
81	Marion, S. C.............	Dec. 28, 1866	William M. Wightman....	F. A. Mood............	40,249	16,390
82	Morganton, N. C......	Dec. 11, 1867	D. S. Doggett.................	F. A. Mood............	38,647	8,270
83	Abbeville, S. C	Dec. 16, 1868	William M. Wightman....	F. M. Kennedy......	40,577	2,417
84	*Cheraw, S. C	Dec. 15, 1869	H. H. Kavanaugh..........	F. M. Kennedy......	42,926	1,536
85	Charleston, S. C	Dec. 7, 1870	G. F. Pierce	F. M. Kennedy......	32,871	1,934
86	Spartanburg, S. C...	Dec. 13, 1871	R. Paine.........................	F. M. Kennedy......	34,872	660
87	Anderson, S. C.........	Dec. 12, 1872	R. Paine.........................	W. C. Power..........	36,163	648
88	Sumter, S. C	Dec. 10, 1873	H. N. McTyeire.............	W. C. Power..........	36,550	424
89	Greenville, S. C.......	Dec. 16, 1874	E. M. Marvin..................	W. C. Power..........	39,083	435
90	Orangeburg, S. C....	Dec. 15, 1875	J. C. Keener...................	W. C. Power..........	40,829	384
91	Chester, S. C............	Dec. 13, 1876	H. H. Kavanaugh	W. C. Power..........	41,886	360
92	Columbia, S. C	Dec. 12, 1877	D. S. Doggett.................	W. C. Power..........	43,341	224
93	Newberry, S. C	Dec. 11, 1878	W. M. Wightman	W. C. Power..........	44,435	
94	Charleston, S. C	Dec. 17, 1879	W. M. Wightman	W. C. Power..........	44,904	
95	Marion, S. C	Dec. 15, 1880	A. M. Shipp....................	W. C. Power..........	46,618	
96	Union, S. C	Dec. 14, 1881	G. F. Pierce....................	W. C. Power..........	47,989	
97	Greenville, S. C.......	Dec. 13, 1882	H. N. McTyeire..............	W. C. Power..........	49,280	
98	Sumter, S. C....... ...	Dec. 12, 1883	A. W. Wilson..................	W. C. Power..........	50,831	
99	Charleston, S. C......	Dec. 17, 1884	H. N. McTyeire..............	W. C. Power..........	52,624	
100	Columbia, S. C.........	Dec. 9, 1885	J. C. Keener...................	W. C. Power..........	54,661	
101	Orangeburg, S. C....	Dec. 15, 1886	J. C. Granbery	W. C. Power..........	62,142	
102	Spartanburg, S. C ...	Nov. 30, 1887	H. N. McTyeire..............	H. F. Chreitzberg.	63,317	
103	Winnsboro, S. C......	Nov. 28, 1888	John C. Keener..............	H. F. Chreitzberg.	65,618	
104	Camden, S. C	Nov. 20, 1889	John C. Keener.......	H. F. Chreitzberg.	67,306	
105	Anderson, S. C	Nov 25, 1890	W. W. Duncan................	H. F. Chreitzberg.	67,299	
106	Darlington, S. C	Dec. 2, 1891	J. C. Granbery...............	H. F. Chreitzberg.	69,514	
107	Charleston, S. C	Nov. 24, 1892	E. R. Hendrix..	H. F. Chreitzberg.	70,062	
108	Sumter, S. C.............	Dec. 9, 1893	E. R. Hendrix.................	E. O. Watson..... ...	71,791	
109	Laurens, S. C...........	Nov. 21, 1894	J. C. Keener...................	E. O. Watson..........	71,535	
110	Rock Hill, S. C.........	Dec. 4, 1895	C. B. Galloway...............	E. O. Watson..........	72,651	
111	Abbeville, S. C.........	Dec. 9, 1896	J. C. Granbery...............	E. O. Watson..........	72,665	

* A large section in State of North Carolina transferred to the North Carolina Conference.

VIII.

NECROLOGICAL RECORD: THE DEAD OF THE SOUTH CAROLINA CONFERENCE, 1788 TO 1896.

NAME.	Place of Birth.	Entered the Itinerancy.	Time of Death.	Age.	Place of Burial.
Woolman Hickson		1782	1788	...	New York, N. Y.
John Major		1783	1788	...	Lincoln Co., Ga.
Henry Bingham	Virginia	1785	1788	...	Cattle Creek Camp G.
James Connor	Buckingham Co., Va.	1787	1789	...	Augusta, Ga.
Wyatt Andrews		1789	1790	...	Cherokee.
John Tunnell		1777	1790	...	Sweet Springs, Tenn.
Lemuel Andrews		1787	1790	...	Santee.
Benjamin Carter	In the West	1787	1792	...	Washington, Ga.
Hardy Herbert	North Carolina	1788	Nov. 20, 1794	25	Norfolk, Va.
Richard Ivy		1781	1790	...	Sussex Co., Va.
Reuben Ellis	North Carolina	1777	Feb., 1796	...	Baltimore, Md.
James King	Gloucester, Va	1794	Sept. 18, 1797	25	Bethel, Charleston.
John N. Jones	Virginia	1790	July 16, 1798	...	Bethel, Charleston.
James Tolleson	South Carolina	1791	Aug., 1800	...	Portsmouth, Va.
Moses Wilson		1795	1803	...	Kershaw Co.
Benjamin Jones	Georgetown Co	1801	1804	30	Bladen Co., N. C.
Tobias Gibson	Marion Co	1792	April 5, 1804	30	Natchez, Miss.
Nicholas Watters	Anne Arundel Co.,Va.	1776	Aug. 10, 1804	65	Bethel, Charleston.
George Dougherty	Newberry	1798	March 23, 1807	...	Wilmington, N. C.
Bennett Kendrick	Virginia	1799	April 5, 1807	...	Marlboro Co.
Thomas Dickinson	North Carolina	1811	1811	...	Cypress Ct.
Samuel Mills	Northampton, N. C.	1802	June 8, 1811	30	Camden.
Jacob Rumph	Orangeburg Co	1808	Sept. 11, 1812	35	Bethel, Charleston.
Lewis Hobbes	Burke Co., Ga	1808	1814	31	Georgia.
Richmond Nolley	Virginia	1808	Nov. 24, 1815	30	Catahoula Parish, La.
William Partridge	Sussex Co., Va	1780	May 17, 1817	63	Sparta, Ga.
Anthony Senter	Lincolnton, N. C	1809	Dec. 23, 1817	32	Georgetown.
Henry Fitzgerald	North Carolina	1818	Sept. 19, 1819	22	Bethel, Charleston.
Charles Dickinson	Moore Co., N. C.	1811	Sept. 1, 1820	36	Washington Co., Ga.
John Dix	Robinson Co., N. C	1818	June 14, 1823	56	North Carolina.
Benjamin Crane		1823	1824	...	
Daniel Asbury	Fairfax Co., Va	1786	1825	63	Catawba Co., N. C.
Isaac Oslin		1824	1825	...	
James Norton		1806	Aug. 26, 1825	38	Columbia.
Benjamin Rhodes	Greenville	1818	1826	35	Georgetown.
Isaac Hartley.	South Carolina	1825	1826	27	Georgetown.
John L. Greaves	South Carolina	1818	1826	...	
John Gamewell		1800	Oct. 7, 1828	...	Near Conwayboro.
Asbury Morgan	Mecklenburg Co., N.C.	1818	Sept. 25, 1828	31	Bethel, Charleston.
John Coleman		1827	1828	...	
George Hill	Charleston	1819	1829	32	Milledgeville, Ga.
John Honour	Charleston	1821	Sept. 19, 1830	60	Trinity, Charleston.
Thomas L. Wynn	Abbeville Co	1817	Oct. 9, 1830	32	Camden.
Trist. Stackhouse	South Carolina	1830	1831	...	Cypress Ct.
Absalom Brown	Fairfield Co	1828	1833	...	Montgomery Co., N. C.
James J. Richardson	Marion Co	1829	July 9, 1833	28	Lincolnton, N. C.
Thomas Neill	Burke Co., N. C	1820	July 21, 1833	27	Newberry.
Isaac Smith	Virginia	1784	July 20, 1834	76	Georgia.
Josiah Freeman	Oglethorpe Co., Va	1822	Nov. 27, 1834	37	Columbia.
Parley W. Clenny	Union Co., N. C	1832	Oct. 5, 1835	23	Rembert's, Sumter Ct.
George W. Huggins	Marion Co	1833	Oct., 1835	27	Horry Co.
Samuel Boseman	North Carolina	1833	1835	29	Richmond Co., N. C.
Angus McPherson	Cumberland Co., N. C.	1826	Nov. 4, 1836	34	Ebenezer, Newberry.
Thomas C. Smith	Richmond Co., N. C	1828	Nov. 27, 1837	30	Montgomery, N. C.
Benjamin Bell	Montgomery Co.,N.C.	1826	Jan. 27, 1858	37	Anson Co., N. C.
John Bunch	Charleston	1812	Sept. 7, 1838	45	Rehoboth,BerkeleyCt.
Thomas D. Turpin	Maryland	1829	July 26, 1838	33	Lowndesville.
William M. Kennedy	North Carolina	1805	Feb. 22, 1840	57	Columbia.
Christian G. Hill	Charleston	1818	Aug. 11, 1840	...	Bethel, Charleston.
Jehu G. Postell	York Co.	1836	April, 1841	50	Charleston.
Bartlett Thomason	Laurens Co	1823	1841	30	Orangeburg Co.
John N. Davies.	Mecklenburg Co.,N.C.	1834	June, 1844	40	Columbia.
Jacob Nipper	Richland Co	1839	1844	32	Darlington, C. H.
Abel Hoyle	Lincoln Co., N. C	1837	Sept. 8, 1844	33	Union Co., N. C.
Newton Gouldelock	Union Co	1842	1845	30	Union Co.

NECROLOGICAL RECORD.—*Continued.*

NAME.	Place of Birth.	Entered the Itinerancy.	Time of Death.	Age.	Place of Burial.
John McMakin............	North Carolina	1837	 1846	35	North Carolina.
John S. Capers...	South Carolina...........	1846	 1846	...	Union, Black Sw'p Ct.
James Jenkins............	Marion Co...	1792	June 24, 1847	83	Camden.
John Tarrant............	Virginia..................	1809	April 1, 1849	64	Anson Co., N. C.
Joseph Moore............	Virginia..................	1791	Feb. 14, 1851	84	Edgefield.
Reddick Bunch...........	South Carolina	1850	Feb. 14, 1851	...	Hardeeville.
Daniel G. McDaniel...	Georgetown, D. C	1811	 1853	62	Camden.
Samuel Dunwody......	Chester Co., Pa.......	1806	July 8, 1854	73	Tab'cle, Abbeville Ct.
Campbell Smith..........	Marlboro Co	1834	Dec. 27, 1854	46	Rutherford Co., N. C.
William Capers..........	St. Thomas Parish.....	1808	Jan. 29, 1855	65	Columbia.
James Dannelly	Columbia Co., Ga.	1818	April 28, 1855	69	Lowndesville.
Jacob Hill.................	Anson Co., N. C.	1811	June 16, 1855	65	Catawba Ct., N. C.
Samuel W. Capers......	Georgetown	1828	June 22, 1855	58	Camden.
John W. J. Harris......	Union Co..................	1848	Sept. 10, 1855	31	Columbia.
William M.Easterling	Colleton Co	1851	Sept. 29, 1855	39	Monroe, N. C.
Edward D. Boyden.	Charleston	1854	 1856	29	Charleston.
Charles S. Walker.....	Charleston	1834	Jan. 18, 1857	41	Spartanburg.
John A. Minnick	Edgefield................	1837	Feb. 26, 1858	46	Waccamaw Neck.
Frederick Rush.........	Orangeburg Co........	1829	Aug. 8, 1858	56	Hebron,Lexington Co.
William E. Boone	Hamlin, N. C	1850	Oct. 29, 1858	28	Aiken.
James L. Belin	All Saints' Parish	1811	May 19, 1859	71	Waccamaw Neck.
J. T. Du Bose............	Darlington Co	1853	July 25, 1859	37	Darlington Co.
William J. Jackson.....	Jackson Co., Ga	1827	Aug. 11, 1859	54	Marlboro Co.
Hugh E. Ogburn........	South Carolina	1838	Jan. 19, 1860	43	Williamsburg Co.
Henry Bass	Berlin, Conn...........	1811	May 13, 1860	73	Tabernacle,Abbeville.
Reddick Pierce..	Halifax Co., N. C......	1805	July 24, 1860	77	Rocky Swamp.
Charles F. Campbell...	Marion Co.................	1859	 1860	25	Marion Co.
A. H. Harmon...........	Cleveland, N. C.......	1848	Aug. 20, 1861	39	Mt.Carmel,Lancaster.
G. G. W. Du Pree......	Greenville..............	1859	Aug. 27, 1861	23	Anson Co., N. C.
Henry H. Durant.......	Horry Co.................	1834	Dec. 3, 1861	47	Spartanburg.
Addison P. Martin......	Laurens Co	1847	Aug. 13, 1862	37	Laurens Co.
J. L. McGregor...........	Anson Co., N. C.	1857	 1862	40	North Carolina.
P. A. M. Williams......	Colleton Co	1837	Jan., 1863	47	Colleton Co.
Lindsey C. Weaver.....	Spartanburg Co........	1859	Feb. 28, 1863	26	Glendale.
A. B. McGilvray.........	Isle Skye, Scotland....	1832	June 9, 1863	64	Greenville Co.
George W. Moore.......	Charleston	1825	Aug. 16, 1863	63	Bethel, Charleston.
James F. Wilson........	Marlboro Co	1800	Jan. 18, 1864	26	Marlboro Co.
William C. Kirkland.	Barnwell Co	1837	March29, 1864	50	Spartanburg.
William M. Wilson.....	....	1860	Sept. 11, 1864	25	Charleston.
Algernon S. Link......	Catawba Co., N. C......	1859	Nov. 14, 1864	27	Catawba Co., N. C.
Samuel Townsend	Marlboro Co	1836	July 31, 1865	50	Columbia.
Daniel N. Ogburn......	Chesterfield...........	1853	 1865	32	Orangeburg.
William A. McSwain..	Stanley Co., N. C......	1839	Jan. 1, 1866	51	Laurens Co.
Hilliard C. Parsons.....	Sumter Co................	1847	Jan. 20, 1866	41	Wadesboro, N. C.
Cornelius McLeod......	Montgomery, N. C.....	1837	April 9, 1866	53	Richland Co.
John D. W. Crook	Orangeburg Co........	1851	May 1, 1866	45	Orangeburg Co.
J. Wesley Miller........	Charleston	1850	Jan. 20, 1866	36	Darlington C. H.
W. A. Hemingway......	Black Mingo	1854	May 19, 1867	30	Manning C. H.
Tracy R. Walsh	South Carolina.........	1830	Oct. 20, 1867	59	Bennettsville.
William Crook...........	Chester Co..............	1825	Nov. 25, 1867	62	York Co.
John P. Morris	Devon, England........	1866	Jan. 24, 1868	21	Darlington C. H.
Bond English.............	Kershaw Co.............	1821	March 4, 1868	71	Sumter C. H. ¾
Hartwell Spain..........	Wake Co., N. C.........	1816	March 9, 1868	73	Summerton.
James Stacy....	Catawba Co.. N. C	1830	May 1, 1868	60	Sumter C. H.
Alexius M. Forster.....	Brunswick, N. C.......	1837	Oct. 28, 1868	80	Cokesbury.
Robert J. Boyd	Chester Co..............	1834	Sept. 3, 1869	63	Marion C H.
W. A. Gamewell........	Darlington Co	1834	Oct. 30, 1869	55	Spartanburg.
M. G. Tuttle	Caldwell Co., N. C	1867	 1869	23	McDowell, N. C.
Evan A. Lemmond......	Union Co., N. C.........	1856	Feb. 17, 1870	55	Anson Co., N. C.
John R. Pickett..........	Fairfield Co.............	1835	March15, 1870	56	Winnsboro.
Edward G. Gage........	Union Co.................	1856	March27, 1870	38	Columbia.
Alexander W. Walker	Charleston..............	1834	 1870	55	Spartanburg.
Charles Betts............	North Carolina	1818	Sept. 30, 1872	72	Marion C. H.
A. L. Smith...............	Marlboro Co	1847	Aug. 25, 1872	49	Spartanburg.
C. Thomason.............	Greenville Co..........	1863	Nov. 23, 1872	31	Unionville.
N. Talley.................	Richmond, Va	1811	May 10, 1873	82	Columbia.
Charles Wilson	Barnwell Co............	1831	April 14, 1873	71	Orangeburg.
J. Lee Dixon.............	Kershaw Co.............	1872	Dec. 19, 1873	44	Columbia.
C. H. Pritchard, Jr.....	Fayetteville, N. C.......	1873	Jan. 20, 1874	23	Greenville.

NECROLOGICAL RECORD.—*Continued.*

NAME.	Place of Birth.	Entered the Itinerancy	Time of Death.	Age.	Place of Burial.
H. Bass Green	Colleton	1872	1874	29	Colleton.
Malcolm V. Wood	Greenville	1872	Aug. 27, 1874	28	Conwayboro.
J. Claudius Miller	Charleston	1870	April 3, 1875	66	Charleston.
A. McCorquodale	Argylshire, Scotland	1830	Nov. 14, 1875	76	Bishopsville.
Edward L. King	Fairfield Co	1839	Nov. 19, 1875	56	Columbia.
William H. Fleming	Charleston	1841	April 16, 1877	56	Charleston.
T. S. Daniel	Edgefield	1839	Aug. 27, 1877	63	Edgefield Co.
R. R. Pegues	Marlboro Co	1855	Oct. 17, 1877	47	Marlboro.
E. J. Pennington	Charleston	1849	Dec. 23, 1877	49	Charleston.
A. R. Danner	Walterboro	1871	Oct. 11, 1878	69	CypressCampGround.
F. M. Kennedy		1854	Feb. 5, 1880	46	Macon, Ga.
J. W. Townsend	Marlboro Co	1823	May 14, 1880	80	Cokesbury.
John R. Coburn	Charleston Co	1829	Sept. 29, 1880	81	Florence.
Duncan J. McMillan	Marion Co	1861	Oct. 6, 1881	...	Graham'sCrossRoads.
Benjamin Boozer	Newberry Co	1875	May 19, 1882	32	Newberry Co.
Wm. M. Wightman	Charleston	1828	Feb. 15, 1882	74	Charleston.
David Derrick	Lexington Co	1827	Jan. 12, 1883	83	Columbia.
John Finger	Lincoln Co., N. C	1848	Jan. 13, 1884	71	Williamston.
L. Scarborough	Montgomery Co., N. C.	1837	May 22, 1884	75	Marion Co.
Samuel J. Hill		1855	June 14, 1884	49	Sumter Co.
John B. Massebeau	Camden	1858	Aug. 25, 1884	48	Spartanburg.
Thomas B. Boyd	Charlotte, N. C	1880	April 4, 1884	43	Orangeburg Co.
Robert L. Harper	Exeter, England	1886	Aug. 17, 1884	39	Iuka, Miss.
William P. Mouzon	Charleston	1838	Jan. 28, 1885	66	Bamberg.
John W. Kelly	Union Co	1841	Feb., 1885	60	Orangeburg Co.
Allison B. Lee	Chester Co	1876	April 15, 1885	36	Orangeburg Co.
John Watts	Chesterfield Co	1825	June 6, 1886	85	Greenville Co.
Hugh A. C. Walker	Antrim Co., Ireland	1831	May 22, 1886	77	Marion Co.
Abner Irvine	Lenoir Co., N. C	1847	Aug. 26, 1886	58	Union Co.
George H. Wells	Green Co., Tenn	1858	Feb. 14, 1886	52	Timmonsville.
Charles C. Fishburn	Barnwell Co	1872	Dec., 1885	40	Bamberg.
James W. Koger	Colleton Co	1878	Jan. 28, 1886	34	Sao Paulo, Brazil.
Dennis J. Simmons	Charleston Co	1841	Jan. 5, 1887	69	St. George's.
Marcus A. McKibben	Mecklenburg Co., N.C.	1836	Jan. 23, 1887	83	Barnwell.
C. D. Rowell	Marion Co	1873	May 1, 1887	57	Jonesville.
Albert M. Shipp	Stokes Co., N. C	1841	June 27, 1887	68	Marlboro Co.
David D. Byars	Spartanburg Co	1849	Sept. 11, 1887	64	Central.
James T. Kilgo	Chester Co	1850	Jan. 4, 1888	68	Marlboro Co.
Abram P. Avant	Marion Co	1844	July 12, 1888	76	Spartanburg.
Lewis M. Little	Lincoln Co., N. C	1840	Dec. 5, 1888	73	Sumter.
William Martin	Mecklenburg Co., N.C.	1828	Jan. 10, 1889	82	Columbia.
Abraham Nettles	Summerville	1836	Nov. 6, 1889	81	Manning.
J. Emory Watson	Laurens Co	1863	June 11, 1889	51	Chester.
John H. Zimmerman	Abbeville Co	1839	March 24, 1889	73	Westminster.
Elias J. Meynardie	Charleston	1848	July 1, 1890	64	Camden.
William Thomas	Lien Regis, England	1868	Dec. 1, 1890	60	Clarendon Co.
Robert C. Oliver	Edgefield Co	1858	Aug. 2, 1891	58	Spartanburg.
Allen A. Gilbert	Walterboro	1880	Aug. 25, 1891	62	Sumter.
John W Murray	Charleston Co	1856	Dec. 2, 1891	60	Lamar.
Basil G. Jones	Davie Co., N. C	1883	Feb. 9, 1891	77	Aiken Co.
Manning Brown	Columbia		July 29, 1892	...	Columbia.
William Hutto	Orangeburg Co	1849	Jan. 19, 1892	64	Williamston.
J. L. Shuford	Cleveland Co., N. C.	1844	March 19, 1892	68	
Landy Wood					
J. B. Platt	Marion Co	1865	Jan 17, 1893	67	Sandy Run.
Whitefoord Smith	Charleston	1833	April 27, 1893	81	Spartanburg.
J. W. McRoy	Kinston, N. C	1859	Aug. 16, 1893	56	Rock Hill.
W. H. Lawton	Hampton Co	1853	Nov. 3, 1893	72	Ninety-Six.
M. A. Connolly	Caldwell Co., N. C	1854	Jan. 28, 1894	65	Kershaw.
J. M. Boyd	Newberry Co	1869	Feb. 25, 1894	62	Spartanburg.
W. L. Pegues	Marlboro Co	1839	July 16, 1894	55	Marlboro Co.
Samuel B. Jones	Charleston	1854	Sept. 8, 1894	66	Spartanburg.
W. T. Capers	Milledgeville, Ga.	1844	Sept. 10, 1894	69	Greenville.
R. N. Wells	Clarendon Co	1847	Dec. 11, 1895	48	Greenville.
R. P. Franks	Laurens Co	1818	Jan. 25, 1895	77	Lowndesville.
D. W. Seale			April 6, 1895	...	Lake City.
C. H. Pritchard	Charleston		March 5, 1896	...	Abbeville.
Samuel Leard	Abbeville	1835	March 8, 1896	...	Raleigh, N. C.
J. A. Mood		1847	April 18, 1896	...	Spartanburg.
W. D. Kirkland	Charleston	1871	May 31, 1896	47	Spartanburg.
Thomas Raysor	Colleton Co	1850	Nov. 23, 1896	69	Orangeburg.

IX.

LIST OF STATIONED PREACHERS IN THE CHARLESTON METH-ODIST EPISCOPAL CHURCHES.

1785. John Tunnell.
1786. Henry Willis and Isaac Green.
1787. Lemuel Green.
1788. Ira Ellis.
1789. No preacher named in the Minutes.
1790. Isaac Smith.
1791. James Parks.
1792. Daniel Smith.
1793. Daniel Smith and Jonathan Jackson.
1794. Joshua Cannon and Isaac Smith.
1795. Philip Bruce.
1796. Benjamin Blanton.
1797. Benjamin Blanton, John N. Jones, and J. King.
1798. John N. Jones and Tobias Gibson.
1799. John Harper and Nicholas Snethen.
1800. George Dougherty and J. Harper.
1801. George Dougherty and J. Harper.
1802. John Garvin and Benjamin Jones.
1803. Bennett Kendrick and Thomas Darley.
1804. Bennett Kendrick and Nicholas Waters.
1805. Buddy W. Wheeler and J. H. Mellard.
1806. L. Myers and Levi Garrison.
1807. Jonathan Jackson and William Owen.
1808. William Phoebus and J. McVean.
1809. Samuel Mills and William M. Kennedy.
1810. William M. Kennedy, T. Mason, and R. Nolley.
1811. Samuel Dunwody, F. Ward, William Capers, and William S. Talley.
1812. F. Ward and J. Rumph.
1813. N. Powers, J. Capers, and S. M. Meek.
1814. S. Dunwody, A. Talley, and J. B. Glenn.
1815. A. Senter, A. Talley, and S. K. Hodges.
1816. J. W. Stanley, E. Christopher, and James O. Andrew.
1817. Solomon Bryan, W. B. Barnett, W. Kennedy, and W. Williams.
1818. L. Myers, A. Talley, and H. Bass.
1819. L. Myers, Z. Dowling, and Henry T. Fitzgerald.
1820. William M. Kennedy, Henry Bass, and J. Murrow.
1821. William M. Kennedy, D. Hall, W. Kennedy, and Asbury Morgan.
1822. James Norton, D. Hall, J. Evans, and R. Flournoy.
1823. John Howard, William Hawkins, Thomas L. Wynn, and Elijah Sinclair.
1824. S. Dunwody, J. Howard, J. Galluchat, Sr., and S. Olin.
1825. William Capers, A. P. Manley, sup., Benjamin L. Hoskins, and S. Olin.
1826. William Capers, H. Bass, and P. N. Maddux.
1827. J. O. Andrew, H. Bass, and N. Laney.
1828. J. O. Andrew, A. Morgan, and Benjamin L. Hoskins.
1829. N. Talley, J. Freeman, and William H. Ellison.
1830. N. Talley, Thomas L. Wynn, and William M. Wightman.
1831. C. Betts, Bond English, and W. Murrah.
1832. William Capers, William Cook, Thomas E. Ledbetter, and William Murrah.
1833. William Capers, J. Holmes, H. A. C. Walker, Reddick Pierce to change after three months with J. K. Morse.
1834. William M. Kennedy, William Martin, and G. F. Pierce.

1835. William M. Kennedy, William Martin, J. J. Allison, and W. A. Gamewell.
1836. William Capers, J. Sewell, J. W. McColl, and W. A. Gamewell.
1837. Bond English, J. Sewell, J. N. Davis, and James W. Welborn.
1838. Bond English, J. E. Evans, and Samuel Armstrong.
1839. N. Talley, J. E. Evans, W. Capers, and P. A. M. Williams.
1840. N. Talley, H. A. C. Walker, and Whitefoord Smith.
1841. Bond English, J. Sewell, J. Stacy, city missionary.
1842. Bond English, H. Spain, and A. M. Shipp.
1843. Cumberland, W. C. Kirkland ; Trinity, James Stacy; Bethel, B. Bass; St. James's, J. Nipper.
1844. Cumberland, S. W. Capers; Trinity, James Stacy; Bethel, William C. Kirkland; St. James's, J. A. Porter.
1845. Cumberland, S. W. Capers; Trinity, T. Huggins; Bethel, C. H. Pritchard; St. James's, D. Derrick.
1846. Cumberland, S. Leard; Trinity, W. Smith; Bethel, C. H. Pritchard; St. James's, J. W. Kelly.
1847. Cumberland, A. M. Forster; Trinity, Whitefoord Smith; Bethel, W. P. Mouzon; St. James's, M. Eaddy.
1848. Cumberland, W. Smith; Trinity, supplied by Alexander Speer, local preacher of Georgia; Bethel, W. P. Mouzon; St. James's, William T. Capers.
1849. Cumberland, W. Smith; Trinity, C. H. Pritchard; Bethel, J. A. Porter; St. James's, A. G. Stacy.
1850. Cumberland, William G. Connor; Trinity, James Stacy; Bethel, Henry M. Mood; St. James's, A. G. Stacy.
1851. Cumberland, W. A. Gamewell; Trinity, W. A. McSwain; Bethel, C. H. Pritchard; St. James's, J. R. Pickett.
1852. Cumberland, W. Smith; Trinity, W. A. McSwain; Bethel, C. H. Pritchard; St. James's, John R. Pickett.
1853. Cumberland, W. Smith, sup., John T. Wightman; Trinity, C. H. Pritchard; Bethel, Joseph Cross; St. James's, Allen McCorquodale.
1854. Cumberland, J. T. Wightman, W. Smith, sup.; Trinity, H. C. Parsons; Bethel, Joseph Cross; St. James's, Allen McCorquodale.
1855. Cumberland, S. Leard; Trinity, J. Cross; Bethel, J. T. Wightman; St. James's, William E. Boone.
1856. Cumberland, William P. Mouzon; Trinity, Joseph Cross; Bethel, J. T. Wightman; St. James's, William E. Boone.
1857. Cumberland, William P. Mouzon; Trinity, John T. Wightman; Bethel, William H. Fleming; Spring Street, W. E. Boone; St. James's, William A. Hemingway.
1858. Cumberland, James Stacy; Trinity, John T. Wightman; City Mission, John W. Kelly; Trinity, William H. Fleming; St. James's, W. A. Hemingway.
1859. Cumberland, James Stacy; City Mission, John W. Kelly; Trinity, William H. Feming; Bethel, William G. Connor; Spring Street, F. M. Kennedy.
1860. Cumberland, John A. Porter; Trinity, William H. Fleming; City Mission, Aaron Wells; Bethel, D. J. Simmons; Spring Street, F. M. Kennedy.
1861. Cumberland, John A. Porter; Trinity, L. R. Walsh; Bethel, W. H. Fleming; Spring Street and City Mission, J. W. Miller.
1862. Cumberland, C. McLeod; Trinity, J. T. Wightman; Bethel, A. M. Chreitzberg; Spring Street, J. W. Humbert.
1863. Trinity and Cumberland, John T. Wightman; Bethel and Spring Street, E. J. Meynardie.
1864. Charleston, E. J. Meynardie, F. Auld.
1865. Charleston, E. J. Meynardie; City Colored Mission, F. A. Mood, W. A. Hodges.
1866. Cumberland, to be supplied; Trinity, E. J. Meynardie; Spring Street, W. A. Hemingway; Bethel, J. T. Wightman.

1867. Cumberland, to be supplied; Trinity, E. J. Meynardie; Bethel, J. T. Wightman; Spring Street, to be supplied.
1868. Trinity and Cumberland, F. A. Mood; Bethel, J. T. Wightman; Spring Street, to be supplied.
1869. Trinity and Cumberland, William P. Mouzon; Bethel, J. T. Wightman; Spring Street, J. R. Pickett.
1870. Trinity and Cumberland, William P. Mouzon; Bethel, T. E. Wannamaker; Spring Street, J. T. Wightman.
1871. Trinity and Cumberland, J. M. Carlisle; Bethel, T. E. Wannamaker; Spring Street, J. T. Wightman.
1872. Trinity and Cumberland, Whitefoord Smith; City Mission, R. D. Smart; Bethel, A. M. Chreitzberg; Spring Street, J. T. Wightman.
1873. Trinity and Cumberland, George H. Wells; Bethel, J. T. Wightman; Spring Street, R. D. Smart.
1874. Trinity and Cumberland, George H. Wells; Bethel, J. T. Wightman; Spring Street, R. D. Smart.
1875. Trinity and Cumberland, George H. Wells; Bethel, J. T. Wightman; Spring Street, W. T. Capers.
1876. Trinity and Cumberland, George H. Wells; Bethel, J. T. Wightman; Spring Street, W. T. Capers.
1877. Trinity, John H. Porter; Bethel, W. H. Fleming; Spring Street, R. L. Harper.
1878. Trinity, R. N. Wells; Bethel, W. C. Power; Spring Street, G. W. Whitman.
1879. Trinity, R. N. Wells; Bethel, W. C. Power; Spring Street, H. F. Chreitzberg.
1880. Trinity, R. N. Wells; Bethel, E. J. Meynardie; Spring Street, H. F. Chreitzberg.
1881. Trinity, A. C. Smith; Bethel, E. J. Meynardie; Spring Street. H. F. Chreitzberg.
1882. Trinity, A. C. Smith; Bethel, E. J. Meynardie; Spring Street, D. J. Simmons.
1883. Trinity, A. C. Smith; Bethel, E. J. Meynardie; Spring Street, J. A. Clifton.
1884. Trinity, J. O. Willson; Bethel, R. N. Wells; Spring Street, William P. Mouzon; City Mission, J. E. Beard.
1885. Trinity, J. O. Willson; Bethel, R. N. Wells; Spring Street, R. H. Jones; Cumberland, J. E. Beard.
1886. Trinity, J. O. Willson; Bethel, R. N. Wells; Spring Street, J. W. Dickson; Cumberland, H. B. Browne.
1887. Trinity, J. O. Willson; Bethel, R. N. Wells; Spring Street, L. F. Beaty; Cumberland, H. B. Browne.
1888. Trinity, R. N. Wells; Bethel, R. D. Smart; Spring Street, J. E. Carlisle, Cumberland, H. B. Browne.
1889. Trinity, R. N. Wells; Bethel, R. D. Smart; Spring Street, J. E. Carlisle, Cumberland, H. B. Browne.
1890. Trinity, R. N. Wells; Bethel, R. D. Smart; Spring Street, J. T. Pate; Cumberland, W. A. Betts.
1891. Trinity, W. A. Rogers; Bethel, R. D. Smart; Spring Street, J. T. Pate; Cumberland, W. A. Betts.
1892. Trinity, W. A. Rogers; Bethel, J. A. Clifton; Spring Street, J. L. Stokes; Cumberland, A. M. Chreitzberg.
1893. Trinity, W. A. Richardson; Bethel, J. A. Clifton; Spring Street, J. L. Stokes; Cumberland, J. C. Younge.
1894. Trinity, W. A. Richardson; Bethel, J. A. Clifton; Spring Street, J. L. Stokes; Cumberland, J. C. Younge.
1895. Trinity, W. A. Richardson; Bethel, J. A. Clifton; Spring Street, J. L. Stokes; Cumberland, J. C. Younge.
1896. Trinity, W. A. Richardson; Bethel, H. W. Bays; Cumberland, J. E. Steadman.

METHODIST CHURCH, ANDERSON, S. C.; REV. G. P. WATSON, PASTOR.

PRESIDING ELDERS ON CHARLESTON DISTRICT FOR ONE HUNDRED AND TEN YEARS.

1786, James Foster.
1787, Beverly Allen.
1788 to 1793, Reuben Ellis.
1794, Philip Bruce.
1795, Isaac Smith.
1796, Enoch George.
1797, Jonathan Jackson.
1798 to 1800, B. Blanton.
1801, James Jenkins.
1802 to 1804, George Dougherty.
1805, 1806, Britton Capel.
1807 to 1809, Lewis Myers.
1810, Reddick Pierce.
1811 to 1813, William M. Kennedy.
1814, 1815, John Collingsworth.
1816, 1817, Alexander Talley.
1818, 1819, James Norton.
1820 to 1823, Lewis Myers.
1824 to 1827, James O. Andrew.
1828 to 1830, William Capers.

1831 to 1834, Henry Bass.
1835 to 1838, Nicholas Talley.
1839 to 1842, Henry Bass.
1843 to 1846, R. J. Boyd.
1847, 1849, S. W. Capers.
1850 to 1853, C. Betts.
1854 to 1857, H. A. C. Walker.
1858 to 1861, William P. Mouzon.
1862, 1863, F. A. Mood.
1864, 1865, T. Raysor.
1866, 1867, F. A. Mood.
1868 to 1871, A. M. Chreitzberg.
1872 to 1875, William P. Mouzon.
1876 to 1879, T. E. Wannamaker.
1880 to 1883, William P. Mouzon.
1884 to 1886, E. J. Meynardie.
1887 to 1890, J. M. Boyd.
1891 to 1894, R. N. Wells.
1895, 1896, W. A. Meadors.

X.

PREACHERS AND PRESIDING ELDERS CONNECTED WITH COLUMBIA, S. C., FROM 1805 TO 1896.

Year.	Preacher in Charge.	Presiding Elder.
1805.	Bennett Kendrick.	George Dougherty.
1806.	Samuel Mills.	George Dougherty.
1807.	Daniel Hall.	Bennett Kendrick.
1808.	Lovick Pierce.	Lewis Myers.
1809.	Reddick Pierce.	Lewis Myers.
1810.	Joseph Travis.	Reddick Pierce.
1811.	Jacob Rumph.	William M. Kennedy.
1812.	John Collingsworth, to change six months with O. Rogers.	Hilliard Judge.
1813.	William S. Talley.	Hilliard Judge.
1814.	Henry D. Green.	Hilliard Judge.
1815.	Samuel Dunwody.	Hilliard Judge.
1816.	Samuel Dunwody.	Anthony Senter.
1817.	Thomas W. Stanley.	Anthony Senter.
1818.	William Capers.	Daniel Asbury.
1819.	James O. Andrew.	Daniel Asbury.
1820.	Isaac Smith.	Daniel Asbury.
1821.	Henry Bass.	Daniel Asbury.
1822.	Tillman Snead.	Henry Bass.
1823.	Nicholas Talley.	Henry Bass.
1824.	Nicholas Talley.	Henry Bass.
1825.	James Norton.	Henry Bass.
1826.	Joseph Holmes.	Robert Adams.
1827.	Joseph Holmes.	Robert Adams.
1828.	William M. Kennedy.	Robert Adams.
1829.	William M. Kennedy.	Robert Adams.
1830.	Joseph Freeman.	William M. Kennedy.
1831.	William Capers.	William M. Kennedy.
1832.	Josiah Freeman.	William M. Kennedy.
1833.	Bond English.	William M. Kennedy.
1834.	H. Spain.	Bond English.
1835.	Malcolm McPherson.	Bond English.
1836.	William M. Kennedy.	Malcolm McPherson.
1837.	William M. Kennedy.	Malcolm McPherson.
1838.	Malcolm McPherson.	H. Spain.
1839.	C. Betts, William P. Mouzon.	H. Spain.
1840.	C. Betts.	H. Spain.
1841.	Whitefoord Smith.	H. Spain.
1842.	Whitefoord Smith.	C. Betts.
1843.	Samuel W. Capers.	C. Betts.
1844.	Joseph H. Wheeler.	C. Betts.
1845.	Joseph H. Wheeler.	C. Betts.
1846.	William Capers.	Nicholas Talley.
1847.	Samuel Leard.	Nicholas Talley.
1848.	Samuel Leard.	Nicholas Talley.
1849.	J. Stacy, J. T. Wightman.	Nicholas Talley.
1850.	W. Smith, F. A. Mood.	Samuel W. Capers.
1851.	Washington Street, W. Smith; Marion Street, T. Mitchell.	Samuel W. Capers.
1852.	Washington Street, H. A. C. Walker; Marion Street, John T. Wightman.	Samuel W. Capers.
1853.	Washington Street, C. Murchison; Marion Street, W. E. Boone.	William Crook.

Year.	Preacher in Charge.	Presiding Elder.
1854.	Washington Street, W. A. Gamewell; Marion Street, F. A. Mood.	William Crook.
1855.	Washington Street, W. A. Gamewell; Marion Street, F. A. Mood.	William Crook.
1856.	Washington Street, C. H. Pritchard; Marion Street, O. A. Darby.	William Crook.
1857.	Washington Street, C. H. Pritchard; Marion Street, A. H. Lester.	W. A. Gamewell.
1858.	Washington Street, John T. Wightman. Marion Street, William C. Power.	W. A. Gamewell.
1859.	Washington Street, John T. Wightman. Marion Street, R. B. Allston.	W. A. Gamewell.
1860.	Washington Street, W. A. Gamewell; Marion Street, J. W. Humbert.	W. A. Gamewell.
1861.	Washington Street, W. A. Gamewell; Marion Street, John W. North.	R. J. Boyd.
1862.	Washington Street, William P. Mouzon; Marion Street, W. T. Capers.	R. J. Boyd.
1863.	Washington Street, William P. Mouzon; Marion Street, W. T. Capers.	R. J. Boyd.
1864.	Washington Street, William P. Mouzon; Marion Street, W. T. Capers.	R. J. Boyd.
1865.	Washington Street, W. G. Connor; Marion Street, F. Auld.	C. H. Pritchard.
1866.	Washington Street, W. T. Capers; Marion Street, E. G. Gage.	C. H. Pritchard.
1867.	D. J. Simmons, William Martin.	C. H. Pritchard.
1868.	Washington Street, William Martin; Marion Street, S. H. Browne.	C. H. Pritchard.
1869.	Washington Street, William Martin; Marion Street, W. W. Mood.	S. H. Browne.
1870.	Washington Street, William Martin; Marion Street, W. W. Mood.	S. H. Browne.
1871.	Washington Street, M. Browne; Marion Street, W. W. Mood.	S. H. Browne.
1872.	Washington Street, M. Browne; Marion Street, W. D. Kirkland.	S. H. Browne.
1873.	Washington Street, O. A. Darby; Marion Street, W. D. Kirkland.	William Martin.
1874.	Washington Street, O. A. Darby, A. Coke Smith; Marion Street, W. D. Kirkland.	W. H. Fleming.
1875.	Washington Street, A. Coke Smith; Marion Street, W. D. Kirkland.	W. H. Fleming.
1876.	Washington Street, A. Coke Smith; Marion Street, J. Walter Dickson.	E. J. Meynardie.
1877.	Washington Street, John T. Wightman; Marion Street, J. Walter Dickson.	E. J. Meynardie.
1878.	Washington Street, John T. Wightman; Marion Street, W. S. Wightman.	E. J. Meynardie.
1879.	Washington Street, A. M. Chreitzberg; Marion Street, G. W. Whitman.	E. J. Meynardie.
1880.	Washington Street, W. T. Capers; Marion Street, J. L. Stokes.	A. M. Chreitzberg.
1881.	Washington Street, R. N. Wells; Marion Street, J. L. Stokes; Mission, L. M. Little.	A. M. Chreitzberg.

Year.	Preacher in Charge.	Presiding Elder.

1882. Washington Street, R. N. Wells;
    Marion Street, J. L. Stokes;
    Mission, L. M. Little.   A. M. Chreitzberg.
1883. Washington Street, William C. Power;
    Marion Street, J. L. Stokes;
    Mission, L. M. Little.   A. M. Chreitzberg.
1884. Washington Street, William C. Power;
    Marion Street, R. P. Franks,
    Mission, C. H. Pritchard.   A. Coke Smith.
1885. Washington Street, William C. Power;
    Marion Street, R. P. Franks ;
    Mission, L. M. Little.   A. Coke Smith.
1886. Washington Street, W. R. Richardson ;
    Marion Street, C. B. Smith;
    Mission, L. M. Little.   A. Coke Smith.
1887. Washington Street, W. R. Richardson;
    Marion Street, T. E. Morris ;
    Mission, L. M. Little.   S. B. Jones.
1888. Washington Street, W. R. Richardson;
    Marion Street, M. Dargan;
    Mission, S. D. Vaughn.   S. B. Jones.
1889. Washington Street, W. R. Richardson;
    Marion Street, M. Dargan;
    Mission, S. D. Vaughn.   S. B. Jones.
1890. Washington Street, H. F. Chreitzberg;
    Marion Street, M. Dargan;
    Mission, S. D. Vaughn.   William C. Power.
1891. Washington Street, H. F. Chreitzberg;
    Marion Street, S. P. H. Elwell;
    Mission, S. D. Vaughn.   William C. Power.
1892. Washington Street, H. F. Chreitzberg;
    Marion Street, S. P. H. Elwell;
    Mission, S. D. Vaughn.   William C. Power.
1893. Washington Street, J. A. Rice;
    Marion Street, S. P. H. Elwell;
    Mission, W. H. Kirton.   William C. Power.
1894. Washington Street, J. A. Rice;
    Marion Street, S. P. H. Elwell;
    Mission, W. H. Kirton.   E. T. Hodges.
1895. Washington Street, W. W. Darr ;
    Marion Street, P. L. Kirton,
    Mission, W. H. Kirton.   J. W. Dickson.
1896. Washington Street, W. W. Daniel;
    Marion Street, P. L. Kirton;
    Mission, W. B. Baker.   J. W. Dickson.